THE STONES OF VENICE

VOLUME III

THE FALL

THE STONES OF VENICE

VOLUME III

THE FALL

John Ruskin

With illustrations drawn by the author

DOVER PUBLICATIONS, INC.
Mineola, New York

DOVER PHOENIX EDITIONS

Bibliographical Note

This Dover edition, first published in 2005, is an unabridged republication of the fourth edition of *The Stones of Venice / Volume the Third / The Fall,* originally published by George Allen, Sunnyside, Orpington, Kent, in 1886. The two original color plates have been reproduced here in black and white. A general index spanning all three volumes appears at the end of Volume III.

All three volumes of *The Stones of Venice* are available from Dover Publications. In addition to this volume, they are: *The Stones of Venice, Volume I, The Foundations* by John Ruskin, ISBN 0-486-44317-5; and *The Stones of Venice, Volume II, The Sea-Stories* by John Ruskin, ISBN 0-486-44318-3.

Library of Congress Cataloging-in-Publication Data

Ruskin, John, 1819–1900.
    The stones of Venice / John Ruskin.
        p. cm.
    Originally published: Sunnyside, Orpington, Kent : George Allen, 1886.
    "With illustrations drawn by the author."
    Includes index.
    ISBN 0-486-44317-5 (v. 1) — ISBN 0-486-44318-3 (v. 2) — ISBN 0-486-44319-1 (v. 3)
        1. Architecture—Italy—Venice. 2. Architecture—Details. 3. Architecture, Gothic. I. Title.

NA1121.V4R7 2005
720'.945'31—dc22

                                                                2005041386

Manufactured in the United States of America
Dover Publications, Inc., 31 East 2nd Street, Mineola, N.Y. 11501

CONTENTS.

THIRD, OR RENAISSANCE PERIOD.

APPENDIX.

LIST OF PLATES.

STONES OF VENICE.

THIRD, OR RENAISSANCE PERIOD.

CHAPTER I.

EARLY RENAISSANCE.

§ I. I TRUST that the reader has been enabled, by the preceding chapters, to form some conception of the magnificence of the streets of Venice during the course of the thirteenth and fourteenth centuries. Yet by all this magnificence she was not supremely distinguished above the other cities of the middle ages. Her early edifices have been preserved to our times by the circuit of her waves; while continual recurrences of ruin have defaced the glory of her sister cities. But such fragments as are still left in their lonely squares, and in the corners of their streets, so far from being inferior to the buildings of Venice, are even more rich, more finished, more admirable in invention, more exuberant in beauty. And although, in the North of Europe, civilisation was less advanced, and the knowledge of the arts was more confined to the ecclesiastical orders, so that, for domestic architecture, the period of perfection must be there placed much later than in Italy, and considered as extending to the middle of the fifteenth century; yet, as each city reached a certain point in civilisation, its streets became decorated with the same magnificence, varied only in style according to the materials at hand, and temper of the people. And I am not aware of any town of wealth and importance in the middle ages, in which some proof does not exist that, at its period of greatest energy and prosperity, its streets were inwrought with rich sculpture, and even (though in this, as before noticed, Venice always stood supreme) glowing with colour and with gold. Now, therefore, let the reader,—forming for himself as vivid and real a conception as he is able, either of a group of Venetian palaces in the fourteenth century, or, if he likes better, of one of the more fantastic but even richer street scenes of Rouen, Antwerp, Cologne, or Nuremberg, and keeping this gorgeous image before him,—go out into any thoroughfare representative, in a general and characteristic way, of the feeling for domestic architecture in modern times : let him, for instance, if in London, walk once up and down Harley Street, or Baker Street, or Gower Street; and then, looking upon this picture and on this, set himself to consider (for this is to be the subject of our following and final inquiry) what have been the causes which have induced so vast a change in the European mind.

§ II. Renaissance architecture is the school which has conducted men's inventive and constructive faculties from the Grand Canal to Gower Street; from the marble shaft, and the lancet arch, and the wreathed leafage, and the glowing and melting harmony of gold and azure, to the square cavity in the brick wall. We have now to consider the causes and the steps of this change; and, as we endeavoured above to investigate the nature of Gothic, here to investigate also the nature of Renaissance.

§ III. Although Renaissance architecture assumes very different forms among different nations, it may be conveniently referred to three heads :—Early Renaissance, consisting of the first corruptions introduced into the Gothic schools : Central or Roman Renaissance, which is the perfectly formed style ; and Grotesque Renaissance, which is the corruption of the Renaissance itself.

§ IV. Now, in order to do full justice to the adverse cause, we will consider the abstract *nature* of the school with reference only to its best or Central examples. The forms of building which must be classed generally under the term *Early* Renaissance are, in many cases, only the extravagances and corruptions of the languid Gothic, for whose errors the classical principle is in nowise answerable. It was stated in the second chapter of the "Seven Lamps," that, unless luxury had enervated and subtlety falsified the Gothic forms, Roman traditions could not have prevailed against them ; and, although these enervated and false conditions are almost instantly coloured by the classical influence, it would be utterly unfair to lay to the charge of that influence the first debasement of the earlier schools, which had lost the strength of their system before they could be struck by the plague.

§ V. The manner, however, of the debasement of all schools of art, so far as it is natural, is in all ages the same ; luxuriance of ornament, refinement of execution, and idle subtleties of fancy, taking the place of true thought and firm handling : and I do not intend to delay the reader long by the Gothic sick-bed, for our task is not so much to watch the wasting of fever in the features of the expiring king, as to trace the character of that Hazael who dipped the cloth in water, and laid it upon his face. Nevertheless, it is necessary to the completeness of our view of the architecture of Venice, as well as to our understanding of the manner in which the Central Renaissance obtained its universal dominion, that we glance briefly at the principal forms into which Venetian Gothic first declined. They are two in number : one the corruption of the Gothic itself; the other a partial return to Byzantine forms : for the Venetian mind having carried the Gothic to a point at which it was dissatisfied, tried to retrace its steps, fell back first upon Byzantine types, and through them passed to the first Roman. But in thus retracing its steps, it does not recover its own lost energy. It revisits the places through which it had passed in the morning light, but it is now with wearied limbs, and under the gloomy shadows of evening.

§ VI. It has just been said that the two principal causes of natural decline in any school are over-luxuriance and over-refinement. The corrupt Gothic of Venice furnishes us with a curious instance of the one, and the corrupt Byzantine of the other. We shall examine them in succession.

Now, observe, first, I do not mean by *luxuriance* of ornament *quantity* of ornament. In the best Gothic in the world there is hardly an inch of stone left unsculptured. But I mean that character of extravagance in the ornament itself which shows that it was addressed to jaded faculties; a violence and coarseness in curvature, a depth of shadow, a lusciousness in arrangement of line, evidently arising out of an incapability of feeling the true beauty of chaste form and restrained power. I do not know any character of design which may be more easily recognised at a glance than this over-lusciousness; and yet it seems to me that at the present day there is nothing so little understood as the essential difference between chasteness and extravagance, whether in colour, shade, or lines. We speak loosely and inaccurately of "overcharged" ornament, with an obscure feeling that there is indeed something in visible Form which is correspondent to Intemperance in moral habits; but without any distinct detection of the character which offends us, far less with any understanding of the most important lesson which there can be no doubt was intended to be conveyed by the universality of this ornamental law.

§ VII. In a word, then, the safeguard of highest beauty, in all visible work, is exactly that which is also the safeguard of conduct in the soul,—Temperance, in the broadest sense; the Temperance which we have seen sitting on an equal throne with Justice amidst the Four Cardinal virtues, and, wanting which, there is not any other virtue which may not lead us into desperate error. Now observe: Temperance, in the nobler sense, does not mean a subdued and imperfect energy; it does not mean a stopping short in any good thing, as in Love or in Faith; but it means the power which governs the most intense energy, and prevents its acting in any way but as it ought. And with respect to things in which there may be excess, it does not mean imperfect enjoyment of them; but the regulation of their quantity, so that the enjoyment of them shall be greatest. For instance, in the matter we have at present in hand, temperance in colour does not mean imperfect or dull enjoyment of colour; but it means that government of colour which shall bring the utmost possible enjoyment out of all hues. A bad colourist does not *love* beautiful colour better than the best colourist does, not half so much. But he indulges in it to excess; he uses it in large masses, and unsubdued; and then it is a law of Nature, a law as universal as that of gravitation, that he shall not be able to enjoy it so much as if he had used it in less quantity. His eye is jaded and satiated, and the blue and red have life in them no more. He tries to paint them bluer and redder, in vain: all the blue has become grey, and gets greyer the more he adds to it; all his crimson has become brown, and gets more sere and autumnal the more he deepens it. But the great painter is sternly temperate in his work; he loves the vivid colour with all his heart; but for a long time he does not allow himself anything like it, nothing but sober browns and dull greys, and colours that have no conceivable beauty in them; but these by his government become lovely: and after bringing out of them all the life and power they possess, and enjoying them to the uttermost,—cautiously, and as the crown of the work, and the consummation of its music, he permits the momentary crimson and azure, and the whole canvas is in a flame.

§ VIII. Again, in curvature, which is the cause of loveliness in all form; the bad designer does not enjoy it more than the great designer, but he indulges in it till his eye is satiated, and he cannot obtain enough of it to touch his jaded feeling for grace. But the great and temperate designer does not allow himself any violent curves; he works much with lines in which the curvature, though always existing, is long before it is perceived. He dwells on all these subdued curvatures to the uttermost, and opposes them with still severer lines to bring them out in fuller sweetness; and, at last, he allows himself a momentary curve of energy, and all the work is, in an instant, full of life and grace.

The curves drawn in Plate VII., p. 216, of the first volume, were chosen entirely to show this character of dignity and restraint, as it appears in the lines of nature, together with the perpetual changefulness of the degrees of curvature in one and the same line; but although the purpose of that plate was carefully explained in the chapter which it illustrates, as well as in the passages of " Modern Painters " therein referred to (vol. ii., pp. 43, 79), so little are we now in the habit of considering the character of abstract lines, that it was thought by many persons that this plate only illustrated Hogarth's reversed line of beauty, even although the curve of the salvia leaf, which was the one taken from that plate for future use, in architecture, was not a reversed or serpentine curve at all. I shall now, however, I hope, be able to show my meaning better.

§ IX. Fig. 1, in Plate I., opposite, is a piece of ornamentation from a Norman-French manuscript of the thirteenth century, and fig. 2 from an Italian one of the fifteenth. Observe in the first its stern moderation in curvature; the gradually united lines *nearly straight*, though none quite straight, used for its main limb, and contrasted with the bold but simple offshoots of its leaves, and the noble spiral from which it shoots, these in their turn opposed by the sharp trefoils and thorny cusps. And see what a reserve of resource there is in the whole; how easy it would have been to make the curves more palpable and the foliage more rich, and how the noble hand has stayed itself, and refused to grant one wave of motion more.

§ X. Then observe the other example, in which, while the same idea is continually repeated, excitement and interest are sought for by means of violent and continual curvatures wholly unrestrained, and rolling hither and thither in confused wantonness. Compare the character of the separate lines in these two examples carefully, and be assured that wherever this redundant and luxurious curvature shows itself in ornamentation, it is a sign of jaded energy and failing invention. Do not confuse it

I.

J. Ruskin.

J.H. Le Keux.

Temperance and Intemperance,
In Curvature

with fulness or richness. Wealth is not necessarily wantonness: a Gothic moulding may be buried half a foot deep in thorns and leaves, and yet will be chaste in every line; and a late Renaissance moulding may be utterly barren and poverty-stricken, and yet will show the disposition to luxury in every line.

§ xi. Plate XX., in the second volume, though prepared for the special illustration of the notices of capitals, becomes peculiarly interesting when considered in relation to the points at present under consideration. The four leaves in the upper row are Byzantine; the two middle rows are transitional, all but fig. 11, which is of the formed Gothic; fig. 12 is perfect Gothic of the finest time (Ducal Palace, oldest part); fig. 13 is Gothic beginning to decline; fig. 14 is Renaissance Gothic in complete corruption.

Now observe, first, the Gothic naturalism advancing gradually from the Byzantine severity; how from the sharp, hard, formalised conventionality of the upper series the leaves gradually expand into more free and flexible animation, until in fig. 12 we have the perfect living leaf as if just fresh gathered out of the dew. And then, in the last two examples, and partly in fig. 11, observe how the forms which can advance no longer in animation, advance, or rather decline, into luxury and effeminacy as the strength of the school expires.

§ xii. In the second place, note that the Byzantine and Gothic schools, however differing in degree of life, are both alike in *temperance*, though the temperance of the Gothic is the nobler, because it consists with entire animation. Observe how severe and subtle the curvatures are in all the leaves from fig. 1 to fig. 12, except only in fig. 11; and observe especially the firmness and strength obtained by the close approximation to the straight line in the lateral ribs of the leaf, fig. 12. The longer the eye rests on these temperate curvatures the more it will enjoy them, but it will assuredly in the end be wearied by the morbid exaggeration of the last example.

§ xiii. Finally, observe—and this is very important—how one and the same character in the work may be a sign of totally

different states of mind, and therefore in one case bad, and in
the other good. The examples, fig. 3 and fig. 12, are both
equally pure in line; but one is subdivided in the extreme,
the other broad in the extreme, and both are beautiful. The
Byzantine mind delighted in the delicacy of subdivision which
nature shows in the fern-leaf or parsley-leaf; and so, also, often
the Gothic mind, much enjoying the oak, thorn, and thistle.
But the builder of the Ducal Palace used great breadth in his
foliage, in order to harmonise with the broad surface of his
mighty wall, and delighted in this breadth as nature delights in
the sweeping freshness of the dock-leaf or water-lily. Both
breadth and subdivision are thus noble, when they are contemplated or conceived by a mind in health; and both become
ignoble, when conceived by a mind jaded and satiated. The subdivision in fig. 13, as compared with the type, fig. 12, which it
was intended to improve, is the sign, not of a mind which loved
intricacy, but of one which could not relish simplicity, which had
not strength enough to enjoy the broad masses of the earlier
leaves, and cut them to pieces idly, like a child tearing the book
which, in its weariness, it cannot read. And on the other hand,
we shall continually find, in other examples of work of the same
period, an unwholesome breadth or heaviness, which results from
the mind having no longer any care for refinement or precision,
nor taking any delight in delicate forms, but making all things
blunted, cumbrous, and dead, losing at the same time the sense
of the elasticity and spring of natural curves. It is as if
the soul of man, itself severed from the root of its health, and
about to fall into corruption, lost the perception of life in
all things around it; and could no more distinguish the wave
of the strong branches, full of muscular strength and sanguine
circulation, from the lax bending of a broken cord, nor the
sinuousness of the edge of the leaf, crushed into deep folds
by the expansion of its living growth, from the wrinkled contraction of its decay.* Thus, in morals, there is a care for

---

* There is a curious instance of this in the modern imitations of the Gothic
capitals of the Casa d' Oro, employed in its restorations. The old capitals look

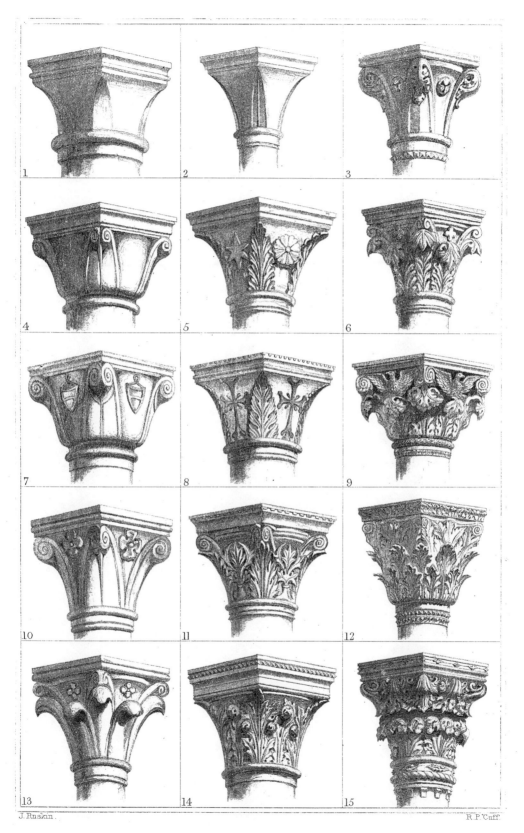

J.Ruskin.

R.P.Cuff.

Gothic Capitals.

trifles which proceeds from love and conscience, and is most holy ; and a care for trifles which comes of idleness and frivolity, and is most base. And so, also, there is a gravity proceeding from thought, which is most noble ; and a gravity proceeding from dulness and mere incapability of enjoyment, which is most base. Now, in the various forms assumed by the later Gothic of Venice, there are one or two features which, under other circumstances, would not have been signs of decline : but, in the particular manner of their occurrence here, indicate the fatal weariness of decay. Of all these features the most distinctive are its crockets and finials.

§ xiv. There is not to be found a single crocket or finial upon any part of the Ducal Palace built during the fourteenth century ; and although they occur on contemporary, and on some much earlier, buildings, they either indicate detached examples of schools not properly Venetian, or are signs of incipient decline.

The reason of this is, that the finial is properly the ornament of gabled architecture ; it is the compliance, in the minor features of the building, with the spirit of its towers, ridged roof, and spires. Venetian building is not gabled, but horizontal in its roofs and general masses ; therefore the finial is a feature contradictory to its spirit, and adopted only in that search for morbid excitement which is the infallible indication of decline. When it occurs earlier, it is on fragments of true gabled architecture ; as, for instance, on the porch of the Carmini.

In proportion to the unjustifiableness of its introduction was the extravagance of the form it assumed ; becoming, sometimes, a tuft at the top of the ogee windows, half as high as the arch itself, and consisting, in the richest examples, of a human figure, half emergent out of a cup of leafage ; as, for instance, in the small archway of the Campo San Zaccaria : while the crockets, as being at the side of the arch, and not so strictly connected with its balance and symmetry, appear to consider themselves at

like clusters of leaves, the modern ones like kneaded masses of dough with holes in them,

greater liberty even than the finials, and fling themselves hither
and thither in the wildest contortions.   Fig. 4, in Plate I., is
the outline of one, carved in stone, from the later Gothic of
St. Mark's; fig. 3 a crocket from the fine Veronese Gothic; in
order to enable the reader to discern the Renaissance character
better by comparison with the examples of curvature above them,
taken from the manuscripts.   And not content with this exube-
rance in the external ornaments of the arch, the finial interferes
with its traceries.   The increased intricacy of these, as such, being
a natural process in the development of Gothic, would have been
no evil; but they are corrupted by the enrichment of the finial
at the point of the cusp,—corrupted, that is to say, in Venice:
for at Verona the finial, in the form of a fleur-de-lis, appears long
previously at the cusp point, with exquisite effect; and in our own
best Northern Gothic it is often used beautifully in this place, as in
the window from Salisbury, Plate XII. (Vol. II.) fig. 2.   But in
Venice, such a treatment of it was utterly contrary to the severe
spirit of the ancient traceries; and the adoption of a leafy finial
at the extremity of the cusps in the door of San Stefano, as
opposed to the simple ball which terminates those of the Ducal
Palace, is an unmistakable indication of a tendency to decline.

In like manner, the enrichment and complication of the jamb
mouldings, which, in other schools, might and did take place in
the healthiest periods, are, at Venice, signs of decline, owing to
the entire inconsistency of such mouldings with the ancient love
of the single square jamb and archivolt.   The process of enrichment in them is shown by the successive examples given in
Plate VII., below.   They are numbered, and explained in the
Appendix.

§ xv. The date at which this corrupt form of Gothic first
prevailed over the early simplicity of the Venetian types can
be determined in an instant on the steps of the choir of the
Church of St. John and Paul.   On our left hand, as we enter, is
the tomb of the Doge Marco Cornaro, who died in 1367.   It is
rich and fully developed Gothic, with crockets and finials, but
not yet attaining any extravagant development.   Opposite to

it is that of the Doge Andrea Morosini, who died in 1382. Its
Gothic is voluptuous, and overwrought: the crockets are bold
and florid, and the enormous finial represents a statue of St.
Michael. There is no excuse for the antiquaries who, having
this tomb before them, could have attributed the severe architecture of the Ducal Palace to a later date; for every one of
the Renaissance errors is here in complete development, though
not so grossly as entirely to destroy the loveliness of the Gothic
forms. In the Porta della Carta, 1423, the vice reaches its
climax.

§ XVI. Against this degraded Gothic, then, came up the Renaissance armies; and their first assault was in the requirement
of universal perfection. For the first time since the destruction
of Rome, the world had seen, in the work of the greatest artists
of the fifteenth century,—in the painting of Ghirlandajo, Masaccio,
Francia, Perugino, Pinturicchio, and Bellini; in the sculpture
of Mino da Fiesole, of Ghiberti, and Verrocchio,—a perfection of
execution and fulness of knowledge which cast all previous art
into the shade, and which, being in the work of those men
united with all that was great in that of former days, did
indeed justify the utmost enthusiasm with which their efforts
were, or could be, regarded. But when this perfection had
once been exhibited in anything, it was required in everything;
the world could no longer be satisfied with less exquisite execution, or less disciplined knowledge. The first thing that it
demanded in all work was, that it should be done in a consummate and learned way; and men altogether forgot that it was
possible to consummate what was contemptible, and to know
what was useless. Imperatively requiring dexterity of touch,
they gradually forgot to look for tenderness of feeling; imperatively requiring accuracy of knowledge, they gradually forgot
to ask for originality of thought. The thought and the feeling
which they despised departed from them, and they were left to
felicitate themselves on their small science and their neat
fingering. This is the history of the first attack of the Renaissance upon the Gothic schools, and of its rapid results; more

fatal and immediate in architecture than in any other art, because there the demand for perfection was less reasonable, and less consistent with the capabilities of the workman ; being utterly opposed to that rudeness or savageness on which, as we saw above, the nobility of the elder schools in great part depends. But, inasmuch as the innovations were founded on some of the most beautiful examples of art, and headed by some of the greatest men that the world ever saw, and as the Gothic with which they interfered was corrupt and valueless, the first appearance of the Renaissance feeling had the appearance of a healthy movement.   A new energy replaced whatever weariness or dulness had affected the Gothic mind ; an exquisite taste and refinement, aided by extended knowledge, furnished the first models of the new school ; and over the whole of Italy a style arose, generally now known as cinque-cento, which in sculpture and painting, as I just stated, produced the noblest masters whom the world ever saw, headed by Michael Angelo, Raphael, and Leonardo ; but which failed of doing the same in architecture, because, as we have seen above, perfection is therein not possible, and failed more totally than it would otherwise have done, because the classical enthusiasm had destroyed the best types of architectural form.

§ XVII. For, observe here very carefully, the Renaissance principle, as it consisted in a demand for universal perfection, is quite distinct from the Renaissance principle as it consists in a demand for classical and Roman *forms* of perfection.   And if I had space to follow out the subject as I should desire, I would first endeavour to ascertain what might have been the course of the art of Europe if no manuscripts of classical authors had been recovered, and no remains of classical architecture left, in the fifteenth century ; so that the executive perfection to which the efforts of all great men had tended for five hundred years, and which now at last was reached, might have been allowed to develope itself in its own natural and proper form, in connection with the architectural structure of earlier schools.   This refinement and perfection had indeed its own perils, and the history of later Italy, as she sank into pleasure and thence into corruption, would probably have been the same whether she had ever learned again to write pure Latin or not. Still the inquiry into the probable cause of the enervation which might naturally have followed the highest exertion of her energies, is a totally distinct one from that into the particular form given to this enervation by her classical learning; and it is matter of considerable regret to me that I cannot treat these two subjects separately : I must be content with marking them for separation in the mind of the reader.

§ XVIII. The effect, then, of the sudden enthusiasm for classical literature, which gained strength during every hour of the fifteenth century, was, as far as respected architecture, to do away with the entire system of Gothic science. The pointed arch, the shadowy vault, the clustered shaft, the heaven-pointing spire, were all swept away; and no structure was any longer permitted but that of the plain cross-beam from pillar to pillar, over the round arch, with square or circular shafts, and a low-gabled roof and pediment : two elements of noble form, which had fortunately existed in Rome, were, however, for that reason, still permitted; the cupola, and, internally, the waggon vault.

§ XIX. These changes in form were all of them unfortunate; and it is almost impossible to do justice to the occasionally exquisite ornamentation of the fifteenth century, on account of its being placed upon edifices of the cold and meagre Roman outline. There is, as far as I know, only one Gothic building in Europe, the Duomo of Florence, in which, though the ornament be of a much earlier school, it is yet so exquisitely finished as to enable us to imagine what might have been the effect of the perfect workmanship of the Renaissance, coming out of the hands of men like Verrocchio and Ghiberti, had it been employed on the magnificent framework of Gothic structure. This is the question which, as I shall note in the concluding chapter, we ought to set ourselves practically to solve in modern times.

§ XX. The changes effected in form, however, were the least part of the evil principles of the Renaissance. As I have just said, its main mistake, in its early stages, was the unwholesome demand for *perfection*, at any cost. I hope enough has been advanced, in the chapter on the Nature of Gothic, to show the reader that perfection is *not* to be had from the general workman, but at the cost of everything,—of his whole life, thought, and energy. And Renaissance Europe thought this a small price to pay for manipulative perfection. Men like Verrocchio and Ghiberti were not to be had every day, nor in every place ; and to require from the common workman execution or knowledge like theirs, was to require him to become their copyist. Their strength was great enough to enable them to join science with invention, method with emotion, finish with fire ; but in them the invention and the fire were first, while Europe saw in them only the method and the finish. This was new to the minds of men, and they pursued it to the neglect of everything else. " This," they cried, " we must have in all our work henceforward :" and they were obeyed. The lower workman secured method and finish, and lost, in exchange for them, his soul.

§ XXI. Now, therefore, do not let me be misunderstood when I speak generally of the evil spirit of the Renaissance. The reader may look through all I have written, from first to last, and he will not find one word but of the most profound reverence for those mighty men who could wear the Renaissance armour of proof, and yet not feel it encumber their living limbs,*—Leonardo and Michael Angelo, Ghirlandajo and Masaccio, Titian and Tintoret. But I speak of the Renaissance as an evil time, because, when it saw those men go burning forth into the battle, it mistook their armour for their strength ; and forthwith encumbered with the painful panoply every stripling who ought to have gone forth only with his own choice of three smooth stones out of the brook.

§ XXII. This, then, the reader must always keep in mind when he is examining for himself any examples of cinque-cento

---

* Not that even these men were able to wear it altogether without harm, as we shall see in the next chapter.

work. When it has been done by a truly great man, whose life and strength could not be oppressed, and who turned to good account the whole science of his day, nothing is more exquisite. I do not believe, for instance, that there is a more glorious work of sculpture existing in the world than that equestrian statue of Bartolomeo Colleone, by Verrocchio, of which, I hope, before these pages are printed, there will be a cast in England. But when the cinque-cento work has been done by those meaner men, who, in the Gothic times, though in a rough way, would yet have found some means of speaking out what was in their hearts, it is utterly inanimate,—a base and helpless copy of more accomplished models ; or, if not this, a mere accumulation of technical skill, in gaining which the workman had surrendered all other powers that were in him.

There is, therefore, of course, an infinite gradation in the art of the period, from the Sistine Chapel down to modern upholstery ; but, for the most part, since in architecture the workman must be of an inferior order, it will be found that this cinque-cento painting and higher religious sculpture is noble, while the cinque-cento architecture, with its subordinate sculpture, is universally bad ; sometimes, however, assuming forms in which the consummate refinement almost atones for the loss of force.

§ XXIII. This is especially the case with that second branch of the Renaissance which, as above noticed, was engrafted at Venice on the Byzantine types. So soon as the classical enthusiasm required the banishment of Gothic forms, it was natural that the Venetian mind should turn back with affection to the Byzantine models in which the round arches and simple shafts, necessitated by recent law, were presented under a form consecrated by the usage of their ancestors. And, accordingly, the first distinct school of architecture* which arose under the new dynasty was one in which the method of inlaying marble, and the general forms of shaft and arch, were adopted from

---

* Appendix 4: " Date of Palaces of Byzantine Renaissance."

the buildings of the twelfth century, and applied with the utmost possible refinements of modern skill. Both at Verona and Venice the resulting architecture is exceedingly beautiful. At Verona it is, indeed, less Byzantine, but possesses a character of richness and tenderness almost peculiar to that city. At Venice it is more severe, but yet adorned with sculpture which, for sharpness of touch and delicacy of minute form, cannot be rivalled, and rendered especially brilliant and beautiful by the introduction of those inlaid circles of coloured marble, serpentine, and porphyry, by which Phillippe de Commynes was so much struck on his first entrance into the city. The two most refined buildings in this style in Venice are, the small Church of the Miracoli, and the Scuola di San Marco beside the Church of St. John and St. Paul. The noblest is the Rio Façade of the Ducal Palace. The Casa Dario, and Casa Manzoni, on the Grand Canal, are exquisite examples of the school, as applied to domestic architecture ; and, in the reach of the Canal between the Casa Foscari and the Rialto, there are several palaces, of which the Casa Contarini (called "delle Figure") is the principal, belonging to the same group, though somewhat later, and remarkable for the association of the Byzantine principles of colour with the severest lines of the Roman pediment, gradually superseding the round arch. The precision of chiselling and delicacy of proportion in the ornament and general lines of these palaces cannot be too highly praised ; and I believe that the traveller in Venice, in general, gives them rather too little attention than too much. But while I would ask him to stay his gondola beside each of them long enough to examine their every line, I must also warn him to observe most carefully the peculiar feebleness and want of soul in the conception of their ornament, which mark them as belonging to a period of decline ; as well as the absurd mode of introduction of their pieces of coloured marble : these, instead of being simply and naturally inserted in the masonry, are placed in small circular or oblong frames of sculpture, like mirrors or pictures, and are represented as suspended by ribands against the wall ; a pair of wings being generally fastened on to the circular tablets, as if to relieve the ribands and knots from their weight, and the whole series tied under the chin of a little cherub at the top, who is nailed against the façade like a hawk on a barn door.

But chiefly let him notice, in the Casa Contarini delle Figure, one most strange incident, seeming to have been permitted, like the choice of the subjects at the three angles of the Ducal Palace, in order to teach us, by a single lesson, the true nature of the style in which it occurs. In the intervals of the windows of the first story, certain shields and torches are attached, in the form of trophies, to the stems of two trees whose boughs have been cut off, and only one or two of their faded leaves left, scarcely observable, but delicately sculptured here and there, beneath the insertions of the severed boughs.

It is as if the workman had intended to leave us an image of the expiring naturalism of the Gothic school. I had not, seen this sculpture when I wrote the passage referring to its period, in the first volume of this work (Chap. XX. § XXXI.) :— " Autumn came,—the leaves were shed,—and the eye was directed to the extremities of the delicate branches. *The Renaissance frosts came, and all perished!*"

§ XXIV. And the hues of this autumn of the early Renaissance are the last which appear in architecture. The winter which succeeded was colourless as it was cold; and although the Venetian painters struggled long against its influence, the numbness of the architecture prevailed over them at last, and the exteriors of all the latter palaces were built only in barren stone. As at this point of our inquiry, therefore, we must bid farewell to colour, I have reserved for this place the continuation of the history of chromatic decoration, from the Byzantine period, when we left it in the fifth chapter of the second volume, down to its final close.

§ XXV. It was above stated, that the principal difference in general form and treatment between the Byzantine and Gothic palaces was the contraction of the marble facing into the narrow spaces between the windows, leaving large fields of brick wall perfectly bare. The reason for this appears to have been, that the Gothic builders were no longer satisfied with the faint and delicate hues of the veined marble ; they wished for some more forcible and piquant mode of decoration, corresponding more completely with the gradually advancing splendour of chivalric costume and heraldic device. What I have said above of the simple habits of life of the thirteenth century, in nowise refers either to costumes of state or of military service ; and any illumination of the thirteenth and early fourteenth centuries (the great period being, it seems to me, from 1250 to 1350), while it shows a peculiar majesty and simplicity in the fall of the robes (often worn over the chain armour), indicates, at the same time, an exquisite brilliancy of colour and power of design in the hems and borders, as well as in the armorial bearings with which they are charged ; and while, as we have seen, a peculiar simplicity is found also in the *forms* of the architecture, corresponding to that of the folds of the robes, its *colours* were constantly increasing in brilliancy and decision, corresponding to those of the quartering of the shield, and of the embroidery of the mantle.

§ XXVI. Whether, indeed, derived from the quarterings of the knights' shields, or from what other source, I know not ; but there is one magnificent attribute of the colouring of the late twelfth, the whole thirteenth, and the early fourteenth century, which I do not find definitely in any previous work, nor afterwards in general art, though constantly, and necessarily, in that of great colourists, namely, the union of one colour with another by reciprocal interference : that is to say, if a mass of red is to be set beside a mass of blue, a piece of the red will be carried into the blue, and a piece of the blue carried into the red ; sometimes in nearly equal portions, as in a shield divided into four quarters, of which the uppermost on one side will be of the same colour as the lowermost on the other ; sometimes in smaller fragments, but, in the periods above named, always definitely and grandly, though in a thousand various ways. And I call it a magnificent principle, for it is an eternal and universal one, not in art only,* but in human life. It is the great principle of Brotherhood, not by equality, nor by likeness, but by giving and receiving ; the souls that are unlike, and the nations that are unlike, and the natures that are unlike, being bound into one noble whole by each receiving something from and of the others' gifts and the others' glory. I have not space to follow out this thought,—it is of infinite extent and application,—but I note it for the reader's pursuit, because I have long believed, and the whole second volume of " Modern Painters " was written to prove, that in whatever has been made by the Deity externally delightful to the human sense of beauty, there is some type of God's nature or of God's laws ; nor are any of His laws, in one sense, greater than the appointment that the most lovely and perfect unity shall be obtained by the taking of one nature into another. I trespass upon too high ground ; and yet I cannot fully show the reader the extent of this law, but by leading him thus far. And it is just because it is so vast and so awful a law, that it has rule over the smallest things ; and there is not a vein of colour on the slightest leaf which the spring winds are at this moment unfolding in the fields around us, but it is an illustration of an ordainment to which the earth and its creatures owe their continuance and their Redemption.

§ XXVII. It is perfectly inconceivable, until it has been made a subject of special inquiry, how perpetually Nature employs this principle in the distribution of her light and shade ; how by the

---

* In the various works which Mr. Prout has written on light and shade, no principle will be found insisted on more strongly than this carrying of the dark into the light, and *vice versa*. It is curious to find the untaught instinct of a merely picturesque artist in the nineteenth century, fixing itself so intensely on a principle which regulated the entire sacred composition of the thirteenth. I say " untaught" instinct, for Mr. Prout was, throughout his life, the discoverer of his own principles ; fortunately so, considering what principles were taught in his time, but unfortunately in the abstract, for there were gifts in him, which, had there been any wholesome influences to cherish them, might have made him one of the greatest men of his age. He was great, under all adverse circumstances, but the mere wreck of what he might have been, if, after the rough training noticed in my pamphlet on Pre-Raphaelitism, as having fitted him for his great function in the world, he had met with a teacher who could have appreciated his powers, and directed them.

most extraordinary adaptations, apparently accidental, but always in exactly the right place, she contrives to bring darkness into light, and light into darkness ; and that so sharply and decisively, that at the very instant when one object changes from light to dark, the thing relieved upon it will change from dark to light, and yet so subtly that the eye will not detect the transition till it looks for it. The secret of a great part of the grandeur in all the noblest compositions is the doing of this delicately in *degree*, and broadly in *mass ;* in colour it may be done much more decisively than in light and shade, and, according to the simplicity of the work, with greater frankness of confession, until, in purely decorative art, as in the illumination, glass-painting, and heraldry of the great periods, we find it reduced to segmental accuracy. Its greatest masters, in high art, are Tintoret, Veronese, and Turner.

§ XXVIII. Together with this great principle of quartering is introduced another, also of very high value as far as regards the delight of the eye, though not of so profound meaning. As soon as colour began to be used in broad and opposed fields, it was perceived that the mass of it destroyed its brilliancy, and it was *tempered* by chequering it with some other colour or colours in smaller quantities, mingled with minute portions of pure white. The two moral principles of which this is the type are those of Temperance and Purity ; the one requiring the fulness of the colour to be subdued, and the other that it shall be subdued without losing either its own purity or that of the colours with which it is associated.

§ XXIX. Hence arose the universal and admirable system of the diapered or chequered backgrounds of early ornamental art. They are completely developed in the thirteenth century, and extend through the whole of the fourteenth, gradually yielding to landscape and other pictorial backgrounds, as the designers lost perception of the purpose of their art, and of the value of colour. The chromatic decoration of the Gothic palaces of Venice was of course founded on these two great principles, which prevailed constantly wherever the true chivalric and Gothic spirit possessed any influence. The windows, with their intermediate spaces of marble, were considered as the objects to be relieved, and variously quartered with vigorous colour. The whole space of the brick wall was considered as a background; it was covered with stucco, and painted in fresco, with diaper patterns.

§ xxx. What? the reader asks in some surprise,—Stucco! and in the great Gothic period? Even so, but *not stucco to imitate stone.* Herein lies all the difference: it is stucco confessed and understood, and laid on the bricks precisely as gesso is laid on canvas, in order to form them into a ground for receiving colour from the human hand,—colour which, if well laid on, might render the brick wall more precious than if it had been built of emeralds. Whenever we wish to paint, we may prepare our paper as we choose; the value of the ground in nowise adds to the value of the picture. A Tintoret on beaten gold would be of no more value than a Tintoret on coarse canvas; the gold would merely be wasted. All that we have to do is to make the ground as good and fit for the colour as possible, by whatever means.

§ xxxi. I am not sure if I am right in applying the term " stucco " to the ground of fresco ; but this is of no consequence : the reader will understand that it was white, and that the whole wall of the palace was considered as the page of a book to be illuminated : but he will understand also that the sea winds are bad librarians ; that, when once the painted stucco began to fade or to fall, the unsightliness of the defaced colour would necessitate its immediate restoration ; and that therefore, of all the chromatic decoration of the Gothic palaces, there is hardly a fragment left.

Happily, in the pictures of Gentile Bellini, the fresco colouring of the Gothic palaces is recorded, as it still remained in his time ; not with rigid accuracy, but quite distinctly enough to enable us, by comparing it with the existing coloured designs in the manuscripts and glass of the period, to ascertain precisely what it must have been.

§ xxxii. The walls were generally covered with chequers of

very warm colour, a russet inclining to scarlet more or less relieved with white, black, and grey; as still seen in the only example which, having been executed in marble, has been perfectly preserved, the front of the Ducal Palace. This, how-ever, owing to the nature of its materials, was a peculiarly simple example; the ground is white, crossed with double bars of pale red, and in the centre of each chequer there is a cross, alternately black with a red centre and red with a black centre where the arms cross. In painted work the grounds would be, of course, as varied and complicated as those of manuscripts; but I only know of one example left, on the Casa Sagredo, where, on some fragments of stucco, a very early chequer background is traceable, composed of crimson quatrefoils inter-laced, with cherubims stretching their wings filling the intervals. A small portion of this ground is seen beside the window taken from the palace, Vol. II. Plate XIII. fig. 1.

§ XXXIII. It ought to be especially noticed, that, in all chequered patterns employed in the coloured designs of these noble periods, the greatest care is taken to mark that they are *grounds* of design rather than designs themselves. Modern architects, in such minor imitations as they are beginning to attempt, endeavour to dispose the parts of the patterns so as to occupy certain symmetrical positions with respect to the parts of the architecture. A Gothic builder never does this: he cuts his ground into pieces of the shape he requires with utter remorselessness, and places his windows or doors upon it with no regard whatever to the lines in which they cut the pattern: and, in illuminations of manuscripts, the chequer itself is constantly changed in the most subtle and arbitrary way, wherever there is the least chance of its regularity attracting the eye, and making it of importance. So *intentional* is this, that a diaper pattern is often set obliquely to the vertical lines of the designs, for fear it should appear in any way connected with them.

§ XXXIV. On these russet or crimson backgrounds the entire space of the series of windows was relieved, for the most part, as a subdued white field of alabaster; and on this delicate and veined white were set the circular disks of purple and green. The arms of the family were of course blazoned in their own proper colours, but I think generally on a pure azure ground; the blue colour is still left behind the shields in the Casa Priuli and one or two more of the palaces which are unrestored, and the blue ground was used also to relieve the sculptures of religious subjects. Finally, all the mouldings, capitals, cornices, cusps, and traceries, were either entirely gilded or profusely touched with gold.

The whole front of a Gothic palace in Venice may, therefore, be simply described as a field of subdued russet, quartered with broad sculptured masses of white and gold; these latter being relieved by smaller inlaid fragments of blue, purple, and deep green.

§ xxxv. Now, from the beginning of the fourteenth century, when painting and architecture were thus united, two processes of change went on simultaneously to the beginning of the seventeenth. The merely decorative chequerings on the walls yielded gradually to more elaborate paintings of figure-subject; first small and quaint, and then enlarging into enormous pictures filled by figures generally colossal. As these paintings became of greater merit and importance, the architecture with which they were associated was less studied; and at last a style was introduced in which the framework of the building was little more interesting than that of a Manchester factory, but the whole space of its walls was covered with the most precious fresco paintings. Such edifices are of course no longer to be considered as forming an architectural school; they were merely large preparations of artist's panels; and Titian, Giorgione, and Veronese, no more conferred merit on the later architecture of Venice, as such, by painting on its façades, than Landseer or Watts could confer merit on that of London by first white-washing and then painting its brick streets from one end to the other.

§ xxxvi. Contemporarily with this change in the relative

values of the colour decoration and the stonework, one equally
important was taking place in the opposite direction, but of
course in another group of buildings.   For in proportion as
the architect felt himself thrust aside or forgotten in one edifice,
he endeavoured to make himself principal in another ; and, in
retaliation for the painter's entire usurpation of certain fields
of design, succeeded in excluding him totally from those in
which his own influence was predominant.   Or, more accurately
speaking, the architects began to be too proud to receive assistance from the colourists ; and these latter sought for ground
which the architect had abandoned for the unrestrained display
of their own skill.   And thus, while one series of edifices is continually becoming feebler in design and richer in superimposed
paintings, another, that of which we have so often spoken as
the earliest or Byzantine Renaissance, fragment by fragment
rejects the pictorial decoration ; supplies its place first with
marbles, and then, as the latter are felt by the architect, daily
increasing in arrogance and deepening in coldness, to be too
bright for his dignity, he casts even these aside one by one :
and when the last porphyry circle has vanished from the façade,
we find two palaces standing side by side, one built, so far as
mere masonry goes, with consummate care and skill, but without
the slightest vestige of colour in any part of it ; the other utterly
without any claim to interest in its architectural form, but
covered from top to bottom with paintings by Veronese.   At
this period, then, we bid farewell to colour, leaving the painters
to their own peculiar field ; and only regretting that they waste
their noblest work on walls, from which in a couple of centuries,
if not before, the greater part of their labour must be effaced.
On the other hand, the architecture whose decline we are tracing,
has now assumed an entirely new condition, that of the Central
or True Renaissance, whose nature we are to examine in the
next chapter.

§ XXXVII. But before leaving these last palaces over which the
Byzantine influence extended itself, there is one more lesson to

be learned from them of much importance to us. Though in many respects debased in style, they are consummate in workmanship, and unstained in honour; there is no imperfection in them, and no dishonesty. That there is absolutely *no* imperfection, is indeed, as we have seen above, a proof of their being wanting in the highest qualities of architecture; but, as lessons in masonry, they have their value, and may well be studied for the excellence they display in methods of levelling stones, for the precision of their inlaying, and other such qualities, which in them are indeed too principal, yet very instructive in their particular way.

§ XXXVIII. For instance, in the inlaid design of the dove with the olive branch, from the Casa Trevisan (Vol. I. Plate XX. p. 358) it is impossible for anything to go beyond the precision with which the olive leaves are cut out of the white marble; and, in some wreaths of laurel below, the rippled edge of each leaf is as finely and easily drawn, as if by a delicate pencil. No Florentine table is more exquisitely finished than the façade of this entire palace; and as ideals of an executive perfection, which, though we must not turn aside from our main path to reach it, may yet with much advantage be kept in our sight and memory, these palaces are most notable amidst the architecture of Europe. The Rio Façade of the Ducal Palace, though very sparing in colour, is yet, as an example of finished masonry in a vast building, one of the finest things, not only in Venice, but in the world. It differs from other work of the Byzantine Renaissance, in being on a very large scale; and it still retains one pure Gothic character, which adds not a little to its nobleness, that of perpetual variety. There is hardly one window of it, or one panel, that is like another; and this continual change so increases its apparent size by confusing the eye, that, though presenting no bold features, or striking masses of any kind, there are few things in Italy more impressive than the vision of it overhead, as the gondola glides from beneath the Bridge of Sighs. And lastly (unless we are to blame these buildings for some pieces of very childish perspective), they are magnificently honest, as well as perfect. I do not remember even any gilding upon them ; all is pure marble, and of the finest kind.*

And therefore, in finally leaving the Ducal Palace,† let us take with us one more lesson, the last which we shall receive from the Stones of Venice, except in the form of a warning.

§ XXXIX. The school of architecture which we have just been examining is, as we have seen above, redeemed from severe condemnation by its careful and noble use of inlaid marbles as means of colour. From that time forward, this art has been unknown or despised ; the frescoes of the swift and daring Venetian painters long contended with the inlaid marbles, out-vying them with colour, indeed more glorious than theirs, but fugitive as the hues of woods in autumn ; and, at last, as the art itself of painting in this mighty manner failed from among men,‡ the modern decorative system established itself, which united the meaninglessness of the veined marble with the evanescence of the fresco, and completed the harmony by falsehood.

§ XL. Since first, in the second chapter of the "Seven Lamps," I endeavoured to show the culpableness, as well as the base-ness, of our common modes of decoration by painted imitation of various woods or marbles, the subject has been discussed in various architectural works, and is evidently becoming one of daily increasing interest. When it is considered how many persons there are whose means of livelihood consist altogether

---

* There may, however, be a kind of dishonesty even in the use of marble, if it is attempted to make the marble look like something else. See the final or Venetian Index, under head " Scalzi."

† Appendix 5 : " Renaissance Side of Ducal Palace."

‡ We have, as far as I *know*, at present among us, only one painter, G. F. Watts, who is capable of design in colour on a large scale. He stands alone among our artists of the old school in his perception of the value of breadth in distant masses, and in the vigour of invention by which such breadth must be sustained ; and his power of expression and depth of thought are not less remarkable than his bold conception of colour effect. Very probably some of the Pre-Raphaelites have the gift also ; I am nearly certain that Rossetti has it, and I think also Millais ; but the experiment has yet to be tried. I wish it could be made in Mr. Hope's church in Margaret Street.

in these spurious arts, and how difficult it is, even for the most candid, to admit a conviction contrary both to their interests and to their inveterate habits of practice and thought, it is rather a matter of wonder that the cause of Truth should have found even a few maintainers, than that it should have encountered a host of adversaries. It has, however, been defended repeatedly by architects themselves, and so successfully, that I believe, so far as the desirableness of this or that method of ornamentation is to be measured by the fact of its simple honesty or dishonesty, there is little need to add anything to what has been already urged upon the subject. But there are some points connected with the practice of imitating marble, which I have been unable to touch upon until now, and by the consideration of which we may be enabled to see something of the *policy* of honesty in this matter, without in the least abandoning the higher ground of principle.

§ XLI. Consider, then, first, what marble seems to have been made for. Over the greater part of the surface of the world, we find that a rock has been providentially distributed, in a manner particularly pointing it out as intended for the service of man. Not altogether a common rock, it is yet rare enough to command a certain degree of interest and attention wherever it is found ; but not so rare as to preclude its use for any purpose to which it is fitted. It is exactly of the consistence which is best adapted for sculpture ; that is to say, neither hard nor brittle, nor flaky nor splintery, but uniformly and delicately, yet not ignobly, soft,—exactly soft enough to allow the sculptor to work it without force, and trace on it the finest lines of finished form ; and yet so hard as never to betray the touch or moulder away beneath the steel ; and so admirably crystallized, and of such permanent elements, that no rain dissolves it, no time changes it, no atmosphere decomposes it ; once shaped, it is shaped for ever, unless subjected to actual violence or attrition. This rock, then, is prepared by Nature for the sculptor and architect, just as paper is prepared by the manufacturer for the artist, with as great—nay, with greater—care, and more perfect adaptation of the material to the requirements. And of this marble paper, some is white and some coloured ; but more is coloured than white, because the white is evidently meant for sculpture, and the coloured for the covering of large surfaces.

§ XLII. Now, if we would take Nature at her word, and use this precious paper which she has taken so much care to provide for us (it is a long process, the making of that paper : the pulp of it needing the subtlest possible solution, and the pressing of it—for it is all hot-pressed—having to be done under the sea, or under something at least as heavy); if, I say, we use it as Nature would have us, consider what advantages would follow. The colours of marble are mingled for us just as if on a pre-pared palette. They are of all shades and hues (except bad ones), some being united and even, some broken, mixed, and inter-rupted, in order to supply, as far as possible, the want of the painter's power of breaking and mingling the colour with the brush. But there is more in the colours than this delicacy of adaptation. There is history in them. By the manner in which they are arranged in every piece of marble, they record the means by which that marble has been produced, and the suc-cessive changes through which it has passed. And in all their veins and zones, and flame-like stainings, or broken and discon-nected lines, they write various legends, never untrue, of the former political state of the mountain kingdom to which they belonged, of its infirmities and fortitudes, convulsions and con-solidations, from the beginning of time.

Now, if we were never in the habit of seeing anything but real marbles, this language of theirs would soon begin to be understood ; that is to say, even the least observant of us would recognise such and such stones as forming a peculiar class, and would begin to inquire where they came from, and, at last, take some feeble interest in the main question, Why they were only to be found in that or the other place, and how they came to make a part of this mountain, and not of that? And in a little while, it would not be possible to stand for a moment at a shop door, leaning against the pillars of it, without remembering or questioning of something well worth the memory or the inquiry, touching the hills of Italy, or Greece, or Africa, or Spain ; and we should be led on from knowledge to knowledge, until even the unsculptured walls of our streets became to us volumes as precious as those of our libraries.

§ XLIII. But the moment we admit imitation of marble, this source of knowledge is destroyed. None of us can be at the pains to go through the work of verification. If we knew that every coloured stone we saw was natural, certain questions, conclusions, interests, would force themselves upon us without any effort of our own ; but we have none of us time to stop in the midst of our daily business, to touch, and pore over, and decide with painful minuteness of investigation, whether such and such a pillar be stucco or stone. And the whole field of this knowledge, which Nature intended us to possess when we were children, is hopelessly shut out from us. Worse than shut out, for the mass of coarse imitations confuses our knowledge acquired from other sources ; and our memory of the marbles we have perhaps once or twice carefully examined, is disturbed and distorted by the inaccuracy of the imitations which are brought before us continually.

§ XLIV. But it will be said, that it is too expensive to employ real marbles in ordinary cases. It may be so : yet not always more expensive than the fitting windows with enormous plate glass, and decorating them with elaborate stucco mouldings, and other useless sources of expenditure in modern building ; nay, not always in the end more expensive than the frequent repainting of the dingy pillars, which a little water dashed against them would refresh from day to day, if they were of true stone. But, granting that it be so, in that very costliness, checking their common use in certain localities, is part of the interest of marbles, considered as history. Where they are not found, Nature has supplied other materials,—clay for brick, or forest for timber,— in the working of which she intends other characters of the human mind to be developed, and by the proper use of which certain local advantages will assuredly be attained, while the delightfulness and meaning of the precious marbles will be felt more forcibly in the districts where they occur, or on the occasions when they may be procured.

§ XLV. It can hardly be necessary to add that, as the imitation of marbles interferes with and checks the knowledge of geography and geology, so the imitation of wood interferes with that of botany ; and that our acquaintance with the nature, uses, and manner of growth of the timber trees of our own and of foreign countries, would probably, in the majority of cases, become accurate and extensive, without any labour or sacrifice of time, were not all inquiry checked, and all observation betrayed, by the wretched labours of the " Grainer."

§ XLVI. But this is not all. As the practice of imitation retards knowledge, so also it retards art.

There is not a meaner occupation for the human mind than the imitation of the stains and striæ of marble and wood. When engaged in any easy and simple mechanical occupation, there is still some liberty for the mind to leave the literal work ; and the clash of the loom or the activity of the fingers will not always prevent the thoughts from some happy expatiation in their own domains. But the grainer must think of what he is doing ; and veritable attention and care, and occasionally considerable skill, are consumed in the doing of a more absolute nothing than I can name in any other department of painful idleness. I know not anything so humiliating as to see a human being, with arms and limbs complete, and apparently a head, and assuredly a soul, yet into the hands of which when you have put a brush and pallet, it cannot do anything with them but imitate a piece of wood. It cannot colour, it has no ideas of colour ; it cannot draw, it has no ideas of form ; it cannot caricature, it has no ideas of humour. It is incapable of anything beyond knots. All its achievement, the entire result of the daily application of its imagination and immortality, is to be such a piece of texture as the sun and dew are sucking up out of the muddy ground, and weaving together, far more finely, in millions of millions of growing branches over every rood of waste woodland and shady hill.

§ XLVII. But what is to be done, the reader asks, with men who are capable of nothing else than this ? Nay, they may be capable of everything else, for all we know, and what we are to do with them I will try to say in the next chapter ; but meanwhile, one word more touching the higher principles of action in this matter, from which we have descended to those of expediency. I trust that some day the language of Types will be more read and understood by us than it has been for centuries ; and when this language, a better one than either Greek or Latin, is again recognized amongst us, we shall find, or remember, that as the other visible elements of the universe—its air, its water, and its flame—set forth, in their pure energies, the lifegiving, purifying, and sanctifying influences of the Deity upon His creatures, so the earth, in its purity, sets forth His eternity and His TRUTH. I have dwelt above on the historical language of stones ; let us not forget this, which is their theological language ; and, as we would not wantonly pollute the fresh waters when they issue forth in their clear glory from the rock, nor stay the mountain winds into pestilential stagnancy, nor mock the sunbeams with artificial and ineffective light ; so let us not, by our own base and barren falsehoods, replace the crystalline strength and burning colour of the earth from which we were born and to which we must return ; the earth which, like our own bodies, though dust in its degradation, is full of splendour when God's hand gathers its atoms ; and which was for ever sanctified by Him, as the symbol no less of His love than of His truth, when He bade the high priest bear the names of the Children of Israel on the clear stones of the Breastplate of Judgment.

CHAPTER II.

ROMAN RENAISSANCE.

§ I. Of all the buildings in Venice, later in date than the final additions to the Ducal Palace, the noblest is, beyond all question, that which, having been condemned by its proprietor, not many years ago, to be pulled down and sold for the value of its materials, was rescued by the Austrian Government, and appropriated—the Government officers having no other use for it—to the business of the Post-Office; though still known to the gondolier by its ancient name, the Casa Grimani. It is composed of three stories of the Corinthian order, at once simple, delicate, and sublime; but on so colossal a scale, that the three-storied palaces on its right and left only reach to the cornice which marks the level of its first floor. Yet it is not at first perceived to be so vast; and it is only when some expedient is employed to hide it from the eye, that by the sudden dwarfing of the whole reach of the Grand Canal, which it commands, we become aware that it is to the majesty of the Casa Grimani that the Rialto itself, and the whole group of neighbouring buildings, owe the greater part of their impressiveness. Nor is the finish of its details less notable than the grandeur of their scale. There is not an erring line, nor a mistaken proportion, throughout its noble front; and the exceeding fineness of the chiselling gives an appearance of lightness to the vast blocks of stone out of whose perfect union that front is composed. The decoration is sparing, but delicate: the first story only simpler than the rest, in that it has pilasters instead of shafts, but all with Corinthian capitals, rich in leafage, and fluted delicately; the rest of the walls flat and smooth, and their mouldings sharp and shallow, so that the bold shafts look like crystals of beryl running through a rock of quartz.

§ II. This palace is the principal type at Venice, and one of the best in Europe, of the central architecture of the Renaissance schools; that carefully studied and perfectly executed architecture to which those schools owe their principal claims to our respect, and which became the model of most of the important works subsequently produced by civilised nations. I have called it the Roman Renaissance, because it is founded, both in its principles of superimposition, and in the style of its ornament, upon the architecture of classic Rome at its best period. The revival of Latin literature both led to its adoption and directed its form; and the most important example of it which exists is the modern Roman basilica of St. Peter's. It had, at its Renaissance or new birth, no resemblance either to Greek, Gothic, or Byzantine forms, except in retaining the use of the round arch, vault, and dome; in the treatment of all details, it was exclusively Latin; the last links of connexion with mediæval tradition having been broken by its builders in their enthusiasm for classical art, and the forms of true Greek or Athenian architecture being still unknown to them. The study of these noble Greek forms has induced various modifications of the Renaissance in our own times; but the conditions which are found most applicable to the uses of modern life are still Roman, and the entire style may most fitly be expressed by the term " Roman Renaissance."

§ III. It is this style, in its purity and fullest form,—represented by such buildings as the Casa Grimani at Venice (built by San Micheli), the Town Hall at Vicenza (by Palladio), St. Peter's at Rome (by Michael Angelo), St. Paul's and Whitehall in London (by Wren and Inigo Jones),— which is the true antagonist of the Gothic school. The intermediate, or corrupt conditions of it, though multiplied over Europe, are no longer admired by architects, or made the subjects of their study; but the finished work of this central school is still, in most cases, the model set before the student of the nineteenth century, as opposed to those Gothic, Romanesque, or Byzantine forms which have long been considered barbarous, and are so still by most of the leading men of the day.   That they are, on the contrary, most noble and beautiful, and that the antagonistic Renaissance is, in the main, unworthy and unadmirable, whatever perfection of a certain kind it may possess, it was my principal purpose to show, when first I undertook the labour of this work.   It has been attempted already to put before the reader the various elements which unite in the Nature of Gothic, and to enable him thus to judge, not merely of the beauty of the forms which that system has produced already, but of its future applicability to the wants of mankind, and endless power over their hearts.   I would now endeavour, in like manner, to set before the reader the Nature of Renaissance, and thus to enable him to compare the two styles under the same light, and with the same enlarged view of their relations to the intellect, and capacities for the service, of man.

§ IV. It will not be necessary for me to enter at length into any examination of its external form.   It uses, whether for its roofs of aperture or roofs proper, the low gable or circular arch : but it differs from Romanesque work in attaching great importance to the horizontal lintel or architrave *above* the arch ; transferring the energy of the principal shafts to the supporting of this horizontal beam, and thus rendering the arch a sub-ordinate, if not altogether a superfluous, feature.   The type of this arrangement has been given already at *c*, Fig. XXXVI., p. 140, Vol. I. : and I might insist at length upon the absurdity of a construction in which the shorter shaft, which has the real weight of wall to carry, is split into two by the taller one, which has nothing to carry at all,—that taller one being strengthened, nevertheless, as if the whole weight of the building bore upon it ; and on the ungracefulness, never conquered in any Palladian work, of the two half-capitals glued, as it were, against the slippery round sides of the central shaft.   But it is not the form of this architecture against which I would plead.   Its defects are shared by many of the noblest forms of earlier building, and might have been entirely atoned for by excellence of spirit.   But it is the moral nature of it which is corrupt, and which it must, therefore, be our principal business to examine and expose.

§ V. The moral, or immoral, elements which unite to form the spirit of Central Renaissance architecture are, I believe, in the main, two,—Pride and Infidelity ; but the pride resolves itself into three main branches,—Pride of Science, Pride of State, and Pride of System : and thus we have four separate mental conditions which must be examined successively.

§ VI. I. PRIDE OF SCIENCE. It would have been more charitable, but more confusing, to have added another element to our list, namely the *Love* of Science ; but the love is included in the pride, and is usually so very subordinate an element, that it does not deserve equality of nomenclature. But, whether pursued in pride or in affection (how far by either we shall see presently), the first notable characteristic of the Renaissance central school is its introduction of accurate knowledge into all its work, so far as it possesses such knowledge ; and its evident conviction that such science is necessary to the excellence of the work, and is the first thing to be expressed therein. So that all the forms introduced, even in its minor ornament, are studied with the utmost care ; the anatomy of all animal structure is thoroughly understood and elaborately expressed, and the whole of the execution skilful and practised in the highest degree. Perspective, linear and aerial, perfect drawing and accurate light and shade in painting, and true anatomy in all representations of the human form, drawn or sculptured, are the first requirements in all the work of this school.

§ VII. Now, first considering all this in the most charitable light, as pursued from a real love of truth, and not from vanity, it would, of course, have been all excellent and admirable, had it been regarded as the aid of art, and not as its essence. But the grand mistake of the Renaissance schools lay in supposing that science and art were the same things, and that to advance in the one was necessarily to perfect the other. Whereas they are, in reality, things not only different, but so opposed that to advance in the one is, in ninety-nine cases out of the hundred, to retrograde in the other. This is the point to which I would at present especially bespeak the reader's attention.

§ VIII. Science and art are commonly distinguished by the nature of their actions; the one as knowing, the other as changing, producing, or creating. But there is a still more important distinction in the nature of the things they deal with. Science deals exclusively with things as they are in themselves; and art exclusively with things as they affect the human sense and human soul.* Her work is to portray the appearances of things, and to deepen the natural impressions which they produce upon living creatures. The work of science is to substitute facts for appearances, and demonstrations for impressions. Both, observe, are equally concerned with truth; the one with truth of aspect, the other with truth of essence. Art does not represent things falsely, but truly as they appear to mankind. Science studies the relations of things to each other: but art studies only their relations to man: and it requires of everything which is submitted to it imperatively this, and only this,—what that thing is to the human eyes and human heart, what it has to say to men, and what it can become to them: a field of question just as much vaster than that of science, as the soul is larger than the material creation.

§ IX. Take a single instance. Science informs us that the sun is ninety-five millions of miles distant from, and 111 times broader than, the earth :† that we and all the planets revolve round it ; and that it revolves on its own axis in 25 days, 14 hours, and 4 minutes. With all this, art has nothing whatsoever to do. It has no care to know anything of this kind. But the things which it does care to know are these: that in the heavens God hath set a tabernacle for the sun, "which is as a bridegroom coming out of his chamber, and rejoiceth as a strong man to run a race. His going forth is from the end of the heaven, and his circuit unto the ends of it, and there is nothing hid from the heat thereof."

---

* Or, more briefly, science has to do with facts, art with phenomena. To science, phenomena are of use only as they lead to facts ; and to art, facts are of use only as they lead to phenomena. I use the word "art" here with reference to the fine arts only; for the lower arts of mechanical production I should reserve the word "manufacture."   [† Written thirty years ago.]

§ X. This, then, being the kind of truth with which art is exclusively concerned, how is such truth as this to be ascertained and accumulated? Evidently, and only, by perception and feeling. Never either by reasoning or report. Nothing must come between Nature and the artist's sight; nothing between God and the artist's soul. Neither calculation nor hearsay,—be it the most subtle of calculations, or the wisest of sayings,—may be allowed to come between the universe, and the witness which art bears to its visible nature. The whole value of that witness depends on its being *eye*-witness; the whole genuineness, acceptableness, and dominion of it depend on the personal assurance of the man who utters it. All its victory depends on the veracity of the one preceding word, "Vidi."

The whole function of the artist in the world is to be a seeing and feeling creature; to be an instrument of such tenderness and sensitiveness, that no shadow, no hue, no line, no instantaneous and evanescent expression of the visible things around him, nor any of the emotions which they are capable of conveying to the spirit which has been given him, shall either be left unrecorded, or fade from the book of record. It is not his business either to think, to judge, to argue, or to know. His place is neither in the closet, nor on the bench, nor at the bar, nor in the library. They are for other men, and other work. He may think, in a by-way; reason, now and then, when he has nothing better to do; know, such fragments of knowledge as he can gather without stooping, or reach without pains; but none of these things are to be his care. The work of his life is to be two-fold only; to see, to feel.

§ XI. Nay, but, the reader perhaps pleads with me, one of the great uses of knowledge is to open the eyes; to make things perceivable which never would have been seen, unless first they had been known.

Not so. This could only be said or believed by those who do not know what the perceptive faculty of a great artist is, in comparison with that of other men. There is no great painter, no great workman in any art, but he sees more with the glance of a moment than he can learn by the labour of a thousand hours.

God has made every man fit for his work; He has given to the man whom He means for a student, the reflective, logical, sequential faculties; and to the man whom He means for an artist, the perceptive, sensitive, retentive faculties. And neither of these men, so far from being able to do the other's work, can even comprehend the way in which it is done. The student has no understanding of the vision, nor the painter of the process; but chiefly, the student has no idea of the colossal grasp of the true painter's vision and sensibility.

The labour of the whole Geological Society, for the last fifty years, has but now arrived at the ascertainment of those truths respecting mountain form which Turner saw and expressed with a few strokes of a camel's hair pencil fifty years ago, when he was a boy. The knowledge of all the laws of the planetary system, and of all the curves of the motion of projectiles, would never enable the man of science to draw a waterfall or a wave; and all the members of Surgeons' Hall helping each other could not at this moment see, or represent, the natural movement of a human body in vigorous action, as a poor dyer's son did two hundred years ago.*

§ XII. But surely, it is still insisted, granting this peculiar faculty to the painter, he will still see more as he knows more, and the more knowledge he obtains, therefore, the better. No; not even so. It is indeed true that, here and there, a piece of knowledge will enable the eye to detect a truth which might otherwise have escaped it; as, for instance, in watching a sunrise, the knowledge of the true nature of the orb may lead the painter to feel more profoundly, and express more fully, the distance between the bars of cloud that cross it, and the sphere of flame that lifts itself slowly beyond them into the infinite heaven. But, for one visible truth to which knowledge thus opens the eyes, it seals them to a thousand : that is to say, if the knowledge occur to the mind so as to occupy its powers of contemplation at the moment when the sight-work is to be done,

---

* Tintoret.

the mind retires inward, fixes itself upon the known fact, and forgets the passing visible ones ; and a *moment* of such forget-fulness loses more to the painter than a day's thought can gain. This is no new or strange assertion.   Every person accustomed to careful reflection of any kind knows that its natural operation is to close his eyes to the external world.   While he is thinking deeply, he neither sees nor feels, even though naturally he may possess strong powers of sight and emotion.   He who, having journeyed all day beside the Leman Lake, asked of his com-panions, at evening, where it was,* probably was not wanting in sensibility ; but he was generally a thinker, not a perceiver. And this instance is only an extreme one of the effect which, in all cases, knowledge, becoming a subject of reflection, produces upon the sensitive faculties   It must be but poor and lifeless knowledge, if it has no tendency to force itself forward, and become ground for reflection, in despite of the succession of external objects.   It will not obey their succession.   The first that comes gives it food enough for its day's work ; it is its habit, its duty, to cast the rest aside, and fasten upon that. The first thing that a thinking and knowing man sees in the course of the day, he will not easily quit.   It is not his way to quit anything without getting to the bottom of it, if possible. But the artist is bound to receive all things on the broad, white, lucid field of his soul, not to grasp at one.   For instance, as the knowing and thinking man watches the sunrise, he sees something in the colour of a ray, or the change of a cloud, that is new to him ; and this he follows out forthwith into a labyrinth of optical and pneumatical laws, perceiving no more clouds nor rays all the morning.   But the painter must catch all the rays, all the colours that come, and see them all truly, all in their real rela-tions and succession ; therefore, everything that occupies room in his mind he must cast aside for the time as completely as may be. The thoughtful man is gone far away to seek ; but the perceiving man must sit still, and open his heart to receive.   The thoughtful

* St. Bernard.

man is knitting and sharpening himself into a two-edged sword, wherewith to pierce. The perceiving man is stretching himself into a four-cornered sheet, wherewith to catch. And all the breadth to which he can expand himself, and all the white emptiness into which he can blanch himself, will not be enough to receive what God has to give him.

§ XIII. What then, it will be indignantly asked, is an utterly ignorant and unthinking man likely to make the best artist? No, not so neither. Knowledge is good for him so long as he can keep it utterly, servilely, subordinate to his own divine work, and trample it under his feet, and out of his way, the moment it is likely to entangle him.

And in this respect, observe, there is an enormous difference between knowledge and education. An artist need not be a *learned* man ; in all probability it will be a disadvantage to him to become so ; but he ought, if possible, always to be an *educated* man : that is, one who has understanding of his own uses and duties in the world, and therefore of the general nature of the things done and existing in the world ; and who has so trained himself, or been trained, as to turn to the best and most courteous account whatever faculties or knowledge he has. The mind of an educated man is greater than the knowledge it possesses ; it is like the vault of heaven, encompassing the earth which lives and flourishes beneath it : but the mind of an uneducated and learned man is like a caoutchouc band, with an everlasting spirit of contraction in it, fastening together papers which it cannot open, and keeps others from opening.

Half our artists are ruined for want of education, and by the possession of knowledge ; the best that I have known have been educated and illiterate. The ideal of an artist, however, is not that he should be illiterate, but well read in the best books, and thoroughly high bred, both in heart and in bearing. In a word, he should be fit for the best society, *and should keep out of it.**

* Society always has a destructive influence upon an artist : first, by its sympathy with his meanest powers ; secondly, by its chilling want of understanding of his greatest ; and, thirdly, by its vain occupation of his time and thoughts. Of

§ xiv. There are, indeed, some kinds of knowledge with which an artist ought to be thoroughly furnished; those, for instance, which enable him to express himself : for this knowledge relieves instead of encumbering his mind, and permits it to attend to its purposes instead of wearying itself about means. The whole mystery of manipulation and manufacture should be familiar to the painter from a child. He should know the chemistry of all colours and materials whatsoever, and should prepare all his colours himself, in a little laboratory of his own. Limiting his chemistry to this one object, the amount of practical science necessary for it, and such accidental discoveries as might fall in his way in the course of his work, of better colours or better methods of preparing them, would be an infinite refreshment to his mind ; a minor subject of interest, to which it might turn when jaded with comfortless labour, or exhausted with feverish invention, and yet which would never interfere with its higher functions, when it chose to address itself to them. Even a considerable amount of manual labour, sturdy colour-grinding and canvas-stretching, would be advantageous ; though this kind of work ought to be in great part done by pupils. For it is one of the conditions of perfect knowledge in these matters, that every great master should have a certain number of pupils, to whom he is to impart all the knowledge of materials and means which he himself possesses, as soon as possible ; so that, at any rate, by the time they are fifteen years old, they may know all that he knows himself in this kind ; that is to say, all that the world of artists know, and his own discoveries besides, and so never be troubled about methods any more. Not that the knowledge even of his own particular methods is to be of purpose confined to himself and his pupils, but that necessarily it must be so in some degree ; for only those who see him at work daily can understand his small and multitudinous ways of practice. These cannot verbally be explained to everybody, nor is it needful that they

course a painter of men must be *among* men ; but it ought to be as a watcher, not as a companion, should ; only let them be concealed from nobody who cares to see them ; in which case, of course, his attendant scholars will know them best.   But all that can be made public in matters of this kind should be so with all speed, every artist throwing his discovery into the common stock, and the whole body of artists taking such pains in this department of science as that there shall be no unsettled questions about any known material or method : that it shall be an entirely ascertained and indisputable matter which is the best white, and which the best brown ; which the strongest canvas, and safest varnish ; and which the shortest and most perfect way of doing everything known up to that time : and if any one discovers a better, he is to make it public forthwith.   All of them taking care to embarrass themselves with no theories or reasons for anything, but to work empirically only : it not being in any wise their business to know whether light moves in rays or in waves ; or whether the blue rays of the spectrum move slower or faster than the rest ; but simply to know how many minutes and seconds such and such a powder must be calcined, to give the brightest blue.

§ xv. Now it is perhaps the most exquisite absurdity of the whole Renaissance system, that while it has encumbered the artist with every species of knowledge that is of no use to him, this one precious and necessary knowledge it has utterly lost.   There is not, I believe, at this moment, a single question which could be put respecting pigments and methods, on which the body of living artists would agree in their answers. The lives of artists are passed in fruitless experiments ; fruitless, because undirected by experience and uncommunicated in their results.   Every man has methods of his own, which he knows to be insufficient, and yet jealously conceals from his fellow-workmen : every colour-man has materials of his own, to which it is rare that the artist can trust : and in the very front of the majestic advance of chemical science, the empirical science of the artist has been annihilated, and the days which should have led us to higher perfection are passed in guessing at, or in mourning over, lost processes ; while the so-called Dark ages, possessing no more knowledge of chemistry than a village herbalist does now, discovered, established, and put into daily practice such methods of operation as have made their work, at this day, the despair of all who look upon it.

§ xvi. And yet even this, to the painter, the safest of sciences, and in some degree necessary, has its temptations, and capabilities of abuse.   For the simplest means are always enough for a great man ; and when once he has obtained a few ordinary colours which he is sure will stand, and a white surface that will not darken, nor moulder, nor rend, he is master of the world, and of his fellow-men.   And, indeed, as if in these times we were bent on furnishing examples of every species of opposite error, while we have suffered the traditions to escape us of the simple methods of doing simple things, which are enough for all the arts, and to all the ages, we have set ourselves to discover fantastic modes of doing fantastic things,—new mixtures and manipulations of metal, and porcelain, and leather, and paper, and every conceivable condition of false substance and cheap work, to our own infinitely multiplied confusion—blinding ourselves daily more and more to the great, changeless, and inevitable truth, that there is but one goodness in art : and that is one which the chemist cannot prepare, nor the merchant cheapen, for it comes only of a rare human hand, and rare human soul.

§ xvii. Within its due limits, however, here is one branch of science which the artist may pursue ; and, within limits still more strict, another also, namely, the science of the appearances of things as they have been ascertained and registered by his fellow-men.   For no day passes but some visible fact is pointed out to us by others, which, without their help, we should not have noticed ; and the accumulation and generalization of visible facts have formed, in the succession of ages, the sciences of light and shade, and perspective, linear and aerial : so that the artist is now at once put in possession of certain truths respecting the appearances of things, which, so pointed out to him, any man may in a few days understand and acknowledge ; but which, without aid, he could not probably discover in his lifetime.   I say, probably could not, because the time which the history of art shows us to have been actually occupied in the discovery and systematization of such truth is no measure of the time *necessary* for such discovery. The lengthened period which elapsed between the earliest and the perfect development of the science of light (if I may so call it) was not occupied in the actual effort to ascertain its laws, but in *acquiring the disposition to make that effort.* It did not take five centuries to find out the appearance of natural objects ; but it took five centuries to make people care about representing them. An artist of the twelfth century did not desire to represent Nature. His work was symbolical and ornamental. So long as it was intelligible and lovely, he had no care to make it like Nature. As, for instance, when an old painter represented the glory round a saint's head by a burnished plate of pure gold, he had no intention of imitating an effect of light. He meant to tell the spectator that the figure so decorated was a saint, and to produce splendour of effect by the golden circle. It was no matter to him what light was like. So soon as it entered into his intention to represent the appearance of light, he was not long in discovering the natural facts necessary for his purpose.

§ xviii. But this being fully allowed, it is still true that the accumulation of facts now known respecting visible phenomena is greater than any man could hope to gather for himself, and that it is well for him to be made acquainted with them ; provided always, that he receive them only at their true value, and do not suffer himself to be misled by them.   I say, at their true value ; that is, an exceedingly small one. All the information which men can receive from the accumulated experience of others is of no use but to enable them more quickly and accurately to see for themselves. It will in nowise take the place of this personal sight. Nothing can be done well in art except by vision. Scientific principles and experiences are helps to the eye, as a microscope is ; and they are of exactly as much use *without* the eye. No science of perspective, or of anything else, will enable us to draw the simplest natural line accurately, unless we see it and feel it. Science is soon at her wits' end. All the professors of perspective in Europe could not, by perspective, draw the line of curve of a sea-beach ; nay, could not outline one pool of the quiet water left among the sand. The eye and hand can do it, nothing else. All the rules of aerial perspective that ever were written, will not tell me how sharply the pines on the hill top are drawn at this moment on the sky. I shall know if I see them, and love them ; not till then. I may study the laws of atmospheric gradation for fourscore years and ten, and I shall not be able to draw so much as a brick-kiln through its own smoke, unless I look at it : and that in an entirely humble and un-scientific manner, ready to see all that the smoke, my master, is ready to show me, and expecting to see nothing more.

§ XIX. So that all the knowledge a man has must be held cheap, and neither trusted nor respected, the moment he comes face to face with Nature. If it help him, well ; if not, but, on the contrary, thrust itself upon him in an impertinent and contradictory temper, and venture to set itself in the slightest degree in opposition to, or comparison with, his sight, let it be disgraced forthwith. And the slave is less likely to take too much upon herself if she has not been bought for a high price. All the knowledge an artist needs will, in these days, come to him almost without his seeking ; if he has far to look for it, he may be sure he does not want it. Prout became Prout without knowing a single rule of perspective to the end of his days ; and all the perspective in the Encyclopædia will never produce us another Prout.

§ XX. And observe, also, knowledge is not only very often unnecessary, but it is often *untrustworthy*. It is inaccurate, and betrays us where the eye would have been true to us. Let us take the single instance of the knowledge of aerial per-spective, of which the moderns are so proud, and see how it betrays us in various ways. First by the conceit of it, which often prevents our enjoying work in which higher and better things were thought of than effects of mist. The other day I showed a fine impression of Albert Durer's "St. Hubert"

to a modern engraver, who had never seen it nor any other of
Albert Durer's works.   He looked at it for a minute contempt-
uously, then turned away : " Ah, I see that man did not know
much about aerial perspective ! "   All the glorious work and
thought of the mighty master, all the redundant landscape,
the living vegetation, the magnificent truth of line, were dead
letters to him, because he happened to have been taught one
particular piece of knowledge which Durer despised.

§ XXI. But not only in the conceit of it, but in the inaccuracy
of it, this science betrays us.   Aerial perspective, as given by
the modern artist, is, in nine cases out of ten, a gross and
ridiculous exaggeration, as is demonstrable in a moment.   The
effect of air in altering the hue and depth of colour is of course
great in the exact proportion of the volume of air between the
observer and the object.   It is not violent within the first few
yards, and then diminished gradually, but it is equal for each
foot of interposing air.   Now in a clear day, and clear
climate, such as that generally presupposed in a work of
fine colour, objects are completely visible at a distance of
ten miles ; visible in light and shade, with gradations between
the two.   Take, then, the faintest possible hue of shadow,
or of any colour, and the most violent and positive possible,
and set them side by side.   The interval between them is
greater than the real difference (for objects may often be seen
clearly much farther than ten miles ; I have seen Mont Blanc
at 120) caused by the ten miles of intervening air between any
given hue of the nearest and most distant objects ; but let us
assume it, in courtesy to the masters of aerial perspective, to be
the real difference.   Then roughly estimating a mile at less than
it really is, also in courtesy to them, or at 5,000 feet, we have
this difference between tints produced by 50,000 feet of air.
Then, ten feet of air will produce the 5,000th part of this difference.   Let the reader take the two extreme tints, and carefully
gradate the one into the other.   Let him divide this gradated
shadow or colour into 5,000 successive parts ; and the difference
in depth between one of these parts and the next is the exact

amount of aerial perspective between one object and another, ten feet behind it, on a clear day.

§ xxii. Now, in Millais' "Huguenot," the figures were standing about three feet from the wall behind them ; and the wise world of critics, which could find no other fault with the picture, professed to have its eyes hurt by the want of an aerial perspective, which, had it been accurately given (as, indeed, I believe it was), would have amounted to the $\frac{10}{3}$ 5,000th, or less than the 15,000th part of the depth of any given colour. It would be interesting to see a picture painted by the critics upon this scientific principle. The aerial perspective usually represented is entirely conventional and ridiculous ; a mere struggle on the part of the pretendedly well-informed, but really ignorant, artist, to express distances by mist which he cannot by drawing.

It is curious that the critical world is just as much offended by the true *presence* of aerial perspective, over distances of fifty miles, and with definite purpose of representing mist, in the works of Turner, as by the true *absence* of aerial perspective, over distances of three feet, and in clear weather, in those of Millais.

§ xxiii. "Well but," still answers the reader, " this kind of error may here and there be occasioned by too much respect for undigested knowledge ; but, on the whole, the gain is greater than the loss, and the fact is, that a picture of the Renaissance period, or by a modern master, does indeed represent Nature more faithfully than one wrought in the ignorance of old times." No, not one whit ; for the most part, less faithfully. Indeed, the outside of Nature is more truly drawn ; the material commonplace, which can be systematized, catalogued, and taught to all painstaking mankind,—forms of ribs and scapulæ,* of eyebrows and lips, and

---

* I intended in this place to have introduced some special consideration of the science of anatomy, which I believe to have been in great part the cause of the decline of modern art ; but I have been anticipated by a writer better able to treat the subject. I have only glanced at his book ; and there is something in the spirit of it which I do not like, and some parts of it are assuredly wrong ; but, respecting anatomy, it seems to me to settle the question indisputably, more especially as being written by a master of the science. I quote two passages, and must refer the reader to the sequel :

curls of hair. Whatever can be measured and handled, dissected and demonstrated,—in a word, whatever is of the body only,—that the schools of knowledge do resolutely and courageously possess themselves of, and portray. But whatever is immeasurable, intangible, indivisible, and of the spirit, that the schools of knowledge do as certainly lose, and blot out of their sight : that is to say, all that is worth art's possessing or recording at all ; for whatever can be arrested, measured, and systematized, we can contemplate as much as we will in Nature herself. But

" *The scientific men of forty centuries* have failed to describe so accurately, so beautifully, so artistically as Homer did, the organic elements constituting the emblems of youth and beauty, and the waste and decay which these sustain by time and age. All these Homer understood better, and has described more truthfully, than the scientific men of forty centuries. . . . .

" Before I approach this question, permit me to make a few remarks on the pre-historic period of Greece ; that era which seems to have produced nearly all the great men.

" On looking attentively at the statues within my observation, I cannot find the slightest foundation for the assertion that their sculptors must have dissected the human frame, and been well acquainted with human anatomy. They, like Homer, had discovered Nature's secret, and bestowed their whole attention on the exterior. The exterior they read profoundly, and studied deeply—the *living exterior* and the *dead*. Above all, they avoided displaying the dead and dissected interior, through the exterior. They had discovered that the interior presents hideous shapes but not forms. Men during the philosophic era of Greece saw all this, each reading the antique to the best of his abilities. The man of genius rediscovered the canon of the ancient masters, and wrought on its principles. The greater number, as now, unequal to this step, merely imitated and copied those who preceded them."—*Great Artists and Great Anatomists.* By R. Knox, M.D. London, Van Voorst, 1852.

Respecting the value of literary knowledge in general as regards art, the reader will also do well to meditate on the following sentences from Hallam's " Literature of Europe ; " remembering at the same time what I have above said, that " the root of all great art in Europe is struck in the thirteenth century," and that the great time is from 1250 to 1350 :

" In Germany, the tenth century, Leibnitz declares, was a golden age of learning compared with the thirteenth."

" The writers of the thirteenth century display an incredible ignorance, not only of pure idiom, but of common grammatical rules."

The fourteenth century was " not superior to the thirteenth in learning. . . . We may justly praise Richard of Bury for his zeal in collecting books. But his erudition appears crude, his style indifferent, and his thoughts superficial."

I doubt the superficialness of the *thoughts* : at all events, this is not a character of the time, though it may be of the writer ; for this would affect art more even than literature.

what we want art to do for us is to stay what is fleeting, and to enlighten what is incomprehensible, to incorporate the things that have no measure, and immortalize the things that have no duration. The dimly seen, momentary glance, the flitting shadow of faint emotion, the imperfect lines of fading thought, and all that by and through such things as these is recorded on the features of man, and all that in man's person and actions, and in the great natural world, is infinite and wonderful; having in it that spirit and power which man may witness, but not weigh; conceive, but not comprehend; love, but not limit; and imagine, but not define;—this, the beginning and the end of the aim of all noble art, we have, in the ancient art, by perception; and we have *not*, in the newer art, by knowledge. Giotto gives it us: Orcagna gives it us; Angelico, Memmi, Pisano,—it matters not who,—all simple and unlearned men, in their measure and manner,—give it us; and the learned men that followed them give it us not, and we, in our supreme learning, own ourselves at this day farther from it than ever.

§ XXIV. "Nay," but it is still answered, "this is because we have not yet brought our knowledge into right use, but have been seeking to accumulate it, rather than to apply it wisely to the ends of art. Let us now do this, and we may achieve all that was done by that elder ignorant art, and infinitely more." No, not so; for as soon as we try to put our knowledge to good use, we shall find that we have much more than we can use, and that what more we have is an encumbrance. All our errors in this respect arise from a gross misconception as to the true nature of knowledge itself. We talk of learned and ignorant men, as if there were a certain quantity of knowledge, which to possess was to be learned, and which not to possess was to be ignorant; instead of considering that knowledge is infinite, and that the man most learned in human estimation is just as far from knowing anything as he ought to know it, as the unlettered peasant. Men are merely on a lower or higher stage of an eminence, whose summit is God's throne, infinitely above all; and there is just as much reason for the wisest as for the simplest man being discontented with his position, as respects the real quantity of knowledge he possesses. And, for both of them, the only true reasons for contentment with the sum of knowledge they possess are these : that it is the kind of knowledge they need for their duty and happiness in life ; that all they have is tested and certain, so far as it is in their power ; that all they have is well in order, and within reach when they need it ; that it has not cost too much time in the getting ; that none of it, once got, has been lost ; and that there is not too much to be easily taken care of.

§ xxv. Consider these requirements a little, and the evils that result in our education and polity from neglecting them. Knowledge is mental food, and is exactly to the spirit what food is to the body (except that the spirit needs several sorts of food, of which knowledge is only one), and it is liable to the same kind of misuses. It may be mixed and disguised by art, till it becomes unwholesome : it may be refined, sweetened, and made palatable, until it has lost all its power of nourishment ; and, even of its best kind, it may be eaten to surfeiting, and minister to disease and death.

§ xxvi. Therefore, with respect to knowledge, we are to reason and act exactly as with respect to food. We no more live to know than we live to eat. We live to contemplate, enjoy, act, adore : and we may know all that is to be known in this world, and what Satan knows in the other, without being able to do any of these. We are to ask, therefore, first, is the knowledge we would have fit food for us, good and simple, not artificial and decorated ? and secondly, how much of it will enable us best for our work ; and will leave our hearts light, and our eyes clear ? For no more than that is to be eaten without the old Eve-sin.

§ xxvii. Observe, also, the difference between tasting knowledge and hoarding it. In this respect it is also like food; since, in some measure, the knowledge of all men is laid up in granaries, for future use ; much of it is at any given moment dormant, not fed upon or enjoyed, but in store. And by all it is to be remembered that knowledge in this form may be kept without air till it rots, or in such unthreshed disorder that it is of no use; and that, however good or orderly, it is still only in being tasted that it becomes of use; and that men may easily starve in their own granaries, men of science, perhaps, most of all, for they are likely to seek accumulation of their store, rather than nourishment from it. Yet let it not be thought that I would undervalue them. The good and great among them are like Joseph, to whom all nations sought to buy corn; or like the sower going forth to sow beside all waters, sending forth thither the feet of the ox and the ass : only let us remember that this is not all men's work. We are not intended to be all keepers of granaries, nor all to be measured by the filling of the storehouse; but many, nay, most of us, are to receive day by day our daily bread, and shall be as well nourished and as fit for our labour, and often, also, fit for nobler and more divine labour, in feeding from the barrel of meal that does not waste and from the cruse of oil that does not fail, than if our barns were filled with plenty, and our presses bursting out with new wine.

§ XXVIII. It is for each man to find his own measure in this matter; in great part, also, for others to find it for him, while he is yet a youth. And the desperate evil of the whole Renaissance system is, that all idea of measure is therein forgotten, that knowledge is thought the one and the only good, and it is never inquired whether men are vivified by it or paralyzed. Let us leave figures. The reader may not believe the analogy I have been pressing so far; but let him consider the subject in itself, let him examine the effect of knowledge in his own heart, and see whether the trees of knowledge and of life are one now, any more than in Paradise. He must feel that the real animating power of knowledge is only in the moment of its being first received, when it fills us with wonder and joy; a joy for which, observe, the previous ignorance is just as necessary as the present knowledge. That man is always happy who is in the presence of something which he cannot know to the full, which he is always going on to know. This is the necessary condition of a finite creature with divinely rooted and divinely directed intelligence; this, therefore, its happy state,—but observe, a state, not of triumph or joy in what it knows, but of joy rather in the continual discovery of new ignorance, continual self-abasement, continual astonishment. Once thoroughly our own, the knowledge ceases to give us pleasure. It may be practically useful to us, it may be good for others, or good for usury to obtain more; but, in itself, once let it be thoroughly familiar, and it is dead. The wonder is gone from it, and all the fine colour which it had when first we drew it up out of the infinite sea. And what does it matter how much or how little of it we have laid aside, when our only enjoyment is still in the casting of that deep-sea line? What does it matter? Nay, in one respect, it matters much, and not to our advantage. For one effect of knowledge is to deaden the force of the imagination and the original energy of the whole man: under the weight of his knowledge he cannot move so lightly as in the days of his simplicity. The pack-horse is furnished for the journey, the war-horse is armed for war; but the freedom of the field and the lightness of the limb are lost for both. Knowledge is, at best, the pilgrim's burden or the soldier's panoply, often a weariness to them both; and the Renaissance knowledge is like the Renaissance armour of plate, binding and cramping the human form; while all good knowledge is like the crusader's chain mail, which throws itself into folds with the body, yet it is rarely so forged as that the clasps and rivets do not gall us. All men feel this, though they do not think of it, nor reason out its consequences. They look back to the days of childhood as of greatest happiness, because those were the days of greatest wonder, greatest sim-plicity, and most vigorous imagination. And the whole dif-ference between a man of genius and other men, it has been said a thousand times, and most truly, is that the first remains in great part a child, seeing with the large eyes of children, in perpetual wonder, not conscious of much knowledge,—conscious, rather, of infinite ignorance, and yet infinite power; a foun-tain of eternal admiration, delight, and creative force within him, meeting the ocean of visible and governable things around him.

That is what we have to make men, so far as we may. All are to be men of genius in their degree,—rivulets or rivers, it does not matter, so that the souls be clear and pure; not dead walls encompassing dead heaps of things known and numbered, but running waters in the sweet wilderness of things unnumbered and unknown, conscious only of the living banks, on which they partly refresh and partly reflect the flowers, and so pass on.

§ xxix. Let each man answer for himself how far his knowledge has made him this, or how far it is loaded upon him as the pyramid is upon the tomb. Let him consider, also, how much of it has cost him labour and time that might have been spent in healthy, happy action, beneficial to all mankind; how many living souls may have been left uncomforted and unhelped by him, while his own eyes were failing by the midnight lamp; how many warm sympathies have died within him as he measured lines or counted letters; how many draughts of ocean air, and steps on mountain turf, and openings of the highest heaven he has lost for his knowledge; how much of that knowledge, so dearly bought, is now forgotten or despised, leaving only the capacity of wonder less within him, and, as it happens in a thousand instances, perhaps even also the capacity of devotion. And let him,—if, after thus dealing with his own heart, he can say that his knowledge has indeed been fruitful to him,—yet consider how many there are who have been forced by the inevitable laws of modern education into toil utterly repugnant to their natures, and that in the extreme, until the whole strength of the young soul was sapped away; and then pronounce with fearfulness how far, and in how many senses, it may indeed be true that the wisdom of this world is foolishness with God.

§ xxx. Now all this possibility of evil, observe, attaches to knowledge pursued for the noblest ends, if it be pursued imprudently. I have assumed, in speaking of its effect both on men generally and on the artist especially, that it was sought in the true love of it, and with all honesty and directness of purpose. But this is granting far too much in its favour. Of knowledge in general, and without qualification, it is said by the Apostle that "it puffeth up ;" and the father of all modern science, writing directly in its praise, yet asserts this danger even in more absolute terms, calling it a "venomousness" in the very nature of knowledge itself.

§ XXXI. There is, indeed, much difference in this respect between the tendencies of different branches of knowledge ; it being a sure rule that exactly in proportion as they are inferior, nugatory, or limited in scope, their power of feeding pride is greater. Thus philology, logic, rhetoric, and the other sciences of the schools, being for the most part ridiculous and trifling, have so pestilent an effect upon those who are devoted to them, that their students cannot conceive of any higher sciences than these, but fancy that all education ends in the knowledge of words : but the true and great sciences, more especially natural history, make men gentle and modest in proportion to the largeness of their apprehension, and just perception of the infiniteness of the things they can never know. And this, it seems to me, is the principal lesson we are intended to be taught by the book of Job ; for there God has thrown open to us the heart of a man most just and holy, and apparently perfect in all things possible to human nature except humility. For this he is tried : and we are shown that no suffering, no self-examination, however honest, however stern, no searching out of the heart by its own bitterness, is enough to convince man of his nothingness before God ; but that the sight of God's creation will do it. For, when the Deity Himself has willed to end the temptation, and to accomplish in Job that for which it was sent, He does not vouchsafe to reason with him, still less does He overwhelm him with terror, or confound him by laying open before his eyes the book of his iniquities. He opens before him only the arch of the dayspring, and the fountains of the deep ; and amidst the covert of the reeds, and on the heaving

waves, He bids him watch the kings of the children of pride,—
" Behold now Behemoth, which I made with thee : " And the
work is done.

§ XXXII Thus, if, I repeat, there is any one lesson in the
whole book which stands forth more definitely than another, it
is this of the holy and humbling influence of natural science on
the human heart.   And yet, even here, it is not the science, but
the perception, to which the good is owing ; and the natural
sciences may become as harmful as any others, when they lose
themselves in classification and catalogue-making.   Still, the
principal danger is with the sciences of words and methods ; and
it was exactly into those sciences that the whole energy of men
during the Renaissance period was thrown.   They discovered
suddenly that the world for ten centuries had been living in
an ungrammatical manner, and they made it forthwith the end of
human existence to be grammatical.   And it mattered thenceforth
nothing what was said, or what was done, so only that it was
said with scholarship, and done with system.   Falsehood in a
Ciceronian dialect had no opposers ; truth in patois no listeners.
A Roman phrase was thought worth any number of Gothic facts.
The sciences ceased at once to be anything more than different
kinds of grammars,—grammar of language, grammar of logic,
grammar of ethics, grammar of art ; and the tongue, wit, and
invention of the human race were supposed to have found their
utmost and most divine mission in syntax and syllogism, perspective and five orders.

Of such knowledge as this, nothing but pride could come ;
and, therefore, I have called the first mental characteristic of the
Renaissance schools the " pride " of science.   If they had reached
any science worthy the name, they might have loved it ; but of
the paltry knowledge they possessed they could only be proud.
There was not anything in it capable of being loved.   Anatomy,
indeed, then first made a subject of accurate study, is a true
science, but not so attractive as to enlist the affections strongly
on its side ; and therefore, like its meaner sisters, it became

merely a ground of pride ; and the one main purpose of the Renaissance artists, in all their work, was to show how much they knew.

§ XXXIII. There were, of course, noble exceptions ; but chiefly belonging to the earliest periods of the Renaissance, when its teaching had not yet produced its full effect. Raphael, Leonardo, and Michael Angelo were all trained in the old school; they all had masters who knew the true ends of art, and had reached them ; masters nearly as great as they were themselves, but imbued with the old religious and earnest spirit, which their disciples receiving from them, and drinking at the same time deeply from all the fountains of knowledge opened in their day, became the world's wonders. Then the dull wondering world believed that their greatness rose out of their new knowledge, instead of out of that ancient religious root, in which to abide was life, from which to be severed was annihilation. And from that day to this, they have tried to produce Michael Angelos and Leonardos by teaching the barren sciences, and still have mourned and marvelled that no more Michael Angelos came ; not perceiving that those great Fathers were only able to receive such nourishment because they were rooted on the rock of all ages, and that our scientific teaching, nowadays, is nothing more nor less than the assiduous watering of trees whose stems are cut through. Nay, I have even granted too much in saying that those great men were able to receive pure nourishment from the sciences ; for my own conviction is, and I know it to be shared by most of those who love Raphael truly,—that he painted best when he knew least. Michael Angelo was betrayed, again and again, into such vain and offensive exhibition of his anatomical knowledge as, to this day, renders his higher powers indiscernible by the greater part of men ; and Leonardo fretted his life away in engineering, so that there is hardly a picture left to bear his name. But, with respect to all who followed, there can be no question that the science they possessed was utterly harmful ; serving merely to draw away the hearts at once from the purposes of art and the power of nature, and to make, out of the canvas and marble, nothing more than materials for the exhibition of petty dexterity and useless knowledge.

§ XXXIV. It is sometimes amusing to watch the naïve and childish way in which this vanity is shown. For instance, when perspective was first invented, the world thought it a mighty discovery, and the greatest men it had in it were as proud of knowing that retiring lines converge, as if all the wisdom of Solomon had been compressed into a vanishing point. And, accordingly, it became nearly impossible for any one to paint a Nativity, but he must turn the stable and manger into a Corinthian arcade, in order to show his knowledge of perspective; and half the best architecture of the time, instead of being adorned with historical sculpture, as of old, was set forth with bas-relief of minor corridors and galleries, thrown into perspective.

Now that perspective can be taught to any schoolboy in a week, we can smile at this vanity. But the fact is, that all pride in knowledge is precisely as ridiculous, whatever its kind, or whatever its degree. There is, indeed, nothing of which man has any right to be proud; but the very last thing of which, with any shadow of reason, he can make his boast is his knowledge, except only that infinitely small portion of it which he has discovered for himself. For what is there to be more proud of in receiving a piece of knowledge from another person, than in receiving a piece of money? Beggars should not be proud, whatever kind of alms they receive. Knowledge is like current coin. A man may have some right to be proud of possessing it, if he has worked for the gold of it, and assayed it, and stamped it, so that it may be received of all men as true; or earned it fairly being already assayed : but if he has done none of these things, but only had it thrown in his face by a passer-by, what cause has he to be proud? And though, in this mendicant fashion, he has heaped together the wealth of Crœsus, would pride any more, for this, become him, as, in some sort, it becomes the man who has laboured for his fortune, however small? So, if a man tells me the sun is larger than the earth, have I any cause for pride in knowing it? or, if any multitude of men tell me any number of things, heaping all their wealth of knowledge upon me, have I any reason to feel proud under the heap ? And is not nearly all the knowledge of which we boast in these days cast upon us in this dishonourable way; worked for by other men ; proved by them, and then forced upon us, even against our wills, and beaten into us in our youth, before we have the wit even to know if it be good or not ? (Mark the distinction between knowledge and thought.) Truly a noble possession to be proud of! Be assured, there is no part of the furniture of a man's mind which he has a right to exult in, but that which he has hewn and fashioned for himself. He who has built himself a hut on a desert heath, and carved his bed, and table, and chair out of the nearest forest, may have some right to take pride in the appliances of his narrow chamber, as assuredly he will have joy in them. But the man who has had a palace built, and adorned, and furnished for him, may, indeed, have many advantages above the other, but he has no reason to be proud of his upholsterer's skill ; and it is ten to one if he has half the joy in his couches of ivory that the other will have in his pallet of pine.

§ xxxv. And observe how we feel this, in the kind of respect we pay to such knowledge as we are indeed capable of estimating the value of. When it is our own, and new to us, we cannot judge of it ; but let it be another's also, and long familiar to us, and see what value we set on it. Consider how we regard a schoolboy fresh from his term's labour. If he begin to display his newly acquired small knowledge to us, and plume himself thereupon, how soon do we silence him with contempt ! But it is not so if the schoolboy begins to feel or see anything. In the strivings of his soul within him he is our equal ; in his power of sight and thought he stands separate from us, and may be a greater than we. We are ready to hear him forthwith. " You saw that? you felt that ? No matter for your being a child ; let us hear."

§ xxxvi. Consider that every generation of men stands in this relation to its successors. It is as the schoolboy : the knowledge of which it is proudest will be as the alphabet to those who follow.   It had better make no noise about its knowledge ; a time will come when its utmost, in that kind, will be food for scorn. Poor fools ! was that all they knew ? and behold how proud they were !   But what we see and feel will never be mocked at.   All men will be thankful to us for telling them that.   " Indeed ! " they will say, " they felt that in their day ? saw that ?   Would God we may be like them, before we go to the home where sight and thought are not ! "

This unhappy and childish pride in knowledge, then, was the first constituent element of the Renaissance mind, and it was enough, of itself, to have cast it into swift decline : but it was aided by another form of pride, which was above called the Pride of State ; and which we have next to examine.

§ xxxvii. II. PRIDE OF STATE.   It was noticed, in the second volume of " Modern Painters," p. 117, that the principle which had most power in retarding the modern school of portraiture was its constant expression of individual vanity and pride.   And the reader cannot fail to have observed that one of the readiest and commonest ways in which the painter ministers to this vanity is by introducing the pedestal or shaft of a column, or some fragment, however simple, of Renaissance architecture, in the background of the portrait.   And this is not merely because such architecture is bolder or grander than, in general, that of the apartments of a private house.   No other architecture would produce the same effect in the same degree.   The richest Gothic, the most massive Norman, would not produce the same sense of exaltation as the simple and meagre lines of the Renaissance.

§ xxxviii. And if we think over this matter a little, we shall soon feel that in those meagre lines there is indeed an expression of aristocracy in its worst characters ; coldness, perfectness of training, incapability of emotion, want of sympathy with the weakness of lower men, blank, hopeless, haughty self-sufficiency. All these characters are written in the Renaissance architecture as plainly as if they were graven on it in words.   For, observe, all other architectures have something in them that common men can enjoy ; some concession to the simplicities of humanity, some daily bread for the hunger of the multitude.   Quaint fancy, rich ornament, bright colour, something that shows a sympathy with men of ordinary minds and hearts ; and this wrought out, at least in the Gothic, with a rudeness showing that the workman did not mind exposing his own ignorance if he could please others.   But the Renaissance is exactly the contrary of all this. It is rigid, cold, inhuman ; incapable of glowing, of stooping, of conceding for an instant.   Whatever excellence it has is refined, high-trained, and deeply erudite ; a kind which the architect well knows no common mind can taste.   He proclaims it to us aloud.   "You cannot feel my work unless you study Vitruvius. I will give you no gay colour, no pleasant sculpture, nothing to make you happy ; for I am a learned man.   All the pleasure you can have in anything I do is in its proud breeding, its rigid formalism, its perfect finish, its cold tranquillity.   I do not work for the vulgar, only for the men of the academy and the court."

§ xxxix. And the instinct of the world felt this in a moment. In the new precision and accurate law of the classical forms, they perceived something peculiarly adapted to the setting forth of state in an appalling manner ; princes delighted in it, and courtiers.   The Gothic was good for God's worship, but this was good for man's worship.   The Gothic had fellowship with all hearts, and was universal, like nature : it could frame a temple for the prayer of nations, or shrink into the poor man's winding stair.   But here was an architecture that would not shrink, that had in it no submission, no mercy.   The proud princes and lords rejoiced in it.   It was full of insult to the poor in its every line. It would not be built of the materials at the poor man's hand ; it would not roof itself with thatch or shingle and black oak beams ; it would not wall itself with rough stone or brick ; it would not pierce itself with small windows where they were needed ; it would not niche itself, wherever there was room for it, in the street corners.   It would be of hewn stone ; it would have its windows and its doors, and its stairs and its pillars, in lordly order and of stately size ; it would have its wings and its corridors, and its halls and its gardens, as if all the earth were its own. And the rugged cottages of the mountaineers, and the fantastic streets of the labouring burgher, were to be thrust out of its way, as of a lower species.

§ XL. It is to be noted, also, that it ministered as much to luxury as to pride. Not to luxury of the eye ; that is a holy luxury : Nature ministers to that in her painted meadows, and sculptured forests, and gilded heavens ; the Gothic builder ministered to that in his twisted traceries, and deep-wrought foliage, and burning casements. The dead Renaissance drew back into its earthliness, out of all that was warm and heavenly ; back into its pride, out of all that was simple and kind ; back into its stateliness, out of all that was impulsive, reverent, and gay. But it understood the luxury of the body ; the terraced and scented and grottoed garden, with its trickling fountains and slumbrous shades ; the spacious hall and lengthened corridor for the summer heat ; the well-closed windows, and perfect fittings and furniture, for defence against the cold : and the soft picture, and frescoed wall and roof, covered with the last lasciviousness of Paganism ;— this it understood and possessed to the full, and still possesses. This is the kind of domestic architecture on which we pride ourselves, even to this day, as an infinite and honourable advance from the rough habits of our ancestors ; from the time when the king's floor was strewn with rushes, and the tapestries swayed before the searching wind in the baron's hall.

§ XLI. Let us hear two stories of those rougher times.

At the debate of King Edwin with his courtiers and priests, whether he ought to receive the Gospel preached to him by Paulinus, one of his nobles spoke as follows :

" The present life, O king ! weighed with the time that is unknown, seems to me like this : When you are sitting at a feast with your earls and thanes in winter time, and the fire is lighted, and the hall is warmed, and it rains and snows, and the storm is loud without, there comes a sparrow, and flies through the house. It comes in at one door, and goes out at the other. While it is within, it is not touched by the winter's storm ; but it is but for the twinkling of an eye, for from winter it comes and to winter it returns.   So also this life of man endureth for a little space ; what goes before, or what follows after, we know not. Wherefore, if this new lore bring anything more certain, it is fit that we should follow it." *

That could not have happened in a Renaissance building. The bird could not have dashed in from the cold into the heat, and from the heat back again into the storm.   It would have had to come up a flight of marble stairs, and through seven or eight antechambers ; and so, if it had ever made its way into the presence-chamber, out again through loggias and corridors innumerable.   And the truth which the bird brought with it, fresh from heaven, has, in like manner, to make its way to the Renaissance mind through many antechambers, hardly, and as a despised thing, if at all.

§ XLII. Hear another story of those early times.

The king of Jerusalem, Godfrey of Bouillon, at the siege of Asshur, or Arsur, gave audience to some emirs from Samaria and Naplous.   They found him seated on the ground on a sack of straw.   They expressing surprise, Godfrey answered them : "May not the earth, out of which we came, and which is to be our dwelling after death, serve us for a seat during life ? "

It is long since such a throne has been set in the reception-chambers of Christendom, or such an answer heard from the lips of a king.

Thus the Renaissance spirit became base both in its abstinence and its indulgence.   Base in its abstinence ; curtailing the bright and playful wealth of form and thought which filled the architecture of the earlier ages with sources of delight for their hardy spirit, pure, simple, and yet rich as the fretwork of flowers and moss watered by some strong and stainless mountain stream : and base in its indulgence ; as it granted to the body what it withdrew from the heart, and exhausted, in smoothing the pavement for the painless feet, and softening the pillow for the sluggish brain, the powers of art which once had hewn rough ladders into

* Churton's "Early English Church."   London, 1840.

the clouds of heaven, and set up the stones by which they rested for houses of God.

§ XLIII. And just in proportion as this courtly sensuality lowered the real nobleness of the men whom birth or fortune raised above their fellows, rose their estimate of their own dignity, together with the insolence and unkindness of its expression, and the grossness of the flattery with which it was fed. Pride is indeed the first and last among the sins of men, and there is no age of the world in which it has not been unveiled in the power and prosperity of the wicked. But there was never in any form of slavery, or of feudal supremacy, a forgetfulness so total of the common majesty of the human soul, and of the brotherly kindness due from man to man, as in the aristocratic follies of the Renaissance. I have not space to follow out this most interesting and extensive subject; but here is a single and very curious example of the kind of flattery with which architectural teaching was mingled, when addressed to the men of rank of the day.

§ XLIV. In St. Mark's library there is a very curious Latin manuscript of the twenty-five books of Averulinus, a Florentine architect, upon the principles of his art. The book was written in or about 1460, and translated into Latin, and richly illuminated for Corvinus, King of Hungary, about 1483. I extract from the third book the following passage on the nature of stones :—" As there are three genera of men,—that is to say, nobles, men of the middle classes, and rustics,—so it appears that there are of stones. For the marbles and common stones of which we have spoken above set forth the rustics. The porphyries and alabasters, and the other harder stones of mingled quality, represent the middle classes, if we are to deal in comparisons ; and by means of these the ancients adorned their temples with incrustations and ornaments in a magnificent manner. And after these come the chalcedonies and sardonyxes, etc., which are so transparent that no spot can exist in them without its being seen. Thus let men endowed with nobility lead a life in which no spot can be found." *

* The advice is good, but illogical; for the spots of marbles are, when

Canute or Cœur de Lion (I name not Godfrey or St. Louis) would have dashed their sceptres against the lips of a man who should have dared to utter to them flattery such as this.   But in the fifteenth century it was rendered and accepted as a matter of course, and the tempers which delighted in it necessarily took pleasure also in every vulgar or false means of marking worldly superiority. And among such false means, largeness of scale in the dwelling-house was of course one of the easiest and most direct. All persons, however senseless or dull, could appreciate size ; it required some exertion of intelligence to enter into the spirit of the quaint carving of the Gothic times, but none to perceive that one heap of stones was higher than another.*   And therefore, while in the execution and manner of work the Renaissance builders zeal-ously vindicated for themselves the attribute of cold and superior learning, they appealed for such approbation as they needed from the multitude to the lowest possible standard of taste : and while the older workman lavished his labour on the minute niche and narrow casement, on the doorways no higher than the head, and the contracted angles of the turreted chamber, the Renaissance builder spared such cost and toil in his detail, that he might spend it in bringing larger stones from a distance ; and restricted himself to rustication and five orders, that he might load the ground with colossal piers, and raise an ambitious barrenness of architecture, as inanimate as it was gigantic, above the feasts and follies of the powerful or the rich.   The Titanic insanity extended itself also into ecclesiastical design : the principal church in Italy was built with little idea of any other admirableness than that which was to result from its being huge ; and the religious impressions of those who enter it are to this day supposed to be dependent, in a great degree, on their discovering that they

frequent enough, thought decorative.   How often has it happened that men of rank have thought sin also decorative, if only bold and frequent !

* Observe, however, that the magnitude spoken of here and in the following passages, is the finished and polished magnitude sought for the sake of pomp : not the rough magnitude sought for the sake of sublimity : respecting which see the "Seven Lamps," chap. iii. §§ 5, 6, and 8.

cannot span the thumbs of the statues which sustain the vessels for holy water.

§ XLV. It is easy to understand how an architecture which thus appealed not less to the lowest instincts of dulness than to the subtlest pride of learning, rapidly found acceptance with a large body of mankind ; and how the spacious pomp of the new manner of design came to be eagerly adopted by the luxurious aristocracies, not only of Venice, but of the other countries of Christendom, now gradually gathering themselves into that insolent and festering isolation, against which the cry of the poor sounded hourly in more ominous unison, bursting at last into thunder (mark where,—first among the planted walks and plashing fountains of the palace wherein the Renaissance luxury attained its utmost height in Europe, Versailles) ; that cry, mingling so much piteousness with its wrath and indignation, " Our soul is filled with the scornful reproof of the wealthy, and with the despitefulness of the proud."

§ XLVI. But of all the evidence bearing upon this subject presented by the various art of the fifteenth century, none is so interesting or so conclusive as that deduced from its tombs. For, exactly in proportion as the pride of life became more insolent, the fear of death became more servile ; and the difference in the manner in which the men of early and later days adorned the sepulchre, confesses a still greater difference in their manner of regarding death.   To those he came as the comforter and the friend, rest in his right hand, hope in his left ; to these as the humiliator, the spoiler, and the avenger.   And, therefore, we find the early tombs at once simple and lovely in adornment, severe and solemn in their expression ; confessing the power, and accepting the peace, of death, openly and joyfully ; and in all their symbols marking that the hope of resurrection lay only in Christ's righteousness ; signed always with this simple utterance of the dead, " I will lay me down in peace, and take my rest ; for it is thou, Lord, only that makest me dwell in safety."   But the tombs of the later ages are a ghastly struggle of mean pride and miserable

terror : the one mustering the statues of the Virtues about
the tomb, disguising the sarcophagus with delicate sculpture,
polishing the false periods of the elaborate epitaph, and filling
with strained animation the features of the portrait statue ;
and the other summoning underneath, out of the niche or
from behind the curtain, the frowning skull, or scythed skeleton,
or some other more terrible image of the enemy in whose
defiance the whiteness of the sepulchre had been set to shine
above the whiteness of the ashes.

§ XLVII. This change in the feeling with which sepulchral
monuments were designed, from the eleventh to the eighteenth
centuries, has been common to the whole of Europe. But,
as Venice is in other respects the centre of the Renaissance
system, so also she exhibits this change in the manner of the
sepulchral monument under circumstances peculiarly calculated
to teach us its true character. For the severe guard which,
in earlier times, she put upon every tendency to personal pomp
and ambition, renders the tombs of her ancient monarchs as
remarkable for modesty and simplicity as for their religious
feeling ; so that, in this respect, they are separated by a considerable interval from the more costly monuments erected at
the same periods to the kings or nobles of other European
states. In later times, on the other hand, as the piety of the
Venetians diminished, their pride overleaped all limits, and the
tombs which, in recent epochs, were erected for men who had
lived only to impoverish or disgrace the state, were as much
more magnificent than those contemporaneously erected for the
nobles of Europe, as the monuments of the great Doges had
been humbler. When, in addition to this, we reflect that the
art of sculpture, considered as expressive of emotion, was at a
low ebb in Venice in the twelfth century, and that in the seventeenth she took the lead in Italy in luxurious work, we shall at
once see that the chain of examples through which the change
of feeling is expressed, must present more remarkable extremes
here than it can in any other city ; extremes so startling that
their impressiveness cannot be diminished, while their intelli-

gibility is greatly increased, by the large number of intermediate types which have fortunately been preserved.

It would, however, too much weary the general reader if, without illustrations, I were to endeavour to lead him step by step through the aisles of St. John and Paul; and I shall therefore confine myself to a slight notice of those features in sepulchral architecture generally which are especially illustrative of the matter at present in hand, and point out the order in which, if possible, the traveller should visit the tombs in Venice, so as to be most deeply impressed with the true character of the lessons they convey.

§ XLVIII. I have not such an acquaintance with the modes of entombment or memorial in the earliest ages of Christianity as would justify me in making any general statement respecting them : but it seems to me that the perfect type of a Christian tomb was not developed until towards the thirteenth century, sooner or later according to the civilization of each country ; that perfect type consisting in the raised and perfectly visible sarcophagus of stone, bearing upon it a recumbent figure, and the whole covered by a canopy. Before that type was entirely developed, and in the more ordinary tombs contemporary with it, we find the simple sarcophagus, often with only a rough block of stone for its lid, sometimes with a low-gabled lid like a cottage roof, derived from Egyptian forms, and bearing, either on the sides or the lid, at least a sculpture of the cross, and sometimes the name of the deceased, and date of erection of the tomb. In more elaborate examples rich figure-sculpture is gradually introduced ; and in the perfect period the sarcophagus, even when it does not bear any recumbent figure, has generally a rich sculpture on its sides representing an angel presenting the dead, in person and dress as he lived, to Christ or to the Madonna, with lateral figures, sometimes of saints, sometimes— as in the tombs of the Dukes of Burgundy at Dijon—of mourners ; but in Venice almost always representing the Annunciation, the angel being placed at one angle of the sarcophagus and the Madonna at the other. The canopy, in a very simple four-square form, or as an arch over a recess, is added above the sarcophagus, long before the life-size recumbent figure appears resting upon it.   By the time that the sculptors had acquired skill enough to give much expression to this figure, the canopy attains an exquisite symmetry and richness ; and, in the most elaborate examples, is surmounted by a statue, generally small, representing the dead person in the full strength and pride of life, while the recumbent figure shows him as he lay in death. And, at this point, the perfect type of the Gothic tomb is reached.

§ XLIX. Of the simple sarcophagus tomb there are many exquisite examples both at Venice and Verona ; the most inter-esting in Venice are those which are set in the recesses of the rude brick front of the Church of St. John and Paul, ornamented only, for the most part, with two crosses set in circles, and the legend with the name of the dead and an " Orate pro anima" in another circle in the centre.   And in this we may note one great proof of superiority in Italian over English tombs : the latter being often enriched with quatrefoils, small shafts, and arches, and other ordinary architectural decorations, which de-stroy their seriousness and solemnity, render them little more than ornamental, and have no religious meaning whatever ; while the Italian sarcophagi are kept massive, smooth, and gloomy,—heavy-lidded dungeons of stone, like rock tombs,— but bearing on their surface, sculptured with tender and narrow lines, the emblem of the cross, not presumptuously nor proudly, but dimly graven upon their granite, like the hope which the human heart holds, but hardly perceives, in its heaviness.

§ L. Among the tombs in front of the Church of St. John and Paul there is one which is peculiarly illustrative of the simplicity of these earlier ages.   It is on the left of the entrance, a massy sarcophagus with low horns as of an altar, placed in a rude recess of the outside wall, shattered and worn, and here and there entangled among wild grass and weeds. Yet it is the tomb of two Doges, Jacopo and Lorenzo Tiepolo, by one of whom nearly the whole ground was given for the erection of the noble church in front of which his unprotected tomb is wasting away. The sarcophagus bears an inscription in the centre, describing the acts of the Doges, of which the letters show that it was added a considerable period after the erection of the tomb: the original legend is still left in other letters on its base, to this effect,

"Lord James, died 1251.   Lord Laurence, died 1288."

At the two corners of the sarcophagus are two angels bearing censers ; and on its lid two birds, with crosses like crests upon their heads. For the sake of the traveller in Venice the reader will, I think, pardon me the momentary irrelevancy of telling the meaning of these symbols.

§ LI. The foundation of the Church of St. John and Paul was laid by the Dominicans about 1234, under the immediate protection of the Senate and the Doge Giacomo Tiepolo, accorded to them in consequence of a miraculous vision appearing to the Doge ; of which the following account is given in popular tradition :

"In the year 1226, the Doge Giacomo Tiepolo dreamed a dream ; and in his dream he saw the little oratory of the Dominicans, and, behold, the ground all around it (now occupied by the church) was covered with roses of the colour of vermilion, and the air was filled with their fragrance. And in the midst of the roses, there were seen flying to and fro a crowd of white doves, with golden crosses upon their heads. And while the Doge looked, and wondered, behold, two angels descended from heaven with golden censers, and passing through the oratory, and forth among the flowers, they filled the place with the smoke of their incense. Then the Doge heard suddenly a clear and loud voice which proclaimed, ' This is the place that I have chosen for my preachers ;' and having heard it, straightway he awoke, and went to the Senate, and declared to them the vision. Then the Senate decreed that forty paces of ground should be given to enlarge the monastery ; and the Doge Tiepolo himself made a still larger grant afterwards."

There is nothing miraculous in the occurrence of such a dream as this to the devout Doge ; and the fact, of which there is no doubt, that the greater part of the land on which the church stands was given by him, is partly a confirmation of the story. But whether the sculptures on the tomb were records of the vision, or the vision a monkish invention from the sculptures on the tomb, the reader will not, I believe, look upon its doves and crosses, or rudely carved angels, any more with disdain ; knowing how, in one way or another, they were connected with a point of deep religious belief.

§ LII. Towards the beginning of the fourteenth century, in Venice, the recumbent figure begins to appear on the sarcophagus, the first dated example being also one of the most beautiful ; the statue of the prophet Simeon, sculptured upon the tomb which was to receive his relics in the church dedicated to him under the name of San Simeone Grande. So soon as the figure appears, the sarcophagus becomes much more richly sculptured, but always with definite religious purpose. It is usually divided into two panels, which are filled with small bas-reliefs of the acts or martyrdom of the patron saints of the deceased : between them, in the centre, Christ, or the Virgin and Child, are richly enthroned, under a curtained canopy ; and the two figures representing the Annunciation are almost always at the angles ; the promise of the Birth of Christ being taken as at once the ground and the type of the promise of eternal life to all men.

§ LIII. These figures are always in Venice most rudely chiselled ; the progress of figure-sculpture being there comparatively tardy. At Verona, where the great Pisan school had strong influence, the monumental sculpture is immeasurably finer ; and so early as about the year 1335,* the consummate form of the Gothic tomb occurs in the monument of Can Grande della Scala at Verona. It is set over the portal of the chapel anciently belonging to the family. The sarcophagus is sculptured with

---

* Can Grande died in 1329 : we can hardly allow more than five years for the erection of his tomb.

shallow bas-reliefs, representing (which is rare in the tombs with which I am acquainted in Italy, unless they are those of saints) the principal achievements of the warrior's life, especially the siege of Vicenza and battle of Placenza; these sculptures, however, form little more than a chased and roughened groundwork for the fully relieved statues representing the Annunciation, projecting boldly from the front of the sarcophagus.   Above, the Lord of Verona is laid in his long robe of civil dignity, wearing the simple bonnet, consisting merely of a fillet bound round the brow, knotted and falling on the shoulder.   He is laid as asleep; his arms crossed upon his body, and his sword by his side. Above him, a bold arched canopy is sustained by two projecting shafts, and on the pinnacle of its roof is the statue of the knight on his war-horse ; his helmet, dragon-winged and crested with the dog's head, tossed back behind his shoulders, and the broad and blazoned drapery floating back from his horse's breast,— so truly drawn by the old workman from the life, that it seems to wave in the wind, and the knight's spear to shake, and his marble horse to be evermore quickening its pace, and starting into heavier and hastier charge, as the silver clouds float past behind it in the sky.

§ LIV. Now observe, in this tomb, as much concession is made to the pride of man as may ever consist with honour, discretion, or dignity.   I do not enter into any question respecting the character of Can Grande, though there can be little doubt that he was one of the best among the nobles of his time ; but that is not to our purpose.   It is not the question whether his wars were just, or his greatness honourably achieved ; but whether, supposing them to have been so, these facts are well and gracefully told upon his tomb.   And I believe there can be no hesitation in the admission of its perfect feeling and truth.   Though beautiful, the tomb is so little conspicuous or intrusive, that it serves only to decorate the portal of the little chapel, and is hardly regarded by the traveller as he enters. When it is examined, the history of the acts of the dead is found subdued into dim and minute ornament upon his coffin ; and the principal aim of the monument is to direct the thoughts to his image as he lies in death, and to the expression of his hope of resurrection; while, seen as by the memory, far away, diminished in the brightness of the sky, there is set the likeness of his armed youth, stately, as it stood of old in the front of battle, and meet to be thus recorded for us, that we may now be able to remember the dignity of the frame, of which those who once looked upon it hardly remembered that it was dust.

§ LV. This, I repeat, is as much as may ever be granted, but this ought always to be granted, to the honour and the affection of men. The tomb which stands beside that of Can Grande, nearest it in the little field of sleep, already shows the traces of erring ambition. It is the tomb of Mastino the Second, in whose reign began the decline of his family. It is altogether exquisite as a work of art; and the evidence of a less wise or noble feeling in its design is found only in this, that the image of a virtue, Fortitude, as belonging to the dead, is placed on the extremity of the sarcophagus, opposite to the Crucifixion. But for this slight circumstance, of which the significance will only be appreciated as we examine the series of later monuments, the composition of this monument of Can Mastino would have been as perfect as its decoration is refined. It consists, like that of Can Grande, of the raised sarcophagus, bearing the recumbent statue, protected by a noble four-square canopy, sculptured with ancient Scripture history. On one side of the sarcophagus is Christ enthroned, with Can Mastino kneeling before Him; on the other, Christ is represented in the mystical form, half-rising from the tomb, meant, I believe, to be at once typical of His passion and resurrection. The lateral panels are occupied by statues of saints. At one extremity of the sarcophagus is the Crucifixion; at the other, a noble statue of Fortitude, with a lion's skin thrown over her shoulders, its head forming a shield upon her breast, her flowing hair bound with a narrow fillet, and a three-edged sword in her gauntleted right hand, drawn back sternly behind her thigh, while, in her left, she bears high the shield of the Scalas,

§ LVI. Close to this monument is another, the stateliest and most sumptuous of the three ; it first arrests the eye of the stranger, and long detains it,—a many pinnacled pile, surrounded by niches with statues of the warrior saints.

It is beautiful, for it still belongs to the noble time, the latter part of the fourteenth century ; but its work is coarser than that of the other, and its pride may well prepare us to learn that it was built for himself, in his own lifetime, by the man whose statue crowns it, Can Signorio della Scala. Now observe, for this is infinitely significant. Can Mastino II. was feeble and wicked, and began the ruin of his house ; his sarcophagus is the first which bears upon it the image of a Virtue, but he lays claim only to Fortitude. Can Signorio was twice a fratricide, the last time when he lay upon his death-bed : *his* tomb bears upon its gables the images of six Virtues,—Faith, Hope, Charity, Prudence, and (I believe) Justice and Fortitude.

§ LVII. Let us now return to Venice, where, in the second chapel counting from right to left, at the west end of the Church of the Frari, there is a very early fourteenth, or perhaps late thirteenth, century tomb, another exquisite example of the perfect Gothic form. It is a knight's ; but there is no inscription upon it, and his name is unknown. It consists of a sarcophagus, supported on bold brackets against the chapel wall, bearing the recumbent figure, protected by a simple canopy in the form of a pointed arch, pinnacled by the knight's crest ; beneath which the shadowy space is painted dark blue, and strewn with stars. The statue itself is rudely carved ; but its lines, as seen from the intended distance, are both tender and masterly. The knight is laid in his mail, only the hands and face being bare. The hauberk and helmet are of chain-mail, the armour for the limbs of jointed steel ; a tunic, fitting close to the breast, and marking the noble swell of it by two narrow embroidered lines, is worn over the mail ; his dagger is at his right side ; his long cross-belted sword, not seen by the spectator from below, at his left. His feet rest on a hound (the hound being his crest), which looks up towards its master.   In general, in tombs of this kind, the face of the statue is slightly turned towards the spectator; in this monument, on the contrary, it is turned away from him, towards the depth of the arch: for there, just above the warrior's breast, is carved a small image of St. Joseph bearing the infant Christ, who looks down upon the resting figure; and to this image its countenance is turned.   The appearance of the entire tomb is as if the warrior had seen the vision of Christ in his dying moments, and had fallen back peacefully upon his pillow, with his eyes still turned to it, and his hands clasped in prayer.

§ LVIII On the opposite side of this chapel is another very lovely tomb, to Duccio degli Alberti, a Florentine ambassador at Venice; noticeable chiefly as being the first in Venice on which any images of the Virtues appear.   We shall return to it presently, but some account must first be given of the more important among the other tombs in Venice belonging to the perfect period.   Of these, by far the most interesting, though not the most elaborate, is that of the great Doge Francesco Dandolo, whose ashes, it might have been thought, were honourable enough to have been permitted to rest undisturbed in the chapter-house of the Frari, where they were first laid.   But, as if there were not room enough, nor waste houses enough, in the desolate city to receive a few convent papers, the monks, wanting an "archivio," have separated the tomb into three pieces : the canopy, a simple arch sustained on brackets, still remains on the blank walls of the desecrated chamber; the sarcophagus has been transported to a kind of museum of antiquities, established in what was once the cloister of Santa Maria della Salute; and the painting which filled the lunette behind it is hung far out of sight, at one end of the sacristy of the same church.   The sarcophagus is completely charged with bas-reliefs; at its two extremities are the types of St. Mark and St. John; in front, a noble sculpture of the death of the Virgin; at the angles, angels holding vases.   The whole space is occupied by the sculpture; there are no spiral shafts or panelled divisions; only a basic plinth below, and crowning plinth above, the sculpture being raised from a deep concave field between the two, but, in order to give piquancy and picturesqueness to the mass of figures, two small trees are introduced at the head and foot of the Madonna's couch, an oak and a stone pine.

§ LIX. It was said above,* in speaking of the frequent disputes of the Venetians with the Pontifical power, which in their early days they had so strenuously supported, that "the humiliation of Francesco Dandolo blotted out the shame of Barbarossa." It is indeed well that the two events should be remembered together. By the help of the Venetians, Alexander III. was enabled, in the twelfth century, to put his foot upon the neck of the emperor Barbarossa, quoting the words of the Psalm, "Thou shalt tread upon the lion and the adder." A hundred and fifty years later, the Venetian ambassador, Francesco Dandolo, unable to obtain even an audience from the Pope, Clement V., to whom he had been sent to pray for a removal of the sentence of excommunication pronounced against the republic, concealed himself (according to the common tradition) beneath the Pontiff's dining-table ; and thence coming out as he sat down to meat, embraced his feet, and obtained, by tearful entreaties, the removal of the terrible sentence.

I say, "according to the common tradition ;" for there are some doubts cast upon the story by its supplement. Most of the Venetian historians assert that Francesco Dandolo's surname of "Dog" was given him first on this occasion, in insult, by the cardinals ; and that the Venetians, in remembrance of the grace which his humiliation had won for them, made it a title of honour to him and to his race. It has, however, been proved † that the surname was borne by the ancestors of Francesco Dandolo long before ; and the falsity of this seal of the legend renders also its circumstances doubtful. But the main fact of grievous humiliation having been undergone, admits of no dispute ; the existence of such a tradition at all is in itself a

* Vol. I. Chap. I. † Sansovino, lib. xiii.

proof of its truth ; it was not one likely to be either invented or
received without foundation ; and it will be well, therefore, that
the reader should remember, in connection with the treatment of
Barbarossa at the door of the Church of St. Mark's, that in the
Vatican, one hundred and fifty years later, a Venetian noble,
a future Doge, submitted to a degradation, of which the current
report among his people was, that he had crept on his hands and
knees from beneath the Pontiff's table to his feet, and had been
spurned as a " dog " by the cardinals present.

§ LX. There are two principal conclusions to be drawn from
this : the obvious one respecting the insolence of the Papal
dominion in the thirteenth century ; the second, that there were
probably most deep piety and humility in the character of the
man who could submit to this insolence for the sake of a benefit
to his country.   Probably no motive would have been strong
enough to obtain such a sacrifice from most men, however unselfish ; but it was, without doubt, made easier to Dandolo by
his profound reverence for the Pontifical office ; a reverence
which, however *we* may now esteem those who claimed it, could
not but have been felt by nearly all good and faithful men at
the time of which we are speaking.   This is the main point
which I wish the reader to remember as we look at his tomb,
this, and the result of it,—that, some years afterwards, when he
was seated on the throne which his piety had saved, "there
were sixty princes' ambassadors in Venice at the same time,
requesting the judgment of the Senate on matters of various
concernment, *so great was the fame of the uncorrupted justice
of the Fathers.*"*

Observe, there are no Virtues on this tomb.   Nothing but
religious history or symbols ; the Death of the Virgin in front,
and the types of St. Mark and St. John at the extremities.

§ LXI. Of the tomb of the Doge Andrea Dandolo, in St.
Mark's, I have spoken before.   It is one of the first in Venice
which presents, in the canopy, the Pisan idea of angels with-

* Tentori, vi. 142, i. 157.

drawing curtains, as of a couch, to look down upon the dead. The sarcophagus is richly decorated with flower-work : the usual figures of the Annunciation are at the sides ; an enthroned Madonna in the centre ; and two bas-reliefs, one of the martyrdom of the Doge's patron saint, St. Andrew, occupy the intermediate spaces. All these tombs have been richly coloured ; the hair of the angels has here been gilded, their wings bedropped with silver, and their garments covered with the most exquisite arabesques. This tomb, and that of St. Isidore in another chapel of St. Mark's, which was begun by this very Doge, Andrea Dandolo, and completed after his death in 1354, are both nearly alike in their treatment, and are, on the whole, the best existing examples of Venetian monumental sculpture.

§ LXII. Of much ruder workmanship, though still most precious, and singularly interesting, from its quaintness, is a sarcophagus in the northernmost chapel, beside the choir of St. John and Paul, charged with two bas-reliefs and many figures, but which bears no inscription. It has, however, a shield with three dolphins on its brackets ; and, as at the feet of the Madonna in its centre there is a small kneeling figure of a Doge, we know it to be the tomb of the Doge Giovanni Dolfino, who came to the throne in 1356.

He was chosen Doge, while, as provveditore, he was in Treviso, defending the city against the King of Hungary. The Venetians sent to the besiegers, praying that their newly elected Doge might be permitted to pass the Hungarian lines. Their request was refused, the Hungarians exulting that they held the Doge of Venice prisoner in Treviso. But Dolfino, with a body of two hundred horse, cut his way through their lines by night, and reached Mestre (Malghera) in safety, where he was met by the Senate. His bravery could not avert the misfortunes which were accumulating on the republic. The Hungarian war was ignominiously terminated by the surrender of Dalmatia ; the Doge's heart was broken, his eyesight failed him, and he died of the plague four years after he had ascended the throne.

§ LXIII. It is perhaps on this account, perhaps in consequence of later injuries, that the tomb has neither effigy nor inscription: that it has been subjected to some violence is evident from the dentil which once crowned its leaf-cornice being now broken away, showing the whole front. But, fortunately, the sculpture of the sarcophagus itself is little injured.

There are two saints, male and female, at its angles, each in a little niche; a Christ, enthroned in the centre, the Doge and Dogaressa kneeling at His feet; in the two intermediate panels, on one side the Epiphany, on the other the Death of the Virgin; the whole supported, as well as crowned, by an elaborate leaf-plinth. The figures under the niches are rudely cut, and of little interest. Not so the central group. Instead of a niche, the Christ is seated under a square tent, or tabernacle, formed by curtains running on rods; the idea, of course, as usual, borrowed from the Pisan one, but here ingeniously applied. The curtains are opened in front, showing those at the back of the tent, behind the seated figure; the perspective of the two retiring sides being very tolerably suggested. Two angels, of half the size of the seated figure, thrust back the near curtains, and look up reverently to the Christ: while again, at their feet, about one-third of *their* size, and half-sheltered, as it seems, by their garments, are the two kneeling figures of the Doge and Dogaressa, though so small and carefully cut, full of life. The Christ raising one hand as to bless, and holding a book upright and open on the knees, does not look either towards them or to the angels, but forward: and there is a very noticeable effort to represent Divine abstraction in the countenance: the idea of the three magnitudes of spiritual being,—the God, the Angel, and the Man,—is also to be observed, aided as it is by the complete subjection of the angelic power to the Divine; for the angels are in attitudes of the most lowly watchfulness of the face of Christ, and appear unconscious of the presence of the human beings who are nestled in the folds of their garments.

§ LXIV. With this interesting but modest tomb of one of the

kings of Venice, it is desirable to compare that of one of her senators, of exactly the same date, which is raised against the western wall of the Frari, at the end of the north aisle. It bears the following remarkable inscription :

" ANNO MCCCLX. PRIMA DIE JULII SEPULTURA . DOMINI . SIMON . DANDOLO . AMADOR . DE . JUSTISIA . E . DESIROSO . DE . ACRESE . EL . BEN . CHOMUM."

The "Amador de Justisia" has perhaps some reference to Simon Dandolo's having been one of the Giunta who condemned the Doge Faliero. The sarcophagus is decorated merely by the Annunciation group, and an enthroned Madonna with a curtain behind her throne, sustained by four tiny angels, who look over it as they hold it up ; but the workmanship of the figures is more than usually beautiful.

§ LXV. Seven years later, a very noble monument was placed on the north side of the choir of St. John and Paul, to the Doge Marco Cornaro, chiefly, with respect to our present subject, noticeable for the absence of religious imagery from the sarcophagus, which is decorated with roses only ; three very beautiful statues of the Madonna and two saints are, however, set in the canopy above. Opposite this tomb, though about fifteen years later in date, is the richest monument of the Gothic period in Venice ; that of the Doge Michele Morosini, who died in 1382. It consists of a highly florid canopy,—an arch crowned by a gable, with pinnacles at the flanks, boldly crocketed, and with a huge finial at the top representing St. Michael,—a medallion of Christ set in the gable ; under the arch, a mosaic, representing the Madonna presenting the Doge to Christ upon the cross ; beneath, as usual, the sarcophagus, with a most noble recumbent figure of the Doge, his face meagre and severe, and sharp in its lines, but exquisite in the form of its small and princely features. The sarcophagus is adorned with elaborate wrinkled leafage, projecting in front of it into seven brackets, from which the statues are broken away : but by which—for there can be no doubt that these last statues represented the theological and cardinal Virtues— we must for a moment pause.

§ LXVI. It was noticed above, that the tomb of the Florentine ambassador, Duccio, was the first in Venice which presented images of the Virtues. Its small lateral statues of Justice and Temperance are exquisitely beautiful, and were, I have no doubt, executed by a Florentine sculptor; the whole range of artistical power and religious feeling being in Florence full half a century in advance of that of Venice. But this is the first truly Venetian tomb which has the Virtues; and it becomes of importance, therefore, to know what was the character of Morosini.

The reader must recollect that I dated the commencement of the fall of Venice from the death of Carlo Zeno, considering that no state could be held as in decline which numbered such a man amongst its citizens. Carlo Zeno was a candidate for the Ducal bonnet together with Michael Morosini; and Morosini was chosen. It might be anticipated, therefore, that there was something more than usually admirable or illustrious in his character. Yet it is difficult to arrive at a just estimate of it, as the reader will at once understand by comparing the following statements :

§ LXVII.   1. "To him (Andrea Contarini) succeeded Morosini, at the age of seventy-four years; a most learned and prudent man, who also reformed several laws."—*Sansovino*, Vite de' Principi.

2. "It was generally believed that, if his reign had been longer, he would have dignified the state by many noble laws and institutes; but by so much as his reign was full of hope, by as much was it short in duration, for he died when he had been at the head of the republic but four months."—*Sabellico*, lib. viii.

3. "He was allowed but a short time to enjoy this high dignity, which he so well deserved by his rare virtues, for God called him to Himself on the 15th of October."—*Muratori*, Annali d' Italia.

4. "Two candidates presented themselves; one was Zeno, the other that Michael Morosini who, during the war, had tripled his fortune by his speculations. The suffrages of the electors fell upon him, and he was proclaimed Doge on the 10th of June."—*Daru*, Histoire de Venise, lib. x.

5. "The choice of the electors was directed to Michaele Morosini, a noble of illustrious birth, derived from a stock which, coeval with the republic itself, had produced the conqueror of Tyre, given a queen to Hungary, and more than one Doge to Venice. The brilliancy of this descent was tarnished in the present chief representative of the family by the most base and grovelling avarice; for at that moment, in the recent war, at which all other Venetians were devoting their whole fortunes to the service of the state, Morosini sought in the distresses

of his country an opening for his own private enrichment, and employed his ducats, not in the assistance of the national wants, but in speculating upon houses which were brought to market at a price far beneath their real value, and which, upon the return of peace, insured the purchaser a fourfold profit. 'What matters the fall of Venice to me, so as I fall not together with her?' was his selfish and sordid reply to some one who expressed surprise at the transaction."—*Sketches of Venetian History.*   Murray, 1831.

§ LXVIII. The writer of the unpretending little history from which the last quotation is taken has not given his authority for this statement, and I could not find it, but believed, from the general accuracy of the book, that some authority might exist better than Daru's.   Under these circumstances, wishing if possible to ascertain the truth, and to clear the character of this great Doge from the accusation, if it proved groundless, I wrote to the Count Carlo Morosini, his descendant, and one of the few remaining representatives of the ancient noblesse of Venice ; one, also, by whom his great ancestral name is revered, and in whom it is exalted.   His answer appears to me altogether conclusive as to the utter fallacy of the reports of Daru and the English history.   I have placed his letter in the close of this volume (Appendix 6), in order that the reader may himself be the judge upon this point ; and I should not have alluded to Daru's report, except for the purpose of contradicting it, but that it still appears to me impossible that any modern historian should have gratuitously invented the whole story, and that, therefore, there must have been a trace, in the documents which Daru himself possessed, of some scandal of this kind raised by Morosini's enemies, perhaps at the very time of the disputed election with Carlo Zeno.   The occurrence of the Virtues upon his tomb, for the first time in Venetian monumental work, and so richly and conspicuously placed, may partly have been in public contradiction of such a floating rumour.   But the face of the statue is a more explicit contradiction still ; it is resolute, thoughtful, serene, and full of beauty ; and we must, therefore, for once, allow the somewhat boastful introduction of the Virtues to have been perfectly just : though the whole tomb is most notable, as furnishing not only the exactly intermediate condition in style between the pure Gothic and its final Renaissance corruption, but, at the same time, the exactly intermediate condition of *feeling* between the pure calmness of early Christianity, and the boastful pomp of the Renaissance faithlessness ; for here we have still the religious humility remaining in the mosaic of the canopy,. which shows the Doge kneeling before the cross, while yet this tendency to self-trust is shown in the surrounding of the coffin by the Virtues.

§ LXIX. The next tomb by the side of which they appear is that of Jacopo Cavalli, in the same chapel of St. John and Paul which contains the tomb of the Doge Delfin. It is peculiarly rich in religious imagery, adorned by boldly cut types of the four Evangelists, and of two saints, while, on projecting brackets in front of it, stood three statues of Faith, Hope, and Charity, now lost, but drawn in Zanotto's work. It is all rich in detail, and its sculptor has been proud of it, thus recording his name below the epitaph :

> " QST OPERA DINTALGIO E FATTO IN PIERA,
> UNVENICIAN LAFE CHANOME POLO,
> NATO DI JACHOMEL CHATAIAPIERA."

> This work of sculpture is done in stone ;
> A Venetian did it, named Paul,
> Son of Jachomel the stone-cutter.

Jacopo Cavalli died in 1384. He was a bold and active Veronese soldier, did the state much service, was therefore ennobled by it, and became the founder of the house of the Cavalli ; but I find no especial reason for the images of the Virtues, especially that of Charity, appearing at his tomb, unless it be this: that at the siege of Feltre, in the war against Leopold of Austria, he refused to assault the city because the Senate would not grant his soldiers the pillage of the town. The feet of the recumbent figure, which is in full armour, rest on a dog, and its head on two lions ; and these animals (neither of which form any part of the knight's bearings) are said by Zanotto to be intended to symbolize his bravery and fidelity. If, however, the lions are meant to set forth courage, it is a pity they should have been represented as howling.

§ LXX. We must next pause for an instant beside the tomb of Michael Steno, now in the northern aisle of St. John and Paul, having been removed there from the destroyed church of the Servi : first, to note its remarkable return to the early simplicity, the sarcophagus being decorated only with two crosses in quatrefoils, though it is of the fifteenth century, Steno dying in 1413 ; and, in the second place, to observe the peculiarity of the epitaph, which eulogizes Steno as having been "amator justitie, pacis, et ubertatis,"—"A lover of justice, peace, and plenty." In the epitaphs of this period, the virtues which are made most account of in public men are those which were most useful to their country. We have already seen one example in the epitaph on Simon Dandolo ; and similar expressions occur constantly in laudatory mentions of their later Doges by the Venetian writers. Thus Sansovino of Marco Cornaro, " Era savio huomo, eloquente, e amava molto la pace el' abbondanza della citta ;" and of Tomaso Mocenigo, " Huomo oltre modo desideroso della pace."

Of the tomb of this last-named Doge mention has before been made. Here, as in Morosini's, the images of the Virtues have no ironical power, although their great conspicuousness marks the increase of the boastful feeling in the treatment of monuments. For the rest, this tomb is the last in Venice which can be considered as belonging to the Gothic period. Its mouldings are already rudely classical, and it has meaningless figures in Roman armour at the angles ; but its tabernacle above is still Gothic, and the recumbent figure is very beautiful. It was carved by two Florentine sculptors in 1423.

§ LXXI. Tomaso Mocenigo was succeeded by the renowned Doge, Francesco Foscari, under whom, it will be remembered, the last additions were made to the Gothic Ducal Palace ; additions which in form only, not in spirit, corresponded to the older portions ; since, during his reign, the transition took place which permits us no longer to consider the Venetian architecture as

Gothic at all.   He died in 1457, and his tomb is the first important example of Renaissance art.

Not, however, a good characteristic example.   It is remarkable chiefly as introducing all the faults of the Renaissance at an early period, when its merits, such as they were, were yet undeveloped.   Its claim to be rated as a classical composition is altogether destroyed by the remnants of Gothic feeling which cling to it here and there in their last forms of degradation; and of which, now that we find them thus corrupted, the sooner we are rid the better.   Thus the sarcophagus is supported by a species of trefoiled arches; the bases of the shafts have still their spurs; and the whole tomb is covered by a pediment, with crockets and a pinnacle.   We shall find that the perfect Renaissance is at least pure in its insipidity, and subtle in its vice; but this monument is remarkable as showing the refuse of one style encumbering the embryo of another, and all principles of life entangled either in the swaddling clothes or the shroud.

§ LXXII. With respect to our present purpose, however, it is a monument of enormous importance. We have to trace, be it remembered, the pride of state in its gradual intrusion upon the sepulchre; and the consequent and correlative vanishing of the expressions of religious feeling and heavenly hope, together with the more and more arrogant setting forth of the virtues of the dead.   Now this tomb is the largest and most costly we have yet seen; but its means of religious expression are limited to a single statue of Christ, small, and used merely as a pinnacle at the top.   The rest of the composition is as curious as it is vulgar. The conceit, so often noticed as having been borrowed from the Pisan school, of angels withdrawing the curtains of the couch to look down upon the dead, was brought forward with increasing prominence by every succeeding sculptor; but, as we draw nearer to the Renaissance period, we find that the *angels* become of less importance, and the *curtains* of more.   With the Pisans, the curtains are introduced as a motive for the angels; with the Renaissance sculptors, the angels are introduced merely as a motive for the curtains, which become every day more huge and elaborate. In the monument of Mocenigo, they have already expanded into a tent, with a pole in the centre of it ; and in that of Foscari, for the first time, the *angels are absent altogether;* while the curtains are arranged in the form of an enormous French tent-bed, and are sustained at the flanks by two diminutive figures in Roman armour ; substituted for the angels, merely that the sculptor might *show his knowledge* of classical costume. And now observe how often a fault in feeling induces also a fault in style. In the old tombs, the angels used to stand on or by the side of the sarcophagus ; but their places are here to be occupied by the Virtues, and therefore, to sustain the diminutive Roman figures at the necessary height, each has a whole Corinthian pillar to himself, a pillar whose shaft is eleven feet high, and some three or four feet round : and because this was not high enough, it is put on a pedestal four feet and a half high ; and has a spurred base besides of its own, a tall capital, then a huge bracket above the capital, and then another pedestal above the bracket, and on the top of all the diminutive figure who has charge of the curtains.

§ LXXIII. Under the canopy, thus arranged, is placed the sarcophagus with its recumbent figure. The statues of the Virgin and the saints have disappeared from it. In their stead, its panels are filled with half length figures of Faith, Hope, and Charity ; while Temperance and Fortitude are at the Doge's feet. Justice and Prudence at his head, figures now the size of life, yet nevertheless recognizable only by their attributes ; for, except that Hope raises her eyes, there is no difference in the character or expression of any of their faces,—they are nothing more than handsome Venetian women, in rather full and courtly dresses, and tolerably well thrown into postures for effect from below. Fortitude could not of course be placed in a graceful one without some sacrifice of her character, but that was of no consequence in the eyes of the sculptors of this period, so she leans back languidly, and nearly overthrows her own column ; while Temperance, and Justice opposite to her, as neither the left hand of the one nor the right hand of the other could be seen from below, have been *left with one hand each*.

§ LXXIV. Still, these figures, coarse and feelingless as they are, have been worked with care, because the principal effect of the tomb depends on them.   But the effigy of the Doge, of which nothing but the sign is visible, has been utterly neglected ; and the ingenuity of the sculptor is not so great, at the best, as that he can afford to be slovenly.   There is, indeed, nothing in the history of Foscari which would lead us to expect anything particularly noble in his face ; but I trust, nevertheless, it has been misrepresented by this despicable carver ; for no words are strong enough to express the baseness of the portraiture. A huge, gross, bony clown's face, with the peculiar sodden and sensual cunning in it which is seen so often in the counte- nances of the worst Romanist priests ; a face part of iron and part of clay, with the immobility of the one, and the foulness of the other, double chinned, blunt-mouthed, bony-cheeked, with its brows drawn down into meagre lines and wrinkles over the eyelid ; the face of a man incapable either of joy or sorrow, unless such as may be caused by the indulgence of passion or the mortification of pride.   Even had he been such a one, a noble workman would not have written it so legibly on his tomb ; and I believe it to be the image of the carver's own mind that is there hewn in the marble, not that of the Doge Foscari.   For the same mind is visible enough throughout, the traces of it mingled with those of the evil taste of the whole time and people.   There is not anything so small but it is shown in some portion of its treatment ; for instance, in the placing of the shields at the back of the great curtain. In earlier times, the shield, as we have seen, was represented as merely suspended against the tomb by a thong, or if sus- tained in any other manner, still its form was simple and un- disguised.   Men in those days used their shields in war, and therefore there was no need to add dignity to their form by external ornament.   That which, through day after day of mortal danger, had borne back from them the waves of battle, could neither be degraded by simplicity, nor exalted by decoration. By its rude leathern thong it seemed to be fastened to their tombs, and the shield of the mighty was not cast away, though capable of defending its master no more.

§ LXXV. It was otherwise in the fifteenth and sixteenth centuries. The changed system of warfare was rapidly doing away with the practical service of the shield ; and the chiefs who directed the battle from a distance, or who passed the greater part of their lives in the council chamber, soon came to regard the shield as nothing more than a field for their armorial bearings. It then became a principal object of their Pride of State to increase the conspicuousness of these marks of family distinction by surrounding them with various and fantastic ornament, generally scroll or flower work, which ot course deprived the shield of all appearance of being intended for a soldier's use. Thus the shield of the Foscari is introduced in two ways. On the sarcophagus, the bearings are three times repeated, enclosed in circular disks, which are sustained each by a couple of naked infants. Above the canopy, two shields of the usual form are set in the centre of circles filled by a radiating ornament of shell flutings which give them the effect of ventilators ; and their circumference is farther adorned by gilt rays, undulating to represent a glory.

§ LXXVI. We now approach that period of the early Renaissance which was noticed in the preceding chapter as being at first a very visible improvement on the corrupted Gothic. The tombs executed during the period of the Byzantine Renaissance exhibit, in the first place, a consummate skill in handling the chisel, perfect science of drawing and anatomy, high appreciation of good classical models, and a grace of composition and delicacy of ornament derived, I believe, principally from the great Florentine sculptors. But, together with this science, they exhibit also, for a short time, some return to the early religious feeling, forming a school of sculpture which corresponds to that of the school of the Bellini in painting ; and the only wonder is that there should not have been more workmen in the fifteenth century doing in marble what Perugino, Francia, and Bellini did on canvas.   There are, indeed, some few, as I have just said, in whom the good and pure temper shows itself: but the sculptor was necessarily led sooner than the painter to an exclusive study of classical models, utterly adverse to the Christian imagination ; and he was also deprived of the great purifying and sacred element of colour, besides having much more of merely mechanical and therefore degrading labour to go through in the realization of his thought.   Hence I do not know any example of sculpture at this period, at least in Venice, which has not conspicuous faults (not faults of imperfection, as in early sculpture, but of purpose and sentiment), staining such beauties as it may possess ; and the whole school soon falls away, and merges into vain pomp and meagre metaphor.

§ LXXVII. The most celebrated monument of this period is that to the Doge Andrea Vendramin, in the Church of St. John and Paul, sculptured about 1480, and before alluded to in the first chapter of the first volume.   It has attracted public admiration, partly by its costliness, partly by the delicacy and precision of its chiselling ; being otherwise a very base and unworthy example of the school, and showing neither invention nor feeling. It has the Virtues, as usual, dressed like heathen goddesses, and totally devoid of expression, though graceful and well studied merely as female figures.   The rest of its sculpture is all of the same kind ; perfect in workmanship, and devoid of thought.   Its dragons are covered with marvellous scales, but have no terror nor sting in them ; its birds are perfect in plumage, but have no song in them ; its children lovely of limb, but have no childishness in them.

§ LXXVIII. Of far other workmanship are the tombs of Pietro and Giovanni Mocenigo, in St. John and Paul, and of Pietro Bernardo in the Frari ; in all which the details are as full of exquisite fancy as they are perfect in execution: and in the two former, and several others of similar feeling, the old religious symbols return ; the Madonna is again seen enthroned under the canopy, and the sarcophagus is decorated with legends ofthe saints.   But the fatal errors of sentiment are, nevertheless, always

traceable.   In the first place, the sculptor is always seen to be
intent upon the exhibition of his skill, more than on producing
any effect on the spectator's mind ; elaborate backgrounds of
landscape, with tricks of perspective, imitations of trees, clouds,
and water, and various other unnecessary adjuncts, merely to
show how marble could be subdued ; together with useless under-
cutting, and over-finish in subordinate parts, continually exhibiting the same cold vanity and unexcited precision of mechanism.
In the second place, the figures have all the peculiar tendency to
posture-making, which, exhibiting itself first painfully in Perugino, rapidly destroyed the veracity of composition in all art.
By posture-making I mean, in general, that action of figures
which results from the painter's considering, in the first place, not
how, under the circumstances, they would actually have walked,
or stood, or looked, but how they may most gracefully and
harmoniously walk or stand.   In the hands of a great man,
posture, like everything else, becomes noble, even when over-
studied, as with Michael Angelo, who was perhaps, more than
any other, the cause of the mischief; but, with inferior men,
this habit of composing attitudes ends necessarily in utter life-
lessness and abortion.   Giotto was, perhaps, of all painters, the
most free from the infection of the poison, always conceiving
an incident naturally, and drawing it unaffectedly ; and the absence of posture-making in the works of the Pre-Raphaelites, as
opposed to the Attitudinarianism of the modern school, has been
both one of their principal virtues, and of the principal causes
of outcry against them.

§ LXXIX. But the most significant change in the treatment
of these tombs, with respect to our immediate object, is in the
form of the sarcophagus.   It was above noted that, exactly in
proportion to the degree of the pride of life expressed in any
monument, would be also the fear of death ; and therefore, as
these tombs increase in splendour, in size, and beauty of workmanship, we perceive a gradual desire to *take away from the
definite character of the sarcophagus.*   In the earliest times, as
we have seen, it was a gloomy mass of stone ; gradually it

became charged with religious sculpture ; but never with the slightest desire to disguise its form, until towards the middle of the fifteenth century. It then becomes enriched with flower-work and hidden by the Virtues ; and, finally, losing its four-square form, it is modelled on graceful types of ancient vases, made as little like a coffin as possible, and refined away in various elegances, till it becomes, at last, a mere pedestal or stage for the portrait statue. This statue, in the meantime, has been gradually coming back to life, through a curious series of transitions. The Vendramin monument is one of the last which shows, or pretends to show, the recumbent figure laid in death. A few years later, this idea became disagreeable to polite minds ; and, lo ! the figures, which before had been laid at rest upon the tomb pillow, raised themselves on their elbows, and began to look round them. The soul of the sixteenth century dared not contemplate its body in death.

§ LXXX. The reader cannot but remember many instances of this form of monument, England being peculiarly rich in examples of them ; although, with her, tomb sculpture, after the fourteenth century, is altogether imitative, and in no degree indicative of the temper of the people. It was from Italy that the authority for the change was derived ; and in Italy only, therefore, that it is truly correspondent to the change in the national mind. There are many monuments in Venice of this semi-animate type, most of them carefully sculptured, and some very admirable as portraits, and for the casting of the drapery, especially those in the Church of San Salvador : but I shall only direct the reader to one, that of Jacopo Pesaro, Bishop of Paphos, in the Church of the Frari ; notable not only as a very skilful piece of sculpture, but for the epitaph, singularly characteristic of the period, and confirmatory of all that I have alleged against it :

" James Pesaro, Bishop of Paphos, who conquered the Turks in war, himself in peace, transported from a noble family among the Venetians to a nobler among the angels, laid here, expects the noblest crown, which the just

Judge shall give to him in that day. He lived the years of Plato. He died 24th March, 1547.*

The mingled classicism and carnal pride of this epitaph surely need no comment. The crown is expected as a right from the justice of the Judge, and the nobility of the Venetian family is only a little lower than that of the angels. The quaint childishness of the " Vixit annos Platonicos " is also very notable.

§ LXXXI. The statue, however, did not long remain in this partially recumbent attitude. Even the expression of peace became painful to the frivolous and thoughtless Italians, and they required the portraiture to be rendered in a manner that should induce no memory of death. The statue rose up, and presented itself in front of the tomb, like an actor upon a stage, surrounded now not merely, or not at all, by the Virtues, but by allegorical figures of Fame and Victory, by genii and muses, by personifications of humbled kingdoms and adoring nations, and by every circumstance of pomp, and symbol of adulation, that flattery could suggest, or insolence could claim.

§ LXXXII. As of the intermediate monumental type, so also of this, the last and most gross, there are unfortunately many examples in our own country ; but the most wonderful, by far, are still at Venice. I shall, however, particularise only two ; the first, that of the Doge John Pesaro, in the Frari. It is to be observed that we have passed over a considerable interval of time ; we are now in the latter half of the seventeenth century ; the progress of corruption has in the meantime been incessant, and sculpture has here lost its taste and learning as well as its feeling. The monument is a huge accumulation of theatrical scenery in marble : four colossal negro caryatides, grinning and horrible, with faces of black marble and white eyes, sustain the first story of it ; above this, two monsters, long-necked, half dog

* " Jacobus Pisaurius Paphi Episcopus, qui Turcos bello, se ipsum pace vincebat, ex nobili inter Venetas, ad nobiliorem inter Angelos familiam delatus, nobilissimam in illa die Coronam justo Judice reddente, hic situs expectat. Vxit annos Platonicos. Obijt MDXLVII. IX. Kal. Aprilis."

and half dragon, sustain an ornamental sarcophagus, on the top of which the full length statue of the Doge in robes of state stands forward with its arms expanded, like an actor courting applause, under a huge canopy of metal, like the roof of a bed, painted crimson and gold ; on each side of him are sitting figures of genii, and unintelligible personifications gesticulating in Roman armour ; below, between the negro caryatides, are two ghastly figures in bronze, half corpse, half skeleton, carrying tablets on which is written the eulogium : but in large letters, graven in gold, the following words are the first and last that strike the eye ; the first two phrases, one on each side, on tablets in the lower story, the last under the portrait statue above :

Vixit annos LXX.   Devixit anno MDCLIX.
" Hic revixit anno MDCLXIX."

We have here, at last, the horrible images of death in violent contrast with the defiant monument, which pretends to bring the resurrection down to earth, " Hic revixit ;" and it seems impossible for false taste and base feeling to sink lower. Yet even this monument is surpassed by one in St. John and Paul.

§ LXXXIII. But before we pass to this, the last with which I shall burden the reader's attention, let us for a moment, and that we may feel the contrast more forcibly, return to a tomb of the early times.

In a dark niche in the outer wall of the outer corridor of St. Mark's,—not even in the church, observe, but in the atrium or porch of it, and on the north side of the church,—is a solid sarcophagus of white marble, raised only about two feet from the ground on four stunted square pillars. Its lid is a mere slab of stone ; on its extremities are sculptured two crosses ; in front of it are two rows of rude figures, the uppermost representing Christ with the Apostles : the lower row is of six figures only, alternately male and female, holding up their hands in the usual attitude of benediction : the sixth is smaller than the rest, and the midmost of the other five has a glory round its head. I cannot tell the meaning of these figures, but be-tween them are suspended censers attached to crosses : a most beautiful symbolic expression of Christ's mediatorial function. The whole is surrounded by a rude wreath of vine leaves, pro-ceeding out of the foot of a cross.

On the bar of marble which separates the two rows of figures are inscribed these words :

> " Here lies the Lord Marin Morosini, Duke."

It is the tomb of the Doge Marino Morosini, who reigned from 1249 to 1252.

§ LXXXIV. From before this rude and solemn sepulchre let us pass to the southern aisle of the church of St. John and Paul ; and there, towering from the pavement to the vaulting of the church, behold a mass of marble, sixty or seventy feet in height, of mingled yellow and white, the yellow carved into the form of an enormous curtain, with ropes, fringes, and tassels, sustained by cherubs ; in front of which, in the now usual stage attitudes, advance the statues of the Doge Ber-tuccio Valier, his son the Doge Silvester Falier, and his son's wife, Elisabeth. The statues of the Doges, though mean and Polonius-like, are partly redeemed by the Ducal robes ; but that of the Dogaressa is a consummation of grossness, vanity, and ugliness,—the figure of a large and wrinkled woman, with elaborate curls in stiff projection round her face, covered from her shoulders to her feet with ruffs, furs, lace, jewels, and embroidery. Beneath and around are scattered Virtues, Vic-tories, Fames, genii,—the entire company of the monumental stage assembled, as before a drop scene,—executed by various sculptors, and deserving attentive study as exhibiting every condition of false taste and feeble conception. The Victory in the centre is peculiarly interesting ; the lion by which she is accompanied, springing on a dragon, has been intended to look terrible, but the incapable sculptor could not conceive any form of dreadfulness, could not even make the lion look angry. It looks only lachrymose ; and its lifted forepaws, there being no spring nor motion in its body, give it the appearance of a dog begging.   The inscriptions under the two principal statues are as follows :

"Bertucius Valier, Duke,
Great in wisdom and eloquence,
Greater in his Hellespontic victory,
Greatest in the Prince his son,
Died in the year 1658."

"Elisabeth Quirina,
The wife of Silvester,
Distinguished by Roman virtue,
By Venetian piety,
And by the Ducal crown,
Died 1708."

The writers of this age were generally anxious to make the world aware that they understood the degrees of comparison, and a large number of epitaphs are principally constructed with this object (compare, in the Latin, that of the Bishop of Paphos, given above): but the latter of these epitaphs is also interesting, from its mention, in an age now altogether given up to the pursuit of worldly honour, of that "Venetian piety" which once truly distinguished the city from all others ; and of which some form and shadow, remaining still, served to point an epitaph, and to feed more cunningly and speciously the pride which could not be satiated with the sumptuousness of the sepulchre.

§ LXXXV. Thus far, then, of the second element of the Renaissance spirit, the Pride of State ; nor need we go farther to learn the reason of the fall of Venice.   She was already likened in her thoughts, and was therefore to be likened in her ruin, to the Virgin of Babylon.   The Pride of State and the Pride of Knowledge were no new passions : the sentence against them had gone forth from everlasting.   "Thou saidst, I shall be a lady for ever, so that thou didst not lay these things to thine heart. . . *Thy wisdom and thy knowledge, it hath perverted thee ;* and thou hast said in thine heart, I am, and none else beside me.   Therefore shall evil come upon thee . . . ; thy merchants from thy youth, they shall wander every one to his quarter ; none shall save thee." *

§ LXXXVI. III. PRIDE OF SYSTEM. I might have illustrated these evil principles from a thousand other sources, but I have not time to pursue the subject farther, and must pass to the third element above named, the Pride of System. It need not detain us so long as either of the others, for it is at once more palpable and less dangerous. The manner in which the pride of the fifteenth century corrupted the sources of know-ledge, and diminished the majesty, while it multiplied the trap-pings, of state, is in general little observed ; but the reader is probably already well and sufficiently aware of the curious tendency to formulization and system which, under the name of philosophy, encumbered the minds of the Renaissance schoolmen. As it was above stated, grammar became the first of sciences ; and whatever subject had to be treated, the first aim of the philosopher was to subject its principles to a code of laws, in the observation of which the merit of the speaker, thinker, or worker, in or on that subject, was thereafter to consist ; so that the whole mind of the world was occupied by the exclusive study of Restraints. The sound of the forging of fetters was heard from sea to sea. The doctors of all the arts and sciences set them-selves daily to the invention of new varieties of cages and manacles ; they themselves wore, instead of gowns, a chain mail, whose purpose was not so much to avert the weapon of the adversary as to restrain the motions of the wearer ; and all the acts, thoughts, and workings of mankind,—poetry, painting, archi-tecture, and philosophy,—were reduced by them merely to so many different forms of fetter-dance.

§ LXXXVII. Now, I am very sure that no reader who has given any attention to the former portions of this work, or the tendency of what else I have written, more especially the last chapter of the "Seven Lamps," will suppose me to underrate the impor-tance, or dispute the authority, of law. It has been necessary

* Isaiah xlvii. 7, 10, 11, 15.

for me to allege these again and again, nor can they ever be too often or too energetically alleged, against the vast masses of men who now disturb or retard the advance of civilization ; heady and high-minded despisers of discipline, and refusers of correction. But law, so far as it can be reduced to form and system, and is not written upon the heart,—as it is, in a Divine loyalty, upon the hearts of the great hierarchies who serve and wait about the throne of the Eternal Lawgiver,—this lower and formally expressible law has, I say, two objects. It is either for the definition and restraint of sin, or the guidance of simplicity ; it either explains, forbids, and punishes wickedness, or it guides the movements and actions both of lifeless things and of the more simple and untaught among responsible agents. And so long, therefore, as sin and foolishness are in the world, so long it will be necessary for men to submit themselves painfully to this lower law, in proportion to their need of being corrected, and to the degree of childishness or simplicity by which they approach more nearly to the condition of the unthinking and inanimate things which are governed by law altogether ; yet yielding, in the manner of their submission to it, a singular lesson to the pride of man,—being obedient more perfectly in proportion to their greatness.* But, so far as men become good and wise, and rise above the state of children, so far they become emancipated from this written law, and invested with the perfect freedom which consists in the fulness and joyfulness of compliance with a higher and unwritten law ; a law so universal, so subtle, so glorious, that nothing but the heart can keep it.

§ LXXXVIII. Now pride opposes itself to the observance of this Divine law in two opposite ways : either by brute resistance, which is the way of the rabble and its leaders, denying or defying law altogether ; or by formal compliance, which is the way of the Pharisee, exalting himself while he pretends to obedience, and making void the infinite and spiritual command-

---

* Compare " Seven Lamps," chap. vii. § 3.

ment by the finite and lettered commandment.   And it is easy to know which law we are obeying : for any law which we magnify and keep through pride, is always the law of the letter ; but that which we love and keep through humility, is the law of the Spirit : and the letter killeth, but the Spirit giveth life.

§ LXXXIX. In the appliance of this universal principle to what we have at present in hand, it is to be noted, that all written or writable law respecting the arts is for the childish and ignorant : that in the beginning of teaching, it is possible to say that this or that must or must not be done ; and laws of colour and shade may be taught, as laws of harmony are to the young scholar in music.   But the moment a man begins to be anything deserving the name of an artist, all this teachable law has become a matter of course with him, and if, thenceforth, he boast himself anywise in the law, or pretend that he lives and works by it, it is a sure sign that he is merely tithing cummin, and that there is no true art nor religion in him.   For the true artist has that inspiration in him which is above all law, or rather which is continually working out such magnificent and perfect obedience to supreme law, as can in nowise be rendered by line and rule.   There are more laws perceived and fulfilled in the single stroke of a great workman, than could be written in a volume.   His science is inexpressibly subtle, directly taught him by his Maker, not in any wise communicable or imitable.*   Neither can any written or definitely observable laws enable us to do any great thing.   It is possible, by measuring and administering quantities of colour, to paint a room wall so that it shall not hurt the eye ; but there are no laws by observing which we can become Titians.   It is possible so to measure and administer syllables as to construct harmonious verse ; but there are no laws by which we can write Iliads.   Out of the poem or the picture, once produced, men may elicit laws by the volume, and study them with advantage, to the better understanding of the existing poem or picture ; but no more

* See the further remarks on Inspiration in the fourth chapter.

write or paint another, than by discovering laws of vegetation they can make a tree to grow. And therefore, wheresoever we find the system and formality of rules much dwelt upon, and spoken of as anything else than a help for children, there we may be sure that noble art is not even understood, far less reached. And thus it was with all the common and public mind in the fifteenth and sixteenth centuries. The greater men, indeed, broke through the thorn hedges; and though much time was lost by the learned among them in writing Latin verses and anagrams, and arranging the framework of quaint sonnets and dexterous syllogisms, till they tore their way through the sapless thicket by force of intellect or of piety; for it was not possible that, either in literature or in painting, rules could be received by any strong mind, so as materially to interfere with its originality: and the crabbed discipline and exact scholarship became an advantage to the men who could pass through and despise them; so that in spite of the rules of the drama we had Shakespeare, and in spite of the rules of art we had Tintoret,— both of them, to this day, doing perpetual violence to the vulgar scholarship and dim-eyed proprieties of the multitude.

§ xc. But in architecture it was not so; for that was the art of the multitude, and was affected by all their errors; and the great men who entered its field, like Michael Angelo, found expression for all the best part of their minds in sculpture, and made the architecture merely its shell. So the simpletons and sophists had their way with it: and the reader can have no conception of the inanities and puerilities of the writers who, with the help of Vitruvius, re-established its "five orders," determined the proportions of each, and gave the various recipes for sublimity and beauty, which have been thenceforward followed to this day, but which may, I believe, in this age of perfect machinery, be followed out still farther. If, indeed, there are only five perfect forms of columns and architraves, and there be a fixed proportion to each, it is certainly possible, with a little ingenuity, so to regulate a stone-cutting machine as that it shall furnish pillars and friezes, to the size ordered, of any of the five orders, on the most perfect Greek models, in any quantity ; an epitome, also, of Vitruvius may be made so simple as to enable any bricklayer to set them up at their proper distances, and we may dispense with our architects altogether.

§ xci. But if this be not so, and there be any truth in the faint persuasion which still lurks in men's mind that architecture *is* an art, and that it requires some gleam of intellect to practise it, then let the whole system of the orders and their proportions be cast out and trampled down as the most vain, barbarous, and paltry deception that was ever stamped on human prejudice ; and let us understand this plain truth, common to all work of man, that, if it be good work, it is not a copy, nor anything done by rule, but a freshly and divinely imagined thing.   Five orders ! There is not a side chapel in any Gothic cathedral but it has fifty orders, the worst of them better than the best of the Greek ones, and all new ; and a single inventive human soul could create a thousand orders in an hour.* And this would have been discovered even in the worst times, but that, as I said, the greatest men of the age found expression for their invention in the other arts, and the best of those who devoted themselves to architecture were in great part occupied in adapting the construction of buildings to new necessities, such as those developed by the invention of gunpowder (introducing a totally new and most interesting science of fortification, which directed the ingenuity of Sanmicheli and many others from its proper channel), and found interest of a meaner kind in the difficulties of reconciling the obsolete architectural laws they had consented to revive, and the forms of Roman architecture which they agreed to copy, with the requirements of the daily life of the sixteenth century.

§ xcii. These, then, were the three principal directions in which the Renaissance pride manifested itself, and its impulses were

---

* That is to say, orders separated by such distinctions as the old Greek ones ; considered with reference to the bearing power of the capital, all orders may be referred to two, as long ago stated ; just as trees may be referred to the two great classes, monocotyledonous and dicotyledonous.

rendered still more fatal by the entrance of another element, inevitably associated with pride. For, as it is written, "He that trusteth in his own heart is a fool," so also it is written, "The fool hath said in his heart, There is no God;" and the self-adulation which influenced not less the learning of the age than its luxury, led gradually to the forgetfulness of all things but self, and to an infidelity only the more fatal because it still retained the form and language of faith.

§ XCIII. IV. INFIDELITY. In noticing the more prominent forms in which this faithlessness manifested itself, it is necessary to distinguish justly between that which was the consequence of respect for Paganism, and that which followed from the corruption of Catholicism. For as the Roman architecture is not to be made answerable for the primal corruption of the Gothic, so neither is the Roman philosophy to be made answerable for the primal corruption of Christianity. Year after year, as the history of the life of Christ sank back into the depth of time, and became obscured by the misty atmosphere of the history of the world,—as intermediate actions and incidents multiplied in number, and countless changes in men's modes of life and tones of thought rendered it more difficult for them to imagine the facts of distant time,—it became daily, almost hourly, a greater effort for the faithful heart to apprehend the entire veracity and vitality of the story of its Redeemer; and more easy for the thoughtless and remiss to deceive themselves as to the true character of the belief they had been taught to profess. And this must have been the case, had the pastors of the Church never failed in their watchfulness, and the Church itself never erred in its practice or doctrine. But when every year that removed the truths of the Gospel into deeper distance, added to them also some false or foolish tradition; when wilful distortion was added to natural obscurity, and the dimness of memory was disguised by the fruitfulness of fiction; when, moreover, the enormous temporal power granted to the clergy attracted into their ranks multitudes of men who, but for such temptation, would not have pretended to the Christian name, so that grievous wolves entered in among them, not sparing the flock ; and when, by the machinations of such men, and the remissness of others, the form and administration of Church doctrine and discipline had become little more than a means of aggrandising the power of the priesthood, it was impossible any longer for men of thoughtfulness or piety to remain in an unquestioning serenity of faith.   The Church had become so mingled with the world that its witness could no longer be received ; and the professing members of it, who were placed in circumstances such as to enable them to become aware of its corruptions, and whom their interest or their simplicity did not bribe or beguile into silence, gradually separated themselves into two vast multitudes of adverse energy, one tending to Reformation, and the other to Infidelity.

§ xcIV. Of these, the last stood, as it were, apart, to watch the course of the struggle between Romanism and Protestantism ; a struggle which, however necessary, was attended with infinite calamity to the Church.   For, in the first place, the Protestant movement was, in reality, not re*formation* but re*animation*.   It poured new life into the Church, but it did not form or define her anew.   In some sort it rather broke down her hedges, so that all they who passed by might pluck off her grapes.   The reformers speedily found that the enemy was never far behind the sower of good seed ; that an evil spirit might enter the ranks of reformation as well as those of resistance : and that though the deadly blight might be checked amidst the wheat, there was no hope of ever ridding the wheat itself from the tares.   New temptations were invented by Satan wherewith to oppose the revived strength of Christianity : as the Romanist, confiding in his human teachers, had ceased to try whether they were teachers sent from God, so the Protestant, confiding in the teaching of the Spirit, believed every spirit, and did not try the spirits whether they were of God. And a thousand enthusiasms and heresies speedily obscured the faith and divided the force of the Reformation.

§ xcv, But the main evils rose out of the antagonism of the

two great parties; primarily, in the mere fact of the existence
of an antagonism.   To the eyes of the unbeliever the Church
of Christ, for the first time since its foundation, bore the
aspect of a house divided against itself.   Not that many forms
of schism had not before arisen in it; but either they had
been obscure and silent, hidden among the shadows of the
Alps and the marshes of the Rhine; or they had been out-
breaks of visible and unmistakable error, cast off by the Church,
rootless, and speedily withering away, while, with much that
was erring and criminal, she still retained within her the pillar
and ground of the truth.   But here was at last a schism in
which truth and authority were at issue.   The body that was
cast off withered away no longer.   It stretched out its boughs
to the sea and its branches to the river, and it was the ancient
trunk that gave signs of decrepitude.   On one side stood the
reanimated faith, in its right hand the Book open, and its left
hand lifted up to heaven, appealing for its proof to the Word
of the Testimony and the power of the Holy Ghost.   On the
other stood, or seemed to stand, all beloved custom and
believed tradition; all that for fifteen hundred years had been
closest to the hearts of men, or most precious for their help.
Long-trusted legend; long-reverenced power; long-practised
discipline; faiths that had ruled the destiny, and sealed the
departure, of souls that could not be told nor numbered for
multitude; prayers, that from the lips of the fathers to those
of the children had distilled like sweet waterfalls, sounding
through the silence of ages, breaking themselves into heavenly
dew to return upon the pastures of the wilderness; hopes, that
had set the face as a flint in the torture, and the sword as a
flame in the battle, that had pointed the purposes and ministered the strength of life, brightened the last glances and shaped
the last syllables of death; charities, that had bound together
the brotherhoods of the mountain and the desert, and had woven
chains of pitying or aspiring communion between this world
and the unfathomable beneath and above; and, more than
these, the spirits of all the innumerable, undoubting dead,

beckoning to the one way by which they had been content to follow the things that belonged unto their peace ;—these all stood on the other side : and the choice must have been a bitter one, even at the best ; but it was rendered tenfold more bitter by the natural, but most sinful, animosity of the two divisions of the Church against each other.

§ xcvi. On one side this animosity was, of course, inevitable. The Romanist party, though still including many Christian men, necessarily included, also, all the worst of those who called themselves Christians. In the fact of its refusing correction, it stood confessed as the Church of the unholy ; and, while it still counted among its adherents many of the simple and believing,—men unacquainted with the corruption of the body to which they belonged, or incapable of accepting any form of doctrine but that which they had been taught from their youth,—it gathered together with them whatever was carnal and sensual in priesthood or in people, all the lovers of power in the one, and of ease in the other. And the rage of these men was, of course, unlimited against those who either disputed their authority, reprehended their manner of life, or cast suspicion upon the popular methods of lulling the conscience in the lifetime, or purchasing salvation on the death-bed.

§ xcvii. Besides this, the reassertion and defence of various tenets which before had been little more than floating errors in the popular mind, but which, definitely attacked by Protestantism, it became necessary to fasten down with a band of iron and brass, gave a form at once more rigid and less rational to the whole body of Romanist Divinity. Multitudes of minds which in other ages might have brought honour and strength to the Church, preaching the more vital truths which it still retained, were now occupied in pleading for arraigned falsehoods, or magnifying disused frivolities : and it can hardly be doubted by any candid observer, that the nascent or latent errors which God pardoned in times of ignorance, became unpardonable when they were formally defined and defended ; the fallacies which were forgiven to the enthusiasm of a multitude, were avenged upon the stubbornness of a Council; that, above all, the great invention of the age, which rendered God's word accessible to every man, left all sins against its light incapable of excuse or expiation; and that from the moment when Rome set herself in direct opposition to the Bible, the judgment was pronounced upon her which made her the scorn and the prey of her own children, and cast her down from the throne where she had magnified herself against heaven, so low, that at last the unimaginable scene of the Bethlehem humiliation was mocked in the temples of Christianity. Judea had seen her God laid in the manger of the beast of burden; it was for Christendom to stable the beast of burden by the altar of her God.

§ XCVIII. Nor, on the other hand, was the opposition of Protestantism to the Papacy less injurious to itself. That opposition was, for the most part, intemperate, undistinguishing, and incautious. It could indeed hardly be otherwise. Fresh bleeding from the sword of Rome, and still trembling at her anathema, the reformed churches were little likely to remember any of her benefits, or to regard any of her teaching. Forced by the Romanist contumely into habits of irreverence, by the Romanist fallacies into habits of disbelief, the self-trusting, rashly-reasoning spirit gained ground among them daily. Sect branched out of sect, presumption rose over presumption; the miracles of the early Church were denied and its martyrs forgotten, though their power and palm were claimed by the members of every persecuted sect; pride, malice, wrath, love of change, masked themselves under the thirst for truth, and mingled with the just resentment of deception, so that it became impossible even for the best and truest men to know the plague of their own hearts; while avarice and impiety openly transformed reformation into robbery, and reproof into sacrilege. Ignorance could as easily lead the foes of the Church, as lull her slumber; men who would once have been the unquestioning recipients, were now the shameless inventors of absurd or perilous superstitions; they who were of the temper that walketh in darkness, gained little by

having discovered their guides to be blind ; and the simplicity of
the faith, ill understood and contumaciously alleged, became an
excuse for the rejection of the highest arts and most tried wisdom
of mankind : while the learned infidel, standing aloof, drew his
own conclusions, both from the rancour of the antagonists, and
from their errors ; believed each in all that he alleged against
the other ; and smiled with superior humanity, as he watched
the winds of the Alps drift the ashes of Jerome, and the dust
of England drink the blood of King Charles.

§ xcix. Now all this evil was, of course, entirely independent
of the renewal of the study of Pagan writers.   But that renewal
found the faith of Christendom already weakened and divided ;
and therefore it was itself productive of an effect tenfold greater
than could have been apprehended from it at another time.   It
acted first, as before noticed, in leading the attention of all men
to words instead of things ; for it was discovered that the language of the middle ages had been corrupt, and the primal object
of every scholar became now to purify his style.   To this study
of words, that of forms being added, both as of matters of the
first importance, half the intellect of the age was at once absorbed
in the base sciences of grammar, logic, and rhetoric ; studies
utterly unworthy of the serious labour of men, and necessarily
rendering those employed upon them incapable of high thoughts
or noble emotion.   Of the debasing tendency of philology, no
proof is needed beyond once reading a grammarian's notes on a
great poet : logic is unnecessary for men who can reason ; and
about as useful to those who cannot as a machine for forcing one
foot in due succession before the other would be to a man who
could not walk : while the study of rhetoric is exclusively one
for men who desire to deceive or be deceived ; he who has the
truth at his heart need never fear the want of persuasion on
his tongue, or, if he fear it, it is because the base rhetoric of
dishonesty keeps the truth from being heard.

§ c. The study of these sciences, therefore, naturally made
men shallow and dishonest in general ; but it had a peculiarly
fatal effect with respect to religion, in the view which men took of

the Bible. Christ's teaching was discovered not to be rhetorical, St. Paul's preaching not to be logical, and the Greek of the New Testament not to be grammatical. The stern truth, the profound pathos, the impatient period, leaping from point to point and leaving the intervals for the hearer to fill, the comparatively Hebraized and unelaborate idiom, had little in them of attraction for the students of phrase and syllogism ; and the chief knowledge of the age became one of the chief stumbling-blocks to its religion.

§ CI. But it was not the grammarian and logician alone who was thus retarded or perverted ; in them there had been small loss. The men who could truly appreciate the higher excellences of the classics were carried away by a current of enthusiasm which withdrew them from every other study. Christianity was still professed as a matter of form, but neither the Bible nor the writings of the Fathers had time left for their perusal, still less heart left for their acceptance. The human mind is not capable of more than a certain amount of admiration or reverence, and that which was given to Horace was withdrawn from David. Religion is, of all subjects, that which will least endure a second place in the heart or thoughts, and a languid and occasional study of it was sure to lead to error or infidelity. On the other hand, what was heartily admired and unceasingly contemplated was soon brought nigh to being believed ; and the systems of Pagan mythology began gradually to assume the places in the human mind from which the unwatched Christianity was wasting. Men did not indeed openly sacrifice to Jupiter, or build silver shrines for Diana, but the ideas of Paganism nevertheless became thoroughly vital and present with them at all times ; and it did not matter in the least, as far as respected the power of true religion, whether the Pagan image was believed in or not, so long as it entirely occupied the thoughts. The scholar of the sixteenth century, if he saw the lightning shining from the east unto the west, thought forthwith of Jupiter, not of the coming of the Son of Man ; if he saw the moon walking in brightness, he thought of Diana, not of the throne which was to be established for ever as a faithful witness in heaven ; and though his heart was but secretly enticed, yet thus he denied the God that is above.*

And, indeed, this double creed, of Christianity confessed and Paganism beloved, was worse than Paganism itself, inasmuch as it refused effective and practical belief altogether. It would have been better to have worshipped Diana and Jupiter at once, than to have gone on through the whole of life naming one God, imagining another, and dreading none. Better, a thousandfold, to have been "a Pagan suckled in some creed outworn," than to have stood by the great sea of Eternity, and seen no God walking on its waves, no heavenly world on its horizon.

§ CII. This fatal result of an enthusiasm for classical literature was hastened and heightened by the misdirection of the powers of art. The imagination of the age was actively set to realise these objects of Pagan belief; and all the most exalted faculties of man, which, up to that period, had been employed in the service of Faith, were now transferred to the service of Fiction. The invention which had formerly been both sanctified and strengthened by labouring under the command of settled intention, and on the ground of assured belief, had now the reins laid upon its neck by passion, and all ground of fact cut from beneath its feet ; and the imagination which formerly had helped men to apprehend the truth, now tempted them to believe a falsehood. The faculties themselves wasted away in their own treason ; one by one they fell in the potter's field; and the Raphael who seemed sent and inspired from heaven that he might paint Apostles and Prophets, sank at once into powerlessness at the feet of Apollo and the Muses.

§ CIII. But this was not all. The habit of using the greatest gifts of imagination upon fictitious subjects, of course destroyed the honour and value of the same imagination used in the cause of truth. Exactly in the proportion in which Jupiters and Mercuries were embodied and believed, in that proportion Virgins

---

* Job xxxi. 26-28 ; Psalm lxxxix. 37.

and Angels were disembodied and disbelieved. The images summoned by art began gradually to assume one average value in the spectator's mind; and incidents from the Iliad and from the Exodus to come within the same degrees of credibility. And, farther, while the powers of the imagination were becoming daily more and more languid, because unsupported by faith, the manual skill and science of the artist were continually on the increase. When these had reached a certain point, they began to be the principal things considered in the picture, and its story or scene to be thought of only as a theme for their manifestation. Observe the difference. In old times, men used their powers of painting to show the objects of faith; in later times, they used the objects of faith that they might show their powers of painting. The distinction is enormous, the difference incalculable as irreconcilable. And thus, the more skilful the artist, the less his subject was regarded; and the hearts of men hardened as their handling softened, until they reached a point when sacred, profane, or sensual subjects were employed, with absolute indifference, for the display of colour and execution; and gradually the mind of Europe congealed into that state of utter apathy,—inconceivable, unless it had been witnessed, and unpardonable, unless by us, who have been infected by it, —which permits us to place the Madonna and the Aphrodite side by side in our galleries, and to pass, with the same unmoved inquiry into the manner of their handling, from a Bacchanal to a Nativity.

Now all this evil, observe, would have been merely the necessary and natural operation of an enthusiasm for the classics, and of a delight in the mere science of the artist, on the most virtuous mind. But this operation took place upon minds enervated by luxury, and which were tempted, at the very same period, to forgetfulness or denial of all religious principle by their own basest instincts. The faith which had been undermined by the genius of Pagans, was overthrown by the crimes of Christians; and the ruin which was begun by scholarship, was completed by sensuality. The characters of the heathen divinities were as suitable to the manners of the time as their forms were agreeable to its taste; and paganism again became, in effect, the religion of Europe. That is to say, the civilised world is at this moment, collectively, just as Pagan as it was in the second century; a small body of believers being now, as they were then, representative of the Church of Christ in the midst of the faithless: but there is just this difference, and this very fatal one, between the second and nineteenth centuries, that the Pagans are nominally and fashionably Christians, and that there is every conceivable variety and shade of belief between the two; so that not only is it most difficult theoretically to mark the point where hesitating trust and failing practice change into definite infidelity, but it has become a point of politeness not to inquire too deeply into our neighbour's religious opinions; and, so that no one be offended by violent breach of external forms, to waive any close examination into the tenets of faith. The fact is, we distrust each other and ourselves so much, that we dare not press this matter; we know that if, on any occasion of general intercourse, we turn to our next neighbour, and put to him some searching or testing question, we shall, in nine cases out of ten, discover him to be only a Christian in his own way, and as far as he thinks proper, and that he doubts of many things which we ourselves do not believe strongly enough to hear doubted without danger. What is in reality cowardice and faithlessness, we call charity; and consider it the part of benevolence sometimes to forgive men's evil practice for the sake of their accurate faith, and sometimes to forgive their confessed heresy for the sake of their admirable practice. And under this shelter of charity, humility, and faintheartedness, the world, unquestioned by others or by itself, mingles with and overwhelms the small body of Christians, legislates for them, moralises for them, reasons for them; and, though itself of course greatly and beneficently influenced by the association, and held much in check by its pretence to Christianity, yet undermines, in nearly the same degree, the sincerity and practical power of Christianity itself, until at last, in the very institutions of which

the administration may be considered as the principal test of the
genuineness of national religion—those devoted to education—
the Pagan system is completely triumphant; and the entire body
of the so-called Christian world has established a system of instruction for its youth, wherein neither the history of Christ's
Church, nor the language of God's law, is considered a study
of the smallest importance ; wherein, of all subjects of human inquiry, his own religion is the one in which a youth's ignorance
is most easily forgiven ; * and in which it is held a light matter
that he should be daily guilty of lying, of debauchery, or of
blasphemy, so only that he write Latin verses accurately, and
with speed.

I believe that in a few years more we shall wake from all
these errors in astonishment, as from evil dreams ; having been
preserved, in the midst of their madness, by those hidden roots
of active and earnest Christianity which God's grace has bound
in the English nation with iron and brass.   But in the Venetian
those roots themselves had withered ; and, from the palace of their
ancient religion, their pride cast them forth hopelessly to the
pasture of the brute.   From pride to infidelity, from infidelity
to the unscrupulous and insatiable pursuit of pleasure, and from
this to irremediable degradation, the transitions were swift, like
the falling of a star.   The great palaces of the haughtiest nobles
of Venice were stayed, before they had risen far above their
foundations, by the blast of a penal poverty ; and the wild grass,
on the unfinished fragments of their mighty shafts, waves at the
tide-mark where the power of the godless people first heard the
" Hitherto shalt thou come."   And the regeneration in which
they had so vainly trusted,—the new birth and clear dawning,
as they thought it, of all art, all knowledge, and all hope,—became

* I shall not forget the impression made upon me at Oxford, when, going up
for my degree, and mentioning to one of the authorities that I had not had
time enough to read the Epistles properly, I was told, that "the Epistles were
separate sciences, and I need not trouble myself about them."

The reader will find some farther notes on this subject in Appendix 7,
" Modern Education."

to them as that dawn which Ezekiel saw on the hills of Israel :
" Behold the Day ; behold, it is come.   The rod hath blossomed,
pride hath budded, violence is risen up into a rod of wickedness.
None of them shall remain, nor of their multitude ; let not the
buyer rejoice, nor the seller mourn, for wrath is upon all the
multitude thereof."

CHAPTER III.

GROTESQUE RENAISSANCE.

§ I. In the close of the last chapter it was noted that the phases of transition in the moral temper of the falling Venetians, during their fall, were from pride to infidelity, and from infidelity to the unscrupulous *pursuit of pleasure*. During the last years of the existence of the state, the minds both of the nobility and the people seem to have been set simply upon the attainment of the means of self-indulgence. There was not strength enough in them to be proud, nor forethought enough to be ambitious. One by one the possessions of the state were abandoned to its enemies; one by one the channels of its trade were forsaken by its own languor, or occupied and closed against it by its more energetic rivals; and the time, the resources, and the thoughts of the nation were exclusively occupied in the invention of such fantastic and costly pleasures as might best amuse their apathy, lull their remorse, or disguise their ruin.

§ II. The architecture raised at Venice during this period is among the worst and basest ever built by the hands of men, being especially distinguished by a spirit of brutal mockery and insolent jest, which, exhausting itself in deformed and monstrous sculpture, can sometimes be hardly otherwise defined than as the perpetuation in stone of the ribaldries of drunkenness. On such a period, and on such work, it is painful to dwell, and I had not originally intended to do so; but I found that the entire spirit of the Renaissance could not be comprehended unless it was followed to its consummation; and that there were many most interesting questions arising out of the study of this particular spirit of jesting, with reference to which I have called it the *Grotesque* Renaissance. For it is not this period alone which is distinguished by such a spirit. There is jest—perpetual, care-less, and not unfrequently obscene—in the most noble work of the Gothic periods; and it becomes, therefore, of the greatest possible importance to examine into the nature and essence of the Grotesque itself, and to ascertain in what respect it is that the jesting of art in its highest flight differs from its jesting in its utmost degradation.

§ III. The place where we may best commence our inquiry is one renowned in the history of Venice, the space of ground before the Church of Santa Maria Formosa; a spot which, after the Rialto and St. Mark's Place, ought to possess a peculiar interest in the mind of the traveller, in consequence of its con-nexion with the most touching and true legend of the Brides of Venice. That legend is related at length in every Venetian history, and, finally, has been told by the poet Rogers, in a way which renders it impossible for any one to tell it after him. I have only, therefore, to remind the reader that the capture of the brides took place in the cathedral church, St. Pietro di Castello; and that this of Santa Maria Formosa is connected with the tale, only because it was yearly visited with prayers by the Venetian maidens, on the anniversary of their ancestors' deliver-ance. For that deliverance, their thanks were to be rendered to the Virgin; and there was no church then dedicated to the Virgin in Venice except this.*

Neither of the cathedral church, nor of this dedicated to St. Mary the Beautiful, is one stone left upon another. But from that which has been raised on the site of the latter, we may receive a most important lesson, introductory to our im-mediate subject, if first we glance back to the traditional history of the church which has been destroyed.

§ IV. No more honourable epithet than "traditional" can be attached to what is recorded concerning it, yet I should grieve to lose the legend of its first erection. The Bishop of Uderzo,

* Mutinelli, Annali Urbani, lib. i. p. 24; and the Chronicle of 1738, quoted by Galliciolli: "Attrovandosi allora la giesia de Sta. Maria Formosa sola giesia del nome della gloriosa Vergine Maria."

driven by the Lombards from his bishopric, as he was praying beheld in a vision the Virgin Mother, who ordered him to found a church in her honour, in the place where he should see a white cloud rest.   And when he went out, the white cloud went before him ; and on the place where it rested he built a church, and it was called the Church of St. Mary the Beautiful, from the love-liness of the form in which she appeared in the vision.*

This first church stood only for about two centuries.   It was rebuilt in 864, and enriched with various relics some fifty years later ; relics belonging principally to St. Nicodemus, and much lamented when they and the church were together destroyed by fire in 1105.

It was then rebuilt in "magnifica forma," much resembling, according to Corner, the architecture of the chancel of St. Mark ;† but the information which I find in various writers, as to the period at which it was reduced to its present condition, is both sparing and contradictory.

§ v. Thus, by Corner, we are told that this church resembling St. Mark's, "remained untouched for more than four centuries, until, in 1689, it was thrown down by an earthquake, and restored by the piety of a rich merchant, Turrin Toroni, "in ornatissima forma ;" and that, for the greater beauty of the renewed church, it had added to it two façades of marble.   With this information that of the Padre dell' Oratorio agrees, only he gives the date of the earlier rebuilding of the church in 1175, and ascribes it to an architect of the name of Barbetta.   But Quadri, in his usually accurate little guide, tells us that this Barbetta rebuilt the church in the fourteenth century ; and that of the two façades, so much admired by Corner, one is of the sixteenth century, and its archi-

---

* Or from the brightness of the cloud, according to the Padre who arranged the " Memorie delle Chiese di Venezia," vol. iii. p. 7.   Compare Corner, p. 42.   This first church was built in 639.

† Perhaps both Corner and the Padre founded their diluted information on the short sentence of Sansovino : " Finalmente, l' anno 1075, fu ridotta a per-fezione da Paolo Barbetta, sul modello del corpo di mezzo della chiesa di S. Marco."   Sansovino, however, gives 842, instead of 864, as the date of the first rebuilding.

tect unknown ; and the rest of the church is of the seventeenth, "in the style of Sansovino."

§ VI. There is no occasion to examine, or endeavour to reconcile, these conflicting accounts. All that it is necessary for the reader to know is, that every vestige of the church in which the ceremony took place was destroyed *at least* as early as 1689 ; and that the ceremony itself, having been abolished in the close of the fourteenth century, is only to be conceived as taking place in that more ancient church, resembling St. Mark's, which, even according to Quadri, existed until that period. I would, therefore, endeavour to fix the reader's mind, for a moment, on the contrast between the former and latter aspect of this plot of ground ; the former, when it had its Byzantine church, and its yearly procession of the Doge and the Brides ; and the latter, when it has its Renaissance church "in the style of Sansovino," and its yearly honouring is done away.

§ VII. And, first, let us consider for a little the significance and nobleness of that early custom of the Venetians, which brought about the attack and the rescue of the year 943 : that there should be but one marriage day for the nobles of the whole nation,* so that all might rejoice together ; and that the sympathy might be full not only of the families who that year beheld the alliance of their children, and prayed for them in one crowd, weeping before the altar, but of all the families of the state, who saw, in the day which brought happiness to others, the anniversary of their own. Imagine the strong bond of brotherhood thus sanctified among them, and consider also the effect on the minds of the youth of the state ; the greater deliberation and openness necessarily given to the contemplation of marriage, to which all the people were solemnly to bear testimony ; the more lofty and unselfish tone which it would give to all their thoughts. It was the exact contrary of stolen marriage. It was marriage to which God and man were taken

---

* Or at least for its principal families. Vide Appendix 8: "Early Venetian Marriages."

for witnesses, and every eye was invoked for its glance, and every tongue for its prayers.*

§ VIII. Later historians have delighted themselves in dwelling on the pageantry of the marriage day itself, but I do not find that they have authority for the splendour of their descriptions. I cannot find a word in the older Chronicles about the jewels or dress of the brides, and I believe the ceremony to have been more quiet and homely than is usually supposed. The only sentence which gives colour to the usual accounts of it is one of Sansovino's, in which he says that the magnificent dress of the brides in his day was founded "on ancient custom."† However this may have been, the circumstances of the rite were otherwise very simple. Each maiden brought her dowry with her in a small "cassetta," or chest; they went first to the cathedral, and waited for the youths, who having come, they heard mass together, and the bishop preached to them and blessed them; and so each bridegroom took his bride and her dowry, and bore her home.

§ IX. It seems that the alarm given by the attack of the pirates put an end to the custom of fixing one day for all marriages: but the main objects of the institution were still attained by the perfect publicity given to the marriages of all

---

* "Nazionale quasi la ceremonia, perciocche per essa nuovi difensori ad acquistar andava la patria, sostegni nuovi le leggi, la libertà."—*Mutinelli.*

† "Vestita, *per antico uso*, di bianco, e con chiome sparse giù per le spalle, conteste con fila d' oro." "Dressed according to ancient usage in white, and with her hair thrown down upon her shoulders, interwoven with threads of gold." This was when she was first brought out of her chamber to be seen by the guests invited to the espousals. "And when the form of the espousal has been gone through, she is led, to the sound of pipes and trumpets, and other musical instruments, round the room, *dancing serenely all the time, and bowing herself before the guests* ("ballando placidamente, e facendo inchini ai convitati"); and so she returns to her chamber: and when other guests have arrived, she again comes forth, and makes the circuit of the chamber. And this is repeated for an hour or somewhat more; and then, accompanied by many ladies who wait for her, she enters a gondola without its felze (canopy), and seated on a somewhat raised seat covered with carpets, with a great number of gondolas following her, she goes to visit the monasteries and convents, wheresoever she has any relations."

the noble families; the bridegroom standing in the court of the Ducal Palace to receive congratulations on his betrothal, and the whole body of the nobility attending the nuptials, and rejoicing, "as at some personal good fortune; since, by the constitution of the state, they are for ever incorporated together, as if of one and the same family."* But the festival of the 2nd of February, after the year 943, seems to have been observed only in memory of the deliverance of the brides, and no longer set apart for public nuptials.

§ x. There is much difficulty in reconciling the various accounts, or distinguishing the inaccurate ones, of the manner of keeping this memorable festival. I shall first give Sansovino's, which is the popular one, and then note the points of importance in the counter statements. Sansovino says that the success of the pursuit of the pirates was owing to the ready help and hard fighting of the men of the district of Sta. Maria Formosa, for the most part trunkmakers; and that they, having been presented after the victory to the Doge and the Senate, were told to ask some favour for their reward. "The good men then said that they desired the Prince, with his wife and the Signory, to visit every year the church of their district, on the day of its feast. And the Prince asking them, 'Suppose it should rain?' they answered, 'We will give you hats to cover you; and if you are thirsty, we will give you to drink.' Whence it is that the Vicar, in the name of the people, presents to the Doge, on his visit, two flasks of malvoisie † and two oranges; and presents to him two gilded hats, bearing the arms of the Pope, of the Prince, and of the Vicar. And thus was instituted the Feast of the Maries, which was called noble and famous because the people from all round came together to behold it. And it was celebrated in this manner : . . ." The

* Sansovino.

† English, "Malmsey." The reader will find a most amusing account of the negotiations between the English and Venetians, touching the supply of London with this wine, in Mr. Brown's translation of the Giustiniani papers. See Appendix IX.

account which follows is somewhat prolix ; but its substance is, briefly, that twelve maidens were elected, two for each division of the city ; and that it was decided by lot which contrade, or quarters of the town, should provide them with dresses. This was done at enormous expense, one contrada contending with another, and even the jewels of the treasury of St. Mark being lent for the occasion to the " Maries," as the twelve damsels were called. They, being thus dressed with gold, and silver, and jewels, went in their galley to St. Mark's for the Doge, who joined them with the Signory, and went first to San Pietro di Castello to hear mass on St. Mark's Day, the 31st of January, and to Santa Maria Formosa on the 2nd of February, the intermediate day being spent in passing in procession through the streets of the city ; " and sometimes there arose quarrels about the places they should pass through, for every one wanted them to pass by his house."

§ XI. Nearly the same account is given by Corner, who, however, does not say anything about the hats or the malvoisie. These, however, we find again in the Matricola de' Casseleri, which, of course, sets the services of the trunkmakers and the privileges obtained by them in the most brilliant light. The quaintness of the old Venetian is hardly to be rendered into English.   " And you must know that the said trunkmakers were the men who were the cause of such victory, and of taking the galley, and of cutting all the Triestines to pieces, because, at that time, they were valiant men and well in order. The which victory was on the 2nd February, on the day of the Madonna of candles. And at the request and entreaties of the said trunkmakers, it was decreed that the Doge, every year, as long as Venice should endure, should go on the eve of the said feast to vespers in the said church, with the Signory. And be it noted, that the Vicar is obliged to give to the Doge two flasks of malvoisie, with two oranges besides. And so it is observed, and will be observed always." The reader must observe the continual confusion between St. Mark's Day the 31st of January, and Candlemas the 2nd of February.

The fact appears to be, that the marriage day in the old republic was St. Mark's Day, and the recovery of the brides was the same day at evening; so that, as we are told by Sansovino, the commemorative festival began on that day, but it was continued to the day of the Purification, that especial thanks might be rendered to the Virgin; and the visit to Sta. Maria Formosa being the most important ceremony of the whole festival, the old chroniclers, and even Sansovino, got confused, and asserted the victory itself to have taken place on the day appointed for that pilgrimage.

§ XII. I doubt not that the reader who is acquainted with the beautiful lines of Rogers is as much grieved as I am at this interference of the "casket-makers" with the achievement which the poet ascribes to the bridegrooms alone; an interference quite as inopportune as that of old Le Balafré with the victory of his nephew, in the unsatisfactory conclusion of "Quentin Durward." I am afraid I cannot get the casket-makers quite out of the way; but it may gratify some of my readers to know that a chronicle of the year 1378, quoted by Galliciolli, denies the agency of the people of Sta. Maria Formosa altogether, in these terms: "Some say that the people of Sta. M. Formosa were those who recovered the *Spoil*" ("preda;" I may notice, in passing, that most of the old chroniclers appear to consider the recovery of the *caskets* rather more a subject of congratulation than that of the brides), "and that, for their reward, they asked the Doge and Signory to visit Sta. M. Formosa; but *this is false*. The going to Sta. M. Formosa was because the thing had succeeded on that day, and because this was then the only church in Venice in honour of the Virgin." But here is again the mistake about the day itself; and besides, if we get rid altogether of the trunkmakers, how are we to account for the ceremony of the oranges and hats, of which the accounts seem authentic? If, however, the reader likes to substitute "carpenters" or "house-builders" for casket-makers, he may do so with great reason (vide Galliciolli, lib. ii. § 1758); but I fear that one or the other body of tradesmen must be allowed to have had no small share in the honour of the victory.

§ XIII. But whatever doubt attaches to the particular circumstances of its origin, there is none respecting the splendour of the festival itself, as it was celebrated for four centuries afterwards. We find that each contrada spent from 800 to 1000 zecchins in the dress of the " Maries" entrusted to it; but I cannot find among how many contradas the twelve Maries were divided; it is also to be supposed that most of the accounts given refer to the later periods of the celebration of the festival. In the beginning of the eleventh century, the good Doge Pietro Orseolo II. left in his will the third of his entire fortune "per la festa delle Marie;" and, in the fourteenth century, so many people came from the rest of Italy to see it, that special police regulations were made for it, and the Council of Ten were twice summoned before it took place.* The expense lavished upon it seems to have increased till the year 1379, when all the resources of the republic were required for the terrible war of Chiozza, and all festivity was for that time put an end to. The issue of the war left the Venetians with neither the power nor the disposition to restore the festival on its ancient scale, and they seem to have been ashamed to exhibit it in reduced splendour. It was entirely abolished.

§ XIV. As if to do away even with its memory, every feature of the surrounding scene which was associated with that festival has been in succeeding ages destroyed. With one solitary exception,† there is not a house left in the whole Piazza of Santa Maria Formosa from whose windows the festa of the Maries has ever been seen : of the church in which they worshipped, not a stone is left, even the form of the ground and direction of the neighbouring canals are changed : and there is now but one landmark to guide the steps of the traveller to the place where the white cloud rested, and the shrine was built to St. Mary the Beautiful. Yet the spot is still worth his pilgrimage, for he may receive a lesson upon it, though a painful one.

---

* "XV. diebus et octo diebus ante festum Mariarum omni anno."—*Galliciolli.* The same precautions were taken before the Feast of the Ascension,

† Casa Vittura.

Let him first fill his mind with the fair images of the ancient festival, and then seek that landmark, the tower of the modern church, built upon the place where the daughters of Venice knelt yearly with her noblest lords; and let him look at the head that is carved on the base of the tower,* still dedicated to St. Mary the Beautiful.

§ xv. A head,—huge, inhuman, and monstrous,—leering in bestial degradation, too foul to be either pictured or described, or to be beheld for more than an instant: yet let it be endured for that instant; for in that head is embodied the type of the evil spirit to which Venice was abandoned in the fourth period of her decline; and it is well that we should see and feel the full horror of it on this spot, and know what pestilence it was that came and breathed upon her beauty, until it melted away like the white cloud from the ancient fields of Santa Maria Formosa.

§ xvi. This head is one of many hundreds which disgrace the latest buildings of the city, all more or less agreeing in their expression of sneering mockery, in most cases enhanced by thrusting out the tongue. Most of them occur upon the bridges, which were among the very last works undertaken by the republic, several, for instance, upon the Bridge of Sighs; and they are evidences of a delight in the contemplation of bestial vice, and the expression of low sarcasm, which is, I believe, the most hopeless state into which the human mind can fall. This spirit of idiotic mockery is, as I have said, the most striking characteristic of the last period of the Renaissance, which, in consequence of the character thus imparted to its sculpture, I have called grotesque; but it must be our immediate task, and it will be a most interesting one, to distinguish between this base grotesqueness, and that magnificent condition of fantastic imagination, which was above noticed as one of the chief elements of the Northern Gothic mind. Nor is this a question of interesting speculation merely: for the distinction between the true and false grotesque is one which the present

---

* The keystone of the arch on its western side facing the canal.

tendencies of the English mind have rendered it practically important to ascertain; and that in a degree which, until he has made some progress in the consideration of the subject, the reader will hardly anticipate.

§ XVII. But, first, I have to note one peculiarity in the late architecture of Venice, which will materially assist us in understanding the true nature of the spirit which is to be the subject of our inquiry; and this peculiarity, singularly enough, is first exemplified in the very façade of Santa Maria Formosa, which is flanked by the grotesque head to which our attention has just been directed. This façade, whose architect is unknown, consists of a pediment, sustained on four Corinthian pilasters, and is, I believe, the earliest in Venice which appears *entirely destitute of every religious symbol, sculpture, or inscription;* unless the cardinal's hat upon the shield in the centre of the pediment be considered a religious symbol. The entire façade is nothing else than a monument to the Admiral Vincenzo Cappello. Two tablets, one between each pair of flanking pillars, record his acts and honours; and, on the corresponding spaces upon the base of the church, are two circular trophies, composed of halberts, arrows, flags, tridents, helmets, and lances: sculptures which are just as valueless in a military as in an ecclesiastical point of view; for being all copied from the forms of Roman arms and armour, they cannot even be referred to for information respecting the costume of the period. Over the door, as the chief ornament of the façade, exactly in the spot which in the " barbarous " St. Mark's is occupied by the figure of Christ, is the statue of Vincenzo Cappello, in Roman armour. He died in 1542; and we have, therefore, the latter part of the sixteenth century fixed as the period when, in Venice, churches were first built to the glory of man, instead of the glory of God.

§ XVIII. Throughout the whole of Scripture history, nothing is more remarkable than the close connexion of punishment with the sin of vainglory. Every other sin is occasionally permitted to remain, for lengthened periods, without definite chastisement; but the forgetfulness of God, and the claim of honour by man, as belonging to himself, are visited at once, whether in Hezekiah, Nebuchadnezzar, or Herod, with the most tremendous punishment. We have already seen that the first reason for the fall of Venice was the manifestation of such a spirit ; and it is most singular to observe the definiteness with which it is here marked,—as if so appointed, that it might be impossible for future ages to miss the lesson. For, in the long inscriptions which record the acts of Vincenzo Cappello, it might at least have been anticipated that some expressions would occur indicative of remaining pretence to religious feeling, or formal acknowledgment of Divine power. But there are none whatever. The name of God does not once occur ; that of St. Mark is found only in the statement that Cappello was a procurator of the church : there is no word touching either on the faith or hope of the deceased ; and the only sentence which alludes to supernatural powers at all, alludes to them under the heathen name of *fates*, in its explanation of what the Admiral Cappello *would* have accomplished, " nisi fata Christianis adversa vetuissent."*

* The inscriptions are as follows :

To the left of the reader—

" VINCENTIUS CAPELLUS MARITIMARUM
RERUM PERITISSIMUS ET ANTIQUORUM
LAUDIBUS PAR, TRIREMIUM ONERARIA
RUM PRÆFECTUS, AB HENRICO VII. BRI
TANNIÆ REGE INSIGNE DONATUS CLAS
SIS LEGATUS V. IMP. DESIG. TER CLAS
SEM DEDUXIT, COLLAPSAM NAVALEM DIS
CIPLINAM RESTITUIT, AD ZACXINTHUM
AURIÆ CÆSARIS LEGATO PRISCAM
VENETAM VIRTUTEM OSTENDIT."

To the right of the reader—

" IN AMBRACIO SINU BARBARUSSUM OTTHO
MANICÆ CLASSIS DUCEM INCLUSIT
POSTRIDIE AD INTERNITIONEM DELETU
RUS NISI FATA CHRISTIANIS ADVERSA
VETUISSENT. IN RYZONICO SINU CASTRO NOVO
EXPUGNATO DIVI MARCI PROCUR
UNIVERSO REIP CONSENSU CREATUS
IN PATRIA MORITUR TOTIUS CIVITATIS
MŒRORE, ANNO ÆTATIS LXXIV. MDCXLII. XIV. KAL. SEPT."

§ XIX. Having taken sufficient note of all the baseness of mind which these facts indicate in the people, we shall not be surprised to find immediate signs of dotage in the conception of their architecture. The churches raised throughout this period are so grossly debased, that even the Italian critics of the present day, who are partially awakened to the true state of art in Italy, though blind, as yet, to its true cause, exhaust their terms of reproach upon these last efforts of the Renaissance builders. The two churches of San Moisè and Santa Maria Zobenigo, which are among the most remarkable in Venice for their manifestation of insolent atheism, are characterised by Lazari, the one as "culmine d' ogni follia architettonica," the other as "orrido ammasso di pietra d' Istria," with added expressions of contempt, as just as it is unmitigated.

§ XX. Now both these churches, which I should like the reader to visit in succession, if possible, after that of Sta. Maria Formosa, agree with that church, and with each other, in being totally destitute of religious symbols, and entirely dedicated to the honour of two Venetian families. In San Moisè, a bust of Vincenzo Fini is set on a tall narrow pyramid above the central door, with this marvellous inscription;

"OMNE FASTIGIVM
VIRTVTE IMPLET
VINCENTIVS FINI."

It is very difficult to translate this : for " fastigium," besides its general sense, has a particular one in architecture, and refers to the part of the building occupied by the bust ; but the main meaning of it is that " Vincenzo Fini fills all height with his virtue." The inscription goes on into farther praise, but this example is enough. Over the two lateral doors are two other laudatory inscriptions of younger members of the Fini family, the dates of death of the three heroes being 1660, 1685, and 1726, marking thus the period of consummate degradation.

§ XXI. In like manner, the Church of Santa Maria Zobenigo is entirely dedicated to the Barbaro family ; the only religious

III

Tho.ˢ Lupton

Noble and Ignoble Grotesque.

J. Ruskin.

symbols with which it is invested being statues of angels blowing brazen trumpets, intended to express the spreading of the fame of the Barbaro family in heaven. At the top of the church is Venice crowned, between Justice and Temperance, Justice holding a pair of grocer's scales, of iron, swinging in the wind. There is a two-necked stone eagle (the Barbaro crest), with a copper crown, in the centre of the pediment. A huge statue of a Barbaro in armour, with a fantastic head-dress, over the central door; and four Barbaros in niches, two on each side of it, strutting statues, in the common stage postures of the period,—Jo. Maria Barbaro, sapiens ordinum; Marinus Barbaro, Senator (reading a speech in a Ciceronian attitude); Franc. Barbaro, legatus in classe (in armour, with high-heeled boots, and looking resolutely fierce); and Carolus Barbaro, sapiens ordinum : the decorations of the façade being completed by two trophies, consisting of drums, trumpets, flags, and cannon; and six plans, sculptured in relief, of the towns of Zara, Candia, Padua, Rome, Corfu, and Spalatro.

§ XXII. When the traveller has sufficiently considered the meaning of this façade, he ought to visit the Church of St. Eustachio, remarkable for the dramatic effect of the group of sculpture on its façade, and then the Church of the Ospeda-letto (see Index, under head Ospedaletto), noticing, on his way, the heads on the foundations of the Palazzo Corner della Regina, and the Palazzo Pesaro, and any other heads carved on the modern bridges, closing with those on the Bridge of Sighs.

He will then have obtained a perfect idea of the style and feeling of the Grotesque Renaissance. I cannot pollute this volume by any illustration of its worst forms, but the head turned to the front, on the right-hand in the opposite Plate, will give the general reader an idea of its most graceful and refined developments. The figure set beside it, on the left, is a piece of noble grotesque, from fourteenth century Gothic; and it must be our present task to ascertain the nature of the difference which exists between the two, by an accurate inquiry into the true essence of the grotesque spirit itself.

§ XXIII. First, then, it seems to me that the grotesque is, in almost all cases, composed of two elements, one ludicrous, the other fearful; that, as one or other of these elements prevails, the grotesque falls into two branches, sportive grotesque and terrible grotesque; but that we cannot legitimately consider it under these two aspects, because there are hardly any examples which do not in some degree combine both elements: there are few grotesques so utterly playful as to be overcast with no shade of fearfulness, and few so fearful as absolutely to exclude all ideas of jest. But although we cannot separate the grotesque itself into two branches, we may easily examine separately the two conditions of mind which it seems to combine; and consider successively what are the kinds of jest, and what the kinds of fearfulness, which may be legitimately expressed in the various walks of art, and how their expressions actually occur in the Gothic and Renaissance schools.

First, then, what are the conditions of playfulness which we may fitly express in noble art, or which (for this is the same thing) are consistent with nobleness in humanity? In other words, what is the proper function of play, with respect not to youth merely, but to all mankind?

§ XXIV. It is a much more serious question than may be at first supposed; for a healthy manner of play is necessary in order to a healthy manner of work: and because the choice of our recreation is, in most cases, left to ourselves, while the nature of our work is as generally fixed by necessity or authority, it may well be doubted whether more distressful consequences may not have resulted from mistaken choice in play than from mistaken direction in labour.

§ XXV. Observe, however, that we are only concerned here with that kind of play which causes laughter or implies re-creation, not with that which consists in the excitement of the energies whether of body or mind. Muscular exertion is, indeed, in youth, one of the conditions of recreation; but neither "the violent bodily labour which children of all ages agree to call play," nor the grave excitement of the mental faculties in games of skill or chance, are in any wise connected with the state of feeling we have here to investigate, namely, that sportiveness which man possesses in common with many inferior creatures, but to which his higher faculties give nobler expression in the various manifestations of wit, humour, and fancy.

With respect to the manner in which this instinct of playfulness is indulged or repressed, mankind are broadly distinguishable into four classes: the men who play wisely; who play necessarily; who play inordinately; and who play not at all.

§ XXVI. First, Those who play wisely. It is evident that the idea of any kind of play can only be associated with the idea of an imperfect, childish, and fatigable nature. As far as men can raise that nature, so that it shall no longer be interested by trifles, or exhausted by toils, they raise it above play; he whose heart is at once fixed upon heaven, and open to the earth, so as to apprehend the importance of heavenly doctrines, and the compass of human sorrow, will have little disposition for jest; and exactly in proportion to the breadth and depth of his character and intellect will be, in general, the incapability of surprise or exuberant and sudden emotion, which must render play impossible. It is, however, evidently not intended that many men should even reach, far less pass their lives in, that solemn state of thoughtfulness, which brings them into the nearest brotherhood with their Divine Master; and the highest and healthiest state which is competent to ordinary humanity appears to be that which, accepting the necessity of recreation, and yielding to the impulses of natural delight springing out of health and innocence, does, indeed, condescend often to playfulness, but never without such deep love of God, of truth, and of humanity, as shall make even its lightest words reverent, its idlest fancies profitable, and its keenest satire indulgent. Wordsworth and Plato furnish us with perhaps the finest and highest examples of this playfulness: in the one case, unmixed with satire, the perfectly simple effusion of that spirit

" Which gives to all the self-same bent,
Whose life is wise and innocent:"

—in Plato, and, by-the-by, in a very wise book of our own times, not unworthy of being named in such companionship, " Friends in Council," mingled with an exquisitely tender and loving satire.

§ XXVII. Secondly, The men who play necessarily. That highest species of playfulness, which we have just been considering, is evidently the condition of a mind, not only highly cultivated, but so habitually trained to intellectual labour that it can bring a considerable force of accurate thought into its moments even of recreation. This is not possible unless so much repose of mind and heart are enjoyed, even at the periods of greatest exertion, that the rest required by the system is diffused over the whole life. To the majority of mankind, such a state is evidently unattainable. They must, perforce, pass a large part of their lives in employments both irksome and toilsome, demanding an expenditure of energy which exhausts the system, and yet consuming that energy upon subjects incapable of interesting the nobler faculties. When such employments are intermitted, those noble instincts, fancy, imagination, and curiosity, are all hungry for the food which the labour of the day has denied to them, while yet the weariness of the body, in a great degree, forbids their application to any serious subject. They therefore exert themselves without any determined purpose, and under no vigorous restraint, but gather, as best they may, such various nourishment, and put themselves to such fantastic exercise, as may soonest indemnify them for their past imprisonment, and prepare them to endure its recurrence. This stretching of the mental limbs as their fetters fall away,—this leaping and dancing of the heart and intellect, when they are restored to the fresh air of heaven, yet half paralyzed by their captivity, and unable to turn themselves to any earnest purpose,—I call necessary play. It is impossible to exaggerate its importance, whether in polity, or in art.

§ XXVIII. Thirdly, The men who play inordinately. The most perfect state of society which, consistently with due understanding of man's nature, it may be permitted us to conceive, would be one in which the whole human race were divided, more or less distinctly, into workers and thinkers ; that is to say, into the two classes who only play wisely or play necessarily. But the number and the toil of the working class are enormously increased, probably more than doubled, by the vices of the men who neither play wisely nor necessarily, but are enabled by circumstances, and permitted by their want of principle, to make amusement the object of their existence. There is not any moment of the lives of such men which is not injurious to others; both because they leave the work undone which was appointed for them, and because they necessarily think wrongly, whenever it becomes compulsory upon them to think at all. The greater portion of the misery of this world arises from the false opinions of men whose idleness has physically incapacitated them from forming true ones. Every duty which we omit obscures some truth which we should have known ; and the guilt of a life spent in the pursuit of pleasure is twofold, partly consisting in the perversion of action, and partly in the dissemination of false-hood.

§ XXIX. There is, however, a less criminal, though hardly less dangerous, condition of mind ; which, though not failing in its more urgent duties, fails in the finer conscientiousness which regulates the degree, and directs the choice, of amusement, at those times when amusement is allowable. The most frequent error in this respect is the want of reverence in approaching subjects of importance or sacredness, and of caution in the expression of thoughts which may encourage like irreverence in others : and these faults are apt to gain upon the mind until it becomes habitually more sensible to what is ludicrous and accidental, than to what is grave and essential, in any subject that is brought before it ; or even, at last, desires to perceive or to know nothing but what may end in jest. Very generally minds of this character are active and able ; and many of them are so far conscientious, that they believe their jesting forwards their work. But it is difficult to calculate the harm they do by destroying the reverence which is our best guide into all truth ; for weakness and evil are easily visible, but greatness and goodness are often latent; and we do infinite mischief by exposing weakness to eyes which cannot comprehend greatness. This error, however, is more connected with abuses of the satirical than of the playful instinct; and I shall have more to say of it presently.

§ XXX. Lastly, The men who do not play at all: those who are so dull or so morose as to be incapable of inventing or enjoying jest, and in whom care, guilt, or pride represses all healthy exhilaration of the fancy; or else men utterly oppressed with labour, and driven too hard by the necessities of the world to be capable of any species of happy relaxation.

§ XXXI. We have now to consider the way in which the presence or absence of joyfulness, in these several classes, is expressed in art.

1. Wise play. The first and noblest class hardly ever speak through art, except seriously; they feel its nobleness too profoundly, and value the time necessary for its production too highly, to employ it in the rendering of trivial thoughts. The playful fancy of a moment may innocently be expressed by the passing word; but he can hardly have learned the preciousness of life who passes days in the elaboration of a jest. And as to what regards the delineation of human character, the nature of all noble art is to epitomize and embrace so much at once, that its subject can never be altogether ludicrous; it must possess all the solemnities of the whole, not the brightness of the partial, truth. For all truth that makes us smile is partial. The novelist amuses us by his relation of a particular incident; but the painter cannot set any one of his characters before us without giving some glimpse of its whole career. That of which the historian informs us in successive pages, it is the task of the painter to inform us of at once, writing upon the countenance not merely the expression of the moment, but the history of the life: and the history of a life can never be a jest.

Whatever part, therefore, of the sportive energy of these men of the highest class would be expressed in verbal wit or humour finds small utterance through their art, and will assuredly be confined, if it occur there at all, to scattered and trivial incidents. But so far as their minds can recreate themselves by the imagination of strange, yet not laughable, forms, which, either in costume, in landscape, or in any other accessories, may be combined with those necessary for their more earnest purposes, we find them delighting in such inventions, and a species of grotesqueness thence arising in all their work, which is indeed one of its most valuable characteristics, but which is so intimately connected with the sublime or terrible form of the grotesque, that it will be better to notice it under that head.

§ XXXII. 2. Necessary play. I have dwelt much, in a former portion of this work, on the justice and desirableness of employing the minds of inferior workmen, and of the lower orders in general, in the production of objects of art of one kind or another. So far as men of this class are compelled to hard manual labour for their daily bread, so far forth their artistical efforts must be rough and ignorant, and their artistical perceptions comparatively dull. Now it is not possible, with blunt perceptions and rude hands, to produce works which shall be pleasing by their beauty; but it is perfectly possible to produce such as shall be interesting by their character or amusing by their satire. For one hard-working man who possesses the finer instincts which decide on perfection of lines and harmonies of colour, twenty possess dry humour or quaint fancy; not because these faculties were originally given to the human race, or to any section of it, in greater degree than the sense of beauty, but because these are exercised in our daily intercourse with each other, and developed by the interest which we take in the affairs of life, while the others are not. And because, therefore, a certain degree of success will probably attend the effort to express this humour or fancy, while comparative failure will assuredly result from an ignorant struggle to reach the forms of solemn beauty, the working man who turns his attention partially to art will probably, and wisely, choose to do that which he can do best, and indulge the pride of an effective satire rather than subject himself to assured mortification in the pursuit of beauty ; and this the more, because we have seen that his application to art is to be playful and recreative, and it is not in recreation that the conditions of perfection can be fulfilled.

§ XXXIII. Now all the forms of art which result from the comparatively recreative exertion of minds more or less blunted or encumbered by other cares and toils, the art which we may call generally art of the wayside, as opposed to that which is the business of men's lives, is, in the best sense of the word, Grotesque. And it is noble or inferior, first according to the tone of the minds which have produced it, and in proportion to their knowledge, wit, love of truth, and kindness ; secondly, according to the degree of strength they have been able to give forth ; but yet, however much we may find in it needing to be forgiven, always delightful so long as it is the work of good and ordinarily intelligent men. And its delightfulness ought mainly to consist *in those very imperfections* which mark it for work done in times of rest. It is not its own merit so much as the enjoyment of him who produced it, which is to be the source of the spectator's pleasure ; it is to the strength of his sympathy, not to the accuracy of his criticism, that it makes appeal ; and no man can indeed be a lover of what is best in the higher walks of art who has not feeling and charity enough to rejoice with the rude sportiveness of hearts that have escaped out of prison, and to be thankful for the flowers which men have laid their burdens down to sow by the wayside.

§ XXXIV. And consider what a vast amount of human work this right understanding of its meaning will make fruitful and admirable to us, which otherwise we could only have passed by with contempt. There is very little architecture in the world which is, in the full sense of the words, good and noble. A few pieces of Italian Gothic and Romanesque, a few scattered fragments of Gothic cathedrals, and perhaps two or three of Greek temples, are all that we possess approaching to an ideal of perfection. All the rest—Egyptian, Norman, Arabian, and most Gothic, and, which is very noticeable, for the most part all the strongest and mightiest—depend for their power on some development of the grotesque spirit; but much more the inferior domestic architecture of the middle ages, and what similar conditions remain to this day in countries from which the life of art had not yet been banished by its laws. The fantastic gables, built up in scroll-work and steps, of the Flemish street; the pinnacled roofs set with their small humorist double windows, as if with so many ears and eyes, of Northern France; the blackened timbers, crossed and carved into every conceivable waywardness of imagination, of Normandy and old England; the rude hewing of the pine timbers of the Swiss cottage; the projecting turrets and bracketed oriels of the German street; these, and a thousand other forms, not in themselves reaching any high degree of excellence, are yet admirable, and most precious, as the fruits of a rejoicing energy in uncultivated minds. It is easier to take away the energy than to add the cultivation; and the only effect of the better knowledge which civilized nations now possess has been, as we have seen in a former chapter, to forbid their being happy, without enabling them to be great.

§ xxxv. It is very necessary, however, with respect to this provincial or rustic architecture, that we should carefully distinguish its truly grotesque from its picturesque elements. In the "Seven Lamps" I defined the picturesque to be "parasitical sublimity," or sublimity belonging to the external or accidental characters of a thing, not to the thing itself. For instance, when a highland cottage roof is covered with fragments of shale instead of slates, it becomes picturesque, because the irregularity and rude fractures of the rocks, and their grey and gloomy colour, give to it something of the savageness, and much of the general aspect, of the slope of a mountain side.

But as a mere cottage roof, it cannot be sublime, and whatever sublimity it derives from the wildness or sternness which the mountains have given it in its covering, is, so far forth, parasitical. The mountain itself would have been grand, which is much more than picturesque ; but the cottage cannot be grand as such, and the parasitical grandeur which it may possess by accidental qualities, is the character for which men have long agreed to use the inaccurate word " Picturesque."

§ XXXVI. On the other hand, beauty cannot be parasitical. There is nothing so small or so contemptible, but it may be beautiful in its own right. The cottage may be beautiful, and the smallest moss that grows on its roof, and the minutest fibre of that moss which the microscope can raise into visible form, and all of them in their own right, not less than the mountains and the sky ; so that we use no peculiar term to express their beauty, however diminutive, but only when the sublime element enters, without sufficient worthiness in the nature of the thing to which it is attached.

§ XXXVII. Now this picturesque element, which is always given, if by nothing else, merely by ruggedness, adds usually very largely to the pleasurableness of grotesque work, especially to that of its inferior kinds ; but it is not for this reason to be confounded with the grotesqueness itself. The knots and rents of the timbers, the irregular lying of the shingles on the roofs, the vigorous light and shadow, the fractures and weather-stains of the old stones, which were so deeply loved and so admirably rendered by our lost Prout, are the picturesque elements of architecture ; the grotesque ones are those which are not produced by the working of nature and of time, but exclusively by the fancy of man ; and, as also for the most part by his indolent and uncultivated fancy, they are always, in some degree, wanting in grandeur, unless the picturesque element be united with them.

§ XXXVIII. 3. Inordinate play. The reader will have some difficulty, I fear, in keeping clearly in his mind the various divisions of our subject ; but, when he has once read the chapter through, he will see their places and coherence.   We have next to consider the expression throughout of the minds of men who indulge themselves in unnecessary play.   It is evident that a large number of these men will be more refined and more highly educated than those who only play necessarily ; their power of pleasure-seeking implies, in general, fortunate circumstances of life.   It is evident also that their play will not be so hearty, so simple, or so joyful ; and this deficiency of brightness will affect it in proportion to its unnecessary and unlawful continuance, until at last it becomes a restless and dissatisfied indulgence in excitement, or a painful delving after exhausted springs of pleasure.

The art through which this temper is expressed will, in all probability, be refined and sensual,—therefore, also assuredly feeble ; and because, in the failure of the joyful energy of the mind, there will fail, also, its perceptions and its sympathies, it will be entirely deficient in expression of character and acuteness of thought, but will be peculiarly restless, manifesting its desire for excitement in idle changes of subject and purpose. Incapable of true imagination, it will seek to supply its place by exaggerations, incoherences, and monstrosities ; and the form of the grotesque to which it gives rise will be an incongruous chain of hackneyed graces, idly thrown together,—prettinesses or sublimities, not of its own invention, associated in forms which will be absurd without being fantastic, and monstrous without being terrible.   And because, in the continual pursuit of pleasure, men lose both cheerfulness and charity, there will be small hilarity, but much malice, in this grotesque ; yet a weak malice, incapable of expressing its own bitterness, not having grasp enough of truth to become forcible, and exhausting itself in impotent or disgusting caricature.

§ XXXIX. Of course, there are infinite ranks and kinds of this grotesque, according to the natural power of the minds which originate it, and to the degree in which they have lost themselves.   Its highest condition is that which first developed itself among the enervated Romans, and which was brought

to the highest perfection of which it was capable by
Raphael in the arabesques of the Vatican. It may be generally
described as an elaborate and luscious form of nonsense. Its
lower conditions are found in the common upholstery and
decorations which, over the whole of civilized Europe, have
sprung from this poisonous root; an artistical pottage, composed of nymphs, cupids, and satyrs, with shreddings of heads
and paws of meek wild beasts, and nondescript vegetables.
And the lowest of all are those which have not even graceful
models to recommend them, but arise out of the corruption
of the higher schools, mingled with clownish or bestial satire,
as is the case in the later Renaissance of Venice, which we
were above examining. It is almost impossible to believe the
depth to which the human mind can be debased in following this
species of grotesque. In a recent Italian garden, the favourite
ornaments frequently consist of stucco images, representing, in
dwarfish caricature, the most disgusting types of manhood and
womanhood which can be found amidst the dissipation of the
modern drawing-room; yet without either veracity or humour,
and dependent, for whatever interest they possess, upon simple
grossness of expression and absurdity of costume. Grossness,
of one kind or another, is, indeed, an unfailing characteristic of
the style; either latent, as in the refined sensuality of the more
graceful arabesques, or, in the worst examples, manifested in
every species of obscene conception and abominable detail. In
the head, described in the opening of this chapter, at Santa
Maria Formosa, the *teeth* are represented as *decayed*.

§ XL. 4. The minds of the fourth class of men, who do
not play at all, are little likely to find expression in any
trivial form of art, except in bitterness of mockery; and this
character at once stamps the work in which it appears as belonging to the class of terrible, rather than of playful, grotesque.
We have, therefore, now to examine the state of mind which
gave rise to this second and more interesting branch of imaginative work.

§ XLI. Two great and principal passions are evidently appointed by the Deity to rule the life of man ; namely, the love of God, and the fear of sin, and of its companion—Death. How many motives we have for Love, how much there is in the universe to kindle our admiration and to claim our gratitude, there are, happily, multitudes among us who both feel and teach. But it has not, I think, been sufficiently considered how evident, throughout the system of creation, is the purpose of God that we should often be affected by Fear ; not the sudden, selfish, and contemptible fear of immediate danger, but the fear which arises out of the contemplation of great powers in destructive operation, and generally from the perception of the presence of death. Nothing appears to me more remarkable than the array of scenic magnificence by which the imagination is appalled, in myriads of instances, when the actual danger is comparatively small ; so that the utmost possible impression of awe shall be produced upon the minds of all, though direct suffering is in-flicted upon few. Consider, for instance, the moral effect of a single thunderstorm. Perhaps two or three persons may be struck dead within a space of a hundred square miles ; and their deaths, unaccompanied by the scenery of the storm, would pro-duce little more than a momentary sadness in the busy hearts of living men. But the preparation for the judgment, by all that mighty gathering of the clouds ; by the questioning of the forest leaves, in their terrified stillness, which way the winds shall go forth ; by the murmuring to each other, deep in the distance, of the destroying angels before they draw forth their swords of fire ; by the march of the funeral darkness in the midst of the noonday, and the rattling of the dome of heaven beneath the chariot-wheels of death ;—on how many minds do not these produce an impression almost as great as the actual witnessing of the fatal issue ! and how strangely are the expressions of the threatening elements fitted to the apprehension of the human soul ! The lurid colour, the long, irregular, convulsive sound, the ghastly shapes of flaming and heaving cloud, are all as true and faithful in their appeal to our instinct of danger, as the moaning or wail-ing of the human voice itself is to our instinct of pity. It is not a reasonable calculating terror which they awake in us ; it is no matter that we count distance by seconds, and measure probability by averages. That shadow of the thunder-cloud will still do its work upon our hearts, and we shall watch it passing away as if we stood upon the threshing-floor of Araunah.

§ XLII. And this is equally the case with respect to all the other destructive phenomena of the universe. From the mightiest of them to the gentlest, from the earthquake to the summer shower, it will be found that they are attended by certain aspects of threatening, which strike terror into the hearts of multitudes more numerous a thousandfold than those who actually suffer from the ministries of judgment ; and that, besides the fearfulness of these immediately dangerous phenomena, there is an occult and subtle horror belonging to many aspects of the creation around us, calculated often to fill us with serious thought, even in our times of quietness and peace. I understand not the most dangerous, because most attractive form of modern infidelity, which, pretending to exalt the beneficence of the Deity, degrades it into a reckless infinitude of mercy, and blind obliteration of the work of sin : and which does this chiefly by dwelling on the manifold appearances of God's kindness on the face of creation. Such kindness is indeed everywhere and always visible ; but not alone. Wrath and threatening are invariably mingled with the love ; and in the utmost solitudes of nature, the existence of Hell seems to me as legibly declared by a thousand spiritual utterances, as that of Heaven.   It is well for us to dwell with thankfulness on the unfolding of the flower, and the falling of the dew, and the sleep of the green fields in the sunshine ; but the blasted trunk, the barren rock, the moaning of the bleak winds, the roar of the black, perilous, merciless whirlpools of the mountain streams, the solemn solitudes of moors and seas, the continual fading of all beauty into darkness, and of all strength into dust, have these no language for us? We may seek to escape their teaching by reasonings touching the good which is wrought out of all evil ; but it is vain sophistry. The good succeeds to the evil as day succeeds the night, but so also the evil to the good. Gerizim and Ebal, birth and death, light and darkness, heaven and hell, divide the existence of man, and his Futurity.*

§ XLIII. And because the thoughts of the choice we have to make between these two ought to rule us continually, not so much in our own actions (for these should, for the most part, be governed by settled habit and principle) as in our manner of regarding the lives of other men, and our own responsibilities with respect to them ; therefore, it seems to me that the healthiest state into which the human mind can be brought is that which is capable of the greatest love and the greatest awe : and this we are taught even in our times of rest ; for when our minds are rightly in tone, the merely pleasurable excitement which they seek with most avidity is that which rises out of the contemplation of beauty or of terribleness. We thirst for both, and according to the height and tone of our feeling desire to see them in noble or inferior forms. Thus there is a Divine beauty, and a terribleness or sublimity coequal with it in rank, which are the subjects of the highest art ; and there is an inferior or ornamental beauty, and an inferior terribleness coequal with it in rank, which are the subjects of grotesque art. And the state of mind in which the terrible form of the grotesque is developed is that which, in some irregular manner, dwells upon certain conditions of terribleness, into the complete depth of which it does not enter for the time.

§ XLIV. Now the things which are the proper subjects of human fear are twofold : those which have the power of Death, and those which have the nature of Sin. Of which there are many ranks, greater or less in power and vice, from the evil

---

* The Love of God is, however, always shown by the predominance, or greater sum, of good in the end ; but never by the annihilation of evil. The modern doubts of eternal punishment are not so much the consequence of benevolence as of feeble powers of reasoning. Every one admits that God brings finite good out of finite evil. Why not, therefore, infinite good out of infinite evil ?

angels themselves down to the serpent which is their type, and which, though of a low and contemptible class, appears to unite the deathful and sinful natures in the most clearly visible and intelligible form ; for there is nothing else which we know of so small strength and occupying so unimportant a place in the economy of creation, which yet is so mortal and so malignant. It is, then, on these two classes of objects that the mind fixes for its excitement, in that mood which gives rise to the terrible grotesque : and its subject will be found always to unite some expression of vice and danger, but regarded in a peculiar temper ; sometimes (A) of predetermined or involuntary apathy, sometimes (B) of mockery, sometimes (C) of diseased and ungoverned imaginativeness.

§ XLV. For observe, the difficulty which, as I above stated, exists in distinguishing the playful from the terrible grotesque arises out of this cause : that the mind, under certain phases of excitement, *plays* with *terror*, and summons images which, if it were in another temper, would be awful, but of which, either in weariness or in irony, it refrains for the time to acknowledge the true terribleness. And the mode in which this refusal takes place distinguishes the noble from the ignoble grotesque. For the master of the noble grotesque knows the depth of all at which he seems to mock, and would feel it at another time, or feel it in a certain undercurrent of thought even while he jests with it ; but the workman of the ignoble grotesque can feel and understand nothing, and mocks at all things with the laughter of the idiot and the cretin.

To work out this distinction completely is the chief difficulty in our present inquiry ; and, in order to do so, let us consider the above-named three conditions of mind in succession, with relation to objects of terror.

§ XLVI. (A) Involuntary or predetermined apathy. We saw above that the grotesque was produced, chiefly in subordinate or ornamental art, by rude, and in some degree uneducated men, and in their times of rest. At such times, and in such subordinate work, it is impossible that they should represent any solemn or terrible subject with a full and serious entrance into its feeling. It is not in the languor of a leisure hour that a man will set his whole soul to conceive the means of representing some important truth, nor to the projecting angle of a timber bracket that he would trust its representation, if conceived. And yet, in this languor, and in this trivial work, he must find some expression of the serious part of his soul, of what there is within him capable of awe, as well as of love. The more noble the man is, the more impossible it will be for him to confine his thoughts to mere loveliness, and that of a low order. Were his powers and his time unlimited, so that, like Frà Angelico, he could paint the Seraphim, in that order of beauty he could find contentment, bringing down heaven to earth. But by the conditions of his being, by his hardworked life, by his feeble powers of execution, by the meanness of his employment and the languor of his heart, he is bound down to earth. It is the world's work that he is doing, and world's work is not to be done without fear. And whatever there is of deep and eternal consciousness within him, thrilling his mind with the sense of the presence of sin and death around him, must be expressed in that slight work, and feeble way, come of it what will. He cannot forget it, among all that he sees of beautiful in nature ; he may not bury himself among the leaves of the violet on the rocks, and of the lily in the glen, and twine out of them garlands of perpetual gladness. He sees more in the earth than these,—misery and wrath, and discordance and danger, and all the work of the dragon and his angels ; this he sees with too deep feeling ever to forget. And though, when he returns to his idle work,—it may be to gild the letters upon the page, or to carve the timbers of the chamber, or the stones of the pinnacle,—he cannot give his strength of thought any more to the woe or to the danger, there is a shadow of them still present with him : and as the bright colours mingle beneath his touch, and the fair leaves and flowers grow at his bidding, strange horrors and phantasms rise by their side ; grisly beasts and venomous serpents, and spectral fiends and nameless inconsistencies of ghastly life, rising out of things most beautiful, and fading back into them again, as the harm and the horror of life do out of its happiness. He has seen these things; he wars with them daily; he cannot but give them their part in his work, though in a state of comparative apathy to them at the time. He is but carving and gilding, and must not turn aside to weep; but he knows that hell is burning on, for all that, and the smoke of it withers his oak-leaves.

§ XLVII. Now, the feelings which give rise to the false or ignoble grotesque, are exactly the reverse of this. In the true grotesque, a man of naturally strong feeling is accidentally or resolutely apathetic; in the false grotesque, a man naturally apathetic is forcing himself into temporary excitement. The horror which is expressed by the one comes upon him whether he will or not; that which is expressed by the other is sought out by him, and elaborated by his art. And therefore, also, because the fear of the one is true, and of true things, however fantastic its expression may be, there will be reality in it, and force. It is not a manufactured terribleness, whose author, when he had finished it, knew not if it would terrify any one else or not: but it is a terribleness taken from the life; a spectre which the workman indeed saw, and which, as it appalled him, will appal us also. But the other workman never felt any Divine fear; he never shuddered when he heard the cry from the burning towers of the earth,

"Venga Medusa; sì lo farem di smalto."

He is stone already, and needs no gentle hand laid upon his eyes to save him.

§ XLVIII. I do not mean what I say in this place to apply to the creations of the imagination. It is not as the creating, but as the *seeing* man, that we are here contemplating the master of the true grotesque. It is because the dreadfulness of the universe around him weighs upon his heart that his work is wild; and therefore through the whole of it we shall find the evidence of deep insight into nature. His beasts and birds, however monstrous, will have profound relations with the true.   He may be an ignorant man, and little acquainted with the laws of nature ; he is certainly a busy man, and has not much time to watch nature ; but he never saw a serpent cross his path, nor a bird flit across the sky, nor a lizard bask upon a stone, without learning so much of the sublimity and inner nature of each as will not suffer him thenceforth to conceive them coldly. He may not be able to carve plumes or scales well ; but his creatures will bite and fly, for all that.   The ignoble workman is the very reverse of this.   He never felt, never looked at nature ; and if he endeavour to imitate the work of the other, all his touches will be made at random, and all his extravagances will be ineffective ; he may knit brows, and twist lips, and lengthen beaks, and sharpen teeth, but it will all be in vain.   He may make his creatures disgusting, but never fearful.

§ XLIX. There is, however, often another cause of difference than this.   The true grotesque being the expression of the *repose* or play of a *serious* mind, there is a false grotesque opposed to it, which is the result of the *full exertion* of a *frivolous* one. There is much grotesque which is wrought out with exquisite care and pains, and as much labour given to it as if it were of the noblest subject ; so that the workman is evidently no longer apathetic, and has no excuse for unconnectedness of thought, or sudden unreasonable fear.   If he awakens horror now, it ought to be in some truly sublime form.   His strength is in his work ; and he must not give way to sudden humour, and fits of erratic fancy.   If he does so, it must be because his mind is naturally frivolous, or is for the time degraded into the delibe- rate pursuit of frivolity.   And herein lies the real distinction between the base grotesque of Raphael and the Renaissance, above alluded to, and the true Gothic grotesque.   Those gro- tesques or arabesques of the Vatican, and other such work, which have become the patterns of ornamentation in modern times, are the fruit of great minds degraded to base objects. The care, skill, and science, applied to the distribution of the leaves, and the drawing of the figures, are intense, admirable, and accurate; therefore, they ought to have produced a grand and serious work, not a tissue of nonsense. If we can draw the human head perfectly, and are masters of its expression and its beauty, we have no business to cut it off, and hang it up by the hair at the end of a garland. If we can draw the human body in the perfection of its grace and movement, we have no business to take away its limbs, and terminate it with a bunch of leaves. Or rather, our doing so will imply that there is something wrong with us; that, if we can consent to use our best powers for such base and vain trifling, there must be something wanting in the powers themselves; and that, however skilful we may be, or however learned, we are wanting both in the earnestness which can apprehend a noble truth, and in the thoughtfulness which can feel a noble fear. No Divine terror will ever be found in the work of the man who wastes a colossal strength in elaborating toys; for the first lesson which that terror is sent to teach us is the value of the human soul and the shortness of mortal time.

§ L. And are we never, then, it will be asked, to possess a refined or perfect ornamentation? Must all decoration be the work of the ignorant and the rude? Not so; but exactly in proportion as the ignorance and rudeness diminish, must the ornamentation become rational and the grotesqueness disappear. The noblest lessons may be taught in ornamentation, the most solemn truths compressed into it. The Book of Genesis, in all the fulness of its incidents, in all the depth of its meaning, is bound within the leaf-borders of the gates of Ghiberti. But Raphael's arabesque is mere elaborate idleness. It has neither meaning nor heart in it; it is an unnatural and monstrous abortion.

§ LI. Now, this passing of the grotesque into higher art, as the mind of the workman becomes informed with better knowledge, and capable of more earnest exertion, takes place in two ways. Either, as his power increases, he devotes himself more and more to the beauty which he now feels himself able to express, and so the grotesque expands, and softens into the beautiful, as in the above-named instance of the gates of Ghiberti; or else, if the mind of the workman be naturally inclined to gloomy contemplation, the imperfection or apathy of his work rises into nobler terribleness, until we reach the point of the grotesque of Albert Durer, where, every now and then, the playfulness or apathy of the painter passes into perfect sublime. Take the Adam and Eve, for instance. When he gave Adam a bough to hold, with a parrot on it, and a tablet hung to it, with " Albertus Durer Noricus faciebat, 1504," thereupon, his mind was not in Paradise. He was half in play, half apathetic with respect to his subject, thinking how to do his work well, as a wise master-graver, and how to receive his just reward of fame. But he rose into the true sublime in the head of Adam, and in the profound truthfulness of every creature that fills the forest. So again, in that magnificent coat of arms, with the lady and the satyr, as he cast the fluttering drapery hither and thither round the helmet, and wove the delicate crown upon the woman's forehead, he was in a kind of play; but there is none in the dreadful skull upon the shield. And in the " Knight and Death," and in the dragons of the illustrations to the Apocalypse, there is neither play nor apathy; but their grotesque is of the ghastly kind which best illustrates the nature of death and sin. And this leads us to the consideration of the second state of mind out of which the noble grotesque is developed; that is to say, the temper of mockery.

§ LII. (B) Mockery, or satire. In the former part of this chapter, when I spoke of the kinds of art which were produced in the recreation of the lower orders, I only spoke of forms of ornament, not of the expression of satire or humour. But it seems probable that nothing is so refreshing to the vulgar mind as some exercise of this faculty, more especially on the failings of their superiors; and that, wherever the lower orders are allowed to express themselves freely, we shall find humour, more or less caustic, becoming a principal feature in their work. The classical and Renaissance manufactures of modern times having silenced the independent language of the operative, his humour and satire pass away in the word-wit which has of late become the especial study of the group of authors headed by Charles Dickens; all this power was formerly thrown into noble art, and became permanently expressed in the sculptures of the cathedral. It was never thought that there was anything discordant or improper in such a position : for the builders evidently felt very deeply a truth of which, in modern times, we are less cognizant ; that folly and sin are, to a certain extent, synonymous, and that it would be well for mankind in general if all could be made to feel that wickedness is as contemptible as it is hateful. So that the vices were permitted to be represented under the most ridiculous forms, and all the coarsest wit of the workman to be exhausted in completing the degradation of the creatures supposed to be subjected to them.

§ LIII. Nor were even the supernatural powers of evil exempt from this species of satire. For with whatever hatred or horror the evil angels were regarded, it was one of the conditions of Christianity that they should also be looked upon as vanquished; and this not merely in their great combat with the King of Saints, but in daily and hourly combats with the weakest of His servants. In proportion to the narrowness of the powers of abstract conception in the workman, the nobleness of the idea of spiritual nature diminished, and the traditions of the encounters of men with fiends in daily temptations were imagined with less terrific circumstances, until the agencies which in such warfare were almost always represented as vanquished with disgrace, became, at last, as much the objects of contempt as of terror.

The superstitions which represented the devil as assuming various contemptible forms or disguises in order to accomplish his purposes aided this gradual degradation of conception, and directed the study of the workman to the most strange and ugly conditions of animal form, until at last, even in the most serious subjects, the fiends are oftener ludicrous than terrible. Nor, indeed, is this altogether avoidable, for it is not possible to

express intense wickedness without some condition of degradation. Malice, subtlety, and pride, in their extreme, cannot be
written upon noble forms ; and I am aware of no effort to represent the Satanic mind in the angelic form which has succeeded
in painting. Milton succeeds only because he separately de-
scribes the movements of the mind, and therefore leaves himself
at liberty to make the form heroic ; but that form is never distinct enough to be painted. Dante, who will not leave even
external forms obscure, degrades them before he can feel them
to be demoniacal ; so also John Bunyan : both of them, I think,
having firmer faith than Milton's in their own creations, and
deeper insight into the nature of sin. Milton makes his fiends
too noble, and misses the foulness, inconstancy, and fury of
wickedness. His Satan possesses some virtues, not the less
virtues for being applied to evil purpose. Courage, resolution,
patience, deliberation in counsel, this latter being eminently
a wise and holy character, as opposed to the " Insania " of
excessive sin : and all this, if not a shallow and false, is a
smoothed and artistical, conception. On the other hand, I have
always felt that there was a peculiar grandeur in the inde-
scribable ungovernable fury of Dante's fiends, ever shortening
its own powers, and disappointing its own purposes ; the deaf,
blind, speechless, unspeakable rage, fierce as the lightning, but
erring from its mark or turning senselessly against itself, and
still further debased by foulness of form and action. Something is indeed to be allowed for the rude feelings of the
time, but I believe all such men as Dante are sent into the
world at the time when they can do their work best ; and that,
it being appointed for him to give to mankind the most vigorous realization possible both of Hell and Heaven, he was born
both in the country and at the time which furnished the most
stern opposition of Horror and Beauty, and permitted it to
be written in the clearest terms. And, therefore, though there
are passages in the " Inferno " which it would be impossible
for any poet now to write, I look upon it as all the more

perfect for them.   For there can be no question but that one
characteristic of excessive vice is indecency, a general baseness in its thoughts and acts concerning the body,* and that
the full portraiture of it cannot be given without marking, and
that in the strongest lines, this tendency to corporeal degradation; which, in the time of Dante, could be done frankly, but
cannot now.   And, therefore, I think the twenty-first and twenty-
second books of the " Inferno" the most perfect portraitures of
fiendish nature which we possess; and, at the same time, in their
mingling of the extreme of horror (for it seems to me that the
silent swiftness of the first demon, " con l' ali aperte e sovra i pie
leggiero," cannot be surpassed in dreadfulness) with ludicrous
actions and images, they present the most perfect instances with
which I am acquainted of the terrible grotesque.   But the
whole of the " Inferno" is full of this grotesque, as well as the
" Faërie Queen;" and these two poems, together with the works
of Albert Durer, will enable the reader to study it in its noblest
forms, without reference to Gothic cathedrals.

§ LIV. Now, just as there are base and noble conditions of the
apathetic grotesque, so also are there of this satirical grotesque.
The condition which might be mistaken for it is that above
described as resulting from the malice of men given to pleasure,
and in which the grossness and foulness are in the workman
as much as in his subject, so that he chooses to represent vice
and disease rather than virtue and beauty, having his chief
delight in contemplating them; though he still mocks at them
with such dull wit as may be in him, because, as Young has said
most truly,

> " 'Tis not in folly not to scorn a fool."

§ LV. Now it is easy to distinguish this grotesque from
its noble counterpart, by merely observing whether any forms
of beauty or dignity are mingled with it or not; for, of course,
the noble grotesque is only employed by its master for good

---

* Let the reader examine, with especial reference to this subject, the general
character of the language of Iago.

purposes, and to contrast with beauty : but the base workman cannot conceive anything but what is base ; and there will be no loveliness in any part of his work, or, at the best, a loveliness measured by line and rule, and dependent on legal shapes of feature. But, without resorting to this test, and merely by examining the ugly grotesque itself, it will be found that, if it belongs to the base school, there will be, first, no Horror in it ; secondly, no Nature in it ; and, thirdly, no Mercy in it.

§ LVI. I say, first, no Horror. For the base soul has no fear of sin, and no hatred of it : and however it may strive to make its work terrible, there will be no genuineness in the fear ; the utmost it can do will be to make its work disgusting.

Secondly, There will be no Nature in it. It appears to be one of the ends proposed by Providence in the appointment of the forms of the brute creation, that the various vices to which mankind are liable should be severally expressed in them so distinctly and clearly as that men could not but understand the lesson ; while yet these conditions of vice might, in the inferior animal, be observed without the disgust and hatred which the same vices would excite, if seen in men, and might be associated with features of interest which would otherwise attract and reward contemplation. Thus, ferocity, cunning, sloth, discontent, gluttony, uncleanness, and cruelty are seen, each in its extreme, in various animals ; and are so vigorously expressed, that, when men desire to indicate the same vices in connexion with human forms, they can do it no better than by borrowing here and there the features of animals. And when the workman is thus led to the contemplation of the animal kingdom, finding therein the expressions of vice which he needs, associated with power, and nobleness, and freedom from disease, if his mind be of right tone he becomes interested in this new study; and all noble grotesque is, therefore, full of the most admirable rendering of animal character. But the ignoble workman is capable of no interest of this kind ; and, being too dull to appreciate, and too idle to execute, the subtle and wonderful lines on which the expression of the lower animal depends, he contents himself with vulgar exaggeration, and leaves his work as false as it is monstrous, a mass of blunt malice and obscene ignorance.

§ LVII. Lastly, there will be no Mercy in it. Wherever the satire of the noble grotesque fixes upon human nature, it does so with much sorrow mingled amidst its indignation : in its highest forms there is an infinite tenderness, like that of the fool in Lear; and even in its more heedless or bitter sarcasm, it never loses sight altogether of the better nature of what it attacks, nor refuses to acknowledge its redeeming or pardonable features. But the ignoble grotesque has no pity : it rejoices in iniquity, and exists only to slander.

§ LVIII. I have not space to follow out the various forms of transition which exist between the two extremes of great and base in the satirical grotesque. The reader must always remember, that although there is an infinite distance between the best and worst, in this kind the interval is filled by endless conditions more or less inclining to the evil or the good; impurity and malice stealing gradually into the nobler forms, and invention and wit elevating the lower, according to the countless minglings of the elements of the human soul.

§ LIX. (c) Ungovernableness of the imagination. The reader is always to keep in mind that if the objects of horror in which the terrible grotesque finds its materials were contemplated in their true light, and with the entire energy of the soul, they would cease to be grotesque, and become altogether sublime ; and that therefore it is some shortening of the power, or the will, of contemplation, and some consequent distortion of the terrible image in which the grotesqueness consists. Now this distortion takes place, it was above asserted, in three ways ; either through apathy, satire, or ungovernableness of imagination. It is this last cause of the grotesque which we have finally to consider ; namely, the error and wildness of the mental impressions, caused by fear operating upon strong powers of imagination, or by the failure of the human faculties in the endeavour to grasp the highest truths.

§ LX. The grotesque which comes to all men in a disturbed

dream is the most intelligible example of this kind, but also the most ignoble; the imagination, in this instance, being entirely deprived of all aid from reason, and incapable of self-government. I believe, however, that the noblest forms of imaginative power are also in some sort ungovernable, and have in them something of the character of dreams; so that the vision, of whatever kind, comes uncalled, and will not submit itself to the seer, but conquers him, and forces him to speak as a prophet, having no power over his words or thoughts.* Only, if the

* This opposition of art to inspiration is long and gracefully dwelt upon by Plato in his "Phædrus;" using, in the course of his argument, almost the words of St. Paul: κάλλιον μαρτυροῦσιν οἱ παλαιοὶ μανίαν σωφροσύνης τὴν ἐκ θεοῦ τῆς παρ' ἀνθρώπων γιγνομένης: "It is the testimony of the ancients, that *the madness which is of God is a nobler thing than the wisdom which is of men;*" and again, "He who sets himself to any work with which the Muses have to do" (*i.e.*, to any of the fine arts) "without madness, thinking that by art alone he can do his work sufficiently, will be found vain and incapable, and the work of temperance and rationalism will be thrust aside and obscured by that of inspiration." The passages to the same effect, relating especially to poetry, are innumerable in nearly all ancient writers; but in this of Plato, the entire compass of the fine arts is intended to be embraced.

No one acquainted with other parts of my writings will suppose me to be an advocate of idle trust in the imagination. But it is in these days just as necessary to allege the supremacy of genius as the necessity of labour; for there never was, perhaps, a period in which the peculiar gift of the painter was so little discerned, in which so many and so vain efforts have been made to replace it by study and toil. This has been peculiarly the case with the German school; and there are few exhibitions of human error more pitiable than the manner in which the inferior members of it, men originally and for ever destitute of the painting faculty, force themselves into an unnatural, encumbered, learned fructification of tasteless fruit, and pass laborious lives in setting obscurely and weakly upon canvas the philosophy, if such it be, which ten minutes' work of a strong man would have put into healthy practice or plain words. I know not anything more melancholy than the sight of the huge German cartoon, with its objective side, and subjective side; and mythological division, and symbolical division, and human and Divine division; its allegorical sense, and literal sense; and ideal point of view, and intellectual point of view; its heroism of well-made armour and knitted brows; its heroinism of graceful attitude and braided hair; its inwoven web of sentiment, and piety, and philosophy; and anatomy, and history, all profound: and twenty innocent dashes of the hand of one God-made painter, poor old Bassan or Bonifazio, were worth it all, and worth it ten thousand times over.

Not that the sentiment or the philosophy is base in itself. They will make a good man, but they will not make a good painter,—no, nor the millionth whole man be trained perfectly, and his mind calm, consistent, and powerful, the vision which comes to him is seen as in a perfect mirror, serenely, and in consistence with the rational powers; but if the mind be imperfect and ill trained, the vision is seen as in a broken mirror, with strange distortions and dis-crepancies, all the passions of the heart breathing upon it in cross ripples, till hardly a trace of it remains unbroken. So that, strictly speaking, the imagination is never governed; it is always the ruling and Divine power: and the rest of the man is to it only as an instrument which it sounds, or a tablet on which it writes; clearly and sublimely if the wax be smooth and the strings true, grotesquely and wildly if they are stained and broken. And thus the " Iliad," the " Inferno," the " Pilgrim's Progress," the "Faërie Queen," are all of them true dreams; only the sleep of the men to whom they came was the deep, living sleep which God sends, with a sacredness in it as of death, the revealer of secrets.

§ LXI. Now, observe in this matter, carefully, the difference between a dim mirror and a distorted one; and do not blame me for pressing the analogy too far, for it will enable me to explain my meaning every way more clearly. Most men's minds are dim mirrors, in which all truth is seen, as St. Paul tells us, darkly: this is the fault most common and most fatal; dulness

---

part of a painter. They would have been good in the work and words of daily life; but they are good for nothing in the cartoon, if they are there alone. And the worst result of the system is the intense conceit into which it cultivates a weak mind. Nothing is so hopeless, so intolerable, as the pride of a foolish man who has passed through a process of thinking, so as actually to have found something out. He believes there is nothing else to be found out in the universe. Whereas the truly great man, on whom the Revela-tions rain till they bear him to the earth with their weight, lays his head in the dust, and speaks thence—often in broken syllables. Vanity is indeed a very equally divided inheritance among mankind; but I think that among the first persons, no emphasis is altogether so strong as that on the German *Ich*. I was once introduced to a German philosopher-painter before Tintoret's " Massacre of the Innocents." He looked at it superciliously, and said it "wanted to be restored." He had been himself several years employed in painting a "Faust" in a red jerkin and blue fire; which made Tintoret appear somewhat dull to him.

of the heart and mistiness of sight, increasing to utter hardness and blindness ; Satan breathing upon the glass, so that if we do not sweep the mist laboriously away, it will take no image. But, even so far as we are able to do this, we have still the distortion to fear, yet not to the same extent, for we can in some sort allow for the distortion of an image, if only we can see it clearly. And the fallen human soul, at its best, must be as a diminishing glass, and that a broken one, to the mighty truths of the universe round it ; and the wider the scope of its glance, and the vaster the truths into which it obtains an insight, the more fantastic their distortion is likely to be, as the winds and vapours trouble the field of the telescope most when it reaches farthest.

§ LXII. Now, so far as the truth is seen by the imagination* in its wholeness and quietness, the vision is sublime ; but so far as it is narrowed and broken by the inconsistencies of the human capacity, it becomes grotesque ; and it would seem to be rare that any very exalted truth should be impressed on the imagination without some grotesqueness : in its aspect, proportioned to the degree of *diminution of breadth* in the grasp which is given of it. Nearly all the dreams recorded in the Bible,—Jacob's, Joseph's ; Pharaoh's, Nebuchadnezzar's,—are grotesques ; and nearly the whole of the accessory scenery in the books of Ezekiel and the Apocalypse. Thus, Jacob's dream revealed to him the ministry of angels ; but because this ministry could not be seen or understood by him in its fulness, it was narrowed to him into a ladder between heaven and earth, which was a grotesque. Joseph's two dreams were evidently intended to be signs of the steadfastness of the Divine purpose towards him, by possessing the clearness of special prophecy ; yet were couched in such imagery, as not to inform him prematurely of his destiny, and only to be understood after their fulfilment. The sun, and moon, and stars were at the period, and are indeed throughout the Bible, the symbols of high authority. It was not revealed to Joseph that he should be

---

* I have before stated (" Modern Painters," vol. ii. pp. 181, 182), that the first function of the imagination is the apprehension of ultimate truth.

lord over all Egypt; but the representation of his family by symbols of the most magnificent dominion, and yet as subject to him, must have been afterwards felt by him as a distinctly prophetic indication of his own supreme power. It was not revealed to him that the occasion of his brethren's special humiliation before him should be their coming to buy corn; but when the event took place, must he not have felt that there was prophetic purpose in the form of the sheaves of wheat which first imaged forth their subjection to him? And these two images of the sun doing obeisance, and the sheaves bowing down,—narrowed and imperfect intimations of great truth which yet could not be otherwise conveyed,—are both grotesques. The kine of Pharaoh eating each other, the gold and clay of Nebuchadnezzar's image, the four beasts full of eyes, and other imagery of Ezekiel and the Apocalypse, are grotesques of the same kind, on which I need not farther insist.

§ LXIII. Such forms, however, ought perhaps to have been arranged under a separate head, as Symbolical Grotesque; but the element of awe enters into them so strongly, as to justify, for all our present purposes, their being classed with the other varieties of terrible grotesque. For even if the symbolic vision itself be not terrible, the sense of what may be veiled behind it becomes all the more awful in proportion to the insignificance or strangeness of the sign itself; and, I believe, this thrill of mingled doubt, fear, and curiosity lies at the very root of the delight which mankind take in symbolism. It was not an accidental necessity for the conveyance of truth by pictures instead of words, which led to its universal adoption wherever art was on the advance; but the Divine fear which necessarily follows on the understanding that a thing is other and greater than it seems; and which, it appears probable, has been rendered peculiarly attractive to the human heart, because God would have us understand that this is true not of invented symbols merely, but of all things amidst which we live; that there is a deeper meaning within them than eye hath seen, or ear hath heard; and that the whole visible creation is a mere perishable symbol of things eternal and true. It

cannot but have been sometimes a subject of wonder with thoughtful men, how fondly, age after age, the Church has cherished the
belief that the four living creatures which surrounded the Apoca-
lyptic throne were symbols of the four Evangelists, and rejoiced
to use those forms in its picture-teaching ; that a calf, a lion,
an eagle, and a beast with a man's face, should in all ages have
been preferred by the Christian world, as expressive of Evangelistic power and inspiration, to the majesty of human form ; and
that quaint grotesques, awkward and often ludicrous caricatures
even of the animals represented, should have been regarded by
all men, not only with contentment, but with awe, and have
superseded all endeavours to represent the characters and persons
of the Evangelistic writers themselves (except in a few instances,
confined principally to works undertaken without a definite religious purpose) ;—this, I say, might appear more than strange to
us, were it not that we ourselves share the awe, and are still
satisfied with the symbol, and that justly.   For, whether we are
conscious of it or not, there is in our hearts, as we gaze upon
the brutal forms that have so holy a signification, an acknowledgment that it was not Matthew, nor Mark, nor Luke, nor
John, in whom the Gospel of Christ was unsealed ; but that the
invisible things of Him from the beginning of the creation are
clearly seen, being understood by the things that are made ;
that the whole world, and all that is therein, be it low or high,
great or small, is a continual Gospel ; and that as the heathen,
in their alienation from God, changed His glory into an image
made like unto corruptible man, and to birds, and four-footed
beasts, the Christian, in his approach to God, is to undo this
work, and to change the corruptible things into the image of
His glory ; believing that there is nothing so base in creation,
but that our faith may give it wings which shall raise us into
companionship with heaven ; and that, on the other hand, there
is nothing so great or so goodly in creation, but that it is a
mean symbol of the Gospel of Christ, and of the things He has
prepared for them that love Him.

§ LXIV. And it is easy to understand, if we follow out this

thought, how, when once the symbolic language was familiarized
to the mind, and its solemnity felt in all its fulness, there was
no likelihood of offence being taken at any repulsive or
feeble characters in execution or conception.   There was no
form so mean, no incident so commonplace, but, if regarded in
this light, it might become sublime; the more vigorous the
fancy and the more faithful the enthusiasm, the greater would
be the likelihood of their delighting in the contemplation of
symbols whose mystery was enhanced by apparent insignificance, or in which the sanctity and majesty of meaning were
contrasted with the utmost uncouthness of external form : nor
with uncouthness merely, but even with every appearance of
malignity or baseness ; the beholder not being revolted even by
this, but comprehending that, as the seeming evil in the framework of creation did not invalidate its Divine authorship, so
neither did the evil or imperfection in the symbol invalidate
its Divine message.   And thus, sometimes, the designer at last
became wanton in his appeal to the piety of his interpreter,
and recklessly poured out the impurity and the savageness of
his own heart, for the mere pleasure of seeing them overlaid
with the fine gold of the sanctuary by the religion of their
beholder.

§ LXV. It is not, however, in every symbolical subject that
the fearful grotesque becomes embodied to the full.   The
element of distortion which affects the intellect when dealing
with subjects above its proper capacity, is as nothing compared
with that which it sustains from the direct impressions of
terror.   It is the trembling of the human soul in the presence
of death which most of all disturbs the images on the intellectual mirror, and invests them with the fitfulness and ghastliness of dreams.   And from the contemplation of death, and
of the pangs which follow his footsteps, arise in men's hearts
the troop of strange and irresistible superstitions which, more
or less melancholy or majestic according to the dignity of the
mind they impress, are yet never without a certain grotesqueness,
following on the paralysis of the reason and over-excitement

of the fancy. I do not mean to deny the actual existence of spiritual manifestations ; I have never weighed the evidence upon the subject ; but with these, if such exist, we are not here concerned. The grotesque which we are examining arises out of that condition of mind which appears to follow naturally upon the contemplation of death, and in which the fancy is brought into morbid action by terror, accompanied by the belief in spiritual presence, and in the possibility of spiritual apparition. Hence are developed its most sublime, because its least voluntary, creations, aided by the fearfulness of the phenomena of nature which are in any wise the ministers of death, and primarily directed by the peculiar ghastliness of expression in the skeleton, itself a species of terrible grotesque in its relation to the perfect human frame.

§ LXVI. Thus, first born from the dusty and dreadful whiteness of the charnel-house, but softened in their forms by the holiest of human affections, went forth the troop of wild and wonderful images, seen through tears, that had the mastery over our Northern hearts for so many ages. The powers of sudden destruction lurking in the woods and waters, in the rocks and clouds ;—kelpie and gnome, Lurlei and Hartz spirits ; the wraith and foreboding phantom ; the spectra of second sight ; the various conceptions of avenging or tormented ghost, haunting the perpetrator of crime, or expiating its commission ; and the half fictitious and contemplative, half visionary and believed images of the presence of death itself, doing its daily work in the chambers of sickness and sin, and waiting for its hour in the fortalices of strength and the high places of pleasure ; —these, partly degrading us by the instinctive and paralyzing terror with which they are attended, and partly ennobling us by leading our thoughts to dwell in the eternal world, fill the last and the most important circle in that great kingdom of dark and distorted power, of which we all must be in some sort the subjects until mortality shall be swallowed up of life ; until the waters of the last fordless river cease to roll their untransparent volume between us and the light of heaven, and

neither death stand between us and our brethren, nor symbols
between us and our God.

§ LXVII. We have now, I believe, obtained a view approaching
to completeness of the various branches of human feeling which
are concerned in the development of this peculiar form of art.
It remains for us only to note, as briefly as possible, what facts
in the actual history of the grotesque bear upon our immediate
subject.

From what we have seen to be its nature, we must, I think,
be led to one most important conclusion ; that wherever the
human mind is healthy and vigorous in all its proportions,
great in imagination and emotion no less than in intellect, and
not overborne by an undue or hardened pre-eminence of the mere
reasoning faculties, there the grotesque will exist in full energy.
And, accordingly, I believe that there is no test of greatness in
periods, nations, or men, more sure than the development, among
them or in them, of a noble grotesque ; and no test of comparative
smallness or limitation, of one kind or another, more sure than
the absence of grotesque invention, or incapability of understanding it.   I think that the central man of all the world, as
representing in perfect balance the imaginative, moral, and
intellectual faculties, all at their highest, is Dante ; and in him
the grotesque reaches at once the most distinct and the most
noble development to which it was ever brought in the human
mind.   The two other greatest men whom Italy has produced,
Michael Angelo and Tintoret, show the same element in no less
original strength, but oppressed in the one by his science, and in
both by the spirit of the age in which they lived ; never, however, absent even in Michael Angelo, but stealing forth continually in a strange and spectral way, lurking in folds of
raiment and knots of wild hair, and mountainous confusions of
crabby limb and cloudy drapery ; and in Tintoret, ruling the
entire conceptions of his greatest works to such a degree that
they are an enigma or an offence, even to this day, to all the
petty disciples of a formal criticism.   Of the grotesque in our own
Shakespeare I need hardly speak, nor of its intolerableness to

his French critics; nor of that of Æschylus and Homer, as opposed to the lower Greek writers; and so I believe it will be found, at all periods, in all minds of the first order.

§ LXVIII. As an index of the greatness of nations, it is a less certain test, or rather, we are not so well agreed on the meaning of the term "greatness" respecting them. A nation may produce a great effect, and take up a high place in the world's history, by the temporary enthusiasm or fury of its multitudes, without being truly great; or on the other hand, the discipline of morality and common sense may extend its physical power or exalt its well-being, while yet its creative and imaginative powers are continually diminishing. And again: a people may take so definite a lead over all the rest of the world in one direction, as to obtain a respect which is not justly due to them if judged on universal grounds. Thus the Greeks perfected the sculpture of the human body; threw their literature into a disciplined form, which has given it a peculiar power over certain conditions of modern mind; and were the most carefully educated race that the world has seen; but a few years hence, I believe, we shall no longer think them a greater people than either the Egyptians or Assyrians.

§ LXIX. If, then, ridding ourselves as far as possible of prejudices owing merely to the school-teaching which remains from the system of the Renaissance, we set ourselves to discover in what races the human soul, taken all in all, reached its highest magnificence, we shall find, I believe, two great families of men one of the East and South, the other of the West and North: the one including the Egyptians, Jews, Arabians, Assyrians, and Persians; the other, I know not whence derived, but seeming to flow forth from Scandinavia, and filling the whole of Europe with its Norman and Gothic energy. And in both these families, wherever they are seen in their utmost nobleness, there the grotesque is developed in its utmost energy; and I hardly know whether most to admire the winged bulls of Nineveh, or the winged dragons of Verona.

§ LXX. The reader who has not before turned his attention

to this subject may, however, at first have some difficulty in distinguishing between the noble grotesque of these great nations, and the barbarous grotesque of mere savageness, as seen in the work of the Hindoo and other Indian nations ; or, more grossly still, in that of the complete savage of the Pacific islands ; or if, as is to be hoped, he instinctively feel the difference, he may yet find difficulty in determining wherein that difference consists. But he will discover, on consideration, that the noble grotesque *involves the true appreciation of beauty*, though the mind may wilfully turn to other images, or the hand resolutely stop short of the perfection, which it must fail, if it endeavoured, to reach ; while the grotesque of the Sandwich islander involves no perception or imagination of anything above itself. He will find that in the exact proportion in which the grotesque results from an incapability of perceiving beauty, it becomes savage or barbarous ; and that there are many stages of progress to be found in it, even in its best times, much truly savage grotesque occurring in the fine Gothic periods, mingled with the other forms of the ignoble grotesque resulting from vicious inclinations or base sportiveness. Nothing is more mysterious in the history of the human mind than the manner in which gross and ludicrous images are mingled with the most solemn subjects in the work of the middle ages, whether of sculpture or illumination ; and although, in great part, such incongruities are to be accounted for on the various principles which I have above endeavoured to define, in many instances they are clearly the result of vice and sensuality. The general greatness or seriousness of an age does not effect the restoration of human nature ; and it would be strange, if, in the midst of the art even of the best periods, when that art was entrusted to myriads of workmen, we found no manifestations of impiety, folly, or impurity.

§ LXXI. It needs only to be added, that in the noble grotesque, as it is partly the result of a morbid state of the imaginative power, that power itself will be always seen in a high degree ; and that therefore our power of judging of the rank of a grotesque work will depend on the degree in which we are in general sensible of the presence of invention. The reader may partly test this power in himself by referring to the Plate given in the opening of this chapter, in which, on the left, is a piece of noble and inventive grotesque, a head of the lion-symbol of St. Mark, from the Veronese Gothic; the other is a head introduced as a boss on the foundation of the Palazzo Corner della Regina at Venice, utterly devoid of invention, made merely monstrous by exaggerations of the eyeballs and cheeks, and generally characteristic of that late Renaissance grotesque of Venice with which we are at present more immediately concerned.*

§ LXXII. The development of that grotesque took place under different laws from those which regulate it in any other European city. For, great as we have seen the Byzantine mind show itself to be in other directions, it was marked as that of a declining nation by the absence of the grotesque element, and, owing to its influence, the early Venetian Gothic remained inferior to all other schools in this particular character. Nothing can well be more wonderful than its instant failure in any attempt at the representation of ludicrous or fearful images, more especially when it is compared with the magnificent grotesque of the neighbouring city of Verona, in which the Lombard influence had full sway. Nor was it until the last links of connexion with Constantinople had been dissolved, that the strength of the Venetian mind could manifest itself in this direction. But it had then a new enemy to encounter. The Renaissance laws altogether checked its imagination in architecture; and it could only obtain permission to express itself by

* Note especially, in connexion with what was advanced in Vol. II., p. 162, § XIII., respecting our English neatness of execution, how the base workman has cut the lines of the architecture neatly and precisely round the abominable head; but the noble workman has used his chisel like a painter's pencil, and sketched the glory with a few irregular lines, anything rather than circular; and struck out the whole head in the same frank and fearless way, leaving the sharp edges of the stone as they first broke, and flinging back the crest of hair from the forehead with half a dozen hammer-strokes, while the poor wretch who did the other was half a day in smoothing its vapid and vermicular curls.

starting forth in the work of the Venetian painters, filling them
with monkeys and dwarfs, even amidst the most serious subjects, and leading Veronese and Tintoret to the most unexpected and wild fantasies of form and colour.

§ LXXIII. We may be deeply thankful for this peculiar reserve
of the Gothic grotesque character to the last days of Venice.
All over the rest of Europe it had been strongest in the days
of imperfect art; magnificently powerful throughout the whole
of the thirteenth century, tamed gradually in the fourteenth
and fifteenth, and expiring in the sixteenth amidst anatomy
and laws of art. But at Venice, it had not been received when
it was elsewhere in triumph, and it fled to the lagoons for
shelter when elsewhere it was oppressed. And it was arrayed
by the Venetian painters in robes of state, and advanced by
them to such honour as it had never received in its days of
widest dominion; while, in return, it bestowed upon their pictures that fulness, piquancy, decision of parts, and mosaic-like
intermingling of fancies, alternately brilliant and sublime, which
were exactly what was most needed for the development of
their unapproachable colour-power.

§ LXXIV. Yet, observe, it by no means follows that because
the grotesque does not appear in the art of a nation, the sense
of it does not exist in the national mind. Except in the form
of caricature, it is hardly traceable in the English work of the
present day; but the minds of our workmen are full of it, if
we would only allow them to give it shape. They express it
daily in gesture and gibe, but are not allowed to do so where
it would be useful. In like manner, though the Byzantine
influence repressed it in the early Venetian architecture, it was
always present in the Venetian mind, and showed itself in
various forms of national custom and festival; *acted* grotesques,
full of wit, feeling, and good-humour. The ceremony of the
hat and the orange, described in the beginning of this chapter,
is one instance out of multitudes. Another, more rude, and
exceedingly characteristic, was that instituted in the twelfth
century in memorial of the submission of Woldaric, the patriarch

of Aquileia, who, having taken up arms against the patriarch of Grado, and being defeated and taken prisoner by the Venetians, was sentenced, not to death, but to send every year on " Fat Thursday" sixty-two large loaves, twelve fat pigs, and a bull, to the Doge; the bull being understood to represent the patriarch, and the twelve pigs his clergy: and the ceremonies of the day consisting in the decapitation of these representatives, and a distribution of their joints among the senators; together with a symbolic record of the attack upon Aquileia, by the erection of a wooden castle in the rooms of the Ducal Palace, which the *Doge and the Senate* attacked and demolished with clubs.   As long as the Doge and the Senate were truly kingly and noble, they were content to let this ceremony be continued; but when they became proud and selfish, and were destroying both themselves and the state by their luxury, they found it inconsistent with their dignity, and it was abolished, as far as the Senate was concerned, in 1549.*

§ LXXV. By these and other similar manifestations, the grotesque spirit is traceable through all the strength of the Venetian people.   But again : it is necessary that we should carefully distinguish between it and the spirit of mere levity.   I said, in the fifth chapter, that the Venetians were distinctively a serious people; serious, that is to say, in the sense in which the English are a more serious people than the French; though the habitual intercourse of our lower classes in London has a tone of humour in it which I believe is untraceable in that of the Parisian populace.   It is one thing to indulge in playful rest, and another to be devoted to the pursuit of pleasure : and gaiety of heart during the reaction after hard labour, and quickened by satisfaction in the accomplished duty or perfected result, is altogether compatible with, nay, even in some sort arises naturally out of, a deep internal seriousness of disposition; this latter being exactly the condition of mind which, as we have seen, leads to the richest developments of the playful grotesque; while, on the contrary, the continual pursuit of pleasure deprives the soul of all alacrity and elasticity, and leaves it

* The decree is quoted by Mutinelli, lib. i. p. 46.

incapable of happy jesting, capable only of that which is bitter, base, and foolish. Thus, throughout the whole of the early career of the Venetians, though there is much jesting, there is no levity ; on the contrary, there is an intense earnestness both in their pursuit of commercial and political successes, and in their devotion to religion,* which led gradually to the formation of that highly wrought mingling of immovable resolution with secret thoughtfulness, which so strangely, sometimes so darkly, distinguishes the Venetian character at the time of their highest power, when the seriousness was left, but the conscientiousness destroyed. And if there be any one sign by which the Venetian countenance, as it is recorded for us, to the very life, by a school of portraiture which has never been equalled (chiefly because no portraiture ever had subjects so noble),—I say, if there be one thing more notable than another in the Venetian features, it is this deep pensiveness and solemnity. In other districts of Italy, the dignity of the heads which occur in the most celebrated compositions is clearly owing to the feeling of the painter. He has visibly raised or idealized his models, and appears always to be veiling the faults or failings of the human nature around him, so that the best of his work is that which has most perfectly taken the colour of his own mind ; and the least impressive, if not the least valuable, that which appears to have been unaffected and unmodified portraiture. But at Venice, all is exactly the reverse of this. The tone of mind in the painter appears often in some degree frivolous or sensual ; delighting in costume, in domestic and grotesque incident, and in studies of the naked form. But the moment he gives himself definitely to portraiture, all is noble and grave ; the more literally true his work, the more majestic ; and the same artist who will produce little beyond what is commonplace in painting a Madonna or an apostle, will rise into unapproachable sublimity when his subject is a member of the Forty, or a Master of the Mint.

Such, then, were the general tone and progress of the Venetian mind, up to the close of the seventeenth century. First, serious,

* See Appendix 9.

religious, and sincere ; then, though serious still, comparatively deprived of conscientiousness, and apt to decline into stern and subtle policy : in the first case, the spirit of the noble grotesque not showing itself in art at all, but only in speech and action ; in the second case, developing itself in painting, through accessories and vivacities of composition, while perfect dignity was always preserved in portraiture. A third phase rapidly developed itself.

§ LXXVI. Once more, and for the last time, let me refer the reader to the important epoch of the death of the Doge Tomaso Mocenigo in 1423, long ago indicated as the commencement of the decline of the Venetian power. That commencement is marked not merely by the words of the dying Prince, but by a great and clearly legible sign. It is recorded, that on the accession of his successor, Foscari, to the throne, " SI FESTEGGIO DALLA CITTA UNO ANNO INTERO : " " The city kept festival for a whole year." Venice had in her childhood sown, in tears, the harvest she was to reap in rejoicing. She now sowed in laughter the seeds of death.

Thenceforward, year after year, the nation drank with deeper thirst from the fountains of forbidden pleasure, and dug for springs, hitherto unknown, in the dark places of the earth. In the ingenuity of indulgence, in the varieties of vanity, Venice surpassed the cities of Christendom, as of old she had surpassed them in fortitude and devotion ; and as once the powers of Europe stood before her judgment-seat, to receive the decisions of her justice, so now the youth of Europe assembled in the halls of her luxury, to learn from her the arts of delight.

It is as needless as it is painful to trace the steps of her final ruin. That ancient curse was upon her, the curse of the Cities of the Plain, " Pride, fulness of bread, and abundance of idleness." By the inner burning of her own passions, as fatal as the fiery rain of Gomorrah, she was consumed from her place among the nations ; and her ashes are choking the channels of the dead, salt sea.

CHAPTER IV.

CONCLUSION.

§ I. I FEAR this chapter will be a rambling one, for it must be a kind of supplement to the preceding pages, and a general recapitulation of the things I have too imperfectly and feebly said.

The grotesques of the seventeenth and eighteenth centuries, the nature of which we examined in the last chapter, close the career of the architecture of Europe. They were the last evidences of any feeling consistent with itself, and capable of directing the efforts of the builder to the formation of anything worthy the name of a style or school. From that time to this, no resuscitation of energy has taken place, nor does any for the present appear possible. How long this impossibility may last, and in what direction with regard to art in general, as well as to our lifeless architecture, our immediate efforts may most profitably be directed, are the questions I would endeavour briefly to consider in the present chapter.

§ II. That modern science, with all its additions to the comforts of life, and to the fields of rational contemplation, has placed the existing races of mankind on a higher platform than any that preceded them, none can doubt for an instant; and I believe the position in which we find ourselves is somewhat analogous to that of thoughtful and laborious youth succeeding a restless and heedless infancy. Not long ago, it was said to me by one of the masters of modern science: "When men invented the locomotive, the child was learning to go; when they invented the telegraph, it was learning to speak." He looked forward to the manhood of mankind as assuredly the nobler in proportion to the slowness of its development. What might not be expected from the prime and middle strength of the order of existence whose infancy had lasted six thousand years? And indeed, I think this the truest, as well as the most cheering, view that we can take of the world's history. Little progress has been made as yet. Base war, lying policy, thoughtless cruelty, senseless improvidence,—all things which, in nations, are analogous to the petulance, cunning, impatience, and carelessness of infancy,—have been, up to this hour, as characteristic of mankind as they were in the earliest periods; so that we must either be driven to doubt of human progress at all, or look upon it as in its very earliest stage. Whether the opportunity is to be permitted us to redeem the hours that we have lost; whether He, in whose sight a thousand years are as one day, has appointed us to be tried by the continued possession of the strange powers with which He has lately endowed us; or whether the periods of childhood and of probation are to cease together, and the youth of mankind is to be one which shall prevail over death, and bloom for ever in the midst of a new heaven and a new earth, are questions with which we have no concern. It is indeed right that we should look for, and hasten, so far as in us lies, the coming of the Day of God; but not that we should check any human efforts by anticipations of its approach. We shall hasten it best by endeavouring to work out the tasks that are appointed for us here ; and, therefore, reasoning as if the world were to continue under its existing dispensation, and the powers which have just been granted to us were to be continued through myriads of future ages.

§ III. It seems to me, then, that the whole human race, so far as their own reason can be trusted, may at present be regarded as just emergent from childhood; and beginning for the first time to feel their strength, to stretch their limbs, and explore the creation around them. If we consider that, till within the last fifty years, the nature of the ground we tread on, of the air we breathe, and of the light by which we see, were not so much as conjecturally conceived by us; that the duration of the globe, and the races of animal life by which it was inhabited, are just

beginning to be apprehended ; and that the scope of the magnificent science which has revealed them is as yet so little received by the public mind, that presumption and ignorance are
still permitted to raise their voices against it unrebuked ; that
perfect veracity in the representation of general nature by art
has never been attempted until the present day, and has in the
present day been resisted with all the energy of the popular
voice ;* that the simplest problems of social science are yet so
little understood, as that doctrines of liberty and equality can
be openly preached, and so successfully as to affect the whole
body of the civilized world with apparently incurable disease ;
that the first principles of commerce were acknowledged by
the English Parliament only a few months ago, in its free trade
measures, and are still so little understood by the million, that
no nation dares to abolish its custom-houses ;† that the simplest
principles of policy are still not so much as stated, far less
received, and that civilized nations persist in the belief that the
subtlety and dishonesty which they know to be ruinous in
dealings between man and man, are serviceable in dealings
between multitude and multitude ; finally, that the scope of
the Christian religion, which we have been taught for two
thousand years, is still so little conceived by us, that we suppose
the laws of charity and of self-sacrifice bear upon individuals
in all their social relations, and yet do not bear upon nations
in any of their political relations ;—when, I say, we thus review
the depth of simplicity in which the human race are

* In the works of Turner and the Pre-Raphaelites.

† Observe, I speak of these various principles as self-evident, only under the
present circumstances of the world, not as if they had always been so ; and I call
them now self-evident, not merely because they seem so to myself, but because
they are felt to be so likewise by all the men in whom I place most trust. But
granting that they are not so, then their very disputability proves the state of
infancy above alleged, as characteristic of the world. For I do not suppose that
any Christian reader will doubt the first great truth, that whatever facts or laws
are important to mankind, God has made ascertainable by mankind ; and that as
the decision of all these questions is of vital importance to the race, that decision
must have been long ago arrived at, unless they were still in a state of childhood,

still plunged with respect to all that it most profoundly concerns them to know, and which might, by them, with most ease have been ascertained, we can hardly determine how far back on the narrow path of human progress we ought to place the generation to which we belong, how far the swaddling clothes are unwound from us, and childish things beginning to be put away.

On the other hand, a power of obtaining veracity in the representation of material and tangible things, which, within certain limits and conditions, is unimpeachable, has now been placed in the hands of all men,* almost without labour. The foundation of every natural science is now at last firmly laid, not a day passing without some addition of buttress and pinnacle to their already magnificent fabric. Social theorems, if fiercely agitated, are therefore the more likely to be at last determined, so that they never can be matters of question more. Human life has been in some sense prolonged by the increased powers of locomotion, and an almost limitless power of converse. Finally, there is hardly any serious mind in Europe but is occupied, more or less, in the investigation of the questions which have so long paralyzed the strength of religious feeling, and shortened the dominion of religious faith. And we may therefore at least look upon ourselves as so far in a definite state of progress, as to justify our caution in guarding against the dangers incident to every period of change, and especially to that from childhood into youth.

§ IV. Those dangers appear, in the main, to be twofold; consisting partly in the pride of vain knowledge, partly in the pursuit of vain pleasure. A few points are still to be noticed with respect to each of these heads.

---

* I intended to have given a sketch in this place (above referred to) of the probable results of the daguerreotype and calotype within the next few years, in modifying the application of the engraver's art, but I have not had time to complete the experiments necessary to enable me to speak with certainty. Of one thing, however, I have little doubt, that an infinite service will soon be done to a large body of our engravers; namely, the making them draughtsmen (in black and white) on paper instead of steel.

Enough, it might be thought, had been said already touching the pride of knowledge ; but I have not yet applied the principles at which we arrived in the third chapter to the practical questions of modern art. And I think those principles, together with what were deduced from the consideration of the nature of Gothic in the second volume, so necessary and vital, not only with respect to the progress of art, but even to the happiness of society, that I will rather run the risk of tediousness than of deficiency in their illustration and enforcement.

In examining the nature of Gothic, we concluded that one of the chief elements of power in that, and in *all good* architecture, was the acceptance of uncultivated and rude energy in the workman. In examining the nature of Renaissance, we concluded that its chief element of weakness was that pride of knowledge which not only prevented all rudeness in expression, but gradually quenched all energy which could only be rudely expressed ; nor only so, but, for the motive and matter of the work itself, preferred science to emotion, and experience to perception.

§ v. The modern mind differs from the Renaissance mind in that its learning is more substantial and extended, and its temper more humble ; but its errors, with respect to the cultivation of art, are precisely the same,—nay, as far as regards execution, even more aggravated. We require, at present, from our general workmen, more perfect finish than was demanded in the most skilful Renaissance periods, except in their very finest productions ; and our leading principles in teaching, and in the patronage which necessarily gives tone to teaching, are, that the goodness of work consists primarily in firmness of handling and accuracy of science, that is to say, in hand-work and head-work ; whereas heart-work, which is the *one* work we want, is not only independent of both, but often, in great degree, inconsistent with either.

§ vi. Here, therefore, let me finally and firmly enunciate the great principle to which all that has hitherto been stated is subservient :—that art is valuable or otherwise, only as it expresses the personality, activity, and living perception of a good and great human soul; that it may express and contain this with little help from execution, and less from science; and that if it have not this, if it show not the vigour, perception, and invention of a mighty human spirit, it is worthless. Worthless, I mean, as *art;* it may be precious in some other way, but, as art, it is nugatory. Once let this be well understood among us, and magnificent consequences will soon follow. Let me repeat it in other terms, so that I may not be misunderstood. All art is great, and good, and true, only so far as it is distinctively the work of *manhood* in its entire and highest sense; that is to say, not the work of limbs and fingers, but of the soul, aided, according to her necessities, by the inferior powers; and therefore distinguished in essence from all products of those inferior powers unhelped by the soul. For as a photograph is not a work of art, though it requires certain delicate manipulations of paper and acid, and subtle calculations of time, in order to bring out a good result; so, neither would a drawing *like* a photograph, made directly from nature, be a work of art, although it would imply many delicate manipulations of the pencil and subtle calculations of effects of colour and shade. It is no more art* to manipulate a camel's-hair pencil, than to manipulate a china tray and a glass vial. It is no more art to lay on colour delicately, than to lay on acid delicately. It is no more art to use the cornea and retina for the reception of an image, than to use a lens and a piece of silvered paper. But the moment that inner part of the man, or rather that entire and only being of the man, of which cornea and retina, fingers and hands, pencils and colours, are all the mere servants and instruments;† that manhood which has light in itself, though the

---

* I mean art in its highest sense. All that men do ingeniously is art, in one sense. In fact, we want a definition of the word "art" much more accurate than any in our minds at present. For, strictly speaking, there is no such thing as "fine" or "high" art. All *art* is a low and common thing, and what we indeed respect is not art at all, but *instinct* or *inspiration* expressed by the help of art.

† "*Socrates.* This, then, was what I asked you; whether that which puts any-

eyeball be sightless, and can gain in strength when the hand and the foot are hewn off and cast into the fire ; the moment this part of the man stands forth with its solemn " Behold, it is I," then the work becomes art indeed, perfect in honour, priceless in value, boundless in power.

§ VII. Yet observe, I do not mean to speak of the body and soul as separable. The man is made up of both : they are to be raised and glorified together, and all art is an expression of the one by and through the other. All that I would insist upon is, the necessity of the whole man being in his work ; the body *must* be in it. Hands and habits must be in it, whether we will or not : but the nobler part of the man may often not be in it. And that nobler part acts principally in love, reverence, and admiration, together with those conditions of thought which arise out of them. For we usually fall into much error by considering the intellectual powers as having dignity in themselves, and separable from the heart ; whereas the truth is, that the intellect becomes noble or ignoble according to the food we give it, and the kind of subjects with which it is conversant. It is not the reasoning power which, of itself, is noble, but the rea-

thing else to service, and the thing which is put to service by it, are always two different things ?

Alcibiades. I think so.

Socrates. What shall we then say of the leather-cutter ? Does he cut his leather with his instruments only, or with his hands also ?

Alcibiades. With his hands also.

Socrates. Does he not use his eyes as well as his hands ?

Alcibiades. Yes.

Socrates. And we agreed that the thing which uses and the thing which is used were different things ?

Alcibiades. Yes.

Socrates. Then the leather-cutter is not the same thing as his eyes or hands ?

Alcibiades. So it appears.

Socrates. Does not, then, man make use of his whole body ?

Alcibiades. Assuredly.

Socrates. Then the man is not the same thing as his body ?

Alcibiades. It seems so.

Socrates. What, then, *is* the man ?

Alcibiades. I know not."

Plato, Alcibiades I,

soning power occupied with its proper objects. Half of the mistakes of metaphysicians have arisen from their not observing this ; namely, that the intellect, going through the same processes, is yet mean or noble according to the matter it deals with, and wastes itself away in mere rotatory motion, if it be set to grind straws and dust. If we reason only respecting words, or lines, or any trifling and finite things, the reason becomes a contemptible faculty ; but reason employed on holy and infinite things, becomes herself holy and infinite. So that, by work of the soul, I mean the reader always to understand the work of the entire immortal creature, proceeding from a quick, perceptive, and eager heart, perfected by the intellect, and finally dealt with by the hands, under the direct guidance of these higher powers.

§ VIII. And now observe, the first important consequence of our fully understanding this pre-eminence of the soul, will be the due understanding of that subordination of knowledge respecting which so much has already been said. For it must be felt at once, that the increase of knowledge, merely as such, does not make the soul larger or smaller ; that in the sight of God, all the knowledge man can gain is as nothing : but that the soul, for which the great scheme of redemption was laid, be it ignorant or be it wise, is all in all ; and in the activity, strength, health, and well-being of this soul, lies the main difference, in His sight, between one man and another. And that which is all in all in God's estimate is also, be assured, all in all in man's labour ; and to have the heart open, and the eyes clear, and the emotions and thoughts warm and quick, and not the knowing of this or the other fact, is the state needed for all mighty doing in this world. And therefore, finally, for this, the weightiest of all reasons, let us take no pride in our knowledge. We may, in a certain sense, be proud of being immortal ; we may be proud of being God's children ; we may be proud of loving, thinking, seeing, and of all that we are by no human teaching : but not of what we have been taught by rote ; not of the ballast and freight of the ship of the spirit, but only of its pilotage, without which all the freight will only sink it faster, and strew the sea more richly with its ruin. There is not at this moment a youth of twenty, having received what we moderns ridiculously call education, but he knows more of everything, except the soul, than Plato or St. Paul did ; but he is not for that reason a greater man, or fitter for his work, or more fit to be heard by others, than Plato or St. Paul.   There is not at this moment a junior student in our schools of painting, who does not know fifty times as much about the art as Giotto did ; but he is not for that reason greater than Giotto ; no, nor his work better, nor fitter for our beholding.   Let him go on to know all that the human intellect can discover and contain in the term of a long life, and he will not be one inch, one line, nearer to Giotto's feet.   But let him leave his academy benches, and, innocently, as one knowing nothing, go out into the highways and hedges, and there rejoice with them that rejoice, and weep with them that weep ; and in the next world, among the companies of the great and good, Giotto will give his hand to him, and lead him into their white circle, and say, " This is our brother."

§ IX. And the second important consequence of our feeling the soul's pre-eminence will be our understanding the soul's language, however broken, or low, or feeble, or obscure in its words ; and chiefly that great symbolic language of past ages, which has now so long been unspoken.   It is strange that the same cold and formal spirit which the Renaissance teaching has raised amongst us, should be equally dead to the languages of imitation and of symbolism ; and should at once disdain the faithful rendering of real nature by the modern school of the Pre-Raphaelites, and the symbolic rendering of imagined nature in the work of the thirteenth century.   But so it is ; and we find the same body of modern artists rejecting Pre-Raphaelitism because it is not ideal ! and thirteenth century work, because it is not real !—their own practice being at once false and un-ideal, and therefore equally opposed to both.

§ X. It is therefore, at this juncture, of much importance to mark for the reader the exact relation of healthy symbolism and of healthy imitation ; and, in order to do so, let us return to one of our Venetian examples of symbolic art, to the central cupola of St. Mark's. On that cupola, as has been already stated, there is a mosaic representing the apostles on the Mount of Olives, with an olive-tree separating each from the other ; and we shall easily arrive at our purpose, by comparing the means which would have been adopted by a modern artist bred in the Renaissance schools,—that is to say, under the influence of Claude and Poussin, and of the common teaching of the present day,—with those adopted by the Byzantine mosaicist to express the nature of these trees.

§ xi. The reader is doubtless aware that the olive is one of the most characteristic and beautiful features of all Southern scenery. On the slopes of the northern Apennines, olives are the usual forest timber ; the whole of the Val d' Arno is wooded with them, every one of its gardens is filled with them, and they grow in orchard-like ranks out of its fields of maize, or corn, or vine ; so that it is physically impossible, in most parts of the neighbourhood of Florence, Pistoja, Lucca, or Pisa, to choose any site of landscape which shall not owe its leading character to the foliage of these trees. What the elm and oak are to England, the olive is to Italy ; nay, more than this, its presence is so constant, that, in the case of at least four-fifths of the drawings made by any artist in North Italy, he must have been somewhat impeded by branches of olive coming between him and the landscape. Its classical associations double its importance in Greece ; and in the Holy Land the remembrances connected with it are of course more touching than can ever belong to any other tree of the field. Now, for many years back, at least one-third out of all the landscapes painted by English artists have been chosen from Italian scenery ; sketches in Greece and in the Holy Land have become as common as sketches on Hampstead Heath ; our galleries also are full of sacred subjects, in which, if any background be introduced at all, the foliage of the olive ought to have been a prominent feature. And here I challenge the untravelled English reader to tell me what an olive-tree is like ?

§ xii. I know he cannot answer my challenge. He has no

more idea of an olive-tree than if olives grew only in the fixed stars. Let him meditate a little on this one fact, and consider its strangeness, and what a wilful and constant closing of the eyes to the most important truths it indicates on the part of the modern artist. Observe, a want of perception, not of science. I do not want painters to tell me any scientific facts about olive-trees. But it had been well for them to have felt and seen the olive-tree; to have loved it for Christ's sake, partly also for the helmed Wisdom's sake which was to the heathen in some sort as that nobler Wisdom which stood at God's right hand, when He founded the earth and established the heavens. To have loved it, even to the hoary dimness of its delicate foliage, subdued and faint of hue, as if the ashes of the Gethsemane agony had been cast upon it for ever; and to have traced, line by line, the gnarled writhing of its intricate branches, and the pointed fretwork of its light and narrow leaves, inlaid on the blue field of the sky, and the small rosy-white stars of its spring blossoming, and the beads of sable fruit scattered by autumn along its topmost boughs —the right, in Israel, of the stranger, the fatherless, and the widow,—and, more than all, the softness of the mantle, silver grey, and tender like the down on a bird's breast, with which, far away, it veils the undulation of the mountains;—these it had been well for them to have seen and drawn, whatever they had left unstudied in the gallery.

§ XIII. And if the reader would know the reason why this has not been done (it is one instance only out of the myriads which might be given of sightlessness in modern art), and will ask the artists themselves, he will be informed of another of the marvellous contradictions and inconsistencies in the base Renaissance art; for it will be answered him, that it is not right, nor according to law, to draw trees so that one should be known from another, but that trees ought to be generalized into a universal idea of a tree: that is to say, that the very school which carries its science in the representation of man down to the dissection of the most minute muscle, refuses so much science to the drawing of a tree as shall distinguish one species from another; and also, while it attends to logic, and rhetoric, and perspective, and atmosphere, and every other circumstance which is trivial, verbal, external, or accidental, in what it either says or sees, it will *not* attend to what is essential and substantial,—being intensely solicitous, for instance, if it draws two trees, one behind the other, that the farthest off shall be as much smaller as mathematics show that it should be, but totally unsolicitous to show, what to the spectator is a far more important matter, whether it is an apple or an orange-tree.

§ XIV. This, however, is not to our immediate purpose. Let it be granted that an idea of an olive-tree is indeed to be given us in a special manner; how, and by what language, this idea is to be conveyed, are questions on which we shall find the world of artists again divided; and it was this division which I wished especially to illustrate by reference to the mosaics of St. Mark's.

Now the main characteristics of an olive-tree are these: It has sharp and slender leaves of a greyish green, nearly grey on the under surface, and resembling, but somewhat smaller than, those of our common willow. Its fruit, when ripe, is black and lustrous; but of course so small, that, unless in great quantity, it is not conspicuous upon the tree. Its trunk and branches are peculiarly fantastic in their twisting, showing their fibres at every turn; and the trunk is often hollow, and even rent into many divisions like separate stems, but the extremities are exquisitely graceful, especially in the setting on of the leaves; and the notable and characteristic effect of the tree in the distance is of a rounded and soft mass or ball of downy foliage.

§ XV. Supposing a modern artist to address himself to the rendering of this tree with his best skill: he will probably draw accurately the twisting of the branches, but yet this will hardly distinguish the tree from an oak: he will also render the colour and intricacy of the foliage, but this will only confuse the idea of an oak with that of a willow. The fruit, and the peculiar grace of the leaves at the extremities, and the fibrous structure of the stems, will all be too minute to be rendered consistently with his artistical feeling of breadth, or with the amount of labour which he considers it dexterous and legitimate to bestow upon the work : but, above all, the rounded and monotonous form of the head of the tree will be at variance with his ideas of "composition ;" he will assuredly disguise or break it, and the main points of the olive-tree will all at last remain untold.

§ XVI. Now observe, the old Byzantine mosaicist begins his work at enormous disadvantage. It is to be some one hundred and fifty feet above the eye, in a dark cupola ; executed not with free touches of the pencil, but with square pieces of glass ; not by his own hand, but by various workmen under his superintendence ; finally, not with a principal purpose of drawing olive-trees, but mainly as a decoration of the cupola. There is to be an olive-tree beside each apostle, and their stems are to be the chief lines which divide the dome. He therefore at once gives up the irregular twisting of the boughs hither and thither, but he will not give up their fibres. Other trees have irregular and fantastic branches, but the knitted cordage of fibres is the olive's own. Again, were he to draw the leaves of their natural size, they would be so small that their forms would be invisible in the darkness ; and were he to draw them so large as that their shape might be seen, they would look like laurel instead of olive. So he arranges them in small clusters of five each, nearly of the shape which the Byzantines give to the petals of the lily, but elongated so as to give the idea of leafage upon a spray ; and these clusters,—his object always, be it remembered, being *decoration* not less than *representation*,— he arranges symmetrically on each side of his branches, laying the whole on a dark ground most truly suggestive of the heavy rounded mass of the tree, which, in its turn, is relieved against the gold of the cupola. Lastly, comes the question respecting the fruit. The whole power and honour of the olive is in its fruit ; and, unless that be represented, nothing is represented. But if the berries were coloured black or green, they would be totally invisible ; if of any other colour, utterly unnatural, and violence would be done to the whole conception. There is but one conceivable means of showing them, namely, to represent them as golden. For the idea of golden fruit of various kinds was already familiar to

IV.

J. Ruskin.   J. C. Armytage.

Mosaics of Olivetree and Flowers.

the mind, as in the apples of the Hesperides, without any violence to the distinctive conception of the fruit itself.*   So the mosaicist introduced small round golden berries into the dark ground between each leaf, and his work was done.

§ XVII. On the opposite plate, the uppermost figure on the left is a tolerably faithful representation of the general effect of one of these decorative olive-trees ; the figure on the right is the head of the tree alone, showing the leaf clusters, berries, and *interlacing* of the boughs as they leave the stem.   Each bough is connected with a separate line of fibre in the trunk, and the junctions of the arms and stem are indicated, down to the very root of the tree, with a truth in structure which may well put to shame the tree anatomy of modern times.

§ XVIII. The white branching figures upon the serpentine band below are two of the clusters of flowers which form the foreground of a mosaic in the atrium.   I have printed the whole plate in blue,† because that colour approaches more nearly than black to the distant effect of the mosaics, of which the darker portions are generally composed of blue, in greater quantity than any other colour.   But the waved background, in this instance, is of various shades of blue and green alternately, with one narrow black band to give it force ; the whole being intended to represent the distant effect and colour of deep grass, and the wavy line to *express its bending motion,* just as the same symbol is used to represent the waves of water.   Then the two white clusters are representative of the distinctly visible herbage close to the spectator, having buds and flowers of two kinds, springing in one case out of the midst of twisted grass, and in the other out of their own proper leaves ; the clusters being kept each so distinctly symmetrical, as to form, when set side by side,

* Thus the grapes pressed by Excesse are partly golden (Spenser, book ii. cant. 12) :
> " Which did themselves amongst the leaves enfold,
> As lurking from the vew of covetous guest,
> That the weake boughes, with so rich load opprest,
> Did bow adowne as overburdened."

† Plate IV appears in black and white in the present edition.

an ornamental border of perfect architectural severity ; and yet each cluster different from the next, and every flower, and bud, and knot of grass, varied in form and thought.   The way the mosaic tesseræ are arranged, so as to give the writhing of the grass blades round the stalks of the flowers, is exceedingly fine.

The three circles below are examples of still more severely conventional forms, adopted, on principle, when the decoration is to be in white and gold, instead of colour ; these ornaments being cut in white marble on the outside of the church, and the ground laid in with gold, though necessarily here represented, like the rest of the plate, in blue.   And it is exceedingly interesting to see how the noble workman, the moment he is restricted to more conventional materials, retires into more conventional forms, and reduces his various leafage into symmetry, now nearly perfect ; yet observe, in the central figure, where the symbolic meaning of the vegetation beside the cross required it to be more distinctly indicated, he has given it life and growth by throwing it into unequal curves on the opposite sides.

§ XIX. I believe the reader will now see, that in these mosaics, which the careless traveller is in the habit of passing by with contempt, there is a depth of feeling and of meaning greater than in most of the best sketches from nature of modern times ; and, without entering into any question whether these conventional representations are as good as, under the required limitations, it was possible to render them, they are at all events good enough completely to illustrate that mode of symbolical expression which appeals altogether to thought, and in nowise trusts to realization.   And little as, in the present state of our schools, such an assertion is likely to be believed, the fact is that this kind of expression is the *only one allowable in noble art*.

§ XX. I pray the reader to have patience with me for a few moments.   I do not mean that no art is noble but Byzantine mosaic ; but that no art is noble which in any wise depends upon direct imitation for its effect upon the mind.   This was asserted in the opening chapters of " Modern Painters," but not upon the highest grounds; the results at which we have now arrived in our investigation of early art will enable me to place it on a loftier and firmer foundation.

§ XXI. We have just seen that all great art is the work of the whole living creature, body and soul, and chiefly of the soul. But it is not only *the work* of the whole creature, it likewise *addresses* the whole creature. That in which the perfect being speaks must also have the perfect being to listen. I am not to spend my utmost spirit, and give all my strength and life to my work, while you, spectator or hearer, will give me only the attention of half your soul. You must be all mine, as I am all yours; it is the only condition on which we can meet each other. All your faculties, all that is in you of greatest and best, must be awake in you, or I have no reward. The painter is not to cast the entire treasure of his human nature into his labour merely to please a part of the beholder: not merely to delight his senses, not merely to amuse his fancy, not merely to beguile him into emotion, not merely to lead him into thought; but to do *all* this. Senses, fancy, feeling, reason, the whole of the beholding spirit, must be stilled in attention or stirred with delight; else the labouring spirit has not done its work well. For observe, it is not merely its *right* to be thus met, face to face, heart to heart; but it is its *duty* to evoke this answering of the other soul: its trumpet call must be so clear, that though the challenge may by dulness or indolence be unanswered, there shall be no error as to the meaning of the appeal; there must be a summons in the work, which it shall be our own fault if we do not obey. We require this of it, we beseech this of it. Most men do not know what is in them till they receive this summons from their fellows: their hearts die within them, sleep settles upon them, the lethargy of the world's miasmata; there is nothing for which they are so thankful as that cry, "Awake, thou that sleepest." And this cry must be most loudly uttered to their noblest faculties; first of all, to the imagination, for that is the most tender, and the soonest struck into numbness by the poisoned air: so that one

of the main functions of art, in its service to man, is to rouse
the imagination from its palsy, like the angel troubling the
Bethesda pool; and the art which does not do this is false
to its duty, and degraded in its nature. It is not enough
that it be well imagined, it must task the beholder also to
imagine well; and this so imperatively, that if he does not
choose to rouse himself to meet the work, he shall not taste it,
nor enjoy it in any wise. Once that he is well awake, the guidance which the artist gives him should be full and authoritative:
the beholder's imagination should not be suffered to take
its own way, or wander hither and thither; but neither must it
be left at rest; and the right point of realization, for any given
work of art, is that which will enable the spectator to complete
it for himself, in the exact way the artist would have him, but
not that which will save him the trouble of effecting the completion. So soon as the idea is entirely conveyed, the artist's
labour should cease; and every touch which he adds beyond
the point when, with the help of the beholder's imagination, the
story ought to have been told, is a degradation to his work.
So that the art is wrong which either realizes its subject completely, or fails in giving such definite aid as shall enable it to
be realized by the beholding imagination.

§ XXII. It follows, therefore, that the quantity of finish or detail which may rightly be bestowed upon any work, depends on
the number and kind of ideas which the artist wishes to convey,
much more than on the amount of realization necessary to
enable the imagination to grasp them. It is true that the differences of judgment formed by one or another observer are in great
degree dependent on their unequal imaginative powers, as well
as their unequal efforts in following the artist's intention; and it
constantly happens that the drawing which appears clear to the
painter in whose mind the thought is formed, is slightly inadequate
to suggest it to the spectator. These causes of false judgment
or imperfect achievement must always exist, but they are of no
importance. For, in nearly every mind, the imaginative power,
however unable to act independently, is so easily helped and so

brightly animated by the most obscure suggestion, that there is no form of artistical language which will not readily be seized by it, if once it set itself intelligently to the task; and even without such effort there are few hieroglyphics of which, once understanding that it is to take them as hieroglyphics, it cannot make itself a pleasant picture.

§ XXIII. Thus, in the case of all sketches, etchings, unfinished engravings, etc., no one ever supposes them to be imitations. Black outlines on white paper cannot produce a deceptive resemblance of anything; and the mind, understanding at once that it is to depend on its own powers for great part of its pleasure, sets itself so actively to the task that it can completely enjoy the rudest outline in which meaning exists. Now, when it is once in this temper, the artist is infinitely to be blamed who insults it by putting anything into his work which is not suggestive: having summoned the imaginative power, he must turn it to account and keep it employed, or it will turn against him in indignation. Whatever he does merely to realize and substantiate an idea is impertinent; he is like a dull story-teller, dwelling on points which the hearer anticipates or disregards. The imagination will say to him : " I knew all that before ; I don't want to be told that. Go on ; or be silent, and let me go on in my own way. I can tell the story better than you."

Observe, then, whenever finish is given for the sake of realization, it is wrong; whenever it is given for the sake of adding ideas, it is right. All true finish consists in the addition of ideas, that is to say, in giving the imagination more food ; for once well awaked, it is ravenous for food : but the painter who finishes in order to substantiate takes the food out of its mouth, and it will turn and rend him.

§ XXIV. Let us go back, for instance, to our olive grove, —or, lest the reader should be tired of olives, let it be an oak copse,—and consider the difference between the substantiating and the imaginative methods of finish in such a subject. A few strokes of the pencil, or dashes of colour, will be enough to

enable the imagination to conceive a tree ; and in those dashes
of colour Sir Joshua Reynolds would have rested, and would
have suffered the imagination to paint what more it liked for
itself, and grow oaks, or olives, or apples, out of the few dashes
of colour at its leisure.   On the other hand, Hobbima, one of
the worst of the realists, smites the imagination on the mouth,
and bids it be silent, while he sets to work to paint his oak of
the right green, and fill up its foliage laboriously with jagged
touches, and furrow the bark all over its branches, so as, if
possible, to deceive us into supposing that we are looking at a
real oak ; which, indeed, we had much better do at once, without
giving any one the trouble to deceive us in the matter.

§ xxv. Now, the truly great artist neither leaves the imagination to itself, like Sir Joshua, nor insults it by realization, like
Hobbima, but finds it continual employment of the happiest
kind.   Having summoned it by his vigorous first touches, he
says to it : "Here is a tree for you, and it is to be an oak.
Now I know that you can make it green and intricate for
yourself, but that is not enough : an oak is not only green and
intricate, but its leaves have most beautiful and fantastic forms,
which I am very sure you are not quite able to complete without help ; so I will draw a cluster or two perfectly for you, and
then you can go on and do all the other clusters.   So far so
good : but the leaves are not enough ; the oak is to be full of
acorns, and you may not be quite able to imagine the way they
grow, nor the pretty contrast of their glossy almond-shaped
nuts with the chasing of their cups ; so I will draw a bunch
or two of acorns for you, and you can fill up the oak with
others like them.   Good : but that is not enough ; it is to be
a bright day in summer, and all the outside leaves are to be
glittering in the sunshine as if their edges were of gold : I
cannot paint this, but you can ; so I will really gild some of the
edges nearest you,* and you can turn the gold into sunshine,

* The reader must not suppose that the use of gold, in this manner, is confined to early art.   Tintoret, the greatest master of pictorial effect that ever
existed, has gilded the ribs of the fig-leaves in his " Resurrection," in the Scuola
di San Rocco.

and cover the tree with it. Well done : but still this is not enough; the tree is so full foliaged and so old that the wood birds come in crowds to build there; they are singing, two or three under the shadow of every bough. I cannot show you them all; but here is a large one on the outside spray, and you can fancy the others inside."

§ XXVI. In this way the calls upon the imagination are multiplied as a great painter finishes ; and from these larger incidents he may proceed into the most minute particulars, and lead the companion imagination to the veins in the leaves and the mosses on the trunk, and the shadows of the dead leaves upon the grass, but always multiplying thoughts, or subjects of thought, never working for the sake of realization ; the amount of realization actually reached depending on his space, his materials, and the nature of the thoughts he wishes to suggest. In the sculpture of an oak-tree, introduced above an Adoration of the Magi on the tomb of the Doge Marco Dolfino (fourteenth century), the sculptor has been content with a few leaves, a single acorn, and a bird ; while, on the other hand, Millais' willow-tree with the robin, in the background of his "Ophelia," or the foreground of Hunt's "Two Gentlemen of Verona," carries the appeal to the imagination into particulars so multiplied and minute, that the work nearly reaches realization. But it does not matter how near realization the work may approach in its fulness, or how far off it may remain in its slightness, so long as realization is not the end proposed, but the informing one spirit of the thoughts of another. And in this greatness and simplicity of purpose all noble art is alike, however slight its means, or however perfect, from the rudest mosaics of St. Mark's to the most tender finishing of the " Huguenot " or the "Ophelia."

§ XXVII. Only observe, in this matter, that a greater degree of realization is often allowed for the sake of colour than would be right without it. For there is not any distinction between the artists of the inferior and the nobler schools more definite than this ; that the first *colour for the sake of realization*, and the second *realize for the sake of colour.* I hope that, in the fifth chapter, enough has been said to show the nobility of colour, though it is a subject on which I would fain enlarge whenever I approach it : for there is none that needs more to be insisted upon, chiefly on account of the opposition of the persons who have no eye for colour, and who, being therefore unable to understand that it is just as divine and distinct in its power as music (only infinitely more varied in its harmonies), talk of it as if it were inferior and servile with respect to the other powers of art :* whereas it is so far from being this, that wherever it enters it must take the mastery, and whatever else is sacrificed for its sake, *it*, at least, must be right. This is partly the case even with music : it is at our choice whether we will accompany a poem with music or not ; but, if we do, the music *must* be right, and neither discordant nor inexpressive. The goodness and sweetness of the poem cannot save it, if the music be harsh or false : but if the music be right, the poem may be insipid or inharmonious, and still saved by the notes to which it is wedded. But this is far more true of colour. If that be wrong, all is wrong. No amount of expression or invention can redeem an ill-coloured picture ; while, on the other hand, if the colour be right, there is nothing it will not raise or redeem ; and, therefore, wherever colour enters at all, anything *may* be sacrificed to it, and, rather than it should be false or feeble, everything *must* be sacrificed to it : so that, when an artist touches colour, it is the same thing as when a poet takes up a musical instru-

* Nothing is more wonderful to me than to hear the pleasure of the eye, in colour, spoken of with disdain as " sensual," while people exalt that of the ear in music. Do they really suppose the eye is a less noble bodily organ than the ear,—that the organ by which nearly all our knowledge of the external universe is communicated to us, and through which we learn to wonder and to love, can be less exalted in its own peculiar delight than the ear, which is only for the communication of the ideas which owe to the eye their very existence ? I do not mean to depreciate music : let it be loved and reverenced as is just ; only let the delight of the eye be reverenced more. The great power of music over the multitude is owing, not to its being less but *more* sensual than colour ; it is so distinctly and so richly sensual, that it can be idly enjoyed ; it is exactly at the point where the lower and higher pleasures of the senses and imagination are balanced ; so that pure and great minds love it for its invention and emotion, and lower minds for its sensual power,

ment; he implies, in so doing, that he is a master, up to a certain point, of that instrument, and can produce sweet sound from it, and is able to fit the course and measure of his words to its tones, which, if he be not able to do, he had better not have touched it. In like manner, to add colour to a drawing is to undertake for the perfection of a visible music, which, if it be false, will utterly and assuredly mar the whole work; if true, proportionately elevate it, according to its power and sweetness. But, in no case ought the colour to be added in order to increase the realization. The drawing or engraving is all that the imagination needs. To "paint" the subject merely to make it more real, is only to insult the imaginative power, and to vulgarize the whole. Hence the common, though little understood feeling, among men of ordinary cultivation, that an inferior sketch is always better than a bad painting; although, in the latter, there may verily be more skill than in the former. For the painter who has presumed to touch colour without perfectly understanding it, not for the colour's sake, nor because he loves it, but for the sake of completion merely, has committed two sins against us; he has dulled the imagination by not trusting it far enough, and then, in this languid state, he oppresses it with base and false colour; for all colour that is not lovely is discordant; there is no mediate condition. So, therefore, when it is permitted to enter at all, it must be with the predetermination that, cost what it will, the colour shall be right and lovely: and I only wish that, in general, it were better understood that a *painter's* business is to *paint*, primarily; and that all expression, and grouping, and conceiving, and what else goes to constitute design, *are of less importance than colour in a coloured work.* And so they were always considered in the noble periods; and sometimes all resemblance to nature whatever (as in painted windows, illuminated manuscripts, and such other work) is sacrificed to the brilliancy of colour; sometimes distinctness of form to its richness, as by Titian, Turner, and Reynolds; and, which is the point on which we are at present insisting, sometimes, in the pursuit of its utmost refinements

on the surfaces of objects, an amount of realization becomes
consistent with noble art, which would otherwise be altogether
inadmissible, that is to say, which no great mind could otherwise have either produced or enjoyed. The extreme finish given
by the Pre-Raphaelites is rendered noble chiefly by their love
of colour.

§ XXVIII. So then, whatever may be the means, or whatever
the more immediate end of any kind of art, all of it that is
good agrees in this, that it is the expression of one soul talking
to another, and is precious according to the greatness of the
soul that utters it. And consider what mighty consequences
follow from our acceptance of this truth! what a key we have
herein given us for the interpretation of the art of all time!
For, as long as we held art to consist in any high manual
skill, or successful imitation of natural objects, or any scientific
and legalized manner of performance whatever, it was necessary
for us to limit our admiration to narrow periods and to few
men. According to our own knowledge and sympathies, the
period chosen might be different, and our rest might be in
Greek statues, or Dutch landscapes, or Italian Madonnas ; but,
whatever our choice, we were therein captive, barred from all
reverence but of our favourite masters, and habitually using the
language of contempt towards the whole of the human race
to whom it had not pleased Heaven to reveal the arcana of the
particular craftsmanship we admired, and who, it might be, had
lived their term of seventy years upon the earth, and fitted
themselves therein for the eternal world, without any clear
understanding, sometimes even with an insolent disregard, of
the laws of perspective and chiaroscuro.

But let us once comprehend the holier nature of the art of
man, and begin to look for the meaning of the spirit, however
syllabled, and the scene is changed; and we are changed also.
Those small and dexterous creatures whom once we worshipped,
those fur-capped divinities with sceptres of camel's hair, peering
and poring in their one-windowed chambers over the minute
preciousness of the laboured canvas; how are they swept away

and crushed into unnoticeable darkness! And in their stead, as the walls of the dismal rooms that enclosed them, and us, are struck by the four winds of Heaven, and rent away, and as the world opens to our sight, lo! far back into all the depths of time, and forth from all the fields that have been sown with human life, how the harvest of the dragon's teeth is springing! how the companies of the gods are ascending out of the earth! The dark stones that have so long been the sepulchres of the thoughts of nations, and the forgotten ruins wherein their faith lay charnelled, give up the dead that were in them; and beneath the Egyptian ranks of sultry and silent rock, and amidst the dim golden lights of the Byzantine dome, and out of the confused and cold shadows of the Northern cloister, behold, the multitudinous souls come forth with singing, gazing on us with the soft eyes of newly comprehended sympathy, and stretching their white arms to us across the grave, in the solemn gladness of everlasting brotherhood.

§ XXIX. The other danger to which, it was above said, we were primarily exposed under our present circumstances of life, is the pursuit of vain pleasure, that is to say, false pleasure; delight, which is not indeed delight; as knowledge vainly accumulated is not indeed knowledge. And this we are exposed to chiefly in the fact of our ceasing to be children. For the child does not seek false pleasure; its pleasures are true, simple, and instinctive: but the youth is apt to abandon his early and true delight for vanities,—seeking to be like men, and sacrificing his natural and pure enjoyments to his pride. In like manner, it seems to me that modern civilization sacrifices much pure and true pleasure to various forms of ostentation from which it can receive no fruit. Consider, for a moment, what kind of pleasures are open to human nature, undiseased. Passing by the consideration of the pleasures of the higher affections, which lie at the root of everything, and considering the definite and practical pleasures of daily life, there is, first, the pleasure of doing good; the greatest of all, only apt to be despised from not being often enough tasted: and then, I know not in what order to put them, nor does it matter,—the pleasure of gaining knowledge ; the pleasure of the excitement of imagination and emotion (or poetry and passion) ; and, lastly, the gratification of the senses, first of the eye, then of the ear, and then of the others in their order.

§ xxx. All these we are apt to make subservient to the desire of praise ; nor unwisely, when the praise sought is God's and the conscience's : but if the sacrifice is made for man's admiration, and knowledge is only sought for praise, passion repressed or affected for praise, and the arts practised for praise, we are feeding on the bitterest apples of Sodom, suffering always ten mortifications for one delight. And it seems to me, that in the modern civilised world we make such sacrifice doubly : first, by labouring for merely ambitious purposes ; and secondly, which is the main point in question, by being ashamed of simple pleasures, more especially of the pleasure in sweet colour and form, a pleasure evidently so necessary to man's perfectness and virtue, that the beauty of colour and form has been given lavishly throughout the whole of creation, so that it may become the food of all, and with such intricacy and subtlety that it may deeply employ the thoughts of all. If we refuse to accept the natural delight which the Deity has thus provided for us, we must either become ascetics, or we must seek for some base and guilty pleasures to replace those of Paradise, which we have denied ourselves.

Some years ago, in passing through some of the cells of the Grande Chartreuse, noticing that the window of each apartment looked across the little garden of its inhabitant to the wall of the cell opposite, and commanded no other view, I asked the monk beside me why the window was not rather made on the side of the cell whence it would open to the solemn fields of the Alpine valley. " We do not come here," he replied, " to look at the mountains."

§ xxxi. The same answer is given, practically, by the men of this century, to every such question ; only the walls with which they enclose themselves are those of Pride, not of Prayer.

But in the middle ages it was otherwise. Not, indeed, in land-scape itself, but in the art which can take the place of it, in the noble colour and form with which they illumined, and into which they wrought, every object around them that was in any wise subjected to their power, they obeyed the laws of their inner nature, and found its proper food. The splendour and fantasy even of dress, which in these days we pretend to despise, or in which, if we even indulge, it is only for the sake of vanity, and therefore to our infinite harm, were in those early days studied for love of their true beauty and honourableness, and became one of the main helps to dignity of character and courtesy of bearing. Look back to what we have been told of the dress of the early Venetians, that it was so invented " that in clothing themselves with it, they might clothe themselves also with modesty and honour ; " * consider what nobleness of expression there is in the dress of any of the portrait figures of the great times ; nay, what perfect beauty, and more than beauty, there is in the folding of the robe round the imagined form even of the saint or of the angel ; and then consider whether the grace of vesture be indeed a thing to be despised. We cannot despise it if we would ; and in all our highest poetry and happiest thought we cling to the magnificence which in daily life we disregard. The essence of modern romance is simply the return of the heart and fancy to the things in which they naturally take pleasure ; and half the influence of the best romances, of Ivanhoe, or Marmion, or the Crusaders, or the Lady of the Lake, is com-pletely dependent upon the accessories of armour and costume. Nay, more than this, deprive the " Iliad " itself of its costume, and consider how much of its power would be lost. And that delight and reverence which we feel in, and by means of, the mere imagination of these accessories, the middle ages had in the vision of them ; the nobleness of dress exercising, as I have said, a perpetual influence upon character, tending in a thousand ways to increase dignity and self-respect, and, together with grace of gesture, to induce serenity of thought.

* Vol. II. Appendix 7.

§ XXXII. I do not mean merely in its magnificence ; the most splendid time was not the best time. It was still in the thirteenth century,—when, as we have seen, simplicity and gorgeousness were justly mingled, and the " leathern girdle and the clasp of bone " were worn, as well as the embroidered mantle,—that the manner of dress seems to have been noblest. The chain mail of the knight, flowing and falling over his form in lapping waves of gloomy strength, was worn under full robes of one colour in the ground, his crest quartered on them, and their borders enriched with subtle illumination. The women wore first a dress close to the form in like manner, and then long and flowing robes, veiling them up to the neck, and delicately embroidered around the hem, the sleeves, and the girdle. The use of plate armour gradually introduced more fantastic types ; the nobleness of the form was lost beneath the steel ; the gradually increasing luxury and vanity of the age strove for continual excitement in more quaint and extravagant devices; and in the fifteenth century, dress reached its point of utmost splendour and fancy, being in many cases still exquisitely graceful, but now, in its morbid magnificence, devoid of all wholesome influence on manners. From this point, like architecture, it was rapidly degraded, and sank through the buff coat, and lace collar, and jack boot, to the bag-wig, tailed coat, and high-heeled shoe ; and so to what it is now.

§ XXXIII. Precisely analogous to this destruction of beauty in dress has been that of beauty in architecture ; its colour, and grace, and fancy, being gradually sacrificed to the base forms of the Renaissance, exactly as the splendour of chivalry has faded into the paltriness of fashion. And observe the form in which the necessary reaction has taken place ; necessary, for it was not possible that one of the strongest instincts of the human race could be deprived altogether of its natural food. Exactly in the degree that the architect withdrew from his buildings the sources of delight which in early days they had so richly possessed, demanding, in accordance with the new principles of taste, the banishment of all happy colour and healthy invention, in that degree the minds of men began to turn to land-scape as their only resource. The picturesque school of art rose up to address those capacities of enjoyment for which, in sculpture, architecture, or the higher walks of painting, there was employment no more ; and the shadows of Rembrandt, and savageness of Salvator, arrested the admiration which was no longer permitted to be rendered to the gloom or the grotesque-ness of the Gothic aisle. And thus the English school of landscape, culminating in Turner, is in reality nothing else than a healthy effort to fill the void which the destruction of Gothic architecture has left.

§ XXXIV. But the void cannot thus be completely filled ; no, nor filled in any considerable degree. The art of landscape-painting will never become thoroughly interesting or sufficing to the minds of men engaged in active life, or concerned prin-cipally with practical subjects. The sentiment and imagination necessary to enter fully into the romantic forms of art are chiefly the characteristics of youth ; so that nearly all men as they advance in years, and some even from their childhood upwards, must be appealed to, if at all, by a direct and sub-stantial art, brought before their daily observation and connected with their daily interests. No form of art answers these con-ditions so well as architecture, which, as it can receive help from every character of mind in the workman, can address every character of mind in the spectator; forcing itself into notice even in his most languid moments, and possessing this chief and peculiar advantage, that it is the property of all men. Pictures and statues may be jealously withdrawn by their possessors from the public gaze, and to a certain degree their safety requires them to be so withdrawn ; but the outsides of our houses belong not so much to us as to the passer-by, and whatever cost and pains we bestow upon them, though too often arising out of ostentation, have at least the effect of benevolence.

§ XXXV. If, then, considering these things, any of my readers should determine, according to their means, to set themselves to the revival of a healthy school of architecture in England, and wish to know in few words how this may be done, the answer is clear and simple. First, let us cast out utterly whatever is connected with the Greek, Roman, or Renaissance architecture, in principle or in form. We have seen above, that the whole mass of the architecture, founded on Greek and Roman models, which we have been in the habit of building for the last three centuries, is utterly devoid of all life, virtue, honourableness, or power of doing good. It is base, unnatural, unfruitful, unenjoyable, and impious. Pagan in its origin, proud and unholy in its revival, paralyzed in its old age, yet making prey in its dotage of all the good and living things that were springing around it in their youth, as the dying and desperate king, who had long fenced himself so strongly with the towers of it, is said to have filled his failing veins with the blood of children ;* an architecture invented, as it seems, to make plagiarists of its architects, slaves of its workmen, and sybarites of its inhabitants ; an architecture in which intellect is idle, invention impossible, but in which all luxury is gratified, and all insolence fortified ;—the first thing we have to do is to cast it out, and shake the dust of it from our feet for ever. Whatever has any connection with the five orders, or with any one of the orders,—whatever is Doric, or Ionic, or Tuscan, or Corinthian, or Composite, or in any wise Grecized or Romanized ; whatever betrays the smallest respect for Vitruvian laws, or conformity with Palladian work,—that we are to endure no more. To cleanse ourselves of these "cast clouts and rotten rags" is the first thing to be done in the court of our prison.

§ XXXVI. Then, to turn our prison into a palace is an easy

---

* Louis the Eleventh. "In the month of March, 1481, Louis was seized with a fit of apoplexy at *St. Bénoît-du-lac-mort*, near Chinon. He remained speechless and bereft of reason three days; and then, but very imperfectly restored, he languished in a miserable state. . . To cure him," says a contemporary historian, "wonderful and terrible medicines were compounded. It was reported among the people that his physicians opened the veins of little children, and made him drink their blood, to correct the poorness of his own."—*Bussey's History of France.* London, 1850.

thing. We have seen above, that exactly in the degree in which Greek and Roman architecture is lifeless, unprofitable, and unchristian, in that same degree our own ancient Gothic is animated, serviceable, and faithful. We have seen that it is flexible to all duty, enduring to all time, instructive to all hearts, honourable and holy in all offices. It is capable alike of all lowliness and all dignity, fit alike for cottage porch or castle gateway; in domestic service familiar, in religious, sublime; simple, and playful, so that childhood may read it, yet clothed with a power that can awe the mightiest, and exalt the loftiest of human spirits: an architecture that kindles every faculty in its workman, and addresses every emotion in its beholder; which, with every stone that is laid on its solemn walls, raises some human heart a step nearer heaven, and which from its birth has been incorporated with the existence, and in all its form is symbolical of the faith, of Christianity. In this architecture let us henceforward build alike the church, the palace, and the cottage; but chiefly let us use it for our civil and domestic buildings. These once ennobled, our ecclesiastical work will be exalted together with them: but churches are not the proper scenes for experiments in untried architecture, nor for exhibitions of unaccustomed beauty. It is certain that we must often fail before we can again build a natural and noble Gothic: let not our temples be the scenes of our failures. It is certain that we must offend many deep-rooted prejudices, before ancient Christian architecture* can be again received by all of us: let not religion be the first source of such offence. We shall meet with difficulties in applying Gothic architecture to churches, which would in nowise affect the designs of civil buildings, for the most beautiful forms of Gothic chapels are not those which are best fitted for Protestant worship. As it was noticed in the second volume,

---

* Observe, I call Gothic "Christian" architecture, not "ecclesiastical." There is a wide difference. I believe it is the only architecture which Christian men should build, but not at all an architecture necessarily connected with the services of their church.

when speaking of the Cathedral of Torcello, it seems not unlikely, that as we study either the science of sound, or the practice of the early Christians, we may see reason to place the pulpit gene- rally at the extremity of the apse or chancel ; an arrangement entirely destructive of the beauty of a Gothic church, as seen in existing examples, and requiring modifications of its design in other parts with which we should be unwise at present to embarrass ourselves ; besides, that the effort to introduce the style exclusively for ecclesiastical purposes, excites against it the strong prejudices of many persons who might otherwise be easily enlisted among its most ardent advocates.   I am quite sure, for instance, that if such noble architecture as has been employed for the interior of the church just built in Margaret Street* had been seen in a civil building, it would have decided the question with many men at once ; whereas, at present, it will be looked upon with fear and suspicion, as the expression of the ecclesiastical principles of a particular party.   But, whether thus regarded or not, this church assuredly decides one question conclusively, that of our present capability of Gothic design.   It is the first piece of architecture I have seen, built in modern days, which is free from all signs of timidity or incapacity.   In general proportion of parts, in refinement and piquancy of mouldings, above all, in force, vitality, and grace of floral ornament, worked in a broad and masculine manner, it challenges fearless comparison with the noblest work of any time.   Having done this, we may do anything ; there need be no limits to our hope or our confidence ; and I believe it to be possible for us, not only to equal, but far to surpass, in some respects, any Gothic yet seen in Northern countries.   In the introduction of figure-sculpture, we must, indeed, for the present, remain utterly inferior, for we have no

---

* Mr. Hope's church, in Margaret Street, Portland Place. I do not altogether like the arrangements of colour in the brickwork ; but these will hardly attract the eye, where so much has been already done with precious and beautiful marble, and is yet to be done in fresco.   Much will depend, however, upon the colouring of this latter portion. I wish that either Holman Hunt or Millais could be prevailed upon to do at least some of these smaller frescoes.

figures to study from. No architectural sculpture was ever good for anything which did not represent the dress and persons of the people living at the time; and our modern dress will *not* form decorations for spandrils and niches. But in floral sculpture we may go far beyond what has yet been done, as well as in refinement of inlaid work and general execution. For, although the glory of Gothic architecture is to receive the rudest work, it refuses not the best; and, when once we have been content to admit the handling of the simplest workman, we shall soon be rewarded by finding many of our simple workmen become cunning ones : and, with the help of modern wealth and science, we may do things like Giotto's campanile, instead of like our own rude cathedrals; but better than Giotto's campanile, insomuch as we may adopt the pure and perfect forms of the Northern Gothic, and work them out with the Italian refinement. It is hardly possible at present to imagine what may be the splendour of buildings designed in the forms of English and French thirteenth century *surface* Gothic, and wrought out with the refinement of Italian art in the details, and with a deliberate resolution, since we cannot have figure-sculpture, to display in them the beauty of every flower and herb of the English fields, each by each; doing as much for every tree that roots itself in our rocks, and every blossom that drinks our summer rains, as our ancestors did for the oak, the ivy, and the rose. Let this be the object of our ambition, and let us begin to approach it, not ambitiously, but in all humility, accepting help from the feeblest hands; and the London of the nineteenth century may yet become as Venice without her despotism, and as Florence without her dispeace.

CHAPTER V.

[ADDED FROM THE TRAVELLERS' EDITION, 1877.]

CASTEL-FRANCO.

§ 1. WITH the words which closed Chap. III.* virtually ended the book which I called " The Stones of Venice,"— meaning, the history of Venice so far as it was written in her ruins : the city itself being even then, in my eyes, dead, in the sense of the death of Jerusalem, when yet her people could love her, dead, and say, " Thy servants think upon her stones, and it pitieth them to see her in the dust."

And her history, so far as it was thus in her desolation graven, is indeed in this book† told truly, and, I find on re-reading it, so clearly, that it greatly amazes me at this date to reflect how no one has ever believed a word I said, though the public have from the first done me the honour to praise my manner of saying it ; and, as far as they found the things I spoke of amusing to themselves, they have deigned for a couple of days or so to look at them,—helped always through the tedium of the business by due quantity of ices at Florian's, music by moonlight on the Grand Canal, paper lamps, and the English papers and magazines at M. Ongaria's, with such illumination as those New Lamps contain—Lunar or Gaseous, enabling pursy Britannia to compare, at her ease, her own culminating and co-operate Prosperity and Virtue with the past wickedness and present out-of-pocketness of the umquhile Queen of the Sea.

---

* The last chapter in the Travellers' Edition.

† As now put into the traveller's hand, free of the encumbrance of minor detail. (*Note to the smaller edition.*)

§ 11. Allowing to the full for the extreme unpleasantness of the facts recorded in this book to the mind of a people set wholly on the pursuit of the same pleasures which ruined Venice, only in ways as witless as hers were witty, I think I can now see a further reason for their non-acceptance of the book's teaching, namely, the entire concealment of my own personal feelings throughout, which gives a continual look of insincerity to my best passages. Everybody praised their " style," partly because they saw it was stippled and laboured, and partly because for that stippling and labouring I had my reward, and got the sentences often into pleasantly sounding tune. But nobody praised the substance, which indeed they never took the trouble to get at ; but, occasionally tasting its roughness here and there, as of a bitter almond put by mistake into a sugarplum, spat it out, and said, "What a pity it had got in."

If, on the contrary, I had written quite naturally, and told, as a more egoistic person would, my own impressions, as thinking *those*, forsooth, and not the history of Venice, the most important business to the world in general, a large number of equally egoistic persons would have instantly felt the sincerity of the selfishness, clapped it, and stroked it, and said, " That's me."

To take an instance in what seemed to me then a little matter, but has become since an important one. In the article of the index, " Ponte de' Sospiri," the reader will find the influence of that building on the public mind ascribed chiefly to the " ignorant sentimentalism of Byron."

Now, these words are precisely true ; and I knew them to be true when I wrote them, and thought it good for the reader to be informed of that truth, namely, that Byron did not know the date of the Bridge of Sighs, nor of the Colleone statue ; and that his feelings about Venice had been founded on an extremely narrow acquaintance with her history. I did not think it at all necessary for the public to know that, in spite of all my carefully collected knowledge, I still felt exactly

as Byron did, in every particular; or that I had formed my
own precious "style" by perpetual reading of him, and imitation of him in various alliterative and despairing poems, of
which the best, the beginning of a Venetian tragedy written
when I was sixteen, has by good luck never seen the light;
but another, a doggerel in imitation of the Giaour, got me
favour in the eyes of Mr. Smith, the publisher of "Friendship's Offering," and made my unwise friends radiantly happy
in the thought that I should certainly be a poet, and as
exquisitely miserable at the first praises of then clear-dawning
Tennyson.

§ III. Nor, again, did I think it would at all advance the
acquaintance of my readers with the principles of Venetian
Gothic or Venetian policy, to be told that for the love of Byron,
I had run the risk of a fever in drawing the under-canal vaults,
and the desolate and mud-buried portico of the ruined Casa
Foscari.

Whether it would have been more becoming in me to tell
them this, or to taunt the ignorance of one who had taught
me so much in points which for his own work were useless
to him, and at the time he wrote, unregarded by anybody
else, may be extremely questioned; but I did not at that
time consult, nor have I much since consulted, becomingness;
vanity, always much,—love, more,—and the truth of the matter
in hand, beyond all things. Which has brought about the
consequences aforesaid; namely, that vain people recognise
the vanity, decorous people the indecorum, and loving people,
I hope, sometimes the love; but that everybody detests and
denies the unexpected truth. And that being so, while every
important fact respecting the art of the Renaissance was calmly
ascertained and inexorably stated in the "Stones of Venice,"
there has nevertheless been a perpetually increasing gabble
ever since, among upholsterers, crockery-mongers, and the
demi-monde of Paris and London, proving at last to everybody's (present) satisfaction that the Sistine Madonna was
meant to decorate snuff-boxes, the Georgics to promote the

manufacture of Dresden shepherdesses, and the powers of
Godhead and Kinghood together to be represented by the
contents of the Green Chamber and the reign of August the
Strong.

The upholsterers and chinamen, however, could never have
got the *Times* newspaper into full cry with them, without the
help of modern science and Apothecaries' Hall ; nor could the
Æsthetic, Phthisic, and otherwise variously sick hospitals and
Hôtels Dieu of the great capitals have produced their Doré
painters and their Eliot novelists, unless the palace or College
of Surgeons had been at one end of their Ponte de' Sospiri,
and the prisons of Iron at the other. So that when I was
last in Venice, while I could not go up the Grand Canal to
call on my dear old friend Rawdon Brown, but in passing
some dozen of brushed-up palaces full of Shylock's properties
got up for the mobs of Piccadilly and the Palais-Royal, I
was finally driven out of my tiny lodgings on the Giudecca
by the rattling and screaming, night and day, of the cranes
and whistles of the steamers which came to unload coals on
the quay. The effort made to do thoughtful work in spite
of their noise was, I doubt not, in great part the cause of
my first illness ; and if the reader cares indeed to see a little
of my true personality, let him buy the numbers of Fors
written in Venice in the winter of 1876.* Which for several
more serious reasons he had better do.

I will not encumber his travelling trunk with reprint of
more than a single sentence of them here ; but these contain quite final statements respecting the history of Venice,
and particulars in the legends of St. Ursula and St. Theodore,
which will be found of material use in the examination of
Carpaccio's paintings, and their contemporary sculpture. These
earlier and perfectly finished works will be found of much
more interest and use by the general visitor if intelligent and
attentive, than the pictures of the more renowned Venetian
masters, always impetuous and often slight, to which attention

* Letters 71 to 77.

is principally directed in the casual notices of this book, and in its terminal index.

§ IV. If, however, in my later books, I have spoken less of the acknowledged heads of the Venetian school, it is not because I love or reverence them less ; but only that I have learned also to estimate more humble labours, and have seen that it was useless to insist, for the ordinary traveller, on the technical merits of the highest examples in an art he had never practised, and on the most imaginative and majestic renderings of legends he had never read.

When you yourself, good reader, first show a natural history book to a child, you must tell it primarily, " That's a goose," " That's a duck," " That's a tomtit," etc.

Well, suppose I take you up to Tintoret's Paradise, and tell you in the same instructive manner,—That's a Saint, that's a Father, that's a Potestas. But you never saw a Saint! you never read a line of a Father! you never heard of such a thing as a Potestas! How can you possibly expect to know whether they are ill done or well, or to get an inch farther forward any-how? The whole canvas must remain for you, to the end of days, a mere big rag all over dirty streaks and blotches, as if Venice had wiped her last palette clean for ever with it. Which indeed she effectually did.

" But if I'm really good, and mean to try to see it, what's to be done?"

Well, you've got to read Homer all through, first, very care-fully ; then, with increasing care, the Prophet Ezekiel ; then, also with always increasing care, the Gospel of St. John, and then—I'll tell you what to do next.

" But have *you?* "

I should rather think so! I knew the Iliad and Odyssey and most of the Apocalypse more or less by heart before I was twelve years old : and have worked under them as my tutors ever since. The Gospel of St. John, everybody, in my young days, knew at least something about, and I've read it myself some thousand times, syllable by syllable. That's all mere

alphabetical work, the knowing it ; but, after knowing it, you've
got to believe some of it, and hope to believe more ; and then,
as I told you, I will tell you what next to do, for then you will
begin to understand some of the things I've been saying for this
last twenty years, and they will lead you as far as, I will not
say Tintoret, for you would have to spend another college-
residence in actual painter's work before you could make
much of *him;* but as far as Gentile Bellini and Giorgione ;
and the rest is according to the time and faculty you can
dispose of.

§ v. When I wrote the passages about Tintoret reprinted in
the following index, I had myself only got far enough to understand his chiaroscuro, and his mysticism in the direction in
which it resembled Turner's ; his properly Venetian mysticism,—
the language of signs and personages, (Iconographie Chrétienne,)
which runs down from Egypt through the Byzantines to Venice
in one unbroken and ever clearer stream,—a sacred language
just as accurately spoken and easily read by its scholars as old
Greek itself, was at that time wholly unknown to me : but
guessed at here and there, or hit upon by chance nearly enough
for use : what farther speciality of imagination there was in this
painter connected with clouds, and seas, and mountains, I
understood beyond any one else, but did not much hope for
sympathy in that perception, any more than with my love for
the Alps ; but told what was there as well and as clearly as I
could, just as I took the angles of the Matterhorn and weighed
the minute-burden of sand in the streams of Chamouni. The
chiaroscuro and other such artistic qualities were seldom much
insisted on to the public, only noted in my private diaries ; and
indeed the mere technique of what may be called upholsterer's
composition, (colour and shade without significance, and addressed to the eye only), had been well mastered and got past
by me as early as the third volume of " Modern Painters." The
reader may perhaps care to see the sort of work done for
this part of my business only : so here is a piece of my diary
for the year 1845, which begins at Genoa, and is not irrelevant

to the matters treated of in this chapter, though I give it only as a "pièce justificative."

PALAZZO DURAZZO.

The Magdalen given to Titian, coarse and vulgar in highest degree, but well painted.

CAPUCINO (Bernard Strozzi), a grand and Velasquez-like portrait of a Bishop.

GUIDO.—Three very valuable heads.   1st, one called la Vestale. She is raising a purple veil, under which she shows a face grand in contour, but flushed and sensual, the under dress rich, fastened by a large ruby at the throat.   It is a fine instance of great dignity of feature, obtained while only the lower part of the forehead is shown.   2nd, Portia, all black and stage-like, drawing-room costume, but fine. 3rd, The Roman daughter, more pale and luminous, rays of light falling across picture.   A fourth, their companion, is a copy, but these three are fine, and the Vestal I think the finest I have ever seen.

DOMENICHINO.—Christ appearing to the Magdalen.   I don't believe the picture.   Abominable in every way, but chiefly in the action and the colour.   A fine instance of exaggerated action on both sides, destroying all appearance of intense feeling.

TITIAN.—St. Catherine of Genoa.   The genuine edition of this is in the Louvre.   This looks like good, but uncompleted work.

GUERCINO.—Andromeda, very poor, but interesting as being an example of the same treatment as the Cleopatra, next noticed, *purple drapery heightening flesh colour.*

PALAZZO BRIGNOLE.

On the right hand in the Strada Nuova.   The effect, to me, imperfect, from its being stucco over bricks.   Only doors and balconies of stone.

GUERCINO.—Cleopatra.   A singular melody of two colours only, with warm white.   The figure lying under curtains of pure purple or lilac, the flesh almost the same tint as the curtains, but paler, and the bed white. Very fine.

RUBENS.—Himself and his wife, a figure of Envy behind with a torch, and a Bacchus, apparently typical of the felicity which excited the former. The whole picture is in warm greys, yellow hinted in the golden brown dress of the woman, all brought into full value by a little piece of pure blue, which appears at the knee through the crimson slashed doublet.

VALERIO CASTELLO.—(Genoese) Rape of Sabines. Very wild and fine, but colours faded; probably never very good. The shades brown and heavy, as if worked on a dark ground.

PAUL VERONESE.—Judith. A very grand picture. The group would be pyramidal, but it is carried to the top of the picture by an enormous mass of dark green curtain, which comes against a bright lilac and blue sky. The figure of the negress who stoops and holds the bag to receive the head, is grand and broad in the highest degree, generally dark, but relieved by white high lights on crimson dress, and by a white fillet round the arm; the headdress, russet and green, connects the warm tones of the figure with the green curtain above.

VANDYKE.—Tribute money. Very bad in colour. Strained and vulgar in expression.

PALAZZO PALLAVICINI.

RAFFAELLE.—Madonna della Colonna. Colour faded and picture hung too high to be seen, but seems very fine. Two green mountains in the distance, close to the head, seem injurious to the picture. Note, with respect to the value of them, the exceeding importance of the distant light in the Bellini of the Louvre.

And so on, for two or three pages more, concluding the study of the collections at Genoa, and, as it came to pass, also concluding my studies in this direction for ever. From Genoa I went on in that spring of 1845, to Lucca, where the tomb of Ilaria di Caretto at once altered the course of my life for me (see Fors Clavigera, Vol. IV., p. 192), and from that day I left the upholsterer's business in art to those who trade in it, and have guided my work, and limited my teaching, only by the sacred laws of truth and devotion which created the perfect schools of Christian art in Florence and Venice.

§ VI. The almost total cessation of reference, in my subsequent writings, to the merely artistic qualities of painting, has naturally enough made its practical students doubt my familiarity with them ; and the occasionally dogmatic statement of the technical excellence of such and such pieces of work, which was indeed founded on an extent of technical study in all the galleries of Europe, except those of Vienna and Madrid, absolutely impossible to painters who must work for their living, seemed to their narrower experience directed only by my humours. Whereas the only humour by which I have allowed myself to be unduly influenced has been that of carrying on my knowledge of the laws of nature and art to the utmost point which the years of active life would allow me to reach, without calculating how far my impaired strength and failing heart might in old age permit me to make the gained knowledge serviceable to others.

Recognizing this error, I hope, not yet wholly too late, and devising, in what may be left to me of time, only to render past work more available, I am deeply thankful to find a rapidly increasing and concentrating energy of help in my scholars; and at the same time, increase of excellent materials for use or reference in works of illustration produced of late years in London and Paris. Among these, the publications of the Arundel Society hold the first rank in purpose and principle, having been from the beginning conducted by a council of gentlemen in the purest endeavour for public utility, and absolutely without taint of self-interest, or encumbrance of operation by personal or national jealousy. Failing often, as could not but be the case when their task was one of supreme difficulty, and before unattempted, they have yet on the whole been successful in producing the most instructive and historically valuable set of engravings that have ever been put within reach of the public; and I am content to close this abstract of my history in Venice, by directing the attention alike of traveller and home student to the plate which this Society has given from the altar-piece by Giorgione in his native hamlet of Castel-Franco.

Content in this instance, and henceforward perhaps always, to be myself also a home student, for I have never seen the picture, I can recognize it by this print as one which unites every artistic quality for which the painting of Venice has become renowned, with a depth of symbolism and nobleness of manner exemplary of all that in any age of art has characterized its highest masters.

§ VII. Primarily observe, it announces itself clearly to you as a work of art, not a mere photograph or colour-stain from nature. I have again and again throughout my books dwelt upon the virtue and even necessity to the intellectual training of men, of effort for the simple rendering of natural or historical fact. Only, I have always said also, that the highest art is *not* this, but something far different from this, and pronouncing itself as such at a glance; as a statue, not a human body—as a picture, not a natural scene. Pre-eminently, Venetian art does so; and Giorgione in no wise intends you to suppose that the Madonna ever sat thus on a pedestal with a coat of arms upon it, or that St. George and St. Francis ever stood, or do now stand, in that manner beside her; but that a living Venetian may, in such vision, most deeply and rightly conceive of her, and of them.

Secondly, observe that the ideas which the picture conveys to you, are of noble, beautiful, and constant things. Not of disease, vice,—thrilling action, or fatal accident.

And that is also one of the chief lessons which in the sum of my work I have given; that, though in many derivative and subordinate ways the action and interest of pictures may be admirable, the greatest pictures represent men and women in peace, clouds and mountains in peace; men and women noble, clouds and mountains beautiful.

Never in the moral or the material universe does the great art of man acknowledge guilt, grief, change, or fear.

Thirdly, and for the present lastly. What the natural or divine facts of the universe *are ;* what God is, or what His work has been, or shall be, no man has ever yet known, nor has any wise man ever attempted, but as a child, to discover. But the utmost reach both towards the reality and the love of all things yet granted to human intellect, has been granted to the thinkers and the workmen who have trusted in the teaching of Christ, and in the spiritual help of the mortals who have tried to serve Him. And the strength, and joy, and height of achievement, of any group or race of mankind has, from the day of Christ's nativity to this hour, been in exact proportion to their power of apprehending, and honesty in obeying the truth of His Gospel.

Which rarely now seen historical fact, it having been permitted me in consistent labour of life to ascertain, I trust in conclusive gathering of that labour enough to prove ; ending this book, contentedly, with three pieces of former statement, made in three different books, respecting the life and power of ancient Venice.

The first shall be the passage in " St. Mark's Rest," describing the election of a Venetian Doge in the eleventh century.

The second, the extract given in " Fors Clavigera," from the oath of the Venetian brotherhood of St. Theodore in the thirteenth.

And the third, the passage in the last volume of " Modern Painters," describing the state of Venice in the days of Giorgione.*

1. " When the Doge Contarini died, the entire multitude of the people of Venice came in armed boats to the Lido,

* See " St. Mark's Rest," Chap. VII., p. 81 ; " Fors Clavigera," Vol. VII., p. 69 ; " Modern Painters," Vol. V., Part IX., Chap. IX., pp. 290-91.

and the Bishop of Venice, and the monks of the new abbey
of St. Nicholas, joined with them in prayer,—the monks in
their church, and the people on the shore and in their boats,
—that God would avert all dangers from their country, and
grant to them such a king as should be worthy to reign over
it. And as they prayed, with one accord, suddenly there rose
up among the multitude the cry, 'Domenico Selvo, we will,
and we approve,' whom a crowd of the nobles brought
instantly forward thereupon, and raised him on their own
shoulders and carried him to his own boat; into which when
he had entered, he put off his shoes from his feet, that he
might in all humility approach the church of St. Mark. And
while the boats began to row from the islands toward Venice,
the monk who saw this, and tells us of it, himself began to
sing the *Te Deum*. All around the voices of the people took
up the hymn, following it with Kyrie Eleison, with such litany
keeping time to their oars in the bright noonday, and rejoicing
on their native sea; all the towers of the city answering
with triumph peals as they drew nearer. They brought their
Doge to the Field of St. Mark, and carried him again on
their shoulders to the porch of the church; there, entering
barefoot, with songs of praise to God round him—'such that
it seemed as if the vaults must fall,'—he prostrated himself
on the earth and gave thanks to God and St. Mark, and
uttered such vow as was in his heart to utter before them.
Rising, he received at the altar the Venetian sceptre, and
thence entering the Ducal Palace, received there the oath of
fealty from the people."*

2. "At which time (1258) we all, with a joyful mind, with
a perfect will, and with a single spirit, to the honour of the
Most Holy Saviour and Lord sir Jesus Christ, and of the

---

* This account of the election of the Doge Selvo is given by Sansovino
("Venetia Descritta," lib. xi. 40: Venice, 1663, p. 477)—saying at the close
of it simply,—"Thus writes Domenico Rino, who was his chaplain, and who
was present at what I have related."—*Part of Note to "St. Mark's Rest."*

glorious Virgin Madonna Saint Mary His Mother, and of the happy and blessed sir Saint Theodore, martyr and cavalier of God,—('martir et cavalier de Dio')—and of all the other saints and saintesses of God," (have set our names,—understood) "to the end that the above sir, sir Saint Theodore, who stands continually before the throne of God, with the other saints, may pray to our Lord Jesus Christ that we all, brothers and sisters, whose names are under-written, may have, by His most sacred pity and mercy, remission of our minds, and pardon of our sins."

3. "Born half-way between the mountains and the sea—that young George of Castelfranco—of the Brave Castle : stout George they called him, George of Georges, so goodly a boy he was—Giorgione.

"Have you ever thought what a world his eyes opened on—fair, searching eyes of youth ? What a world of mighty life, from those mountain rocks to the shore ; of loveliest life, when he went down, yet so young, to the marble city—and became himself as a fiery heart to it ?

"A city of marble, did I say ? nay, rather a golden city, paved with emeralds. For truly, every pinnacle and turret glanced or glowed, overlaid with gold, or bossed with jasper. Beneath, the unsullied sea drew in deep breathing, to and fro, its eddies of green wave. Deep-hearted, majestic, terrible as the sea,—the men of Venice moved in sway of power and war ; pure as her pillars of alabaster, stood her mothers and maidens ; from foot to brow, all noble, walked her knights; the low bronzed gleaming of sea-rusted armour shot angrily under their blood-red mantle-folds. Fearless, faithful, patient, impenetrable, implacable,—every word a fate—sate her senate. In hope and honour, lulled by flowing of wave around their isles of sacred sand, each with his name written, and the cross graved at his side, lay her dead. A wonderful piece of world.   Rather, itself a world.   It lay along the face of the waters, no larger, as its captains saw it from their masts

at evening, than a bar of sunset that could not pass away;
but for its power, it must have seemed to them as if they
were sailing in the expanse of heaven, and this a great
planet, whose orient edge widened through ether, a world
from which all ignoble care and petty thoughts were banished,
with all the common and poor elements of life. No foulness,
nor tumult, in those tremulous streets, that filled or fell beneath
the moon; but rippled music of majestic change or thrilling
silence. No weak walls could rise above them; no low-
roofed cottage, nor straw-built shed. Only the strength as
of rock, and the finished setting of stones most precious.
And around them, far as the eye could reach, still the soft
moving of stainless waters, proudly pure; as not the flower,
so neither the thorn nor the thistle could grow in the glancing
fields. Ethereal strength of Alps, dream-like, vanishing in
high procession beyond the Torcellan shore; blue islands of
Paduan hills, poised in the golden west. Above, free winds
and fiery clouds ranging at their will;—brightness out of the
north, and balm from the south, and the stars of the evening
and morning clear in the limitless light of arched heaven and
circling sea."

APPENDIX.

I. ARCHITECT OF THE DUCAL PALACE.

POPULAR tradition, and a large number of the chroniclers, ascribe the building of the Ducal Palace to that Filippo Calendario who suffered death for his share in the conspiracy of Faliero. He was certainly one of the leading architects of the time, and had for several years the superintendence of the works of the Palace; but it appears, from the documents collected by the Abbé Cadorin, that the first designer of the Palace, the man to whom we owe the adaptation of the Frari traceries to civil architecture, was Pietro Baseggio, who is spoken of expressly as "formerly the Chief Master of our New Palace," * in the decree of 1361, quoted by Cadorin, and who, at his death, left Calendario his executor. Other documents collected by Zanotto, in his work on "Venezia e le sue Lagune," show that Calendario was for a long time at sea, under the commands of the Signory, returning to Venice only three or four years before his death; and that therefore the entire management of the works of the Palace, in the most important period, must have been entrusted to Baseggio.

It is quite impossible, however, in the present state of the Palace, to distinguish one architect's work from another in the older parts; and I have not in the text embarrassed the reader by any attempt at close definition of epochs before the great junction of the Piazzetta Façade with the older palace in the fifteenth century. Here, however, it is necessary that I should briefly state the observations I was able to make on the relative dates of the earlier portions.

In the description of the Fig-tree angle, given in the eighth chapter of Vol. II., I said that it seemed to me somewhat earlier than that of the Vine, and the reader might be surprised at the apparent opposition of this statement to my supposition that the Palace was built gradually round from the

* "Olim *magistri* prothi palatii nostri novi."—*Cadorin*, p. 127.

Rio Façade to the Piazzetta. But in the two great open arcades there is no succession of work traceable; from the Vine angle to the junction with the fifteenth century work, above and below, all seems nearly of the same date, the only question being of the accidental precedence of workmanship of one capital or another; and I think, from its style, that the Fig-tree angle must have been first completed. But in the upper stories of the Palace there are enormous differences of style. On the Rio Façade, in the upper story, are several series of massive windows of the third order, corresponding exactly in mouldings and manner of workmanship to those of the chapter-house of the Frari, and consequently carrying us back to a very early date in the fourteenth century: several of the capitals of these windows, and two richly sculptured string-courses in the wall below, are of Byzantine workmanship, and in all probability fragments of the Ziani Palace. The traceried windows on the Rio Façade, and the two eastern windows on the Sea Façade, are all of the finest early fourteenth century work, masculine and noble in their capitals and bases to the highest degree, and evidently contemporary with the very earliest portions of the lower arcades. But the moment we come to the windows of the Great Council Chamber the style is debased. The mouldings are the same, but they are coarsely worked, and the heads set amidst the leafage of the capitals quite valueless and vile.

I have not the least doubt that these window-jambs and traceries were restored after the great fire ; * and various other restorations have taken place since, beginning with the removal of the traceries from all the windows except the northern one of the Sala del Scrutinio, behind the Porta della Carta, where they are still left. I made out four periods of restoration among these windows, each baser than the preceding. It is not worth troubling the reader about them, but the traveller who is interested in the subject may compare two of them in the same window; the one nearer the sea of the two belonging to the little room at the top of the Palace on the Piazzetta Façade, between the Sala del Gran Consiglio and that of the Scrutinio. The seaward jamb of that window is of the first, and the opposite jamb of the second, period of these restorations. These are all the points of separation in date which I could discover by internal evidence. But much more might be made out by any Venetian antiquary whose time permitted him thoroughly to examine any existing documents which allude to or describe the parts of the Palace spoken of

* A print, dated 1585, barbarously inaccurate, as all prints were at that time, but still in some respects to be depended upon, represents all the windows on the façade full of traceries, and the circles above, between them, occupied by quatrefoils.

in the important decrees of 1340, 1342, and 1344; for the first of these decrees speaks of certain "columns looking towards the Canal"* or sea, as then existing, and I presume these columns to have been part of the Ziani Palace, corresponding to the part of that palace on the Piazzetta where were the "red columns" between which Calendario was executed; and a great deal more might be determined by any one who would thoroughly unravel the obscure language of those decrees.

Meantime, in order to complete the evidence respecting the main dates stated in the text, I have collected here such notices of the building of the Ducal Palace as appeared to me of most importance in the various chronicles I examined. I could not give them all in the text, as they repeat each other, and would have been tedious; but they will be interesting to the antiquary, and it is to be especially noted in all of them how the Palazzo *Vecchio* is invariably distinguished, either directly or by implication, from the Palazzo Nuovo. I shall first translate the piece of the Zancarol Chronicle given by Cadorin, which has chiefly misled the Venetian antiquaries. I wish I could put the rich old Italian into old English, but must be content to lose its raciness, as it is necessary that the reader should be fully acquainted with its facts.

"It was decreed that none should dare to propose to the Signory of Venice to ruin the *old* palace and rebuild it new and more richly, and there was a penalty of one thousand ducats against any one who should break it. Then the Doge, wishing to set forward the public good, said to the Signory, . . . that they ought to rebuild the façades of the *old* palace, and that it ought to be restored to do honour to the nation; and so soon as he had done speaking, the Avogadori demanded the penalty from the Doge, for having disobeyed the law; and the Doge with ready mind paid it, remaining in his opinion that the said fabric ought to be built. And so, in the year 1422, on the 20th day of September, it was passed in the Council of the Pregadi that the said new palace should be begun, and the expense should be borne by the Signori del Sal; and so, on the 24th day of March, 1424, it was begun to throw down the *old* palace, and to build it anew."—*Cadorin*, p. 129.

The day of the month, and the council in which the decree was passed, are erroneously given by this Chronicle. Cadorin has printed the words of the decree itself, which passed in the Great Council on the 27th September: and these words are, fortunately, much to our present purpose.

---

* "Lata tanto, quantum est ambulum existens super columnis versus canale respicientibus,"

For, as more than one façade is spoken of in the above extract, the Marchese Selvatico was induced to believe that both the front to the sea and that to the Piazzetta had been destroyed; whereas, the "façades" spoken of are evidently those of the Ziani Palace. For the words of the decree (which are much more trustworthy than those of the Chronicle, even if there were any inconsistency between them) run thus: "Palatium nostrum fabricetur et fiat in forma decora et convenienti, quod respondeat *solemnissimo principio palatii nostri novi.*" Thus the new council chamber and façade to the sea are called the "most venerable beginning of our *new* Palace;" and the rest was ordered to be designed in accordance with these, as was actually the case as far as the Porta della Carta. But the Renaissance architects who thenceforward proceeded with the fabric, broke through the design, and built everything else according to their own humours.

The question may be considered as set at rest by these words of the decree, even without any internal or any farther documentary evidence. But rather for the sake of impressing the facts thoroughly on the reader's mind, than of any additional proof, I shall quote a few more of the best accredited Chronicles.

The passage given by Bettio from the Sivos Chronicle, is a very important parallel with that from the Zancarol above:

"Essendo molto vecchio, e quasi rovinoso el Palazzo sopra la piazza, fo deliberato di far quella parte tutta da novo, et continuarla com' è quella della Sala grande, et cosi il Lunedi 27 Marzo 1424 fu dato principio a ruinare detto Palazzo vecchio dalla parte ch' è verso panateria, cioè della Giustizia, ch' è nelli occhi di sopra le colonne fino alla Chiesa, et fo fatto anco la porta grande, com' è al presente, con la sala che si addimanda la Libraria." *

We have here all the facts told us in so many words: the "old palace" is definitely stated to have been "on the piazza," and it is to be rebuilt "like the part of the great saloon." The very point from which the newer buildings commenced is told us; but here the chronicler has carried his attempt at accuracy too far. The point of junction is, as stated above, at the third pillar beyond the medallion of Venice; and I am much at a loss to understand what could have been the disposition of these three pillars where they joined the Ziani Palace, and how they were connected with the arcade of the inner cortile. But with these difficulties, as they do not bear on the immediate question, it is of no use to trouble the reader.

* Bettio, p. 28.

The next passage I shall give is from a Chronicle in the Marcian Library, bearing title, "Supposta di Zancaruol;" but in which I could not find the passage given by Cadorin from, I believe, a manuscript of this Chronicle at Vienna. There occurs instead of it the following, thus headed :

"Come *la parte nova* del Palazzo fuo hedificata *novamente.*

"El Palazzo novo de Venesia quella parte che xe verso la Chiesia de S. Marcho fuo prexo chel se fesse del 1422 e fosse pagado la spexa per li officiali del sal. E fuo fatto per sovrastante G. Nicolo Barberigo cum provision de ducati X doro al mexe e fuo fabricado e fatto nobelissimo. Come fin ancho di el sta e fuo grande honor a la Signori a de Venesia e a la sua Citta."

This entry, which itself bears no date, but comes between others dated 22nd July and 27th December, is interesting, because it shows the first transition of the idea of *newness*, from the Grand Council Chamber to the part built under Foscari. For when Mocenigo's wishes had been fulfilled, and the old palace of Ziani had been destroyed, and another built in its stead, the Great Council Chamber, which was "the new palace" compared with Ziani's, became "the old palace" compared with Foscari's ; and thus we have, in the body of the above extract, the whole building called "the new palace of Venice;" but in the heading of it, we have "the new *part* of the palace" applied to the part built by Foscari, in contradistinction to the Council Chamber.

The next entry I give is important, because the writing of the MS. in which it occurs, No. 53 in the Correr Museum, shows it to be probably not later than the end of the fifteenth century :

"El palazo nuovo de Venixia zoe quella parte che se sora la piazza verso la giesia di Miss. San Marcho del 1422 fo principiado, el qual fo fato e finito molto belo, chome al presente se vede nobilissimo, et a la fabricha de quello fo deputado Miss. Nicolo Barberigo, soprastante con ducati dieci doro al mexe."

We have here the part built by Foscari distinctly called the Palazzo Nuovo, as opposed to the Great Council Chamber, which had now completely taken the position of the Palazzo Vecchio, and is actually so called by Sansovino. In the copy of the Chronicle of Paolo Morosini, and in the MSS. numbered respectively 57, 59, 74, and 76 in the Correr Museum, the passage above given from No. 53 is variously repeated with slight modifications and curtailments; the entry in the Morosini Chronicle being headed, "Come fu principiato il palazo che guarda sopra la piaza grande di S. Marco," and proceeding in the words, "El Palazo

Nuovo di Venetia, cioe quella partechee sopra la piaza," etc.; the writers being cautious, in all these instances, to *limit their statement* to the part facing the Piazza, that no reader might suppose the Council Chamber to have been built or begun at the same time; though, as long as to the end of the sixteenth century, we find the Council Chamber still included in the expression " Palazzo Nuovo." Thus, in the MS. No. 75 in the Correr Museum, which is about that date, we have " Del 1422, a di 20, Settembre fu preso nel consegio grando de dover *compir* el Palazo Novo e dovesen fare la spessa li officialli del Sal (61, M. 2, B)." And so long as this is the case, the " Palazzo Vecchio " always means the Ziani Palace. Thus, in the next page of this same MS. we have "a di 27 Marzo (1424 by context) fo pncipia a butar zosso, el *Palazzo Vecchio* per refarlo da novo, e poi se he " (and so it is done); and in the MS. No. 81, " Del 1424, fo gittado zoso el *Palazzo Vecchio* per refarlo de nuovo, a di 27 Marzo." But in the time of Sansovino the Ziani Palace was quite forgotten; the Council Chamber was then the *old* palace, and Foscari's part was the new. His account of the " Palazzo Publico " will now be perfectly intelligible; but, as the work itself is easily accessible, I shall not burden the reader with any farther extracts, only noticing that the chequering of the façade with red and white marbles, which he ascribes to Foscari, may or may not be of so late a date, as there is nothing in the style of the work which can be produced as evidence.

2. THEOLOGY OF SPENSER.

The following analysis of the first book of the " Faërie Queen " may be interesting to readers who have been in the habit of reading the noble poem too hastily to connect its parts completely together, and may perhaps induce them to more careful study of the rest of the poem.

The Redcrosse Knight is Holiness,—the " Pietas " of St. Mark's, the " Devotio " of Orcagna,—meaning, I think, in general, Reverence and Godly Fear.

This Virtue, in the opening of the book, has Truth (or Una) at its side, but presently enters the Wandering Wood, and encounters the serpent Error; that is to say, Error in her universal form, the first enemy of Reverence and Holiness; and more especially Error as founded on learning; for when Holiness strangles her,

> " Her vomit *full of bookes and papers was*,
> With loathly frogs and toades, which eyes did lacke."

Having vanquished this first open and palpable form of Error, as

Reverence and Religion must always vanquish it, the Knight encounters Hypocrisy, or Archimagus: Holiness cannot detect Hypocrisy, but believes him, and goes home with him; whereupon, Hypocrisy succeeds in separating Holiness from Truth; and the Knight (Holiness) and Lady (Truth) go forth separately from the house of Archimagus.

Now observe; the moment Godly Fear, or Holiness, is separated from Truth, he meets Infidelity, or the Knight Sans Foy; Infidelity having Falsehood, or Duessa, riding behind him. The instant the Redcrosse Knight is aware of the attack of Infidelity, he

> "Gan fairly couch his speare, and towards ride."

He vanquishes and slays Infidelity; but is deceived by his companion, Falsehood, and takes her for his lady: thus showing the condition of Religion, when, after being attacked by Doubt, and remaining victorious, it is nevertheless seduced, by any form of Falsehood, to pay reverence where it ought not. This, then, is the first fortune of Godly Fear separated from Truth. The poet then returns to Truth, separated from Godly Fear. She is immediately attended by a lion, or Violence, which makes her dreaded wherever she comes; and when she enters the mart of superstition, this Lion tears Kirkrapine in pieces: showing how Truth, separated from Godliness, does indeed put an end to the abuses of superstition, but does so violently and desperately. She then meets again with Hypocrisy, whom she mistakes for her own lord, or Godly Fear, and travels a little way under his guardianship (Hypocrisy thus not unfrequently appearing to defend the Truth), until they are both met by Lawlessness, or the Knight Sans Loy, whom Hypocrisy cannot resist. Lawlessness overthrows Hypocrisy, and seizes upon Truth, first slaying her lion attendant: showing that the first aim of licence is to destroy the force and authority of Truth. Sans Loy then takes Truth captive, and bears her away. Now this Lawlessness is the "unrighteousness," or "adikia," of St. Paul; and his bearing Truth away captive is a type of those "who hold the truth in unrighteousness,"—that is to say, generally, of men who, knowing what is true, make the truth give way to their own purposes, or use it only to forward them, as is the case with so many of the popular leaders of the present day. Una is then delivered from Sans Loy by the satyrs, to show that Nature, in the end, must work out the deliverance of the truth, although, where it has been captive to Lawlessness, that deliverance can only be obtained through Savageness, and a return to barbarism. Una is then taken from among the satyrs by Satyrane, the son of a satyr and a "lady myld, fair Thyamis" (typifying the early steps of renewed civilization, and its rough and hardy character, " nousled up in life and manners wilde "), who, meeting again with Sans Loy, enters instantly into rough and prolonged combat with him : showing how the early organization of a hardy nation must be wrought out through much discouragement from Lawlessness. This contest the poet leaving for the time undecided, returns to trace the adventures of the Redcrosse Knight, or Godly Fear, who, having vanquished Infidelity, presently is led by Falsehood to the house of Pride : thus showing how religion, separated from truth, is first tempted by doubts of God, and then by the pride of life. The description of this house of Pride is one of the most elaborate and noble pieces in the poem ; and here we begin to get at the proposed system of Virtues and Vices. For Pride, as Queen, has six other vices yoked in her chariot ; namely, first, Idleness, then Gluttony, Lust, Avarice, Envy, and Anger, all driven on by " Sathan, with a smarting whip in hand." From these lower vices and their company, Godly Fear, though lodging in the house of Pride, holds aloof ; but he is challenged, and has a hard battle to fight with Sans Joy, the brother of Sans Foy : showing, that though he has conquered Infidelity, and does not give himself up to the allurements of Pride, he is yet exposed, so long as he dwells in her house, to distress of mind and loss of his accustomed rejoicing before God. He, however, having partly conquered Despondency, or Sans Joy, Falsehood goes down to Hades, in order to obtain drugs to maintain the power or life of Despondency ; but, meantime, the Knight leaves the house of Pride : Falsehood pursues and overtakes him, and finds him by a fountain side, of which the waters are

> " Dull and slow,
> And all that drinke thereof do faint and feeble grow."

Of which the meaning is, that Godly Fear, after passing through the house of Pride, is exposed to drowsiness and feebleness of watch ; as, after Peter's boast, came Peter's sleeping, from weakness of the flesh, and then, last of all, Peter's fall. And so it follows, for the Redcrosse Knight, being overcome with faintness by drinking of the fountain, is thereupon attacked by the giant Orgoglio, overcome, and thrown by him into a dungeon. This Orgoglio is Orgueil, or Carnal Pride ; not the pride of life, spiritual and subtle, but the common and vulgar pride in the power of this world : and his throwing the Redcrosse Knight into a dungeon is a type of the captivity of true religion under the temporal power of corrupt churches, more especially of the Church of Rome ; and of its gradually wasting away in unknown places, while Carnal Pride has the pre-eminence over all things. That Spenser means especially the pride of the Papacy, is shown by the 16th stanza of the book; for there the giant Orgoglio is said to have taken Duessa, or Falsehood, for his "deare," and to have set upon her head a triple crown, and endowed her with royal majesty, and made her to ride upon a seven-headed beast.

In the meantime, the dwarf, the attendant of the Redcrosse Knight, takes his arms, and finding Una, tells her of the captivity of her lord. Una, in the midst of her mourning, meets Prince Arthur, in whom, as Spenser himself tells us, is set forth generally Magnificence; but who, as is shown by the choice of the hero's name, is more especially the magnificence, or literally, "great doing," of the kingdom of England. This power of England, going forth with Truth, attacks Orgoglio, or the Pride of Papacy, slays him; strips Duessa, or Falsehood, naked; and liberates the Redcrosse Knight. The magnificent and well-known description of Despair follows, by whom the Redcrosse Knight is hard bested, on account of his past errors and captivity, and is only saved by Truth, who, perceiving him to be still feeble, brings him to the house of Cœlia, called, in the argument of the canto, Holiness, but properly, Heavenly Grace, the mother of the Virtues. Her "three daughters, well upbrought," are Faith, Hope, and Charity. Her porter is Humility; because Humility opens the door of Heavenly Grace. Zeal and Reverence are her chamberlains, introducing the new-comers to her presence; her groom, or servant, is Obedience; and her physician, Patience. Under the commands of Charity, the matron Mercy rules over her hospital, under whose care the Knight is healed of his sickness; and it is to be especially noticed how much importance Spenser, though never ceasing to chastise all hypocrisies and mere observances of form, attaches to true and faithful *penance* in effecting this cure. Having his strength restored to him, the Knight is trusted to the guidance of Mercy, who, leading him forth by a narrow and thorny way, first instructs him in the seven works of Mercy, and then leads him to the hill of Heavenly Contemplation; whence, having a sight of the New Jerusalem, as Christian of the Delectable Mountains, he goes forth to the final victory over Satan, the old serpent, with which the book closes.

3. AUSTRIAN GOVERNMENT IN ITALY.

I cannot close these volumes without expressing my astonishment and regret at the facility with which the English allow themselves to be misled by any representations, however openly groundless or ridiculous,

proceeding from the Italian Liberal party, respecting the present administration of the Austrian Government. I do not choose here to enter into
any political discussion, or express any political opinion; but it is due to
justice to state the simple facts which came under my notice during my
residence in Italy. I was living at Venice through two entire winters,
and in the habit of familiar association both with Italians and Austrians,
my own antiquarian vocations rendering such association possible without
exciting the distrust of either party. During this whole period, I never
once was able to ascertain, from any liberal Italian, that he had a single
definite ground of complaint against the Government. There was much
general grumbling and vague discontent : but I never was able to bring
one of them to the point, or to discover what it was that they wanted,
or in what way they felt themselves injured ; nor did I ever myself witness
an instance of oppression on the part of the Government, though several
of much kindness and consideration. The indignation of those of my own
countrymen and countrywomen whom I happened to see during their
sojourn in Venice was always vivid, but by no means large in its grounds.
English ladies on their first arrival invariably began the conversation
with the same remark : " What a dreadful thing it was to be ground under
the iron heel of despotism !" Upon closer inquiries it always appeared
that being "ground under the heel of despotism" was a poetical expression for being asked for one's passport at San Juliano, and required to
fetch it from San Lorenzo, full a mile and a quarter distant. In like
manner, travellers, after two or three days' residence in the city, used to
return with pitiful lamentations over "the misery of the Italian people."
Upon inquiring what instances they had met with of this misery, it invariably turned out that their gondoliers, after being paid three times
their proper fare, had asked for something to drink, and had attributed
the fact of their being thirsty to the Austrian Government. The misery
of the Italians consists in having three festa days a week, and doing in
their days of exertion about one-fourth as much work as an English
labourer.

There is, indeed, much true distress occasioned by the measures which
the Government is sometimes compelled to take in order to repress
sedition; but the blame of this lies with those whose occupation is the
excitement of sedition. So also there is much grievous harm done to
works of art by the occupation of the country by so large an army; but
for the mode in which that army is quartered, the Italian municipalities
are answerable, not the Austrians. Whenever I was shocked by finding,
as above-mentioned at Milan, a cloister, or a palace, occupied by soldiery,

I always discovered, on investigation, that the place had been given by the municipality; and that, beyond requiring that lodging for a certain number of men should be found in such and such a quarter of the town, the Austrians had nothing to do with the matter. This does not, however, make the mischief less: and it is strange, if we think of it, to see Italy, with all her precious works of art, made a continual battle-field; as if no other place for settling their disputes could be found by the European powers, than where every random shot may destroy what a king's ransom cannot restore.* It is exactly as if the tumults in Paris could be settled no otherwise than by fighting them out in the Gallery of the Louvre.

4. DATE OF THE PALACES OF THE BYZANTINE RENAISSANCE.

In the sixth article of the Appendix to the first volume, the question of the date of the Casa Dario and Casa Trevisan was deferred until I could obtain from my friend Mr. Rawdon Brown, to whom the former palace once belònged, some more distinct data respecting this subject than I possessed myself.

.Speaking first of the Casa Dario, he says : " Fontana dates it from about the year 1450, and considers it the earliest specimen of the architecture founded by Pietro Lombardo, and followed by his sons, Tullio and Antonio. In a Sanuto autograph miscellany, purchased by me long ago, and which I gave to St. Mark's Library, are two letters from Giovanni Dario, dated 10th and 11th July, 1485, in the neighbourhood of Adrianople; where the Turkish camp found itself, and Bajazet II. received presents from the Soldan of Egypt, from the Schah of the Indies (query Grand Mogul), and from the King of Hungary : of these matters, Dario's letters give many curious details. Then, in the *printed* Malipiero Annals, page 136 (which err, I think, by a year), the Secretary Dario's negotiations at the Porte are alluded to ; and in date of 1484 he is stated to have returned to Venice, having quarrelled with the Venetian bailiff at Constantinople : the annalist adds, that ' Giovanni Dario was a native of Candia, and that the Republic

---

* In the bombardment of Venice in 1848, hardly a single palace escaped without three or four balls through its roof : three came into the Scuola di San Rocco, tearing their way through the pictures of Tintoret, of which the ragged fragments were still hanging from the ceiling in 1851 ; and the shells had reached to within a hundred yards of St. Mark's Church itself, at the time of the capitulation.

was so well satisfied with him for having concluded peace with Bajazet, that he received, as a gift from his country, an estate at Noventa, in the Paduan territory, worth 1,500 ducats, and 600 ducats in cash for the dower of one of his daughters.' These largesses probably enabled him to build his house about the year 1486, and are doubtless hinted at in the inscription, which I restored A.D. 1837 ; *it had no date*, and ran thus, URBIS . GENIO . JOANNES . DARIVS.   In the Venetian history of Paolo Morosini, page 594, it is also mentioned that Giovanni Dario was, moreover, the Secretary who concluded the peace between Mahomet, the conqueror of Constantinople, and Venice, A.D. 1478 : but, unless he built his house by proxy, that date has nothing to do with it ; and, in my mind, the fact of the present, and the inscription, warrant one's dating it 1486, and not 1450.

"The Trevisan-Cappello House, in Canonica, was once the property (A.D. 1578) of a Venetian dame fond of cray-fish, according to a letter of hers in the archives, whereby she thanks one of her lovers for some which he had sent her from Treviso to Florence, of which she was then Grand Duchess. Her name has perhaps found its way into the English annuals. Did you ever hear of Bianca Cappello ? She bought that house of the Trevisana family, by whom Selva (in Cicognara) and Fontana (following Selva) say it was ordered of the Lombardi, at the commencement of the sixteenth century : but the inscription on its façade, thus,

SOLI	HONOR. ET
DEO	GLORIA,

reminding one both of the Dario House, and of the words NON NOBIS DOMINE inscribed on the façade of the Loredano Vendramin Palace at S. Marcuola (now the property of the Duchess of Berri), of which Selva found proof in the Vendramin archives that it was commenced by Sante Lombardo, A.D. 1481, is in favour of its being classed among the works of the fifteenth century."

5. RENAISSANCE SIDE OF DUCAL PALACE.

In passing along the Rio del Palazzo the traveller ought especially to observe the base of the Renaissance building, formed by alternately depressed and raised pyramids, the depressed portions being *casts* of the projecting ones, which are truncated on the summits. The work cannot be called rustication, for it is cut as sharply and delicately as a piece of ivory, but it thoroughly answers the end which rustication proposes, and misses: it gives the base of the building a look of crystalline hardness, actually resembling, and that very closely, the appearance presented by the fracture of a piece of cap quartz; while yet the light and shade of its alternate recesses and projections are so varied as to produce the utmost possible degree of delight to the eye attainable by a geometrical pattern so simple. Yet, with all this high merit, it is not a base which could be brought into general use. Its brilliancy and piquancy are here set off with exquisite skill by its opposition to mouldings, in the upper part of the building, of an almost effeminate delicacy, and its complexity is rendered delightful by its contrast with the ruder bases of the other buildings of the city; but it would look meagre if it were employed to sustain bolder masses above, and would become wearisome if the eye were once thoroughly familiarized with it by repetition.

6. CHARACTER OF THE DOGE MICHELE MOROSINI.

The following extracts from the letter of Count Charles Morosini, above mentioned, appear to set the question at rest.

" It is our unhappy destiny that, during the glory of the Venetian republic, no one took the care to leave us a faithful and conscientious history: but I hardly know whether this misfortune should be laid to the charge of the historians themselves, or of those commentators who have destroyed their trustworthiness by new accounts of things, invented by themselves. As for the poor Morosini, we may perhaps save his honour by assembling a conclave of our historians, in order to receive their united sentence; for, in this case, he would have the absolute majority on his side, nearly all the authors bearing testimony to his love for his country and to the magnanimity of his heart. I must tell you that the history of Daru is not looked upon with esteem by well-informed men; and it is said that he seems to have no other object in view than to obscure the glory of all actions. I know not on what authority the English writer depends; but he has, perhaps, merely copied the statement of Daru. . . . . . I have consulted an ancient and authentic MS. belonging to the Venieri family, a MS. well known, and certainly better worthy of confidence than Daru's History, and it says nothing of M. Morosini but that he was elected Doge to the delight and joy of all men. Neither do the Savina or Dolfin Chronicles say a word of the shameful speculation ; and our best informed men say that the reproach cast by some historians against the Doge perhaps arose from a mistaken interpretation of the words pronounced by him, and reported by Marin Sanuto, that 'the speculation would sooner or later have been advantageous to the country.'   But this single consideration is enough to induce us to form a favourable conclusion respecting the honour of this man, namely, that he was not elected Doge until after he had been entrusted with many honourable embassies to the Genoese and Carrarese, as well as to the King of Hungary and Amadeus of Savoy ; and if in these embassies he had not shown himself a true lover of his country, the Republic not only would not again have entrusted him with offices so honourable, but would never have rewarded him with the dignity of Doge, therein to succeed such a man as Andrea Contarini ; and the war of Chioggia, during which it is said that he tripled his fortune by speculations, took place during the reign of Contarini, 1379, 1380, while Morosini was absent on foreign embassies."

7. MODERN EDUCATION.

The following fragmentary notes on this subject have been set down at different times.   I have been accidentally prevented from arranging them properly for publication, but there are one or two truths in them which it is better to express insufficiently than not at all.

By a large body of the people of England and of Europe a man is called educated if he can write Latin verses and construe a Greek chorus.   By some few more enlightened persons it is confessed that the construction of hexameters is not in itself an important end of human existence ; but they say, that the general discipline which a course of classical reading gives to the intellectual powers is the final object of our scholastical institutions.

But it seems to me there is no small error even in this last and more philosophical theory.   I believe that what it is most honourable to know, it is also most profitable to learn ; and that the science which it is the highest power to possess, it is also the best exercise to acquire.

And if this be so, the question as to what should be the materiel of education, becomes singularly simplified.   It might be matter of dispute what processes have the greatest effect in developing the intellect ; but it can hardly be disputed what facts it is most advisable that a man entering into life should accurately know.

I believe, in brief, that he ought to know three things :

First, Where he is.

Secondly, Where he is going.

Thirdly, What he had best do under those circumstances.

First, Where he is.—That is to say, what sort of a world he has got into; how large it is; what kind of creatures live in it, and how; what it is made of, and what may be made of it.

Secondly, Where he is going.—That is to say, what chances or reports there are of any other world besides this; what seems to be the nature of that other world; and whether, for information respecting it, he had better consult the Bible, Koran, or Council of Trent.

Thirdly, What he had best do under those circumstances.—That is to say, what kind of faculties he possesses; what are the present state and wants of mankind; what is his place in society; and what are the readiest means in his power of attaining happiness and diffusing it. The man who knows these things, and who has had his will so subdued in the learning them, that he is ready to do what he knows he ought, I should call educated; and the man who knows them not,—uneducated, though he could talk all the tongues of Babel.

Our present European system of so-called education ignores, or despises, not one, nor the other, but all the three, of these great branches of human knowledge.

First, It despises Natural History.—Until within the last year or two, the instruction in the physical sciences given at Oxford consisted of a course of twelve or fourteen lectures on the Elements of Mechanics or Pneumatics, and permission to ride out to Shotover with the Professor of Geology. I do not know the specialties of the system pursued in the academies of the Continent; but their practical result is, that unless a man's natural instincts urge him to the pursuit of the physical sciences too strongly to be resisted, he enters into life utterly ignorant of them. I cannot, within my present limits, even so much as count the various directions in which this ignorance does evil. But the main mischief of it is, that it leaves the greater number of men without the natural food which God intended for their intellects. For one man who is fitted for the study of words, fifty are fitted for the study of things, and were intended to have a perpetual, simple, and religious delight in watching the processes, or admiring the creatures, of the natural universe. Deprived of this source of pleasure, nothing is left to them but ambition or dissipation; and the vices of the upper classes of Europe are, I believe, chiefly to be attributed to this single cause.

Secondly, It despises Religion.—I do not say it despises "Theology,"

that is to say, *Talk* about God.   But it despises " Religion ;" that is to say,
the " binding" or training to God's service.   There is much talk and much
teaching in all our academies, of which the effect is not to bind, but to
loosen, the elements of religious faith.   Of the ten or twelve young men
who, at Oxford, were my especial friends, who sat with me under the same
lectures on Divinity, or were punished with me for missing lecture by
being sent to evening prayers,* four are now zealous Romanists,—a large
average out of twelve ; and while thus our own universities profess to
teach Protestantism, and do not, the universities on the Continent profess to teach Romanism, and do not,—sending forth only rebels and
infidels.   During long residence on the Continent, I do not remember
meeting with above two or three young men who either believed in
revelation, or had the grace to hesitate in the assertion of their infidelity.

Whence, it seems to me, we may gather one of two things : either
that there is nothing in any European form of religion so reasonable or
ascertained, as that it can be taught securely to our youth, or fastened in
their minds by any rivets of proof which they shall not be able to loosen
the moment they begin to think ; or else, that no means are taken to
train them in such demonstrable creeds.

It seems to me the duty of a rational nation to ascertain (and to be
at some pains in the matter) which of these suppositions is true ; and, if
indeed no proof can be given of any supernatural fact, or Divine doctrine, stronger than a youth just out of his teens can overthrow in the
first stirrings of serious thought, to confess this boldly ; to get rid of
the expense of an Establishment, and the hypocrisy of a Liturgy ; to
exhibit its cathedrals as curious memorials of a bygone superstition,
and, abandoning all thoughts of the next world, to set itself to make
the best it can of this.

But if, on the other hand, there *does* exist any evidence by which the
probability of certain religious facts may be shown, as clearly, even, as the
probabilities of things not absolutely ascertained in astronomical or geological science, let this evidence be set before all our youth so distinctly,
and the facts for which it appears inculcated upon them so steadily,
that although it may be possible for the evil conduct of after life to efface,
or for its earnest and protracted meditation to modify, the impressions
of early years, it may not be possible for our young men, the instant
they emerge from their academies, to scatter themselves like a flock of

---

* A *Mohammedan* youth is punished, I believe, for such misdemeanours, by being *kept
away* from prayers.

wildfowl risen out of a marsh, and drift away on every irregular wind of heresy and apostasy.

Lastly, Our system of European education despises Politics.—That is to say, the science of the relations and duties of men to each other. One would imagine, indeed, by a glance at the state of the world, that there was no such science. And, indeed, it is one still in its infancy.

It implies, in its full sense, the knowledge of the operations of the virtues and vices of men upon themselves and society; the understanding of the ranks and offices of their intellectual and bodily powers in their various adaptations to art, science, and industry; the understanding of the proper offices of art, science, and labour themselves, as well as of the foundations of jurisprudence, and broad principles of commerce; all this being coupled with practical knowledge of the present state and wants of mankind.

What, it will be said, and is all this to be taught to schoolboys? No; but the first elements of it, all that are necessary to be known by an individual in order to his acting wisely in any station of life, might be taught, not only to every schoolboy, but to every peasant. The impossibility of equality among men; the good which arises from their inequality; the compensating circumstances in different states and fortunes; the honourableness of every man who is worthily filling his appointed place in society, however humble; the proper relations of poor and rich, governor and governed; the nature of wealth, and mode of its circulation; the difference between productive and unproductive labour; the relation of the products of the mind and hand; the true value of works of the higher arts, and the possible amount of their production; the meaning of " Civilization," its advantages and dangers; the meaning of the term " Refinement;" the possibilities of possessing refinement in a low station, and of losing it in a high one; and, above all, the significance of almost every act of a man's daily life, in its ultimate operation upon himself and others;—all this might be, and ought to be, taught to every boy in the kingdom, so completely, that it should be just as impossible to introduce an absurd or licentious doctrine among our adult population, as a new version of the multiplication table. Nor am I altogether without hope that some day it may enter into the heads of the tutors of our schools to try whether it is not as easy to make an Eton boy's mind as sensitive to falseness in policy, as his ear is at present to falseness in prosody.

I know that this is much to hope. That English ministers of religion should ever come to desire rather to make a youth acquainted with the powers of Nature and of God, than with the powers of Greek particles;

that they should ever think it more useful to show him how the great universe rolls upon its course in heaven, than how the syllables are fitted in a tragic metre ; that they should hold it more advisable for him to be fixed in the principles of religion than in those of syntax ; or, finally, that they should ever come to apprehend that a youth likely to go straight out of college into parliament, might not unadvisably know as much of the Peninsular as of the Peloponnesian War, and be as well acquainted with the state of modern Italy as of old Etruria ;—all this, however unreasonably, I *do* hope, and mean to work for. For though I have not yet abandoned all expectation of a better world than this, I believe this in which we live is not so good as it might be. I know there are many people who suppose French revolutions, Italian insurrections, Caffre wars, and such other scenic effects of modern policy, to be among the normal conditions of humanity. I know there are many who think the atmosphere of rapine, rebellion, and misery which wraps the lower orders of Europe more closely every day, is as natural a phenomenon as a hot summer. But God forbid ! There are ills which flesh is heir to, and troubles to which man is born ; but the troubles which he is born to are as sparks which fly *upward*, not as flames burning to the nethermost Hell. The Poor we must have with us always, and sorrow is inseparable from any hour of life ; but we may make their poverty such as shall inherit the earth, and the sorrow such as shall be hallowed by the hand of the Comforter with everlasting comfort. We *can*, if we will but shake off this lethargy and dreaming that is upon us, and take the pains to think and act like men, we can, I say, make kingdoms to be like well-governed households, in which, indeed, while no care or kindness can prevent occasional heart-burnings, nor any foresight or piety anticipate all the vicissitudes of fortune, or avert every stroke of calamity, yet the unity of their affection and fellowship remains unbroken, and their distress is neither embittered by division, prolonged by imprudence, nor darkened by dishonour.

    *   *   *   *   *   *   *   *

The great leading error of modern times is the mistaking erudition for education. I call it the leading error, for I believe that, with little difficulty, nearly every other might be shown to have root in it ; and, most assuredly, the worst that are fallen into on the subject of art.

Education then, briefly, is the leading human souls to what is best, and making what is best out of them ; and these two objects are always attainable together, and by the same means ; the training which makes men happiest in themselves also makes them most serviceable to others. True education, then, has respect, first to the ends which are proposable to the man, or attainable by him; and, secondly, to the material of which the man is made. So far as it is able, it chooses the end according to the material: but it cannot always choose the end, for the position of many persons in life is fixed by necessity; still less can it choose the material; and, therefore, all it can do is to fit the one to the other as wisely as may be.

But the first point to be understood is that the material is as various as the ends; that not only one man is unlike another, but *every* man is essentially different from *every* other, so that no training, no forming, nor informing, will ever make two persons alike in thought or in power. Among all men, whether of the upper or lower orders, the differences are eternal and irreconcilable, between one individual and another, born under absolutely the same circumstances. One man is made of agate, another of oak; one of slate, another of clay. The education of the first is polishing; of the second, seasoning; of the third, rending; of the fourth, moulding. It is of no use to season the agate; it is vain to try to polish the slate; but both are fitted, by the qualities they possess, for services in which they may be honoured.

Now the cry for the education of the lower classes, which is heard every day more widely and loudly, is a wise and a sacred cry, provided it be extended into one for the education of *all* classes, with definite respect to the work each man has to do, and the substance of which he is made. But it is a foolish and vain cry, if it be understood, as in the plurality of cases it is meant to be, for the expression of mere craving after knowledge, irrespective of the simple purposes of the life that now is, and blessings of that which is to come.

One great fallacy into which men are apt to fall when they are reasoning on this subject is: that light, as such, is always good; and darkness, as such, always evil. Far from it. Light untempered would be annihilation. It is good to them that sit in darkness and in the shadow of death; but, to those that faint in the wilderness, so also is the shadow of the great rock in a weary land. If the sunshine is good, so also the cloud of the latter rain. Light is only beautiful, only available for life, when it is tempered with shadow; pure light is fearful, and unendurable by humanity. And it is not less ridiculous to say that the light, as such, is good in itself, than to say that the darkness is good in itself. Both are rendered safe, healthy, and useful by the other; the night by the day, the day by the night; and we could just as easily live without the dawn as without the sunset, so long as we are human. Of the celestial city we are told there shall be " no night there," and then we shall know even as also we are known : but the night and the mystery have both their service here ; and our business is not to strive to turn the night into day, but to be sure that we are as they that watch for the morning.

Therefore, in the education either of lower or upper classes, it matters not the least how much or how little they know, provided they know just what will fit them to do their work, and to be happy in it. What the sum or the nature of their knowledge ought to be at a given time or in a given case, is a totally different question : the main thing to be understood is, that a man is not educated, in any sense whatsoever, because he can read Latin, or write English, or can behave well in a drawing-room ; but that he is only educated if he is happy, busy, beneficent, and effective in the world ; that millions of peasants are therefore at this moment better educated than most of those who call themselves gentlemen ; and that the means taken to "educate" the lower classes in any other sense may very often be productive of a precisely opposite result.

Observe, I do not say, nor do I believe, that the lower classes ought not to be better educated, in millions of ways, than they are. I believe *every man in a Christian kingdom ought to be equally well educated.* But I would have it education to purpose ; stern, practical, irresistible, in moral habits, in bodily strength and beauty, in all faculties of mind capable of being developed under the circumstances of the individual, and especially in the technical knowledge of his own business ; but yet, infinitely various in its effort, directed to make one youth humble, and another confident ; to tranquillize this mind, to put some spark of ambition into that ; now to urge, and now to restrain : and in the doing of all this, considering knowledge as one only out of myriads of means in its hands, or myriads of gifts at its disposal ; and giving it or withholding it as a good husbandman waters his garden, giving the full shower only to the thirsty plants, and at times when they are thirsty ; whereas at present we pour it upon the heads of our youth as the snow falls on the Alps, on one and another alike, till they can bear no more, and then take honour to ourselves because here and there a river descends from their crests into the valleys, not observing that we have made the loaded hills themselves barren for ever.

Finally, I hold it for indisputable, that the first duty of a state is to see that every child born therein shall be well housed, clothed, fed, and educated, till it attain years of discretion. But in order to the effecting this, the government must have an authority over the people of which we now do not so much as dream ; and I cannot in this place pursue the subject farther.

8. EARLY VENETIAN MARRIAGES.

Galliciolli, lib. ii. § 1757, insinuates a doubt of the general custom, saying, "It would be more reasonable to suppose that only twelve maidens were married in public on St. Mark's Day;" and Sandi also speaks of twelve only. All evidence, however, is clearly in favour of the popular tradition; the most curious fact connected with the subject being the mention, by Herodotus, of the mode of marriage practised among the Illyrian "Veneti" of his time, who presented their maidens for marriage on one day in each year; and, with the price paid for those who were beautiful, gave dowries to those who had no personal attractions.

It is very curious to find the traces of this custom existing, though in a softened form, in Christian times. Still, I admit that there is little confidence to be placed in the mere concurrence of the Venetian Chroniclers, who, for the most part, copied from each other: but the best and most complete account I have read is that quoted by Galliciolli from the "Matricola de' Casseleri," written in 1449; and, in that account, the words are quite unmistakable. "It was anciently the custom of Venice, that *all the brides* (novizze) of Venice, when they married, should be married by the bishop, in the Church of S. Pietro di Castello, on St. Mark's Day, which is the 31st of January." Rogers quotes Navagiero to the same effect; and Sansovino is more explicit still. "It was the custom to contract marriages openly; and when the deliberations were completed, the damsels assembled themselves in St. Pietro di Castello, for the feast of St. Mary, in February."

9. CHARACTER OF THE VENETIAN ARISTOCRACY.

The following noble answer of a Venetian ambassador, Giustiniani, on the occasion of an insult offered him at the court of Henry the Eighth, is as illustrative of the dignity which there yet remained in the character and thoughts of the Venetian noble, as descriptive, in few words, of the early faith and deeds of his nation. He writes thus to the Doge, from London, on the 15th of April, 1516:

"By my last, in date of the 30th ult., I informed you that the countenances of some of these lords evinced neither friendship nor good-will, and that much language had been used to me of a nature bordering not merely on arrogance, but even on outrage; and not having specified this in the foregoing letters, I think fit now to mention it in detail. Finding myself at the court, and talking familiarly about other matters, two lay lords, great personages in this kingdom, inquired of me 'whence it came that your Excellency was of such slippery faith, now favouring one party and then the other ?' Although these words ought to have irritated me, I answered them with all discretion, 'that you did keep, and ever had kept, your faith; the maintenance of which has placed you in great trouble, and subjected you to wars of longer duration than you would otherwise have experienced; descending to particulars in justification of your Sublimity.' Whereupon one of them replied, '*Isti Veneti sunt piscatores.*'* Marvellous was the command I then had over myself in not giving vent to expressions which might have proved injurious to your Signory; and with extreme moderation I rejoined, 'that had he been at Venice, and seen our Senate, and the Venetian nobility, he perhaps would not speak thus; and more-over, were he well read in our history, both concerning the origin of our city, and the grandeur of your Excellency's feats, neither the one nor the other would seem to him those of fishermen; yet,' said I, 'did fishermen found the Christian faith, and we have been those fishermen who defended it against the forces of the Infidel, our fishing-boats being galleys and ships, our hooks the treasure of St. Mark, and our bait the life-blood of our citizens, who died for the Christian faith.' "

I take this most interesting passage from a volume of despatches addressed from London to the Signory of Venice, by the ambassador Giustiniani, during the years 1516—1519; despatches not only full of matters of historical interest, but of the most delightful everyday description of all that went on at the English court. They were translated by Mr. Brown from the original letters, and will, I believe, soon be published, and I hope also, read and enjoyed: for I cannot close these volumes without expressing a conviction, which has long been forcing itself upon my mind, that *restored* history is of little more value than restored painting or architecture; that the only history worth reading is that written at the time of which it treats, the history of what was done and seen, heard out of the mouths of the men who did and saw. One fresh draught of such history is worth more than a thousand volumes of abstracts, and reasonings, and suppositions, and theories; and I believe that, as we get wiser, we shall take little trouble about the history of nations who have left no distinct records of themselves, but spend our time only in the examination of the faithful documents which, in any period of the world, have been left, either in the form of art or literature, portraying the scenes, or recording the events, which in those days were actually passing before the eyes of men.

---

* "Those Venetians are fishermen,"

V.

Byzantine Bases.

J. Ruskin.

R. P. Cuff.

10. FINAL APPENDIX.

The statements respecting the dates of Venetian buildings, made throughout the preceding pages, are founded, as above stated, on careful and personal examination of all the mouldings, or other features available as evidence, of every palace of importance in the city. Three parts, at least, of the time occupied in the completion of the work have been necessarily devoted to the collection of these evidences, of which it would be quite useless to lay the mass before the reader ; but of which the leading points must be succinctly stated, in order to show the nature of my authority for any of the conclusions expressed in the text.

I have therefore collected in the plates which illustrate this article of the Appendix, for the examination of any reader who may be interested by them, as many examples of the evidence-bearing details as are sufficient for the proof required, especially including all the exceptional forms ; so that the reader may rest assured that if I had been able to lay before him all the evidence in my possession, it would have been still more conclusive than the portion now submitted to him.

We must examine in succession the Bases, Doorways and Jambs, Capitals, Archivolts, Cornices, and Tracery Bars, of Venetian architecture.

I. BASES.

The principal points we have to notice are the similarity and simplicity of the Byzantine bases in general, and the distinction between those of Torcello and Murano, and of St. Mark's, as tending to prove the earlier dates attributed in the text to the island churches. I have sufficiently illustrated the forms of the Gothic bases in Plates X., XI., and XIII. of the first volume, so that I here note chiefly the Byzantine or Romanesque ones, adding two Gothic forms for the sake of comparison.

The most characteristic examples, then, are collected in Plate V. opposite ; namely :

1, 2, 3, 4. In the upper gallery of apse of Murano.

5. Lower shafts of apse.   Murano.

6. Casa Falier.

7. Small shafts of panels.   Casa Farsetti.

8. Great shafts and plinth.   Casa Farsetti.

PLATE V. Vol. III.

9. Great lower shafts.   Fondaco de' Turchi.

10. Ducal Palace, upper arcade.

11. General late Gothic form.

12. Tomb of Dogaressa Vital Michele, in St. Mark's atrium.

Now, observe, first, the enormous difference in style between the bases 1 to 5, and the rest in the upper row, that is to say, between the bases of Murano and the twelfth and thirteenth century bases of Venice ; and, secondly, the difference between the bases 16 to 20 and the rest in the lower row, that is to say, between the bases of Torcello (with those of St. Mark's which belong to the nave, and which may therefore be supposed to be part of the earlier church) and the later ones of the St. Mark's façade.

Secondly, Note the fellowship between 5 and 6, one of the evidences of the early date of the Casa Falier.

Thirdly, Observe the slurring of the upper roll into the cavetto, in 13, 14, and 15, and the consequent relationship established between three most important buildings, the Rio Foscari House, Terraced House, and Madonnetta House.

Fourthly, Byzantine bases, if they have an incision between the upper roll and cavetto, are very apt to approach the form of fig. 23, in which the upper roll is cut out of the flat block, and the ledge beneath it is sloping. Compare Nos. 7, 8, 9, 21, 22, 23, 24, 25, 26. On the other hand, the later Gothic base, 11, has always its upper roll well developed, and, generally, the fillet between it and the cavetto vertical. The sloping fillet is indeed found down to late periods ; and the vertical fillet, as in No. 12, in Byzantine ones ; but still, when a base has such a sloping fillet and peculiarly graceful sweeping cavetto as those of No. 10, looking as if they would run into one line with each other, it is strong presumptive evidence of its belonging to an early, rather than a late period.

The base 12 is the boldest example I could find of the exceptional form in early times ; but observe in this, that the upper roll is larger than the lower. This is *never* the case in late Gothic, where the proportion is always as in fig. 11. Observe that in Nos. 8 and 9 the upper rolls are

at least as large as the lower, an important evidence of the dates of the
Casa Farsetti and Fondaco de' Turchi.

Lastly, Note the peculiarly steep profile of No. 22, with reference to
what is said of this base in Vol. II., Appendix 9.

II. DOORWAYS AND JAMBS.

The entrances to St. Mark's consist, as above mentioned, of great circular or ogee porches; underneath which the real open entrances, in
which the valves of the bronze doors play, are square-headed.

The mouldings of the jambs of these doors are highly curious, and
the most characteristic are therefore repre-
sented in one view. The outsides of the
jambs are lowest.

a. Northern lateral door.
b. First northern door of the façade.
c. Second door of the façade.
d. Fourth door of the façade.
e. Central door of the façade.

Fig. 1.

a   *b*   *e*   *d*   *c*

I wish the reader especially to note the arbitrary character of the curves and incisions; all evidently being drawn by hand, none being segments of circles, none like another, none influenced by any visible law. I do not give these mouldings as beautiful; they are, for the most part, very poor in effect, but they are singularly characteristic of the free work of the time.

The kind of door to which these mouldings belong, is shown, with the other groups of doors, in Plate XIV., Vol. II., fig. 6 *a*. Then 6 *b*, 6 *c*, 6 *d* represent the groups of doors in which the Byzantine influence remained energetic, admitting slowly the forms of the pointed Gothic; 7 *a*, with the gable above, is the intermediate group between the Byzantine and Gothic schools; 7 *b*, 7 *c*, 7 *d*, 7 *e* are the advanced guards of the Gothic and Lombardic invasions, representative of a large number of thirteenth century arcades and doors. Observe that 6 *d* is shown to be of a late school by its finial, and 6 *e* of the latest school by its finial, complete ogee arch (instead of round or pointed), and abandonment of the lintel.

These examples, with the exception of 6 *a*, which is a general form, are all actually existing doors; namely:

6 *b*. In the Fondamenta Venier, near St. Maria della Salute.

6 *c*. In the Calle delle Botteri, between the Rialto and San Cassan.

6 *d*. Main door of San Gregorio.

6 *e*. Door of a palace in Rio San Paternian.

7 *a*. Door of a small courtyard near house of Marco Polo.

7 *b*. Arcade in narrow canal, at the side of Casa Barbaro.

7 *c*. At the turn of the canal, close to the Ponte dell' Angelo.

7 *d*. In Rio San Paternian (a ruinous house).

7 *e*. At the turn of the canal on which the Sotto Portico della Stua opens, near San Zaccaria.

If the reader will take a magnifying glass to the figure 6 *d*, he will see that its square ornaments, of which, in the real door, each contains a rose, diminish to the apex of the arch; a very interesting and characteristic circumstance, showing the subtle feeling of the Gothic builders. They must needs diminish the ornamentation, in order to sympathize with the delicacy of the point of the arch. The magnifying glass will also show the Bondumieri shield in No. 7 *d*, and the Leze shield in No. 7 *e*, both introduced on the keystones in the grand early manner. The mouldings of these various doors will be noticed under the head "Archivolt."

Now, throughout the city we find a number of doors resembling the square doors of St. Mark, and occurring with rare exceptions either in buildings of the Byzantine period, or imbedded in restored houses; never in a single instance forming a connected portion of any late building;

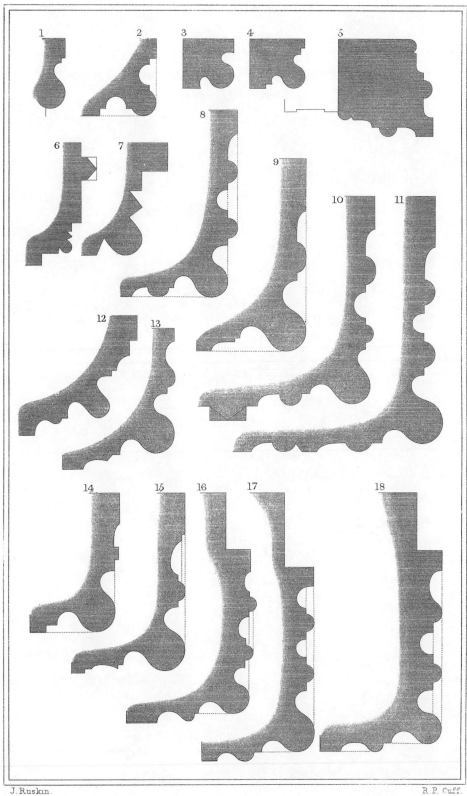

VI

J. Ruskin.

R. P. Cuff.

Byzantine Jambs.

and they therefore furnish a most important piece of evidence, wherever they are part of the original structure of a *Gothic* building, that such building is one of the advanced guards of the Gothic school, and belongs to its earliest period.

On Plate VI., opposite, are assembled all the important examples I could find in Venice of these mouldings. The reader will see at a glance their peculiar character, and unmistakable likeness to each other. The following are the references:

1. Door in Calle Mocenigo.
2. Angle of tomb of Dogaressa Vital Michele.
3. Door in Sotto Portico, St. Apollonia (near Ponte di Canonica).
4. Door in Calle della Verona (another like it is close by).
5. Angle of Tomb of Doge Marino Morosini.
6, 7. Door in Calle Mocenigo.
8. Door in Campo S. Margherita.

PLATE VI.
Vol. III.

9. Door at Traghetto San Samuele, on south side of Grand Canal.
10. Door at Ponte St. Toma.
11. Great door of Church of Servi.
12. In Calle della Chiesa, Campo San Filippo e Giacomo.
13. Door of house in Calle di Rimedio (page 254, Vol. II.).
14. Door in Fondaco de' Turchi.
15. Door in Fondamenta Malcanton, near Campo S. Margherita.
16. Door in south side of Canna Reggio.
17, 18. Doors in Sotto Portico dei Squellini.

The principal points to be noted in these mouldings are their curious differences of level, as marked by the dotted lines, more especially in 14, 15, 16, and the systematic projection of the outer or lower mouldings in 16, 17, 18. Then, as points of evidence, observe that 1 is the jamb and 6 the archivolt (7 the angle on a larger scale) of the brick door given in my folio work from Ramo di rimpetto Mocenigo, one of the evidences of the early date of that door; 8 is the jamb of the door in Campo Santa Margherita (also given in my folio work), fixing the early date of that also; 10 is from a Gothic door opening off the Ponte St. Toma; and 11 is also from a Gothic building. All the rest are from Byzantine work, or from ruins. The angle of the tomb of Marino Morosini (5) is given for comparison only.

The doors with the mouldings 17, 18, are from the two ends of a small dark passage, called the Sotto Portico dei Squellini, opening near

Ponte Cappello, on the Rio Marin : 14 is the outside one, arranged as usual, and at *a*, in the rough stone, are places for the staples of the door valve ; 15, at the other end of the passage, opening into the little Corte dei Squellini, is set with the part *a* outwards, it also having places for hinges ; but it is curious that the rich moulding should be set in towards the dark passage, though natural that the doors should both open one way.

The next plate, VII., will show the principal characters of the Gothic jambs, and the total difference between them and the Byzantine ones. Two more Byzantine forms, 1 and 2, are given here for the sake of comparison ; then 3, 4, and 5 are the common profiles of simple jambs of doors in the Gothic period ; 6 is one of the jambs of the Frari windows, continuous into the archivolt, and meeting the traceries, where the line is set upon it at the extremity of its main slope ; 7 and 8 are jambs of the Ducal palace windows, in which the great semicircle is the half shaft which sustains the traceries, and the rest of the profile is continuous in the archivolt : 17, 18, and 19 are the principal piers of the Ducal Palace ; and 20, from St. Fermo of Verona, is put with them in order to show the step of transition from the Byzantine form 2 to the Gothic chamfer, which is hardly represented at Venice. The other profiles on the plate are all late Gothic, given to show the gradual increase of complexity without any gain of power. The open lines in 12, 14, 16, etc., are the parts of the profile cut into flowers or cable mouldings ; and so much incised as to show the constant outline of the cavetto or curve beneath them. The following are the references :

1. Door in house of Marco Polo.
2. Old door in a restored church of St. Cassan.
3, 4, 5. Common jambs of Gothic doors.
6. Frari windows.
7, 8. Ducal Palace windows.
9. Casa Priuli, great entrance.
10. San Stefano, great door.
11. San Gregorio, door opening to the water.
12. Lateral door, Frari.
13. Door of Campo San Zaccaria.
14. Madonna dell' Orto.
15. San Gregorio, door in the façade.
16. Great lateral door, Frari.
17. Pilaster at Vine angle, Ducal Palace.
18. Pier, inner cortile, Ducal Palace.
19. Pier, under the medallion of Venice, on the Piazzetta façade of the Ducal Palace.

PLATE VII.
Vol. III.

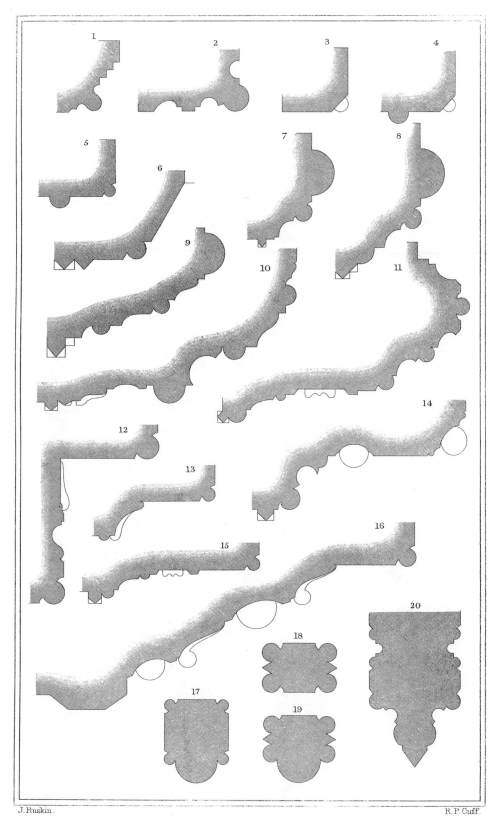

VII

J.Ruskin.

R.P.Cuff.

Gothic Jambs

III. CAPITALS.

I shall here notice the various facts I have omitted in the text of the work.

First, with respect to the Byzantine capitals represented in Plate VII., Vol. II. (p. 131), I omitted to notice that figs. 6 and 7 represent two sides of the same capital at Murano (though one is necessarily drawn on a smaller scale than the other). Fig. 7 is the side turned to the light, and fig. 6 to the shade, the inner part, which is quite concealed, not being touched at all.

We have here a conclusive proof that these capitals were cut for their place in the apse; therefore I have always considered them as tests of Venetian workmanship, and, on the strength of that proof, have occasionally spoken of capitals as of true Venetian work, which M. Lazari supposes to be of the Lower Empire. No. 11, from St. Mark's, was not above noticed. The way in which the cross is gradually left in deeper relief as the sides slope inwards, and away from it, is highly picturesque and curious.

No. 9 has been reduced from a larger drawing, and some of the life and character of the curves lost in consequence. It is chiefly given to show the irregular and fearless freedom of the Byzantine designers, no two parts of the foliage being correspondent; in the original it is of white marble, the ground being coloured blue.

Plate X., Vol. II. (p. 137), represents the four principal orders of Venetian capitals in their greatest simplicity, and the profiles of the most interesting examples of each. The figures 1 and 4 are the two great concave and convex groups; and 2 and 3 the transitional. Above each type of form I have put also an example of the group of flowers which represent it in nature: fig. 1 has a lily; fig. 2 a variety of the Tulipa sylvestris; figs. 3 and 4 forms of the magnolia. I prepared this plate in the early spring, when I could not get any other examples,* or I would rather have had two different species for figs. 3 and 4; but the half-open magnolia will answer the purpose, showing the beauty of the triple curvature in the sides.

I do not say that the forms of the capitals are actually taken from

---

* I am afraid that the kind friend, Lady Trevelyan, who helped me to finish this plate, will not like to be thanked here; but I cannot let her send into Devonshire for magnolias, and draw them for me, *without* thanking her.

flowers, though assuredly so in some instances, and partially so in the decoration of nearly all. But they were designed by men of pure and natural feeling for beauty, who therefore instinctively adopted the forms represented, which are afterwards proved to be beautiful by their frequent occurrence in common flowers.

The convex forms, 3 and 4, are put lowest in the plate only because they are heaviest; they are the earliest in date, and have already been enough examined.

I have added a plate to this volume (Plate XII.), which should have appeared in illustration of the fifth chapter of Vol. II., but was not finished in time. It represents the central capital and two of the lateral ones of the Fondaco de' Turchi, the central one drawn very large in order to show the excessive simplicity of its chiselling, together with the care and sharpness of it, each leaf being expressed by a series of sharp furrows and ridges. Some slight errors in the large tracings from which the engraving was made have, however, occasioned a loss of spring in the curves, and the little fig. 4 of Plate X., Vol. II., gives a truer idea of the distant effect of the capital.

The profiles given in Plate X., Vol. II., are the following:

1. *a.* Main capitals, upper arcade, Madonnetta House.
   b. Main capitals, upper arcade, Casa Falier.
   c. Lateral capitals, upper arcade, Fondaco de' Turchi.
   d. Small pillars of St. Mark's pulpit.
   e. Casa Farsetti.
   f. Inner capitals of arcade of Ducal Palace.
   g. Plinth of the house* at Apostoli.
   h. Main capitals of house at Apostoli.
   i. Main capitals, upper arcade, Fondaco de' Turchi.

PLATE X. 2. *a.* Lower arcade, Fondaco de' Turchi.
Vol. II.   *b, c.* Lower pillars, house at Apostoli.
   d. San Simeon Grande.
   e. Restored house on Grand Canal. Three of the old arches left.
   f. Upper arcade, Ducal Palace.
   g. Windows of third order, central shaft, Ducal Palace.
   h. Windows of third order, lateral shaft, Ducal Palace.
   i. Ducal Palace, main shafts.
   k. Piazzetta shafts.

* That is, the house in the parish of the Apostoli, on the Grand Canal, noticed in page 253, Vol. II.; and see also Venetian Index, under head "Apostoli."

    3. *a.* St. Mark's nave.

       b, c. Lily capitals, St. Mark's.

    4. *a.* Fondaco de' Turchi, central shaft, upper arcade.

PLATE X.   *b.* Murano, upper arcade.

Vol. II.   *c.* Murano, lower arcade.

       d. Tomb of St. Isidore.

       e. General late Gothic profile.

The last two sections are convex in effect, though not in reality ; the bulging lines being carved into bold flower-work.

The capitals belonging to the groups 1 and 2, in the Byzantine times, have already been illustrated in Plate VIII., Vol. II. ; we have yet to trace their succession in the Gothic times. This is done in Plate II. of this volume, which we will now examine carefully. The following are the capitals represented in that plate :

    1. Small shafts of St. Mark's pulpit.

    2. From the transitional house in the Calle di Rimedio (conf. p. 259, Vol. II.).

    3. General simplest form of the middle Gothic capital.

    4. Nave of San Giacomo de Lorio.

    5. Casa Falier.

    6. Early Gothic house in Campo Sta. M^a· Mater Domini.

PLATE II.   7. House at the Apostoli.

Vol. III.   8. Piazzetta shafts.

    9. Ducal Palace, upper arcade.

    10. Palace of Marco Querini.

    11. Fondaco de' Turchi.

    12. Gothic palaces in Campo San Polo.

    13. Windows of fourth order, Plate XVI., Vol. II.

    14. Nave of Church of San Stefano.

    15. Late Gothic palace at the Miracoli.

The two lateral columns form a consecutive series : the central column is a group of exceptional character, running parallel with both. We will take the lateral ones first. 1. Capital of pulpit of St. Mark's (representative of the simplest concave forms of the Byzantine period). Look back to Plate VIII., Vol. II., and observe that while all the forms in that plate are contemporaneous, we are now going to follow a series *consecutive* in time, which begins from figure 1, either in that plate or in this ; that is to say, with the simplest possible condition to be found at the time ;

and which proceeds to develop itself into gradually increasing richness, while the *already rich* capitals of the old school die at its side. In the forms 14 and 15 (Plate VIII.) the Byzantine school expired; but from the Byzantine simple capital (1, Plate II. above) which was co-existent with them, sprang another hardy race of capitals, whose succession we have now to trace.

The form 1, Plate II., is evidently the simplest conceivable condition of the truncated capital, long ago represented generally at p. 105, Vol. I., being only rounded a little on its side to fit it to the shaft. The next step was to place a leaf beneath each of the truncations (fig. 4, Plate II., San Giacomo de Lorio), the end of the leaf curling over at the top in a somewhat formal spiral, partly connected with the traditional volute of the Corinthian capital. The sides are then enriched by the addition of some ornament, as a shield (fig. 7) or rose (fig. 10), and we have the formed capital of the early Gothic. Fig. 10, being from the palace of Marco Querini, is certainly not later than the middle of the thirteenth century (see Vol. II., p. 256), and fig. 7 is, I believe, of the same date; it is one of the bearing capitals of the lower story of the palace at the Apostoli, and is remarkably fine in the treatment of its angle leaves, which are not deeply under-cut, but show their magnificent sweeping under surface all the way down, not as a leaf surface, but treated like the gorget of a helmet, with a curved line across it like that where the gorget meets the mail. I never saw anything finer in simple design. Fig. 10 is given chiefly as a certification of date, and to show the treatment of the capitals of this school on a small scale. Observe the more expansive head in proportion to the diameter of the shaft, the leaves being drawn from the angles, as if gathered in the hand, till their edges meet; and compare the rule given in Vol. I., Chap. IX., § XIV. The capitals of the remarkable house, of which a portion is represented in Fig. XXXI., p. 256, Vol. II., are most curious and pure examples of this condition; with experimental trefoils, roses, and leaves introduced between their volutes. When compared with those of the Querini Palace, they form one of the most important evidences of the date of the building.

Fig. 13. One of the bearing capitals, already drawn on a small scale in the windows represented in Plate XVI., Vol. II.

Now, observe, the capital of the form of fig. 10 appeared sufficient to the Venetians for all ordinary purposes; and they used it in common windows to the latest Gothic periods, but yet with certain differences which at once show the lateness of work. In the first place, the rose, which at first was flat and quatrefoiled, becomes, after some experiments, a round ball dividing into three leaves, closely resembling our English ball-flower, and probably derived from it; and, in other cases, forming a bold projecting bud in various degrees of contraction or expansion. In the second place, the extremities of the angle leaves are wrought into rich flowing lobes, and bent back so as to lap against their own breasts; showing lateness of date in exact proportion to the looseness of curvature. Fig. 3 represents the general aspect of these later capitals, which may be conveniently called the rose capitals of Venice; two are seen on service, in Plate VIII., Vol. I., showing comparatively early date by the experimental form of the six-foiled rose. But for elaborate edifices this form was not sufficiently rich; and there was felt to be something awkward in the junction of the leaves at the bottom. Therefore, four other shorter leaves were added at the sides, as in fig. 13, Plate II., and as generally represented in Plate X., Vol. II., fig. 1. This was a good and noble step, taken very early in the thirteenth century; and all the best Venetian capitals were thenceforth of this form. Those which followed, and rested in the common rose type, were languid and unfortunate: I do not know a single good example of them after the first half of the thirteenth century.

But the form reached in fig. 13 was quickly felt to be of great value and power. One would have thought it might have been taken straight from the Corinthian type; but it is clearly the work of men who were making experiments for themselves. For instance, in the central capital of Fig. XXXI., p. 256, Vol. II., there is a trial condition of it, with the intermediate leaf set behind those at the angles (the reader had better take a magnifying glass to this woodcut; it will show the character of the capitals better). Two other experimental forms occur in ·the Casa Cicogna (p. 265, Vol. II.), and supply one of the evidences which fix the date of that palace. But the form soon was determined as in fig. 13, and then means were sought of recommending it by farther decoration.

The leaves which are used in fig. 13, it will be observed, have lost the Corinthian volute, and are now pure and plain leaves, such as were used in the Lombardic Gothic of the early thirteenth century all over Italy. Now in a round-arched gateway at Verona, certainly not later than 1300, the pointed leaves of this pure form are used in one portion of the mouldings, and in another are enriched by having their surfaces carved each into a beautiful ribbed and pointed leaf. The capital, fig. 6, Plate II., is nothing more than fig. 13 so enriched; and the two conditions are quite contemporary, fig. 13 being from a beautiful series of fourth-order windows in Campo Sta. Ma. Mater Domini already drawn in my folio work,

Fig. 13 is representative of the richest conditions of Gothic capital which existed at the close of the thirteenth century. The builder of the Ducal Palace amplified them into the form of fig. 9, but varying the leafage in disposition and division of lobes in every capital; and the workmen trained under him executed many noble capitals for the Gothic palaces of the early fourteenth century, of which fig. 12, from a palace in the Campo St. Polo, is one of the most beautiful examples. In figs. 9 and 12 the reader sees the Venetian Gothic capital in its noblest development. The next step was to such forms as fig. 15, which is generally characteristic of the late fourteenth and early fifteenth century Gothic, and of which I hope the reader will at once perceive the exaggeration and corruption.

This capital is from a palace near the Miracoli, and is remarkable for the delicate, though corrupt, ornament on its abacus, which is precisely the same as that on the pillars of the screen of St. Mark's. That screen is a monument of very great value, for it shows the entire corruption of the Gothic power, and the style of the later palaces accurately and completely defined in all its parts, and is dated 1380; thus at once furnishing us with a limited date, which throws all the noble work of the Early Ducal Palace, and all that is like it in Venice, thoroughly back into the middle of the fourteenth century at the latest.

Fig. 2 is the simplest condition of the capital universally employed in the windows of the second order, noticed above, Vol. II., pp. 253, 254, as belonging to a style of great importance in the transitional architecture of Venice. Observe, that in all the capitals given in the lateral columns in Plate II., the points of the leaves *turn over*. But in this central group they lie *flat* against the angle of the capital, and form a peculiarly light and lovely succession of forms, occurring only in their purity in the windows of the second order, and in some important monuments connected with them.

In fig. 2 the leaf at the angle is cut, exactly in the manner of an Egyptian bas-relief, *into* the stone, with a raised edge round it, and a raised rib up the centre; and this mode of execution, seen also in figs. 4 and 7, is one of the collateral evidences of early date. But in figs. 5 and 8, where more elaborate effect was required, the leaf is thrown out boldly with an even edge from the surface of the capital, and enriched on its own surface: and as the treatment of fig. 2 corresponds with that of fig. 4, so that of fig. 5 corresponds with that of fig. 6; 2 and 5 having the upright leaf, 4 and 6 the bending leaves; but all contemporary.

Fig. 5 is the central capital of the windows of Casa Falier, drawn in Plate XV., Vol. II.; and one of the leaves set on its angles is drawn larger at fig. 7, Plate XX., Vol. II. It has no rib, but a sharp raised ridge down its centre; and its lobes, of which the reader will observe the curious form,—round in the middle one, truncated in the sides,—are wrought with a precision and care which I have hardly ever seen equalled : but of this more presently.

The next figure (8, Plate II.) is the most important capital of the whole transitional period, that employed on the two columns of the Piazzetta. These pillars are said to have been *raised* in the close of the twelfth century, but I cannot find even the most meagre account of their bases, capitals, or, which seems to me most wonderful, of that noble winged lion, one of the grandest things produced by mediæval art, which all men admire, and none can draw. I have never yet seen a faithful represen-tation of his firm, fierce, and fiery strength. I believe that both he and the capital which bears him are late thirteenth century work. I have not been up to the lion, and cannot answer for it; but if it be not thirteenth century work, it is as good ; and respecting the capitals, there can be small question. They are of exactly the date of the oldest tombs, bearing crosses, outside of St. John and Paul ; and are associated with all the other work of the transitional period, from 1250 to 1300 (the bases of these pillars, representing the trades of Venice, ought, by-the-bye, to have been mentioned as among the best early efforts of Venetian grotesque) ; and, besides, their abaci are formed by four reduplications of the dentilled mouldings of St. Mark's, which never occur after the year 1300.

Nothing can be more beautiful or original than the adaptation of these broad bearing abaci; but as they have nothing to do with the capital itself, and could not easily be brought into the space, they are omitted in Plate II., where fig. 8 shows the bell of the capital only. Its profile is curiously subtle,—apparently concave everywhere, but in reality concave (all the way down) only on the angles, and slightly convex at the sides (the profile through the side being 2 *k*, Plate X., Vol. II.) ; in this subtlety of curvature, as well as in the simple cross, showing the influence of early times.

The leaf on the angle, of which more presently, is fig. 5, Plate XX., Vol. II.

Connected with this school of transitional capitals we find a form in the later Gothic, such as fig. 14, from the Church of San Stefano ; but which appears in part derived from an old and rich Byzantine type, of which fig. 11, from the Fondaco de' Turchi, is a characteristic example.

I must now take the reader one step farther, and ask him to examine, finally, the treatment of the leaves, down to the cutting of their most minute lobes, in the series of capitals of which we have hitherto only sketched the general forms.

In all capitals with nodding leaves, such as 6 and 9 in Plate II., the real form of the leaf is not to be seen, except in perspective; but, in order to render the comparison more easy, I have in Plate XX., Vol. II., opened all the leaves out, as if they were to be dried in a herbarium, only leaving the furrows and sinuosities of surface, but laying the outside contour nearly flat upon the page, except for a particular reason in figs. 2, 10, 11, and 15.

I shall first, as usual, give the references, and then note the points of interest.

PLATE XX.
Vol. II.

1, 2, 3. Fondaco de' Turchi, upper arcade.
4. Greek pillars brought from St. Jean d'Acre.
5. Piazzetta shafts.
6. Madonnetta House.
7. Càsa Falier.
8. Palace near St. Eustachio.
9. Tombs, outside of St. John and Paul.
10. Tomb of Giovanni Soranzo.
11. Tomb of Andrea Dandolo.
12, 13, 14. Ducal Palace.

N.B.—The upper row, 1 to 4, is Byzantine, the next transitional, the last two Gothic.

Fig. 1. The leaf of the capital No. 6, Plate VIII., Vol. II. Each lobe of the leaf has a sharp furrow up to its point, from its root.

Fig. 2. The leaf of the capital on the right hand, at the top of Plate XII. in this volume. The lobes worked in the same manner, with deep black drill holes between their points.

Fig. 3. One of the leaves of fig. 14, Plate VIII., Vol. II., fully unfolded. The lobes worked in the same manner, but left shallow, so as not to destroy the breadth of light; the central line being drawn by drill holes, and the interstices between the lobes cut black and deep.

Fig. 4. Leaf with flower; pure Byzantine work, showing whence the treatment of all the other leaves has been derived.

Fig. 6. For the sake of symmetry, this is put in the centre: it is the earliest of the three in this row; taken from the Madonnetta House, where the capitals have leaves both at their sides and angles. The tall angle leaf, with its two lateral ones, is given in the plate; and there is a remarkable distinction in the mode of workmanship of these leaves, which, though found in a palace of the Byzantine period, is indicative of a tendency to transition ; namely, that the sharp furrow is now drawn *only to the central lobe* of each division of the leaf, and the rest of the surface of the leaf is left nearly flat, a slight concavity only marking the division of the extremities.   At the base of these leaves they are perfectly flat, only cut by the sharp and narrow furrow, as an elevated tableland is by ravines.

Fig. 5. A more advanced condition ; the fold at the recess, between each division of the leaf, carefully expressed, and the concave or depressed portions of the extremities marked more deeply, as well as the central furrow, and the rib added in the centre.

Fig. 7. A contemporary, but more finished form ; the sharp furrows becoming softer, and the whole leaf more flexible.

Fig. 8. An exquisite form of the same period, but showing still more advanced naturalism, from. a very early group of third-order windows, near the Church of St. Eustachio on the Grand Canal.

Fig. 9. Of the same time, from a small capital of an angle shaft of the sarcophagi at the *side* of St. John and Paul, in the little square which is adorned by the Colleone statue.   This leaf is very quaint and pretty in giving its midmost lateral divisions only two lobes each, instead of the usual three or four.

Fig. 10. Leaf employed in the cornice of the tomb of the Doge Giovanni Soranzo, who died in 1312.   It nods over, and has three ribs on its upper surface ; thus giving us the completed ideal form of the leaf, but its execution is still very archaic and severe.

Now the next example, fig. 11, is from the tomb of the Doge Andrea Dandolo, and therefore executed between 1354 and 1360 ; and this leaf shows the Gothic naturalism and refinement of curvature fully developed. In this forty years' interval, then, the principal advance of Gothic sculpture is to be placed.

I had prepared a complete series of examples, showing this advance, and the various ways in which the separations of the ribs, a most characteristic feature, are more and more delicately and scientifically treated, from the beginning to the middle of the fourteenth century ; but I feared that no general reader would care to follow me into these minutiæ, and have cancelled this portion of the work, at least for the present, the main point being, that the reader should feel the full extent of the change, which he can hardly fail to do in looking from fig. 10 to figs. 11 and 12.   I believe that fig. 12 is the earlier of the two ; and it is assuredly the finer, having all the elasticity and simplicity of the earliest forms, with perfect flexibility added.   In fig. 11 there is a perilous element beginning to develop itself in one feature, namely, the extremities of the leaves, which, instead of merely nodding over, now curl completely round into a kind of ball. This occurs early, and in the finest Gothic work, especially in cornices and other running mouldings : but it is a fatal symptom, a beginning of the intemperance of the later Gothic, and it was followed out with singular avidity; the ball of coiled leafage increasing in size and complexity, and at last becoming the principal feature of the work; the light striking on its vigorous projection, as in fig. 14. Nearly all the Renaissance Gothic of Venice depends upon these balls for effect, a late capital being generally composed merely of an upper and lower range of leaves terminating in this manner.

It is very singular and notable how, in this loss of *temperance*, there is loss of *life*. For truly healthy and living leaves do not bind themselves into knots at the extremities. They bend, and wave, and nod, but never curl. It is in disease or in death, by blight, or frost, or poison only, that leaves in general assume this ingathered form. It is the flame of autumn that has shrivelled them, or the web of the caterpillar that has bound them : and thus the last forms of the Venetian leafage set forth the fate of the Venetian pride ; and, in their utmost luxuriance and abandonment, perish as if eaten of worms.

And now, by glancing back to Plate X., Vol. II., the reader will see in a moment the kind of evidence which is found of the date of capitals in their profiles merely. Observe, we have seen that the treatment of the leaves in the Madonnetta House seemed " indicative of a tendency to transition." Note their profile, 1 *a*, and its close correspondence with 1 *h*, which is actually of a transitional capital from the upper arcade of second-order windows in the Apostoli Palace ; yet both shown to be very close to the Byzantine period, if not belonging to it, by their fellowship with the profile *i*, from the Fondaco de' Turchi. Then note the close correspondence of all the other profiles in that line, which belong to the concave capitals or plinths of the Byzantine palaces, and note their composition, the abacus being, in idea, merely an echo or reduplication of the capital itself; as seen in perfect simplicity in the profile *f*, which is a roll under a *tall* concave curve forming the bell of the capital, with a roll and *short* concave curve for its abacus. This peculiar abacus is an unfailing test of early date ; and our finding this simple profile used for the Ducal Palace (*f*), is strongly confirmatory of all our former conclusions.

Then the next row, 2, are the Byzantine and early Gothic semi-convex curves, in their pure forms, having no roll below ; but often with a roll added, as at *f*, and in certain early Gothic conditions curiously fused into it, with a cavetto between, as *b*, *c*, *d*. But the more archaic form is at *f*

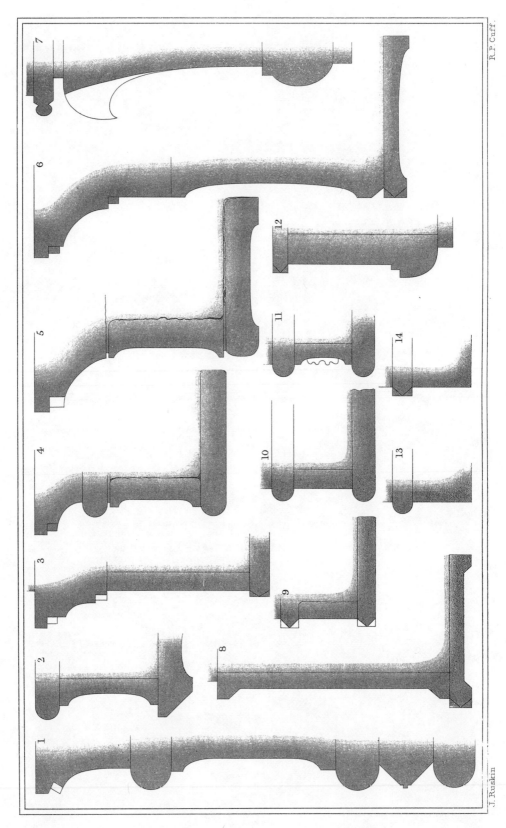

VIII

J. Ruskin

R.P. Cuff.

Byzantine Archivolts.

and k; and as these two profiles are from the Ducal Palace and Piazzetta shafts, they join again with the rest of the evidence of their early date. The profiles i and k are both most beautiful; i is that of the great capitals of the Ducal Palace, and the small profiles between it and k are the varieties used on the fillet at its base. The profile i should have had leaves springing from it, as 1 h has, only more boldly, but there was no room for them.

The reader cannot fail to discern at a glance the fellowship of the whole series of profiles, 2 a to k, nor can he but with equal ease observe a marked difference in 4 d and 4 e from any others in the plate; the bulging outlines of leafage being indicative of the luxuriant and flowing masses, no longer expressible with a simple line, but to be considered only as confined within it, of the later Gothic. Now d is a dated pro-file from the tomb of St. Isidore, 1355, which by its dog-tooth abacus and heavy leafage distinguishes itself from all the other profiles, and therefore throws them back into the first half of the century. But, observe, it still retains the noble swelling root. This character soon after vanishes; and, in 1380, the profile e, at once heavy, feeble, and ungraceful, with a meagre and valueless abacus hardly discernible, is characteristic of all the capitals of Venice.

Note, finally, this contraction of the abacus. Compare 4 c, which is the earliest form in the plate, from Murano, with 4 e, which is the latest. The other profiles show the gradual process of change; only observe, in 3 a the abacus is not drawn; it is so bold that it would not come into the plate without reducing the bell curve to too small a scale.

So much for the evidence derivable from the capitals; we have next to examine that of the archivolts or arch mouldings.

IV. ARCHIVOLTS.

In Plate VIII., opposite, are arranged in one view all the conditions of Byzantine archivolt employed in Venice, on a large scale. It will be seen in an instant that there can be no mistaking the manner of their masonry. The soffit of the arch is the horizontal line at the bottom of all these profiles, and each of them (except 13, 14) is composed of two slabs of marble, one for the soffit, another for the face of the arch; the one on the soffit is worked on the edge into a roll (fig. 10) or dentil (fig. 9), and the one on the face is bordered on the other side by another piece let edgeways into the wall, and also worked into a roll or dentil: in the richer archivolts a cornice is added to this roll, as in figs. 1

and 4, or takes its place, as in figs. 1, 3, 5, and 6; and in such richer examples the facestone, and often the soffit, are sculptured, the sculpture being cut into their surfaces, as indicated in fig. 11.   The concavities cut in the facestones of 1, 2, 4, 5, 6, are all indicative of sculpture in effect like that of Fig. XXVI., p. 251, Vol. II., of which archivolt fig. 5 here is the actual profile.   The following are the references to the whole:

    1. Rio Foscari House.
    2. Terraced House, entrance door.
    3. Small porticos of St. Mark's, external arches.
    4. Arch on the canal at Ponte St. Toma.
    5. Arch of Corte del Remer.

PLATE VIII.   6. Great outermost archivolt of central door, St. Mark's.
Vol. III.   7. Inner archivolt of southern porch of St. Mark's façade.
    8. Inner archivolt of central entrance, St. Mark's.
    9. Fondaco de' Turchi, main arcade.
    10. Byzantine restored house on Grand Canal, lower arcade.
    11. Terraced House, upper arcade.
    12. Inner archivolt of northern porch of façade, St. Mark's.
    13 and 14.   Transitional forms.

There is little to be noted respecting these forms, except that, in fig. 1, the two lower rolls, with the angular projections between, represent the fall of the mouldings of two proximate arches on the abacus of the bearing shaft; their two cornices meeting each other, and being gradually narrowed into the little angular intermediate piece, their sculptures being slurred into the contracted space, a curious proof of the earliness of the work.   The real archivolt moulding is the same as fig. 4 *c c*, including only the midmost of the three rolls in fig. 1.

It will be noticed that 2, 5, 6, and 8 are sculptured on the soffits as well as the faces; 9 is the common profile of arches decorated only with coloured marble, the facestone being coloured, the soffit white.   The effect of such a moulding is seen in the small windows at the right hand of Fig. XXVI., p. 251, Vol. II.

The reader will now see that there is but little difficulty in identifying Byzantine work, the archivolt mouldings being so similar among themselves, and so unlike any others.   We have next to examine the Gothic forms.

Figs. 13 and 14 in Plate VIII. represent the first brick mouldings of the transitional period, occurring in such instances as Fig. XXIII. or Fig. XXXIII., Vol. II. (the soffit stone of the Byzantine mouldings being taken away), and this profile, translated into solid stone, forms the almost universal moulding of the windows of the second order.   These

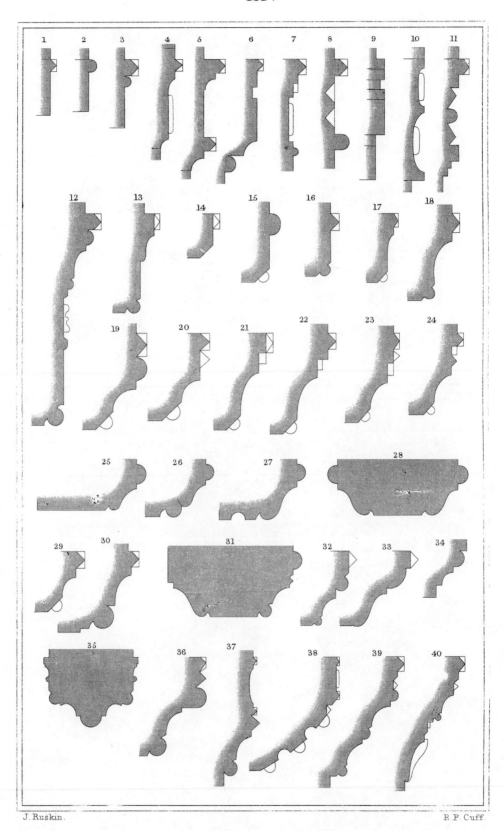

Gothic Archivolts.

two brick mouldings are repeated, for the sake of comparison, at the top of Plate IX. opposite; and the upper range of mouldings which they commence, in that plate, are the brick mouldings of Venice in the early Gothic period. All the forms below are in stone; and the moulding 2, translated into stone, forms the universal archivolt of the early pointed arches of Venice, and windows of second and third orders. The moulding 1 is much rarer, and used for the most part in doors only.

The reader will see at once the resemblance of character in the various flat brick mouldings, 3 to 11. They belong to such arches as 1 and 2 in Plate XVII., Vol. II.; or *6 b, 6 c*, in Plate XIV., Vol. II., 7 and 8 being actually the mouldings of those two doors; the whole group being perfectly defined, and separate from all the other Gothic work in Venice, and clearly the result of an effort to imitate, in brickwork, the effect of the flat sculptured archivolts of the Byzantine times. (See Vol. II. Chap. VII. § xxxvii.)

Then comes the group 14 to 18 in stone, derived from the mouldings 1 and 2; first by truncation, 14; then by beading the truncated angle, 15, 16. The occurrence of the profile 16 in the three beautiful windows represented in the uppermost figure of Plate XVIII., Vol. I., renders that group of peculiar interest, and is strong evidence of its antiquity. Then a cavetto is added, 17; first shallow and then deeper, 18, which is the common archivolt moulding of the central Gothic door and window; but, in the windows of the early fourth order, this moulding is complicated by various additions of dog-tooth mouldings under the dentil, as in 20; or the *gabled* dentil (see fig. 20, Plate IX., p. 260, Vol. I.), as fig. 21; or both, as figs. 23, 24. All these varieties expire in the advanced period, and the established moulding for windows is 29. The intermediate group, 25 to 28, I found only in the high windows of the third order in the Ducal Palace, or in the Chapter-house of the Frari, or in the arcades of the Ducal Palace; the great outside lower arcade of the Ducal Palace has the profile 31, the left-hand side being the innermost.

Now observe, all these archivolts, without exception, assume that the spectator looks from the outside only: none are complete on both sides; they are essentially *window* mouldings, and have no resemblance to those of our perfect Gothic arches prepared for traceries. If they were all completely drawn in the plate, they should be as fig. 25, having a great depth of wall behind the mouldings, but it was useless to represent this in every case. The Ducal Palace begins to show mouldings on both sides, 28, 31; and 35 is a *complete* arch moulding from the apse of the Frari. That moulding, though so perfectly developed, is earlier than the Ducal Palace, and, with other features of the building, indicates the

completeness of the Gothic system, which made the architect of t
Ducal Palace found his work principally upon that church.

The other examples in this plate show the various modes of combin
tion employed in richer archivolts.   The triple change of slope in 38
very curious.   The references are as follows:

1. Transitional to the second order.

2. Common second order.

3. Brick, at Corte del Forno, round arch.

4. Door at San Giovanni Grisostomo.

5. Door at Sotto Portico della Stua.

6. Door in Campo St. Luca, of rich brickwork.

7. Round door at Fondamenta Venier.

8. Pointed door.   Fig. 6 *c*, Plate XIV., Vol. II.

9. Great pointed arch, Salizzada San Lio.

10. Round door near Fondaco de' Turchi.

11. Door with Lion, at Ponte della Corona.

12. San Gregorio, façade.

13. St. John and Paul, nave.

PLATE IX.   14. Rare early fourth order, at San Cassan.

Vol. III.   15. General early Gothic archivolt.

16. Same, from door in Rio San G. Grisostomo.

17. Casa Vittura.

18. Casa Sagredo, unique thirds.   Page 257, Vol. II.

19. Murano Palace, unique fourths.*

20. Pointed door of Four-Evangelist House.†

21. Keystone door in Campo St. M. Formosa.

22. Rare fourths, at St. Pantaleon.

23. Rare fourths, Casa Papadopoli.

24. Rare fourths, Chess house.‡

25. Thirds of Frari Cloister.

26. Great pointed arch of Frari Cloister.

27. Unique thirds, Ducal Palace.

28. Inner cortile, pointed arches, Ducal Palace.

29. Common fourth and fifth order archivolt.

* Close to the bridge over the main channel through Murano is a massive four-squ
Gothic palace, containing some curious traceries, and many *unique* transitional forms
window, among which these windows of the fourth order occur, with a roll within th
dentil band.

† Thus, for the sake of convenience, we may generally call the palace with the emble
of the Evangelists on its spandrils, p. 265, Vol. II.

‡ The house with chequers like a chess-board on its spandrils, given in my folio work.

X.

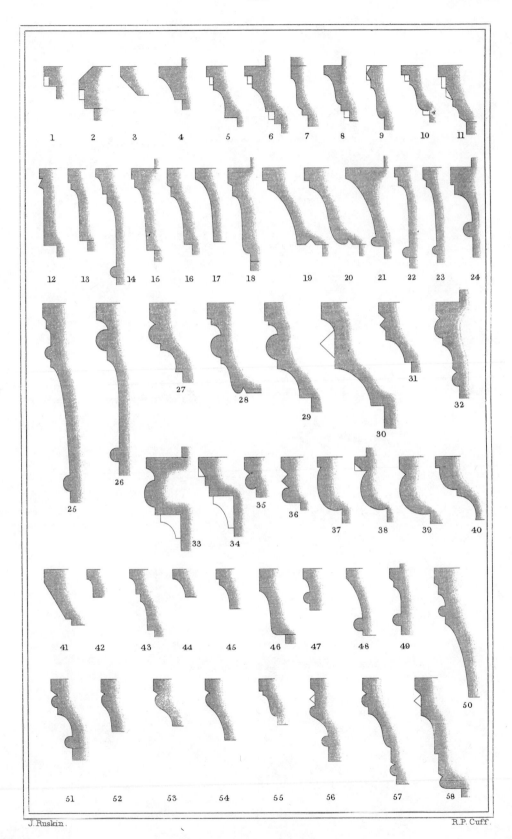

J. Ruskin.

R.P. Cuff.

Cornices and Abaci.

30. Unique thirds, Ducal Palace.

31. Ducal Palace, lower arcade.

32. Casa Priuli, arches in the inner court.

33. Circle above the central window, Ducal Palace.

34. Murano apse.

PLATE IX.   35. Acute-pointed arch, Frari.

Vol. III.   36. Door of Accademia delle belle Arti.

37. Door in Calle Tiossi, near Four-Evangelist House.

38. Door in Campo San Polo.

39. Door of palace at Ponte Marcello.

40. Door of a palace close to the Church of the Miracoli.

V. CORNICES.

Plate X. represents, in one view, the cornices or string-courses of Venice, and the abaci of its capitals, early and late; these two features being inseparably connected, as explained at p. 113, Vol. I.

The evidence given by these mouldings is exceedingly clear. The two upper lines in the Plate, 1—11, 12—24, are all plinths from Byzantine buildings. The reader will at once observe their unmistakable resemblances. The row 41 to 50 are contemporary abaci of capitals; 52, 53, 54, 56, are examples of late Gothic abaci; and observe, especially, these are all rounded at the *top* of the cavetto, but the Byzantine abaci are rounded, if at all, at the *bottom* of the cavetto (see 7, 8, 9, 10, 20, 28, 46). Consider what a valuable test of date this is, in any disputable building.

Again, compare 28, 29, one from St. Mark's, the other from the Ducal Palace, and observe the close resemblance, giving further evidence of early date in the palace.

25 and 50 are drawn to the same scale. The former is the wall-cornice, the latter the abacus of the great shafts, in the Casa Loredan; the one passing into the other, as seen in Fig. XXVIII., p. 113, Vol. I. It is curious to watch the change in proportion, while the moulding, all but the lower roll, remains the same.

The following are the references:

1. Common plinth of St. Mark's.

2. Plinth above lily capitals, St. Mark's.

PLATE X.   3, 4. Plinths in early surface Gothic.

Vol. III.   5. Plinth of door in Campo St. Luca.

6. Plinth of treasury door, St. Mark's.

7. Archivolts of nave, St. Mark's.

8. Archivolts of treasury door, St. Mark's.

9. Moulding of circular window in St. John and Paul.

10. Chief decorated narrow plinth, St. Mark's.

11. Plinth of door, Campo St. Margherita.

12. Plinth of tomb of Doge Vital Falier.

13. Lower plinth, Fondaco de' Turchi, and Terraced House.

14. Running plinth of Corte del Remer.

15. Highest plinth at top of Fondaco de' Turchi.

16. Common Byzantine plinth.

17. Running plinth of Casa Falier.

18. Plinth of arch at Ponte St. Toma.

19, 20, 21. Plinths of tomb of Doge Vital Falier.

22. Plinth of window in Calle del Pistor.

23. Plinth of tomb of Dogaressa Vital Michele.

24. Archivolt in the Frari.

25. Running plinth, Casa Loredan.

26. Running plinth, under pointed arch, in Salizzada San Lio.

27. Running plinth, Casa Erizzo.

PLATE X.   28. Circles in portico of St. Mark's.
Vol. III.
29. Ducal Palace cornice, lower arcade.

30. Ducal Palace cornice, upper arcade.

31. Central Gothic plinth.

32. Late Gothic plinth.

33. Late Gothic plinth, Casa degli Ambasciatori.

34. Late Gothic plinth, palace near the Jesuiti.

35, 36. Central balcony cornice.

37. Plinth of St. Mark's balustrade.

38. Cornice of the Frari, in brick, cabled.

39. Central balcony plinth.

40. Uppermost cornice, Ducal Palace.

41. Abacus of lily capitals, St. Mark's.

42. Abacus, Fondaco de' Turchi.

43. Abacus, large capital of Terraced House.

44. Abacus, Fondaco de' Turchi.

45. Abacus, Ducal Palace, upper arcade.

46. Abacus, Corte del Remer.

47. Abacus, small pillars, St. Mark's pulpit.

48. Abacus, Murano and Torcello.

It is only farther to be noted, that these mouldings are used, in various proportions, for all kinds of purposes: sometimes for true cornices; sometimes for window-sills; sometimes, 3 and 4 (in the Gothic time) especially, for dripstones of gables: 11 and such others form little plinths or abaci at the spring of arches, such as those shown at *a*, Fig. XXIII., p. 241, Vol. II. Finally, a large number of superb Byzantine cornices occur, of the form shown at the top of the arch in Plate V., Vol. II., having a profile like 16 or 19 here; with nodding leaves of acanthus thrown out from it, being, in fact, merely one range of the leaves of a Byzantine capital unwrapped, and formed into a continuous line. I had prepared a large mass of materials for the illustration of these cornices, and the Gothic ones connected with them; but found the subject would take up another volume, and was forced, for the present, to abandon it. The lower series of profiles, 7 to 12 in Plate XV., Vol. I., shows how the leaf-ornament is laid on the simple early cornices.

VI. TRACERIES.

We have only one subject more to examine, the character of the early and late tracery bars.

The reader may perhaps have been surprised at the small attention given to traceries in the course of the preceding volumes: but the reason is, that there are no *complicated* traceries at Venice belonging to the good Gothic time, with the single exception of those of the Casa Cicogna; and the magnificent arcades of the Ducal Palace Gothic are so simple as to require little explanation.

There are, however, two curious circumstances in the later traceries; the first, that they are universally considered by the builder (as the old Byzantines considered sculptured surfaces of stone) as material out of which a certain portion is *to be cut*, to fill his window. A fine Northern Gothic tracery is a complete and systematic arrangement of arches and foliation, *adjusted* to the form of the window; but a Venetian tracery is a piece of a larger composition, cut to the shade of the window. In the Porta della Carta, in the Church of the Madonna dell' Orto, in the Casa Bernardo on the Grand Canal, in the old Church of the Misericordia, and wherever else there are rich traceries in Venice, it will always be found that a certain arrangement of quatrefoils and other figures has been planned as if it were to extend indefinitely into miles of arcade ; and out of this colossal piece of marble lace, a piece in the shape of a window is cut, mercilessly and fearlessly ; whatever fragments and odd shapes of interstice, remnants of this or that figure of the divided foliation, may occur at the edge of the window, it matters not ; all are cut across, and shut in by the great outer archivolt.

It is very curious to find the Venetians treating what in other countries became of so great individual importance, merely as a kind of diaper ground, like that of their chequered colours on the walls. There is great grandeur in the idea, though the system of their traceries was spoilt by it : but they always treated their buildings as masses of colour rather than of line ; and the great traceries of the Ducal Palace itself are not spared any more than those of the minor palaces. They are cut off at the flanks in the middle of their quatrefoils, and the terminal mouldings take up part of the breadth of the poor half of a quatrefoil at the extremity.

One other circumstance is notable also. In good Northern Gothic the tracery bars are of a constant profile, the same on both sides ; and if the plan of the tracery leaves any interstices so small that there is not room for the full profile of the tracery bar all round them, those interstices are entirely closed, the tracery bars being supposed to have met each other. But in Venice, if an interstice becomes anywhere inconveniently small, the tracery bar is sacrificed, cut away, or in some way altered in profile, in order to afford more room for the light, especially in the early traceries, so that one side of a tracery bar is often quite different from the other. For instance, in the bars 1 and 2, Plate XI., from the Frari and St. John and Paul, the uppermost side is towards a great opening, and there was room for the bevel or slope to the cusp ; but in the other side the opening was too small, and the bar falls vertically to the cusp. In 5 the upper-most side is to the narrow aperture, and the lower to the small one ; and in fig. 9, from the Casa Cicogna, the uppermost side is to the apertures of the tracery, the lowermost to the arches beneath, the great roll following

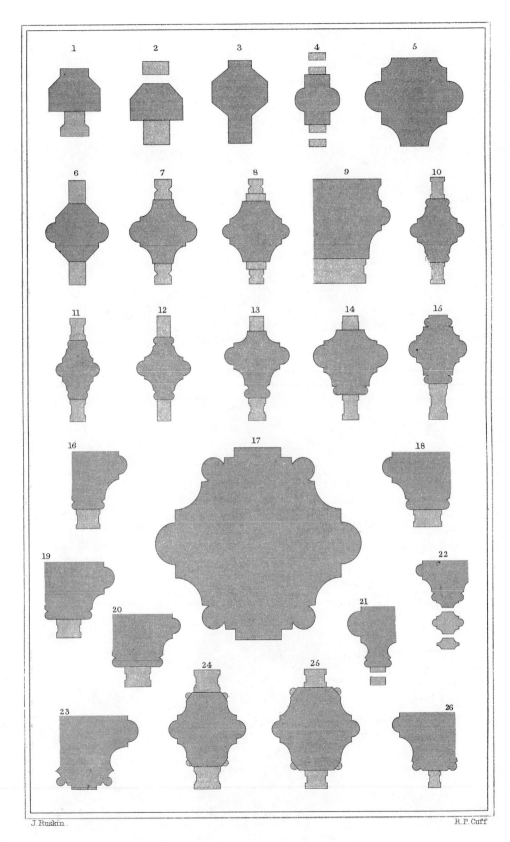

XI

J. Ruskin.

R.P. Cuff

Tracery Bars

the design of the tracery; while 13 and 14 are left without the roll
at the base of their cavettos on the uppermost sides, which are turned to
narrow apertures. The earliness of the Casa Cicogna tracery is seen in
a moment by its being moulded on the face only. It is in fact nothing
more than a series of quatrefoiled apertures in the solid wall of the
house, with mouldings on their faces, and magnificent arches of pure
pointed fifth order sustaining them below.

The following are the references to the figures in the plate :

1. Frari.
2. Apse, St. John and Paul.
3. Frari.
4. Ducal Palace, inner court, upper window.
5. Madonna dell' Orto.
6. St. John and Paul.
7. Casa Bernardo.
8. Casa Contarini Fasan.
9. Casa Cicogna.
10, 11. Frari.
12. Murano Palace (see note, p. 254).
13. Misericordia.
14. Palace of the younger Foscari.*

PLATE XI.　15. Casa d' Oro; great single windows.
Vol. III.　16. Hotel Danieli.
17. Ducal Palace.
18. Casa Erizzo, on Grand Canal.
19. Main story, Casa Cavalli.
20. Younger Foscari.
21. Ducal Palace, traceried windows.
22. Porta della Carta.
23. Casa d' Oro.
24. Casa d' Oro, upper story.
25. Casa Facanon.
26. Casa Cavalli, near Post-Office.

It will be seen at a glance that, except in the very early fillet traceries
of the Frari and St. John and Paul, Venetian work consists of roll
traceries of one general pattern. It will be seen also, that 10 and 11

* The palace next the Casa Foscari, on the Grand Canal, sometimes said to have
belonged to the son of the Doge.

from the Frari, furnish the first examples of the form afterwards completely developed in 17, the tracery bar of the Ducal Palace ; but that
this bar differs from them in greater strength and squareness, and in
adding a recess between its smaller roll and the cusp.   Observe, that
this is done for strength chiefly ; as in the contemporary tracery (21)
of the upper windows, no such additional thickness is used.

Figure 17 is slightly inaccurate.   The little curved recesses behind
the smaller roll are not equal on each side ; that next the cusp is smallest,
being about $\frac{5}{8}$ of an inch, while that next the cavetto is about $\frac{7}{8}$; to such
an extent of subtlety did the old builders carry their love of change.

The return of the cavetto in 21, 23, and 26 is comparatively rare,
and is generally a sign of later date.

The reader must observe that the great sturdiness of the form of the
bars, 5, 9, 17, 24, 25, is a consequence of the peculiar office of Venetian
traceries in supporting the mass of the building above, already noticed
at p. 239 of Vol. II. ; and indeed the forms of the Venetian Gothic are,
in many other ways, influenced by the dif-
ficulty of obtaining stability on sandy foundations.   One thing is especially noticeable in
all their arrangements of traceries ; namely, the
endeavour to obtain equal and horizontal pressure along the whole breadth of the building, not the divided and local pressures of
Northern Gothic.   This object is considerably
aided by the structure of the balconies, which
are of great service in knitting the shafts together, forming complete tie-beams of marble,
as well as a kind of rivets, at their bases.   For
instance, at *b*, Fig. II., is represented the
masonry of the base of the upper arcade of
the Ducal Palace, showing the root of one
of its main shafts, with the binding balconies.
The solid stones which form the foundation
are much broader than the balcony shafts, so
that the socketed arrangement is not seen : it
is shown as it would appear in a longitudinal
section.   The balconies are not let into the
circular shafts, but fitted to their circular

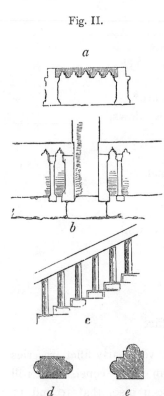

Fig. II.

a

b

c

d   *e*

curves, so as to grasp them, and riveted with metal ; and the bars of stone which form the tops of the balconies are of great strength and depth, the small trefoiled arches being cut out of them as in Fig. III., so as hardly to diminish their binding power. In the lighter independent balconies they are often cut deeper; but in all cases the bar of stone is nearly independent of the small shafts placed beneath it, and would stand firm though these were removed, as at *a*, Fig. II., supported

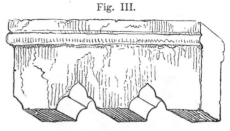

Fig. III.

either by the main shafts of the traceries, or by its own small pilasters with semi-shafts at their sides, of the plan *d*, Fig. II., in a continuous balcony, and *e* at the angle of one.

There is one more very curious circumstance illustrative of the Venetian desire to obtain horizontal pressure. In all the Gothic staircases with which I am acquainted, out of Venice, in which vertical shafts are used to support an inclined line, those shafts are connected by arches rising each above the other, with a little bracket above the capitals, on the side where it is necessary to raise the arch; or else, though less gracefully, with a longer curve to the lowest side of the arch.

But the Venetians seem to have had a morbid horror of arches which were not *on a level*. They could not endure the appearance of the roof of one arch bearing against the side of another; and rather than introduce the idea of obliquity into bearing curves, they abandoned the arch principle altogether: so that even in their richest Gothic staircases, where trefoiled arches, exquisitely decorated, are used on the landings, they ran the shafts on the sloping stair simply into the bar of stone above them, and used the excessively ugly and valueless arrangement *c*, Fig. II., rather than sacrifice the sacred horizontality of their arch system.

It will be noted, in Plate XI., that the form and character of the tracery bars themselves are independent of the position or projection of the cusps on their flat sides. In this respect, also, Venetian traceries are peculiar, the example 22 of the Porta della Carta being the only one in the plate which is subordinated according to the Northern system. In every other case the form of the aperture is determined, either by a flat and solid cusp as in 6, or by a pierced cusp as in 4. The effect of the pierced cusp is seen in the uppermost figure, Plate XVIII., Vol. II.; and its derivation from the solid cusp will be understood, at once, from the woodcut below, Fig. IV., which represents a series of the flanking stones of any arch of the fifth order, such as *f* in Plate III., Vol. I.

The first on the left shows the condition of cusp in a perfectly simple and early Gothic arch, 2 and 3 are those of common arches of the fifth

Fig. IV.

I   2   3   4   5

order, 4 is the condition in more studied examples of the Gothic advanced guard, and 5 connects them all with the system of traceries. Introducing the common archivolt mouldings on the projecting edge of 2 and 3, we obtain the bold and deep fifth-order window, used down to the close of the fourteenth century or even later, and always grand in its depth of cusp, and consequently of shadow; but the narrow cusp 4 occurs also in very early work, and is piquant when set beneath a bold flat archivolt, as in Fig. V., from the Corte del Forno at Santa Marina. The pierced cusp gives a peculiar lightness and brilliancy to the window, but is not so sublime. In the richer buildings the surface of the flat and solid cusp is decorated with a shallow trefoil (see Plate VIII., Vol. I.), or, when the cusp is small, with a triangular incision only, as seen in figs. 7 and 8, Plate XI.

Fig. V.

The recesses on the sides of the other cusps indicate their single or double lines of foliation. The cusp of the Ducal Palace has a fillet only round its edge, and a ball of red marble on its truncated point, and is perfect in its grand simplicity; but in general the cusps of Venice are far inferior to those of Verona and of the other cities of Italy, chiefly because there was always some confusion in the mind of the designer between true cusps and the mere bending inwards of the arch of the fourth order.　The two series, 4 *a* to 4 *e,* and 5 *a* to 5 *e,* in Plate XIV., Vol. II., are arranged so as to show this connection, as well as the varieties of curvature in the trefoiled arches of the fourth and fifth orders, which, though apparently slight on so small a scale, are of enormous importance in distant effect; a house in which the joints of the cusps project as much as in 5 *c,* being quite piquant and grotesque when compared with one in which the cusps are subdued to the form 5 *b.*　4 *d* and 4 *e* are Veronese forms, wonderfully effective and spirited; the latter occurs at Verona only, but the former at Venice also.　5 *d* occurs in Venice, but is very rare; and 5 *e* I found only once, on the narrow canal close to the entrance door of the Hotel Danieli.　It was partly walled up, but I obtained leave to take down the brickwork and lay open one side of the arch, which may still be seen.

The above particulars are enough to enable the reader to judge of the distinctness of evidence which the details of Venetian architecture bear to its dates.　Farther explanation of the plates would be vainly tedious: but the architect who uses these volumes in Venice will find them of value, in enabling him instantly to class the mouldings which may interest him; and for this reason I have given a larger number of examples than would otherwise have been sufficient for my purpose.

II. ADDITIONAL NOTES: FROM THE " TRAVELLERS' EDITION" OF " STONES OF VENICE."

Chap. I., § XVI., p. 11, line 10: "*Against this degraded Gothic, then, came up the Renaissance armies.*"

Note *b.*—I request the reader's earnest attention to the now following analysis.　I feel inclined to say of it as Albert Durer of his engraving, ' Sir,—it cannot be better done.'

Chap. I., § XX., p. 14, line 17: " *The lower workman secured method and finish, and lost, in exchange for them, his soul.*"

Note *c.*—See the examination to be given in "St. Mark's Rest," of the clever work on the restored porch of St. Mark's.

Chap. I., § XXI., p. 14, line 20: " *The reader . . . will not find one word but of the most profound reverence for . . . Leonardo and Michael Angelo, Ghirlandajo . . .*,"

Note *d.*—He will find plenty of words *now,* of extreme irreverence towards Leonardo, Michael Angelo, and Ghirlandajo. But I was only breaking my way through old prejudices, in 1851, and was still encumbered with the dust of them. But I think the reader will do me the justice to observe how carefully and temperately the advance was made ; so that I have now only to confirm or complete its statements ; and nothing of real good was ever denied by me, in the enemy's ranks. See the passage just following of the Colleone statue.

Chap. I., § XXIII., p. 16, line 4 : "*At Verona it is, indeed, less Byzantine, but possesses a character of richness and tenderness almost peculiar to that city.*"

Note *e.*—Alas, the noblest example of it, Fra Giocondo's exquisite loggia, has been daubed and damned by the modern restorer, into a caricature worse than a Christmas clown's. The exquisite colours of the Renaissance fresco, pure as rose-leaves and dark laurel—the modern Italian decorator thinks ' Sporco,' and replaces by buff-colour of oil-cloth, and Prussian green—spluttering his gold about wherever the devil prompts him, to enrich the whole.

Chap. I., § XXIII., p. 16, line 15 : "*The Casa Dario, and the Casa Manzoni, on the Grand Canal, are exquisite examples of the school*" [*of Renaissance-Byzantine*].

Note *f.*—No : these are not so good. Strangely I have omitted mention here of the palace I knew best of all. See § 38. The entire school is limited to a period of forty years—1480-1520.

Chap. I., § XXXII., p. 21, last line : "*The walls were generally covered with chequers . . . crimson quatrefoils interlaced, with cherubims stretching their wings filling the intervals.*"

Note *h.*—All now whitewashed by "Progresso." Progressive Italy performs always two fresco operations in due order. First, blind whitewash, to show that she can do something in Italy. Then soot, in imitation of England.

Chap. I., § XXXIII., p. 22, line 32 : "*A diaper pattern is often set obliquely.*"

Note *i.*—*Always,* in the best work.

Chap. I., § XXXIV., p. 23, line 12 : "*A field of subdued russet, quartered with broad sculptured masses of white and gold.*"

Note *k.*—See, again and again, Carpaccio's and Bellini's backgrounds.

Delicate, instead of broad, in the italicized sentence, would have been a better word; the white and gold lines being often mere threads.

Chap. I., § xxxvi., p. 24, line 25: "*Covered from top to bottom with paintings by Veronese.*"

Note *l.*—I must really give myself another pat, and "good dog." How absolutely accurate and true this account is, the reader may see for himself in a moment by going to the Church of St. Sebastian, where he will see literally the last bits of porphyry vanishing from the façade, and the roof " covered with paintings," which were indeed once by Paul Veronese, and are now by the pupils of the Venetian Academy.

Chap. I., § xxxix., p. 26, last line : add,—Note written, I believe, in 1852.

Chap. II., § 1, p. 32, line 7: "*The Post Office.*"
Note *b.*—Now removed elsewhere.

Chap. II., § xxxii., p. 55, line 8: "*The natural sciences may become as harmful as any others, when they lose themselves in classification and cata-logue-making.*"

Note *a.*—I had not at this time conceived the possibility of their losing themselves in the contemplation of death instead of life ; and becoming the bigots of corruption.

I have italicized the pregnant sentence above [*—it is not the science, but the perception*].

Chap. II., §§ xlvi.—lxxxv.   [Chap. III. of Travellers' Edition].
Note *a.*—The substance of this present chapter will be gradually illus-trated by the publications of the Arundel Society on the " Tombs of Italy."

Chap. II., §§ xcii.—ciii.   [Chap. IV. of Travellers' Edition.]
Note *a.*—I should re-write [this] now, in effect the same, but with much better sense of its close application to ourselves.   In the original, the Renaissance Pride was divided into three heads, Pride of State, of Know-ledge, and of System ; but the last was insufficiently treated, and would lead us into quite other fields of weed, if we followed it now.   For Venice in her wig and high-soled shoes thought just as much of herself as an English engineer—or an English banker—or an English Member of Parliament for the borough of Puddlecombe—or the Duke of D—— building the profit-able port of Barrow, and had set herself to just such profitable business.

Chap. II., § xciv., p. 101, line 18 : "*The Protestant movement was, in reality, not re-*FORMATION *but re-*ANIMATION."

Note *b.*—I was here still writing as a Protestant, and did not ask myself what sort of "animation," on the whole, was in the English and German Noblesse of the Reforming Party. Carlyle and Froude have together told us whatever was best in them. But the really efficient force in the whole business was—primarily, resolve to have everything their own way ; and secondly, resolve to steal the Church lands and moneys. Of course the Church had misused, else it would never have lost them : but the whole question is, to my clearer knowledge of it, one of contention between various manners of temporal misbehaviour : the doctrines of the two parties are little more than their war-cries,—and in the applications of them both alike false.

The most true and beautiful analysis of the entire debate that I know in literature is given in three of Scott's novels —if you know how to read them—"The Monastery," "The Abbot," and "Old Mortality."

Chap. II., § xciv., p. 101, line 20 : "*In some sort it rather broke down her hedges.*"

Note *c.*—*Rather* so, certainly ! Life had been before a labyrinth ; but became then, a desert. See Part IV. of the Bible of Amiens, describing the old pavement of the cathedral.

Chap. II., § xcvii., p. 104, line 2 : "*The great invention of the age, which rendered God's word accessible to every man.*"

Note *d.*—What a little Edgworthian gosling I still was, when I wrote this ! See "Harry and Lucy," vol. ii., p. 274, on the subject of the misery of the Dark Ages in only possessing manuscripts. "And then came the Dark Ages," said Lucy, "and in the Dark Ages I suppose people fell asleep and *could not think of glass*, or anything else ! " This is the state of the model British-manufactured young lady's mind, in the year 1825. (Compare also the passage on the " Honour of Knighthood conferred on Sir Richard Arkwright "—and its money representation,—Vol. I., p. 229.) I hope St. George's Museum at Sheffield has already shown some Yorkshire and Lancashire Protestants what a manuscript of the Bible was once, in Bolton and Furness.

Chap. II., § xcvii., p. 104, line 5 : "*Rome set herself in direct opposition to the Bible.*"

Note *e.*—To the popular distribution of the Bible, I meant. But it had nothing whatever to do with the matter. Anybody may write out for themselves in ten minutes more Bible than they will learn to obey in ten years.

For the rest the main meaning of this paragraph is right enough, else I had not reprinted it, and the end of it is not strong enough. The most beautiful Norman church in Chartres is a hay-loft, at this moment,—such the holy zeal of the Catholic world, going pettifogging about in proclamation of its Immaculate Conceptions, etc.

Chap. II., § xcviii., end; p. 105.

Note *f.*—A good concentrated paragraph, but full of literary coxcombry. I was very proud of it when I had got it finished, and am now only woful over the waste of time. There is no use whatever in this history of blunders. We have little time enough, in human life, to watch men who are doing right, and to help them.

Chap. II., § xcix., p. 105, line 21 : "*Grammar, logic, and rhetoric ; studies utterly unworthy of the serious labour of men.*"

Note *g.*—The reader had, perhaps, better take breath. But it's all right, or nearly so, with a little expansion. Logic and rhetoric are indeed studies only for fools and hypocrites ; all strong heads reason as easily as they walk, and all strong lips speak for truth's sake, and not emotion's. But grammar at a certain time of life is decidedly an expedient study,— and at any time of life an amusing one, if people have a turn for it. It should never be much more than play. Whether we say "two and two makes four," or "two and two make," is of small consequence ; but no accuracy of grammar will make it a safe statement that two and two make five. Of 'grammar,' in the original grand sense of the word, see " Mornings in Florence," Part V., "The Strait Gate."

Chap. II., § ci., p. 106, line 19 : "*That which was given to Horace was withdrawn from David.*"

Note *h.*—True ; but a good deal *ought* to be given to Horace, nevertheless.

Chap. II., § cii., p. 107, line 26 : "*Raphael . . . . sank at once into powerlessness at the feet of Apollo and the Muses.*"

Note *i.*—True, again, in general ; yet the Parnassus is the greatest of the Vatican Raphael frescoes.

Chap. II., § ciii., p. 109, line 4 : "*The world is . . . . as Pagan as it was in the second century.*"

Note *k.*—I wish it were! But the worship of Bacteria and Holothuriæ had not been instituted when this was written.

Chap. II., § CIII., p. 110, line 7 : "*Of all subjects of human inquiry his own religion is the one in which a youth's ignorance is most easily forgiven*" [*in modern Universities*].

Note *l.*—This paragraph is a very good one ; but already superannuated. The enemy is now not Latin Verse, but Cockney Prose.

Chap. II., § CIII., p. 110, line 13 : "*I believe that in a few years more we shall wake from all these errors.*"

Note *m.*—Carlyle allows two hundred or so,—I hope too liberally.

Chap. III., § IV., p. 113 ; last line : "*The bishop of Uderzo.*"

Note.—Altinum. See clearer statement in " St. Mark's Rest."

Chap. III., § VII., p. 115, note : "*Or at least for its principal families.*"

Add—But the evidence is in favour of the totality.

Chap. III., § XXII., p. 125, line 28 : "*Grotesque Renaissance.*"

Note.—We are again (1881) so fast sinking to the level of it that the English connoisseur will perhaps admire both. But he may be assured of the historical fact that it is a constant sign of national decrepitude.

Chap. III., § LXVII., p. 158, line 26 : "*Michael Angelo.*"

Note *a.*—I had not at this time extricated myself from the false reverence for Michael Angelo in which I had been brought up. It held me longer than any other youthful formalism. The real relations between Michael Angelo and Tintoret are given in my Oxford lecture on the subject.

VENETIAN INDEX.

VENETIAN INDEX.

In the Venetian Index, I have named every building of importance in the city of Venice itself, or near it ; supplying, for the convenience of the traveller, short notices of those to which I had no occasion to allude in the text of the work ; and making the whole as complete a guide as I could, with such added directions as I should have given to any private friend visiting the city. As, however, in many cases, the opinions I have expressed differ widely from those usually received ; and, in other instances, subjects which may be of much interest to the traveller, have not come within the scope of my inquiry ; the reader had better take Lazari's small Guide in his hand also, as he will find in it both the information I have been unable to furnish, and the expression of most of the received opinions upon any subject of art.

Various inconsistencies will be noticed in the manner of indicating the buildings, some being named in Italian, some in English, and some half in one, and half in the other. But these inconsistencies are permitted in order to save trouble, and make the Index more practically useful. For instance, I believe the traveller will generally look for " Mark," rather than for " Marco," when he wishes to find the reference to St. Mark's Church ; but I think he will look for Rocco, rather than for Roch, when he is seeking for the account of the Scuola di San Rocco. So also I have altered the character in which the titles of the plates are printed, from the black letter in the first volume, to the plain Roman in the second and third ; finding experimentally that the former character was not easily legible, and conceiving that the book would be none the worse for this practical illustration of its own principles, in a daring sacrifice of symmetry to convenience.

Alphabetical Indices will, however, be of little use, unless another, and a very different kind of Index, be arranged in the mind of the reader ; an Index explanatory of the principal purposes and contents of the various parts of this essay. It is difficult to analyze the nature of the reluctance with which either a writer or painter takes it upon him to explain the meaning of his own work, even in cases where, without such explanation, it must in a measure remain always disputable : but I am persuaded that this reluctance is, in most instances, carried too far ; and that, wherever there really is a serious purpose in a book or a picture, the author does wrong who, either in modesty or vanity (both feelings have their share in producing the dislike of personal interpretation), trusts entirely to the patience and intelligence of the readers or spectators to penetrate into their significance. At all events, I will, as far as possible, spare such trouble with respect to these volumes, by stating here, finally and clearly, both what they intend and what they contain ; and this the rather because I have lately noticed, with some surprise, certain reviewers announcing as a discovery, what I thought I had lain palpably on the surface of the book, namely, that " if Mr. Ruskin be right, all the architects, and all the architectural teaching of the last three hundred years, must have been wrong." That is indeed precisely the fact ; and the very thing I meant to say, which indeed I thought I had said over and over again. I believe the architects of the last three centuries to have been wrong ; wrong without exception ; wrong totally, and from the foundation. This is exactly the point I have been endeavouring to prove, from the beginning of this work to the end of it. But as it seems not yet to have been stated clearly enough, I will here try to put my entire theorem into an unmistakable form.

The various nations who attained eminence in the arts before the time of Christ, each of them, produced forms of architecture which in their various degrees of merit were almost exactly indicative of the degrees of intellectual and moral energy of the nations which originated them ; and each reached its greatest perfection at the time when the true energy and prosperity of the people who had invented it were at their culminating point. Many of these various styles of architecture were good, considered in relation to the times and races which gave birth to them ; but none were absolutely good or perfect, or fitted for the practice of all future time.

The advent of Christianity for the first time rendered possible the full development of the soul of man, and therefore the full development of the arts of man.

Christianity gave birth to a new architecture, not only immeasurably superior to all that had preceded it, but demonstrably the best architecture that *can* exist; perfect in construction and decoration, and fit for the practice of all time.

This architecture, commonly called "Gothic," though in conception perfect, like the theory of a Christian character, never reached an actual perfection, having been retarded and corrupted by various adverse influences; but it reached its highest perfection, hitherto manifested, about the close of the thirteenth century, being then indicative of a peculiar energy in the Christian mind of Europe.

In the course of the fifteenth century, owing to various causes which I have endeavoured to trace in the preceding pages, the Christianity of Europe was undermined; and a Pagan architecture was introduced, in imitation of that of the Greeks and Romans.

The architecture of the Greeks and Romans themselves was not good, but it was natural, and, as I said before, good in some respects, and for a particular time.

But the imitative architecture introduced first in the fifteenth century, and practised ever since, was neither good nor natural. It was good in no respect, and for no time. All the architects who have built in that style have built what was worthless; and therefore the greater part of the architecture which has been built for the last three hundred years, and which we are now building, is worthless. We must give up this style totally, despise it and forget it, and build henceforward only in that perfect and Christian style hitherto called Gothic, which is everlastingly the best.

This is the theorem of these volumes.

In support of this theorem, the first volume contains, in its first chapter, a sketch of the actual history of Christian architecture, up to the period of the Reformation; and, in the subsequent chapters, an analysis of the entire system of the laws of architectural construction and decoration, deducing from those laws positive conclusions as to the best forms and manners of building for all time.

The second volume contains, in its first five chapters, an account of one of the most important and least known forms of Christian architecture, as exhibited in Venice, together with an analysis of its nature in the fourth chapter; and, which is a peculiarly important part of this section, an account of the power of colour over the human mind.

The sixth chapter of the second volume contains an analysis of the nature of Gothic architecture, properly so called, and shows that in its external form it complies precisely with the abstract laws of structure and beauty, investigated in the first volume. The seventh and eighth chapters of the second volume illustrate the nature of Gothic architecture by various Venetian examples. The third volume investigates, in its first chapter, the causes and manner of the corruption of Gothic architecture ; in its second chapter, defines the nature of the Pagan architecture which superseded it ; in the third chapter, shows the connection of that Pagan architecture with the various characters of mind which brought about the destruction of the Venetian nation ; and, in the fourth chapter, points out the dangerous tendencies in the modern mind which the practice of such an architecture indicates.

Such is the intention of the preceding pages, which I hope will no more be doubted or mistaken. As far as regards the manner of its fulfilment, though I hope, in the course of other inquiries, to add much to the elucidation of the points in dispute, I cannot feel it necessary to apologise for the imperfect handling of a subject which the labour of a long life, had I been able to bestow it, must still have left imperfectly treated.

I have endeavoured to make the following index as useful as possible to the traveller by indicating only the objects which are really worth his study. A traveller's interest, stimulated as it is into strange vigour by the freshness of every impression, and deepened by the sacredness of the charm of association which long familiarity with any scene too fatally wears away,* is too precious a thing to be heedlessly wasted ; and as it is physically impossible to see and to understand more than a certain quantity of art in a given time, the attention bestowed on second-rate works, in such a city as Venice, is not merely lost, but actually harmful,—deadening the interest and confusing the memory with respect to those which it is a duty to enjoy, and a disgrace to forget. The reader need not fear

* "Am I in Italy ? Is this the Mincius ?
Are those the distant turrets of Verona ?
And shall I sup where Juliet at the masque
Saw her loved Montague, and now sleeps by him ?
Such questions hourly do I ask myself ;
And not a stone in a crossway inscribed
'To Mantua,' 'To Ferrara,' but excites
Surprise, and doubt, and self-congratulation."

Alas ! after a few short months, spent even in the scenes dearest to history, we can feel thus no more.

being misled by any omissions; for I have conscientiously pointed out every characteristic example, even of the styles which I dislike, and have referred to Lazari in all instances in which my own information failed: but if he is in anywise willing to trust me, I should recommend him to devote his principal attention, if he is fond of paintings, to the works of Tintoret, Paul Veronese, and John Bellini; not of course neglecting Titian, yet remembering that Titian can be well and thoroughly studied in almost any great European gallery, while Tintoret and Bellini can be judged of *only* in Venice, and Paul Veronese, though gloriously represented by the two great pictures in the Louvre, and many others throughout Europe, is yet not to be fully estimated until he is seen at play among the fantastic chequers of the Venetian ceilings.

I have supplied somewhat copious notices of the pictures of Tintoret, because they are much injured, difficult to read, and entirely neglected by other writers on art. I cannot express the astonishment and indignation I felt on finding, in Kugler's handbook, a paltry cenacolo, painted probably in a couple of hours for a couple of zecchins, for the monks of St. Trovaso, quoted as characteristic of this master; just as foolish readers quote separate stanzas of Peter Bell or the Idiot Boy, as characteristic of Wordsworth. Finally, the reader is requested to observe, that the dates assigned to the various buildings named in the following index, are almost without exception conjectural; that is to say, founded exclusively on the internal evidence of which a portion has been given in the Final Appendix. It is likely, therefore, that here and there, in particular instances, farther inquiry may prove me to have been deceived; but such occasional errors are not of the smallest importance with respect to the general conclusions of the preceding pages, which will be found to rest on too broad a basis to be disturbed.

[1881. The delay in the publication of the second volume of the "Travellers' Edition" was caused by my wish to complete this index into some more generally serviceable form. But I find that now-a-days, as soon as I begin to speak of anything anywhere, it is sure to be moved somewhere else; and now, at last, in desperation, I print the old index almost as it was, cutting out of it only the often-repeated statements that such and such churches or pictures were of "no importance." The modern traveller is but too likely to say so for himself. In my last edition of "Murray's Guide to Northern Italy," I find the visitor advised how to see all the remarkable objects in Venice in a single day.]

A.

ACCADEMIA DELLE BELLE ARTE. Notice above the door the two bas-reliefs of St. Leonard and St. Christopher, chiefly remarkable for their rude cutting at so late a date, 1377 ; but the niches under which they stand are unusual in their bent gables, and in the little crosses within circles which fill their cusps. The traveller is generally too much struck by Titian's great picture of the "Assumption," to be able to pay proper attention to the other works in this gallery. Let him, however, ask himself candidly, how much of his admiration is dependent merely upon the picture being larger than any other in the room, and having bright masses of red and blue in it ; let him be assured, that the picture is in reality not one whit the better for being either large, or gaudy in colour ; and he will then be better disposed to give the pains necessary to discover the merit of the more profound and solemn works of Bellini and Tintoret. One of the most wonderful works in the whole gallery is Tintoret's "Death of Abel," on the left of the "Assumption ;" the "Adam and Eve," on the right of it, is hardly inferior ; and both are more characteristic examples of the master, and in many respects better pictures, than the much vaunted "Miracle of St. Mark." All the works of Bellini in this room are of great beauty and interest. In the great room, that which contains Titian's "Presentation of the Virgin," the traveller should examine carefully all the pictures by Vittor Carpaccio and Gentile Bellini, which represent scenes in ancient Venice ; they are full of interesting architecture and costume. Marco Basaiti's "Agony in the Garden" is a lovely example of the religious school. The Tintorets in this room are all second rate, but most of the Veroneses are good, and the large ones are magnificent.

[1877. I leave this article as originally written ; the sixth chapter of ' St. Mark's Rest' now containing a careful notice of as many pictures as travellers are likely to have time to look at.]

ALIGA. See GIORGIO.

ALVISE, CHURCH OF ST. I have never been in this church, but Lazari dates its interior, with decision, as of the year 1388, and it may be worth a glance, if the traveller has time.

ANDREA, CHURCH OF ST. Well worth visiting for the sake of the peculiarly sweet and melancholy effect of its little grass-grown campo, opening to the lagoon and the Alps. The sculpture over the door, " The Miraculous Draught of Fishes," is a quaint piece of Renaissance work. Note the distant rocky landscape, and the oar of the existing gondola floating by St. Andrew's boat. The church is of the later Gothic period, much defaced, but still picturesque. The lateral windows are bluntly trefoiled, and good of their time.

[1877. All now defaced and defiled by factory and railroad bridges. A mere woe and desolation.]

ANGELI, CHURCH DEGLI, at Murano. The sculpture of the "Annunciation" over the entrance-gate is graceful. In exploring Murano, it is worth while to row up the great canal thus far for the sake of the opening to the lagoon.

APOSTOLI, CHURCH OF THE. The exterior is nothing. There is said to be a picture by Veronese in the interior, "The Fall of the Manna." I have not seen it; but if it be of importance, the traveller should compare it carefully with Tintoret's, in the Scuola di San Rocco, and in San Giorgio Maggiore.

[1877. It is an imitation of that in San Giorgio, almost invisible, and not worth losing time upon.]

APOSTOLI, PALACE AT, II. 253, on the Grand Canal, near the Rialto, opposite the fruit-market. A most important transitional palace. Its sculpture in the first story is peculiarly rich and curious; I think Venetian, in imitation of Byzantine. The sea story and first floor are of the first half of the thirteenth century, the rest modern. Observe that only one wing of the sea story is left, the other half having been modernized. The traveller should land to look at the capital drawn in Plate II. of Vol. III., fig. 7.

ARSENAL. Its gateway is a curiously picturesque example of Renaissance workmanship, admirably sharp and expressive in its ornamental sculpture; it is in many parts like some of the best Byzantine work. The Greek lions in front of it appear to me to deserve more praise than they have received; though they are awkwardly balanced between conventional and imitative representation, having neither the severity proper to the one, nor the veracity necessary for the other.

[1877. No, there's no good in them; they are stupid work of the Greek decadence,—mere cumber of ground: but at least decently quiet, not strutting or sprawling or mouthing like lions of modern notion. Pacific at least—not insolent lumber. The traveller who cares for Turner should look with remembering attention at the internal angle of the Arsenal canal. Turner made its brick walls one flame of spiritual fire, in his mystic drawing of them, now in our National Gallery.]

B.

BADOER, PALAZZO, in the Campo San Giovanni in Bragola. A magnificent example of the fourteenth century Gothic, circa 1310—1320, anterior to the Ducal Palace, and showing beautiful ranges of the fifth-order window, with fragments of the original balconies, and the usual lateral window larger than any of the rest. In the centre of its arcade on the first floor is the inlaid ornament drawn in Plate VIII., Vol. I. The fresco painting on the walls is of later date; and I believe the heads which form the finials have been inserted afterwards also, the original windows having been pure fifth order.

The building is now a ruin, inhabited by the lowest orders; the first floor, when I was last in Venice, by a laundress.

[1877. Restored and destroyed.]

BAFFO, PALAZZO, in the Campo St. Maurizio. The commonest late Renaissance. A few olive-leaves and vestiges of two figures still remain upon it, of the frescoes by Paul Veronese with which it was once adorned.

[1877. All but gone now; nor were they Paul's—only some clever imitations.]

BARBARIGO, PALAZZO, on the Grand Canal, next the Casa Pisani. Late Renaissance; noticeable only as a house in which some of the best pictures of Titian were allowed to be ruined by damp, and out of which they were then sold to the Emperor of Russia.

BARBARO, PALAZZO, on the Grand Canal, next the Palazzo Cavalli. These two buildings form the principal objects in the foreground of the view which almost every artist seizes on his first traverse of the Grand Canal, the Church of the Salute forming a most graceful distance. Neither is, however, of much value, except in general effect; but the Barbaro is the best, and the pointed arcade in its side wall, seen from the narrow canal between it and the Cavalli, is good Gothic of the earliest fourteenth century type.

BARTOLOMEO, CHURCH OF ST. I did not go to look at the works of Sebastian del Piombo which it contains, fully crediting M. Lazari's statement, that they have been "Barbaramente sfigurati da mani imperite, che pretendevano ristaurarli." Otherwise the church is of no importance.

BECCHERIE. See QUERINI.

BEMBO, PALAZZO, on the Grand Canal, next the Casa Manin. A noble Gothic pile, circa 1350—1380, which, before it was painted by the modern Venetians with the two most valuable colours of Tintoret, Bianco e Nero, by being whitewashed above, and turned into a coal warehouse below, must have been among the most noble in effect on the whole Grand Canal. It still forms a beautiful group with the Rialto, some large shipping being generally anchored at its quay. Its sea story and entresol are of earlier date, I believe, than the rest; the doors of the former are Byzantine (see above, Final Appendix, under head "Jambs"); and above the entresol is a beautiful Byzantine cornice, built into the wall, and harmonizing well with the Gothic work.

BEMBO, PALAZZO, in the Calle Magno, at the Campo de' due Pozzi, close to the Arsenal. Noticed by Lazari and Selvatico as having a very interesting staircase. It is early Gothic, circa 1330, but not a whit more interesting than many others of similar date and design. See "Contarini Porta de Ferro," "Morosini," "Sanudo," and "Minelli."

BENEDETTO, CAMPO OF ST. Do not fail to see the superb, though partially ruinous, Gothic palace fronting this little square. It is very late Gothic, just passing into Renaissance; unique in Venice, in masculine character, united with the delicacy of the incipient style. Observe especially the brackets of the balconies, the flower-work on the cornices, and the arabesques on the angles of the balconies themselves.

BERNARDO, PALAZZO, on the Grand Canal. A very noble pile of early fifteenth century Gothic, founded on the Ducal Palace. The traceries in its lateral windows are both rich and unusual.

BERNARDO, PALAZZO, at St. Polo. A glorious palace, on a narrow canal, in a part of Venice now inhabited by the lower orders only. It is rather late central Gothic, circa 1380—1400, but of the finest kind, and superb in its effect of colour when seen from the side. A capital in the interior court is much praised by Selvatico and Lazari, because its "foglie d' acanto" (anything, by the by, *but* acanthus), "quasi agitate da vento si attorcigliano d' intorno alla campana, *concetto non indegno della bell' epoca greca!*" Does this mean "epoca Bisantina?" The capital is simply a translation into Gothic sculpture of the Byzantine ones of St. Mark's and the Fondaco de' Turchi (see Plate VIII., Vol. I., fig. 14), and is far inferior to either. But, taken as a whole, I think that, after the Ducal Palace, this is the noblest in effect of all in Venice.

BRENTA, Banks of the, I. 344. Villas on the, I. 345.

BUSINELLO, CASA, II. 389.

BYZANTINE PALACES generally, II. 118.

C.

CAMERLENGHI, PALACE OF THE, beside the Rialto. A graceful work of the early Renaissance (1525) passing into Roman Renaissance. Its details are inferior to most of the work of the school. The "Camerlenghi," properly " Camerlenghi di Comune," were the three officers or ministers who had care of the administration of public expenses.

Cancellaria, II. 292.

Cappello, Palazzo, at St. Aponal. Of no interest. Some say that Bianca Cappello fled from it; but the tradition seems to fluctuate between the various houses belonging to her family.

Carità, Church of the. Once an interesting Gothic church of the fourteenth century, lately defaced, and applied to some of the usual important purposes of the modern Italians. The effect of its ancient façade may partly be guessed at from the pictures of Canaletto, but only guessed at; Canaletto being less to be trusted for renderings of details, than the rudest and most ignorant painter of the thirteenth century.

Carmini, Church of the. A most interesting church, of late thirteenth century work, but much altered and defaced. Its nàve, in which the early shafts and capitals of the pure truncate form are unaltered, is very fine in effect; its lateral porch is quaint and beautiful, decorated with Byzantine circular sculptures (of which the central one is given in Vol. II., Plate XI., fig. 5), and supported on two shafts whose capitals are the most archaic examples of the pure Rose form that I know in Venice.

There is a glorious Tintoret over the first altar on the right in entering; the "Circumcision of Christ." I do not know an aged head either more beautiful or more picturesque than that of the high priest. The cloister is full of notable tombs, nearly all dated; one, of the fifteenth century, to the left on entering, is interesting from the colour still left on the leaves and flowers of its sculptured roses.

Cassano, Church of St. This church must on no account be missed, as it contains three Tintorets, of which one, the "Crucifixion," is among the finest in Europe. There is nothing worth notice in the building itself, except the jamb of an ancient door (left in the Renaissance buildings, facing the canal), which has been given among the examples of Byzantine jambs; and the traveller may therefore devote his entire attention to the three pictures in the chancel.

1. *The Crucifixion.* (On the left of the high altar.) It is refreshing to find a picture taken care of, and in a bright, though not a good light, so that such parts of it as are seen at all are seen well. It is also in a better state than most pictures in galleries, and most remarkable for its new and strange treatment of the subject. It seems to have been

painted more for the artist's own delight, than with any laboured attempt at composition; the horizon is so low, that the spectator must fancy himself lying at full length on the grass, or rather among the brambles and luxuriant weeds, of which the foreground is entirely composed. Among these, the seamless robe of Christ has fallen at the foot of the cross; the rambling briars and wild grasses thrown here and there over its folds of rich, but pale, crimson. Behind them, and seen through them, the heads of a troop of Roman soldiers are raised against the sky; and, above them, their spears and halberds form a thin forest against the horizontal clouds. The three crosses are put on the extreme right of the picture, and its centre is occupied by the executioners, one of whom, standing on a ladder, receives from the other at once the sponge and the tablet with the letters INRI. The Madonna and St. John are on the extreme left, superbly painted, like all the rest, but quite subordinate. In fact, the whole mind of the painter seems to have been set upon making the principals accessory, and the accessories principal. We look first at the grass, and then at the scarlet robe; and then at the clump of distant spears, and then at the sky, and last of all at the cross. As a piece of colour, the picture is notable for its extreme modesty. There is not a single very full or bright tint in any part, and yet the colour is delighted in throughout; not the slightest touch of it but is delicious. It is worth notice also, and especially, because this picture being in a fresh state, we are sure of one fact, that, like nearly all other great colourists, Tintoret was afraid of light greens in his vegetation. He often uses dark blue greens in his shadowed trees, but here where the grass is in full light, it is all painted with various hues of sober brown, more especially where it crosses the crimson robe. The handling of the whole is in his noblest manner; and I consider the picture generally quite beyond all price. It was cleaned, I believe, some years ago, but not injured, or at least as little injured as it is possible for a picture to be which has undergone any cleaning process whatsoever.

2. *The Resurrection.* (Over the high altar.) The lower part of this picture is entirely concealed by a miniature temple, about five feet high, on the top of the altar; certainly an insult little expected by Tintoret, as, by getting on steps, and looking over the said temple, one may see that the lower figures of the picture are the most laboured. It is strange that the painter never seemed able to conceive this subject with any power, and in the present work he is marvellously hampered by various types and conventionalities. It is not a painting of the

Resurrection, but of Roman Catholic saints, *thinking* about the Resurrection. On one side of the tomb is a bishop in full robes, on the other a female saint, I know not who; beneath it, an angel playing on an organ, and a cherub blowing it; and other cherubs flying about the sky, with flowers; the whole conception being a mass of Renaissance absurdities. It is, moreover, heavily painted, over-done, and over-finished; and the forms of the cherubs utterly heavy and vulgar. I cannot help fancying the picture has been restored in some way or another, but there is still great power in parts of it. If it be a really untouched Tintoret, it is a highly curious example of failure from over-labour on a subject into which his mind was not thrown; the colour is hot and harsh, and felt to be so more painfully, from its opposition to the grand coolness and chastity of the "Crucifixion." The face of the angel playing the organ is highly elaborated; so, also, the flying cherubs.

3. *The Descent into Hades*. (On the right-hand side of the high altar.) Much injured and little to be regretted. I never was more puzzled by any picture, the painting being throughout careless, and in some places utterly bad, and yet not like modern work; the principal figure, however, of Eve, has either been re-done, or is scholar's work altogether, as, I suspect, most of the rest of the picture. It looks as if Tintoret had sketched it when he was ill, left it to a bad scholar to work on with, and then finished it in a hurry: but he has assuredly had something to do with it; it is not likely that anybody else would have refused all aid from the usual spectral company with which common painters fill the scene. Bronzino, for instance, covers his canvas with every form of monster that his sluggish imagination could coin. Tintoret admits only a somewhat haggard Adam, a graceful Eve, two or three Venetians in court dress, seen amongst the smoke, and a Satan represented as a handsome youth, recognizable only by the claws on his feet. The picture is dark and spoiled, but I am pretty sure there are no demons or spectres in it. This is quite in accordance with the master's caprice, but it considerably diminishes the interest of a work in other ways unsatisfactory. There may once have been something impressive in the shooting in of the rays at the top of the cavern, as well as in the strange grass that grows in the bottom, whose infernal character is indicated by its all being knotted together; but so little of these parts can be seen, that it is not worth spending time on a work certainly unworthy of the master, and in great part probably never seen by him.

CATTARINA, CHURCH OF ST., said to contain a *chef-d'œuvre* of Paul Veronese, the "Marriage of St. Catherine." I have not seen it.

CAVALLI, PALAZZO, opposite the Academy of Arts. An imposing pile, on the Grand Canal, of Renaissance Gothic, but of little merit in the details; and the effect of its traceries has been of late destroyed by the fittings of modern external blinds. Its balconies are good, of the later Gothic type. See "BARBARO."

CAVALLI, PALAZZO, next the Casa Grimani (or Post-Office), but on the other side of the narrow canal. Good Gothic, founded on the Ducal Palace, circa 1380. The capitals of the first story are remarkably rich in the deep fillets at the necks. The crests, heads of seahorses, inserted between the windows, appear to be later, but are very fine of their kind.

CICOGNA, PALAZZO, at San Sebastiano, II. 265.

CLEMENTE, CHURCH OF ST. On an island to the south of Venice, from which the view of the city is peculiarly beautiful. See "SCALZI."

CONTARINI, PORTA DI FERRO, PALAZZO, near the Church of St. John and Paul, so called from the beautiful ironwork on a door, which was some time ago taken down by the proprietor and sold. Mr. Rawdon Brown rescued some of the ornaments from the hands of the blacksmith who had bought them for old iron. The head of the door is a very interesting stone arch of the early thirteenth century, already drawn in my folio work. In the interior court is a beautiful remnant of staircase, with a piece of balcony at the top, circa 1350, and one of the most richly and carefully wrought in Venice. The palace, judging by these remnants (all that are now left of it, except a single traceried window of the same date at the turn of the stair), must once have been among the most magnificent in Venice.

CONTARINI (DELLE FIGURE), PALAZZO, on the Grand Canal, III. 17.

CONTARINI DAI SCRIGNI, PALAZZO, on the Grand Canal. A Gothic building, founded on the Ducal Palace. Two Renaissance statues in niches at the sides give it its name.

CONTARINI FASAN, PALAZZO, on the Grand Canal, II. 245. The richest work of the fifteenth century domestic Gothic in Venice, but notable more for riches than excellence of design. In one respect, however, it deserves to be regarded with attention, as showing how much beauty and dignity may be bestowed on a very small and unimportant dwelling-house by Gothic sculpture. Foolish criticisms upon it have appeared in English accounts of foreign buildings, objecting to it on the ground of its being "ill-proportioned;" the simple fact

being, that there was no room in this part of the canal for a wider house,
and that its builder made its rooms as comfortable as he could, and
its windows and balconies of a convenient size for those who were to
see through them, and stand on them, and left the " proportions " outside to take care of themselves ; which indeed they have very sufficiently
done ; for though the house thus honestly confesses its diminutive-
ness, it is nevertheless one of the principal ornaments of the very
noblest reach of the Grand Canal, and would be nearly as great a loss,
if it were destroyed, as the Church of La Salute itself.

CORNER DELLA CA' GRANDE, PALAZZO, on the Grand Canal. One of
the worst and coldest buildings of the central Renaissance. It is on
a grand scale, and is a conspicuous object, rising over the roofs of
the neighbouring houses in the various aspects of the entrance of the
Grand Canal, and in the general view of Venice from San Clemente.

CORNER DELLA REGINA, PALAZZO. A late Renaissance building of no
merit or interest.

CORNER SPINELLI, PALAZZO, on the Grand Canal. A graceful and
interesting example of the early Renaissance, remarkable for its pretty
circular balconies.

CORRER, RACCOLTA. [Carpaccio's portrait-study of the two ladies with
their pets is the most interesting piece of his finished execution
existing in Venice. The Visitation, slight but lovely. The Man-
tegna ? or John Bellini ? (the Transfiguration), of the most pathetic
interest. And there are many other curious and some beautiful minor
pictures. 1877.]

D.

DANDOLO, PALAZZO, on the Grand Canal. Between the Casa Loredan and
Casa Bembo is a range of modern buildings, some of which occupy,
I believe, the site of the palace once inhabited by the Doge Henry
Dandolo. Fragments of early architecture of the Byzantine school may
still be traced in many places among their foundations, and two doors
in the foundation of the Casa Bembo itself belong to the same group.
There is only one existing palace, however, of any value, on this spot,
a very small but rich Gothic one of about 1300, with two groups of
fourth-order windows in its second and third stories, and some Byzantine circular mouldings built into it above. This is still reported to
have belonged to the family of Dandolo, and ought to be carefully
preserved, as it is one of the most interesting and ancient Gothic
palaces which yet remain.

DANIELI, ALBERGO. See NANI.

DA PONTE, PALAZZO. Of no interest.

DARIO, PALAZZO, I. 13 (Plate I.).

DOGANA DI MARE, at the separation of the Grand Canal from the Giudecca. A barbarous building of the time of the Grotesque Renaissance (1676), rendered interesting only by its position. The statue of Fortune forming the weathercock, standing on the world, is alike characteristic of the conceits of the time, and of the hopes and principles of the last days of Venice.

DONATO, CHURCH OF ST., at Murano, II. 31.

DONA', PALAZZO, on the Grand Canal. I believe the palace described under this name as of the twelfth century, by M. Lazari, is that which I have called the Braided House, II. 132, 389.

D'ORO, CASA. A noble pile of very quaint Gothic, once superb in general effect, but now destroyed by restorations. I saw the beautiful slabs of red marble, which formed the bases of its balconies, and were carved into noble spiral mouldings of strange sections, half a foot deep, dashed to pieces when I was last in Venice ; its glorious interior staircase, by far the most interesting Gothic monument of the kind in Venice, had been carried away, piece by piece, and sold for waste marble, two years before. Of what remains, the most beautiful portions are, or were, when I last saw them, the capitals of the windows in the upper story, most glorious sculpture of the fourteenth century. The fantastic window traceries are, I think, later ; but the rest of the architecture of this palace is anomalous, and I cannot venture to give any decided opinion respecting it. Parts of its mouldings are quite Byzantine in character, but look somewhat like imitations.

DUCAL PALACE, I. 29 ; history of, II. 281, etc., III. 200 ; plan and section of, II. 282, 283 ; description of, II. 306, etc. ; series of its capitals, II. 329, etc. ; spandrils of, I. 290, 397 ; shafts of, I. 396 ; traceries of, derived from those of the Frari, II. 234 ; angles of, II. 240 ; main balcony of, II. 246 ; base of, III. 224 ; Rio Façade of, III. 25 ; paintings in, II. 374. The multitude of works by various masters which cover the walls of this palace is so great that the traveller is in general merely wearied and confused by them. He had better refuse all attention except to the following works :[*]

---

[*] [I leave this notice of the Ducal Palace as originally written. Everything is changed or confused, now, I believe : and the text will only be useful to travellers who have time to correct it for themselves to present need. For fuller account of Tintoret's Paradise, see my pamphlet on Michael Angelo and Tintoret. 1877.]

1. *Paradise*, by Tintoret; at the extremity of the Great Council-chamber. I found it impossible to count the number of figures in this picture, of which the grouping is so intricate, that at the upper part it is not easy to distinguish one figure from another; but I counted 150 important figures in one half of it alone; so that, as there are nearly as many in subordinate positions, the total number cannot be under 500. I believe this is, on the whole, Tintoret's *chef-d'œuvre;* though it is so vast that no one takes the trouble to read it, and therefore less wonderful pictures are preferred to it. I have not myself been able to study except a few fragments of it, all executed in his finest manner; but it may assist a hurried observer to point out to him that the whole composition is divided into concentric zones, represented one above another like the stories of a cupola, round the figures of Christ and the Madonna, at the central and highest point: both these figures are exceedingly dignified and beautiful. Between each zone or belt of the nearer figures, the white distances of heaven are seen filled with floating spirits. The picture is on the whole wonderfully preserved, and the most precious thing that Venice possesses. She will not possess it long; for the Venetian academicians, finding it exceedingly unlike their own works, declare it to want harmony, and are going to retouch it to their own ideas of perfection.

2. *Siege of Zara;* the first picture on the right on entering the Sala del Scrutinio. It is a mere battle piece, in which the figures, like the arrows, are put in by the score. There are high merits in the thing, and so much invention that it is possible Tintoret may have made the sketch for it; but, if executed by him at all, he has done it merely in the temper in which a sign-painter meets the wishes of an ambitious landlord. He seems to have been ordered to represent all the events of the battle at once; and to have felt that, provided he gave men, arrows, and ships enough, his employers would be perfectly satisfied. The picture is a vast one, some thirty feet by fifteen.

Various other pictures will be pointed out by the custode, in these two rooms, as worthy of attention, but they are only historically, not artistically, interesting. The works of Paul Veronese on the ceiling have been repainted; and the rest of the pictures on the walls are by second-rate men. The traveller must, once for all, be warned against mistaking the works of Domenico Robusti (Domenico Tintoretto), a very miserable painter, for those of his illustrious father, Jacopo.

3. *The Doge Grimani kneeling before Faith*, by Titian; in the Sala

delle quattro Porte. To be observed with care, as one of the most striking examples of Titian's want of feeling and coarseness of conception. (See above, Vol. I., p. 11.) As a work of mere art, it is, however, of great value. The traveller who has been accustomed to deride Turner's indistinctness of touch, ought to examine carefully the mode of painting the Venice in the distance at the bottom of this picture.

4. *Frescoes on the roof of the Sala delle quattro Porte*, by Tintoret. Once magnificent beyond description, now mere wrecks (the plaster crumbling away in large flakes), but yet deserving of the most earnest study.

5. *Christ taken down from the Cross*, by Tintoret ; at the upper end of the Sala dei Pregadi. One of the most interesting mythic pictures of Venice, two Doges being represented beside the body of Christ, and a most noble painting ; executed, however, for distant effect, and seen best from the end of the room.

6. *Venice, Queen of the Sea*, by Tintoret. Central compartment of the ceiling, in the Sala dei Pregadi. Notable for the sweep of its vast green surges, and for the daring character of its entire conception, though it is wild and careless, and in many respects unworthy of the master. Note the way in which he has used the fantastic forms of the sea-weeds, with respect to what was above stated (III. 158), as to his love of the grotesque.

7. *The Doge Loredano in prayer to the Virgin*, by Tintoret ; in the same room. Sickly and pale in colour, yet a grand work ; to be studied, however, more for the sake of seeing what a great man does " to order," when he is wearied of what is required from him, than for its own merit.

8. *St. George and the Princess.* There are, besides the " Paradise," only six pictures in the Ducal Palace, as far as I know, which Tintoret painted carefully, and these are all exceedingly fine : the most finished of those are in the Anti-Collegio ; but those that are most majestic and characteristic of the master are two oblong ones, made to fill the panels of the walls in the Anti-Chiesetta ; these two, each, I suppose, about eight feet by six, are in his most quiet and noble manner. There is excessively little colour in them, their prevalent tone being a greyish brown opposed with grey, black, and a very warm russet. They are thinly painted, perfect in tone, and quite untouched. The first of them is " St. George and the Dragon," the subject being treated in a new and curious way.

The principal figure is the princess, who sits astride on the dragon's neck, holding him by a bridle of silken riband; St. George stands above and behind her, holding his hands over her head as if to bless her, or to keep the dragon quiet by heavenly power; and a monk stands by on the right, looking gravely on. There is no expression or life in the dragon, though the white flashes in its eye are very ghastly : but the whole thing is entirely typical; and the princess is not so much represented riding on the dragon, as supposed to be placed by St. George in an attitude of perfect victory over her chief enemy. She has a full rich dress of dull red, but her figure is somewhat ungraceful. St. George is in grey armour and grey drapery, and has a beautiful face; his figure entirely dark against the distant sky. There is a study for this picture in the Manfrini Palace.

9. *St. Andrew and St. Jerome.* This, the companion picture, has even less colour than its opposite. It is nearly all brown and grey ; the fig-leaves and olive-leaves brown, the faces brown, the dresses brown, and St. Andrew holding a great brown cross. There is nothing that can be called colour, except the grey of the sky, which approaches in some places a little to blue, and a single piece of dirty brick-red in St. Jerome's dress ; and yet Tintoret's greatness hardly ever shows more than in the management of such sober tints. I would rather have these two small brown pictures, and two others in the Academy perfectly brown also in their general tone—the " Cain and Abel " and the " Adam and Eve,"—than all the other small pictures in Venice put together which he painted in bright colours for altar pieces ; but I never saw two pictures which so nearly approached grisailles as these, and yet were delicious pieces of colour. I do not know if I am right in calling one of the saints St. Andrew. He stands holding a great upright wooden cross against the sky. St. Jerome reclines at his feet, against a rock over which some glorious fig-leaves and olive branches are shooting ; every line of them studied with the most exquisite care, and yet cast with perfect freedom.

10. *Bacchus and Ariadne.* The most beautiful of the four careful pictures by Tintoret, which occupy the angles of the Anti-Collegio. Once one of the noblest pictures in the world, but now miserably faded, the sun being allowed to fall on it all day long. The design of the forms of the leafage round the head of the Bacchus, and the floating grace of the female figure above, will, however, always give interest to this picture, unless it be repainted.

The other three Tintorets in this room are careful and fine, but far inferior to the " Bacchus ; " and the " Vulcan and the Cyclops " is a singularly meagre and vulgar study of common models.

11. *Europa*, by Paul Veronese ; in the same room. One of the very few pictures which both possess, and deserve, a high reputation.

12. *Venice enthroned*, by Paul Veronese ; on the roof of the same room. One of the grandest pieces of frank colour in the Ducal Palace.

13. *Venice, and the Doge Sebastian Venier;* at the upper end of the Sala del Collegio. An unrivalled Paul Veronese, far finer even than the " Europa."

14. *Marriage of St. Catherine*, by Tintoret; in the same room. An inferior picture, but the figure of St. Catherine is quite exquisite. Note how her veil falls over her form, showing the sky through it, as an alpine cascade falls over a marble rock.

There are three other Tintorets on the walls of this room, but all inferior, though full of power. Note especially the painting of the lion's wings, and of the coloured carpet, in the one nearest the throne, the Doge Alvise Mocenigo adoring the Redeemer.*

The roof is entirely by Paul Veronese, and the traveller who really loves painting ought to get leave to come to this room whenever he chooses ; and should pass the sunny summer mornings there again and again, wandering now and then into the Anti-Collegio and Sala dei Pregadi, and coming back to rest under the wings of the couched lion at the feet of the " Mocenigo." He will no otherwise enter so deeply into the heart of Venice.

E.

ERIZZO, PALAZZO, near the Arsenal, II. 262.

ERIZZO, PALAZZO, on the Grand Canal, nearly opposite the Fondaco de' Turchi. A Gothic palace, with a single range of windows founded on the Ducal traceries, and bold capitals. It has been above referred to in the notice of tracery bars.

EUFEMIA, CHURCH OF ST. A small and defaced, but very curious, early Gothic church on the Giudecca. Not worth visiting, unless the traveller is seriously interested in architecture.

EUROPA, ALBERGO ALL'. Once a Giustiniani palace. Good Gothic, circa 1400, but much altered.

EVANGELISTI, CASA DEGLI, II. 265.

* [I was happy enough to obtain the original sketch for this picture, in Venice (it had been long in the possession of Signor Nerly) : and after being the most honoured of all pictures at Denmark Hill, until my father's death, it is now given to my school in Oxford.]

F.

FACANON, PALAZZO (ALLA FAVA).   A fair example of the fifteenth century
    Gothic, founded on Ducal Palace.

FALIER, PALAZZO, at the Apostoli.   Above, II. 254.

FANTINO, CHURCH OF ST.   Said to contain a John Bellini, otherwise of
    no importance.

FARSETTI, PALAZZO, on the Grand Canal, II. 124, 390.

FELICE, CHURCH OF ST.   Said to contain a Tintoret, which, if untouched,
    I should conjecture, from Lazari's statement of its subject, St. Deme-
    trius armed, with one of the Ghisi family in prayer, must be very fine.
    Otherwise the church is of no importance.

FERRO, PALAZZO, on the Grand Canal.   Fifteenth century Gothic, very
    hard and bad.

FONDACO DE' TURCHI, I. 319; II. 119, 121, 237.   The opposite plate,
    representing three of its capitals, has been several times referred to.

FONDACO DE' TEDESCHI.   A huge and ugly building near the Rialto,
    rendered, however, peculiarly interesting by remnants of the frescoes by
    Giorgione with which it was once covered.   See Vol. II. 79, and III. 23.

FORMOSA, CHURCH OF SANTA MARIA, III. 113, 122.

FOSCA, CHURCH OF ST.   Notable for its exceedingly picturesque cam-
    panile, of late Gothic, but uninjured by restorations, and peculiarly
    Venetian in being crowned by the cupola instead of the pyramid, which
    would have been employed at the same period in any other Italian
    city.

FOSCARI, PALAZZO, on the Grand Canal.   The noblest example in Venice
    of the fifteenth century Gothic, founded on the Ducal Palace, but
    lately restored and spoiled, all but the stonework of the main
    windows.   The restoration was necessary, however: for, when I was in
    Venice in 1845, this palace was a foul ruin; its great hall a mass of
    mud, used as the back receptacle of a stonemason's yard; and its
    rooms whitewashed, and scribbled over with indecent caricatures.   It
    has since been partially strengthened and put in order; but as the
    Venetian municipality have now given it to the Austrians to be used
    as barracks, it will probably soon be reduced to its former condition.
    The lower palaces at the side of this building are said by some to have
    belonged to the younger Foscari.   See "GIUSTINIANI."

FRANCESCO DELLA VIGNA, CHURCH OF ST.   Base Renaissance, but must
    be visited in order to see the John Bellini in the Cappella Santa.
    The late sculpture, in the Cappella Giustiniani, appears from Lazari's

XII

J. Ruskin.

J. H. Le Keux.

Capitals of Fondaco de' Turchi.

statement to be deserving of careful study. This church is said also to contain two pictures by Paul Veronese.

FRARI, CHURCH OF THE. Founded in 1250, and continued at various subsequent periods. The apse and adjoining chapels are the earliest portions, and their traceries have been above noticed (II. 234) as the origin of those of the Ducal Palace. The best view of the apse, which is a very noble example of Italian Gothic, is from the door of the Scuola di San Rocco.* The doors of the church are all later than any other portion of it, very elaborate Renaissance Gothic. The interior is good Gothic, but not interesting, except in its monuments. Of these, the following are noticed in the text of this volume :

That of Duccio degli Alberti, at pages 74, 80; of the unknown knight, opposite that of Duccio, III. 73 ; of Francesco Foscari, III. 84 ; of Giovanni Pesaro, 91 ; of Jacopo Pesaro, 90.

Besides these tombs, the traveller ought to notice carefully that of Pietro Bernardo, a first-rate example of Renaissance work ; nothing can be more detestable or mindless in general design, or more beautiful in execution. Examine especially the griffins, fixed in admiration of bouquets at the bottom. The fruit and flowers which arrest the attention of the griffins may well arrest the traveller's also; nothing can be finer of their kind. The tomb of Canova, *by* Canova, cannot be missed ; consummate in science, intolerable in affectation, ridiculous in conception, null and void to the uttermost in invention and feeling. The equestrian statue of Paolo Savelli is spirited ; the monument of the Beato Pacifico, a curious example of Renaissance Gothic with wild crockets (all in terra cotta). There are several good Vivarinis in the church, but its chief pictorial treasure is the John Bellini in the sacristy, the most finished and delicate example of the master in Venice. [1877. The Pesaro Titian was forgotten, I suppose, in this article, because I thought it as well known as the Assumption. I hold it now the best Titian in Venice ; the powers of portraiture and disciplined composition, shown in it, placing it far above the showy masses of commonplace cherubs and merely picturesque men, in the Assumption.]

G.

GIACOMO DE LORIO, CHURCH OF ST. A most interesting church, of the early thirteenth century, but grievously restored. Its capitals have

* [Now destroyed by restoration. 1877.]

been already noticed as characteristic of the earliest Gothic; and it is
said to contain four works of Paul Veronese, but I have not examined
them.   The pulpit is admired by the Italians, but is utterly worthless.
The verd-antique pillar in the south transept is a very noble example
of the "Jewel Shaft."   See the note at p. 82, Vol. II.

GIACOMO DI RIALTO, CHURCH OF ST.   A picturesque little church, on
the Piazza di Rialto.   It has been grievously restored, but the pillars
and capitals of its nave are certainly of the eleventh century; those of
its portico are of good central Gothic; and it will surely not be left
unvisited, on this ground, if on no other, that it stands on the site,
and still retains the name, of the first church ever built on that
Rialto which formed the nucleus of future Venice, and became afterwards the mart of her merchants.

GIOBBE, CHURCH OF ST., near the Canna Reggio.   Its principal entrance is a very fine example of early Renaissance sculpture.   Note
in it, especially, its beautiful use of the flower of the convolvulus.
There are said to be still more beautiful examples of the same period,
in the interior.   The cloister, though much defaced, is of the Gothic
period, and worth a glance.

GIORGIO DE' GRECI, CHURCH OF ST.   The Greek Church.   It contains
no valuable objects of art, but its service is worth attending by those
who have never seen the Greek ritual.

GIORGIO DE' SCHIAVONI, CHURCH OF ST.   Said to contain a very precious
series of paintings by Vittor Carpaccio.   [1877. See "St. Mark's
Rest."   First Supplement, "The Shrine of the Slaves."]

GIORGIO IN ALGA (St. George in the seaweed), CHURCH OF ST.   Unimportant in itself, but the most beautiful view of Venice at sunset is from
a point at about two-thirds of the distance from the city to the island.
[1877. From the island itself, now, the nearer view is spoiled by loath-
some mud-castings and machines.   But all is spoiled from what it was.
The Campanile, good early Gothic, had its top knocked off to get space
for an observatory in the siege.]

GIORGIO MAGGIORE, CHURCH OF ST.   A building which owes its interesting
effect chiefly to its isolated position, being seen over a great space
of lagoon.   The traveller should especially notice in its façade the
manner in which the central Renaissance architects (of whose style this
church is a renowned example) endeavoured to fit the laws they had
established to the requirements of their age.   Churches were required
with aisles and clerestories, that is to say, with a high central nave and
lower wings; and the question was, how to face this form with pillars of

one proportion. The noble Romanesque architects built story above story, as at Pisa and Lucca; but the base Palladian architects dared not do this. They must needs retain some image of the Greek temple, but the Greek temple was all of one height, a low gable roof being borne on ranges of equal pillars. So the Palladian builders raised first a Greek temple with pilasters for shafts ; and, *through the middle of its roof, or horizontal beam,* that is to say, of the cornice which externally represented this beam, they lifted another temple on pedestals, adding these barbarous appendages to the shafts, which otherwise would not have been high enough ; fragments of the divided cornice or tie-beam being left between the shafts, and the great door of the church thrust in between the pedestals. It is impossible to conceive a design more gross, more barbarous, more childish in conception, more servile in plagiarism, more insipid in result, more contemptible under every point of rational regard.

Observe, also, that when Palladio had got his pediment at the top of the church, he did not know what to do with it : he had no idea of decorating it except by a round hole in the middle. (The traveller should compare, both in construction and decoration, the Church of the Redentore with this of San Giorgio.) Now, a dark penetration is often a most precious assistance to a building dependent upon colour for its effect ; for a cavity is the only means in the architect's power of obtaining certain and vigorous shadow ; and for this purpose, a circular penetration, surrounded by a deep russet marble moulding, is beautifully used in the centre of the white field on the side of the Portico of St. Mark's. But Palladio had given up colour, and pierced his pediment with a circular cavity, merely because he had not wit enough to fill it with sculpture. The interior of the church is like a large assembly room, and would have been undeserving of a moment's attention, but that it contains some most precious pictures, namely :

1. *Gathering the Manna.* (On the left hand of the high altar.) One of Tintoret's most remarkable landscapes. A brook flowing through a mountainous country, studded with thickets and palm-trees : the congregation have been long in the Wilderness, and are employed in various manufactures much more than in gathering the manna. One group is forging, another grinding manna in a mill, another making shoes, one woman making a piece of dress, some washing ; the main purpose of Tintoret being evidently to indicate the *continuity* of the supply of heavenly food. Another painter would have made the congregation hurrying to gather it, and wondering at it ; Tintoret at once makes us

remember that they have been fed with it " by the space of forty years."
It is a large picture, full of interest and power, but scattered in effect,
and not striking except from its elaborate landscape.

2. *The Last Supper.* (Opposite the former.) These two pictures
have been painted for their places, the subjects being illustrative of the
sacrifice of the mass. This latter is remarkable for its entire homeliness
in the general treatment of the subject ; the entertainment being represented like any large supper in a second-rate Italian inn, the figures
being all comparatively uninteresting ; but we are reminded that the
subject is a sacred one, not only by the strong light shining from the
head of Christ, but because the smoke of the lamp which hangs over
the table turns, as it rises, into a multitude of angels, all painted
in grey, the colour of the smoke ; and so writhed and twisted together
that the eye hardly at first distinguishes them from the vapour out of
which they are formed, ghosts of countenances and filmy wings filling
up the intervals between the completed heads. The idea is highly
characteristic of the master. The picture has been grievously injured,
but still shows miracles of skill in the expression of candlelight mixed
with twilight ; variously reflected rays, and half tones of the dimly
lighted chamber, mingled with the beams of the lantern and those from
the head of Christ, flashing along the metal and glass upon the table, and
under it along the floor, and dying away into the recesses of the room.

3. *Martyrdom of various Saints.* (Altar piece of the third altar in
the south aisle.) A moderately sized picture, and now a very disagreeable one, owing to the violent red into which the colour that formed
the glory of the angel at the top is changed. It has been hastily
painted, and only shows the artist's power in the energy of the figure
of an executioner drawing a bow, and in the magnificent ease with
which the other figures are thrown together in all manner of wild
groups and defiances of probability. Stones and arrows are flying
about in the air at random.

4. *Coronation of the Virgin.* (Fourth altar in the same aisle.)
Painted more for the sake of the portraits at the bottom, than of the
Virgin at the top. A good picture, but somewhat tame for Tintoret, and
much injured. The principal figure, in black, is still, however, very fine.

5. *Resurrection of Christ.* (At the end of the north aisle, in the
chapel beside the choir.) Another picture painted chiefly for the sake
of the included portraits, and remarkably cold in general conception ;
Its colour has, however, been gay and delicate, lilac, yellow, and blue
being largely used in it. The flag which our Saviour bears in His

hand has been once as bright as the sail of a Venetian fishing-boat, but the colours are now all chilled, and the picture is rather crude than brilliant ; a mere wreck of what it was, and all covered with droppings of wax at the bottom.

6. *Martyrdom of St. Stephen.* (Altar piece in the north transept.) The saint is in a rich prelate's dress, looking as if he had just been saying mass, kneeling in the foreground, and perfectly serene. The stones are flying about him like hail, and the ground is covered with them as thickly as if it were a river bed. But in the midst of them, at the saint's right hand, there is a book lying, crushed, but open, two or three stones which have torn one of its leaves lying upon it. The freedom and ease with which the leaf is crumpled is just as charac-teristic of the master as any of the grander features ; no one but Tintoret could have so crushed a leaf ; but the idea is still more cha-racteristic of him, for the book is evidently meant for the Mosaic History which Stephen had just been expounding, and its being crushed by the stones shows how the blind rage of the Jews was violating their own law in the murder of Stephen. In the upper part of the picture are three figures,—Christ, the Father, and St. Michael. Christ of course at the right hand of the Father, as Stephen saw Him standing ; but there is little dignity in this part of the conception. In the middle of the picture, which is also the middle distance, are three or four men throwing stones, with Tintoret's usual vigour of gesture, and behind them an immense and confused crowd ; so that, at first, we wonder where St. Paul is ; but presently we observe that, in the front of this crowd, and *almost exactly in the centre of the picture*, there is a figure seated on the ground, very noble and quiet, and with some loose garments thrown across its knees. It is dressed in vigorous black and red. The figure of the Father in the sky above is dressed in black and red also, and these two figures are the centres of colour to the whole design. It is almost impossible to praise too highly the refinement of conception which withdrew the unconverted St. Paul into the distance, so as entirely to separate him from the immediate interest of the scene, and yet marked the dignity to which he was afterwards to be raised, by investing him with the colours which occurred nowhere else in the picture except in the dress which veils the form of the Godhead. It is also to be noted as an interesting example of the value which the painter put upon colour only ; another composer would have thought it necessary to exalt the future apostle by some peculiar dignity of action or expression. The posture of the figure is indeed

grand, but inconspicuous ; Tintoret does not depend upon it, and thinks that the figure is quite ennobled enough by being made a key-note of colour.

It is also worth observing how boldly imaginative is the treatment which covers the ground with piles of stones, and yet leaves the martyr apparently unwounded.   Another painter would have covered him with blood, and elaborated the expression of pain upon his countenance. Tintoret leaves us under no doubt as to what manner of death he is dying ; he makes the air hurtle with the stones, but he does not choose to make his picture disgusting, or even painful.   The face of the martyr is serene, and exulting ; and we leave the picture, remembering only how " he fell asleep."

GIOVANELLI, PALAZZO, at the Ponte di Noale.   A fine example of fifteenth century Gothic, founded on the Ducal Palace.

GIOVANNI E PAOLO, CHURCH OF ST.*   Foundation of, III. 69.   An impressive church, though none of its Gothic is comparable with that of the North, or with that of Verona.   The western door is interesting as one of the last conditions of Gothic design passing into Renaissance, very rich and beautiful of its kind, especially the wreath of fruit and flowers which forms its principal moulding.   The statue of Bartolomeo Colleone, in the little square beside the church, is certainly one of the noblest works in Italy.   I have never seen anything approaching it in animation, in vigour of portraiture, or nobleness of line.   The reader will need Lazari's Guide in making the circuit of the church, which is full of interesting monuments: but I wish especially to direct his attention to two pictures, besides the celebrated Peter Martyr : namely,

1. *The Crucifixion*, by Tintoret ; on the wall of the left-hand aisle, just before turning into the transept.   A picture fifteen feet long by eleven or twelve high.   I do not believe that either the " Miracle of St. Mark," or the great " Crucifixion" in the Scuola di San Rocco, cost Tintoret more pains than this comparatively small work, which is now utterly neglected, covered with filth and cobwebs, and fearfully injured. As a piece of colour, and light and shade, it is altogether marvellous. Of all the fifty figures which the picture contains, there is not one which in any way injures or contends with another ; nay, there is not a single fold of garment or touch of the pencil which could be spared ; every virtue of Tintoret, as a painter, is there in its highest degree,—colour at once the most intense and the most delicate, the utmost decision in

---

* I have always called this church, in the text, simply " St. John and Paul," not Sts. John and Paul ; just as the Venetians say San Giovanni e Paolo, and not Santi G., etc.

the arrangement of masses of light, and yet half tones and modulations of endless variety; and all executed with a magnificence of handling which no words are energetic enough to describe. I have hardly ever seen a picture in which there was so much decision, and so little impetuosity, and in which so little was conceded to haste, to accident, or to weakness. It is too infinite a work to be describable; but among its minor passages of extreme beauty, should especially be noticed the manner in which the accumulated forms of the human body, which fill the picture from end to end, are prevented from being felt heavy, by the grace and elasticity of two or three sprays of leafage which spring from a broken root in the foreground, and rise conspicuous in shadow against an interstice filled by the pale blue, grey, and golden light in which the distant crowd is invested, the office of this foliage being, in an artistical point of view, correspondent to that of the trees set by the sculptors of the Ducal Palace on its angles. But they have a far more important meaning in the picture than any artistical one. If the spectator will look carefully at the root which I have called broken, he will find that, in reality, it is not broken, but cut: the other branches of the young tree having *lately been cut away*. When we remember that one of the principal incidents in the great San Rocco Crucifixion is the ass feeding on withered palm-leaves, we shall be at no loss to understand the great painter's purpose in lifting the branch of this mutilated olive against the dim light of the distant sky; while, close beside it, St. Joseph of Arimathea drags along the dust a white garment, —observe, the principal light of the picture,—stained with the blood of that King before whom, five days before, His crucifiers had strewn their own garments in the way.

2. *Our Lady with the Camerlenghi.* (In the centre chapel of the three on the right of the choir.) A remarkable instance of the theoretical manner of representing scriptural facts, which, at this time, as noted in the second chapter of this volume, was undermining the belief of the facts themselves. Three Venetian chamberlains desired to have their portraits painted, and at the same time to express their devotion to the Madonna; to that end they are painted kneeling before her, and in order to account for their all three being together, and to give a thread or clue to the story of the picture, they are represented as the Three Magi; but lest the spectator should think it strange that the Magi should be in the dress of Venetian chamberlains, the scene is marked as a mere ideality, by surrounding the person of the Virgin with saints who lived five hundred years after her. She has for attendants St. Theodore,

St. Sebastian, and St. Carlo (query St. Joseph). One hardly knows whether most to regret the spirit which was losing sight of the verities of religious history in imaginative abstractions, or to praise the modesty and piety which desired rather to be represented as kneeling before the Virgin than in the discharge or among the insignia of important offices of state.

As an "Adoration of the Magi," the picture is, of course, sufficiently absurd : the St. Sebastian leans back in the corner to be out of the way; the three Magi kneel, without the slightest appearance of emotion, to a Madonna seated in a Venetian loggia of the fifteenth century, and three Venetian servants behind bear their offerings in a very homely sack, tied up at the mouth. As a piece of portraiture and artistical composition, the work is altogether perfect, perhaps the best piece of Tintoret's portrait-painting in existence. It is very carefully and steadily wrought, and arranged with consummate skill on a difficult plan. The canvas is a long oblong, I think about eighteen or twenty feet long, by about seven high; one might almost fancy the painter had been puzzled to bring the piece into use, the figures being all thrown into positions which a little diminish their height. The nearest chamberlain is kneeling, the two behind him bowing themselves slightly, the attendants behind bowing lower, the Madonna sitting, the St. Theodore sitting still lower on the steps at her feet, and the St. Sebastian leaning back, so that all the lines of the picture incline more or less from right to left as they ascend. This slope, which gives unity to the detached groups, is carefully exhibited by what a mathematician would call co-ordinates,—the upright pillars of the loggia and the horizontal clouds of the beautiful sky. The colour is very quiet, but rich and deep, the local tones being brought out with intense force, and the cast shadows subdued, the manner being much more that of Titian than of Tintoret. The sky appears full of light, though it is as dark as the flesh of the faces ; and the forms of its floating clouds, as well as of the hills over which they rise, are drawn with a deep remembrance of reality. There are hundreds of pictures of Tintoret's more amazing than this, but I hardly know one that I more love.

The reader ought especially to study the sculpture round the altar of the Cappella del Rosario, as an example of the abuse of the sculptor's art ; every accessory being laboured out with much ingenuity and intense effort to turn sculpture into painting, the grass, trees, and landscape being as far realized as possible, and in alto-relievo. These bas-reliefs are by various artists, and therefore exhibit the folly of the age, not the error of an individual.

The following alphabetical list of the tombs in this church which are alluded to as described in the text, with references to the pages where they are mentioned, will save some trouble :

Cavalli, Jacopo, III. 82.
Cornaro, Marco, III. 10.
Dolfin, Giovanni, III. 77.
Giustiniani, Marco, I. 306.
Mocenigo, Giovanni, III. 88.

Mocenigo, Pietro, III. 88.
Mocenigo, Tomaso, I. 7, 25, III. 83.
Morosini, Michele, III. 80.
Steno, Michele, III. 83.
Vendramin, Andrea, I. 26, III. 88.

GIOVANNI GRISOSTOMO, CHURCH OF ST. One of the most important in Venice. It is early Renaissance, containing some good sculpture, but chiefly notable as containing a noble Sebastian del· Piombo, and a John Bellini, which a few years hence, unless it be " restored," will be esteemed one of the most precious pictures in Italy, and among the most perfect in the world. John Bellini is the only artist who appears to me to have united, in equal and magnificent measures, justness of drawing, nobleness of colouring, and perfect manliness of treatment, with the purest religious feeling. He did, as far as it is possible to do it, instinctively and unaffectedly, what the Caracci only pretended to do. Titian colours better, but has not his piety. Leonardo draws better, but has not his colour. Angelico is more heavenly, but has not his manliness, far less his powers of art.

GIOVANNI ELEMOSINARIO, CHURCH OF ST. Said to contain a Titian and a Bonifazio. Of no other interest. [1877. 1398-1410, Selvatico. Its campanile is the most interesting piece of central Gothic remaining comparatively intact in Venice. It stands on four detached piers ; a greengrocer's shop in the space between them ; the stable tower for its roof. There are three lovely bits of heraldry, carved on three square stones, on its side towards the Rialto. Selvatico gives no ground for his date ; I believe 1298-1310 more probable. The Titian, only visible to me by the sacristan's single candle, seems languid and affected.]

GIOVANNI IN BRAGOLA, CHURCH OF ST. A Gothic church of the fourteenth century, small but interesting, and said to contain some precious works by Cima da Conegliano, and one by John Bellini.

GIOVANNI, S., SCUOLA DI. A fine example of the Byzantine Renaissance, mixed with remnants of good late Gothic. The little exterior cortile is sweet in feeling, and Lazari praises highly the work of the interior staircase.

GIUDECCA. The crescent-shaped island (or series of islands) which forms the most northern extremity of the city of Venice, though separated by a broad channel from the main city. Commonly said to derive its name from the number of Jews who lived upon it; but Lazari derives it from the word "judicato," in Venetian dialect "Zudegà," it having been in old time "adjudged" as a kind of prison territory to the more dangerous and turbulent citizens. It is now inhabited only by the poor, and covered by desolate groups of miserable dwellings, divided by stagnant canals.

Its two principal churches, the Redentore and St. Eufemia, are named in their alphabetical order.

GIUSEPPE DI CASTELLO, CHURCH OF ST. Said to contain a Paul Veronese : otherwise of no importance.

GIUSTINIANI, PALAZZO, on the Grand Canal, now Albergo all' Europa. Good late fourteenth century Gothic, but much altered.

GIUSTINIANI, PALAZZO, next the Casa Foscari, on the Grand Canal. Lazari, I know not on what authority, says that this palace was built by the Giustiniani family before 1428. It is one of those founded directly on the Ducal Palace, together with the Casa Foscari at its side : and there could have been no doubt of their date on this ground ; but it would be interesting, after what we have seen of the progress of the Ducal Palace, to ascertain the exact year of the erection of any of these imitations.

This palace contains some unusually rich detached windows, full of tracery, of which the profiles are given in the Appendix, under the title of the Palace of the Younger Foscari, it being popularly reported to have belonged to the son of the Doge.

GIUSTINIAN LOLIN, PALAZZO, on the Grand Canal. Of no importance.

GRASSI, PALAZZO, on the Grand Canal, now Albergo all' Imperator d' Austria. Of no importance.

GREGORIO, CHURCH OF ST., on the Grand Canal. An important church of the fourteenth century, now desecrated, but still interesting. Its apse is on the little canal crossing from the Grand Canal to the Giudecca, beside the Church of the Salute, and is very characteristic of the rude ecclesiastical Gothic contemporary with the Ducal Palace. The entrance to its cloisters, from the Grand Canal, is somewhat later ; a noble square door, with two windows on each side of it, the grandest examples in Venice of the late window of the fourth order.

The cloister, to which this door gives entrance, is exactly contemporary with the finest work of the Ducal Palace, circa 1350. It is the loveliest cortile I know in Venice ; its capitals consummate in design and execution ; and the low wall on which they stand showing remnants of sculpture unique, as far as I know, in such application.

GRIMANI, PALAZZO, on the Grand Canal, III. 32.

There are several other palaces in Venice belonging to this family, but none of any architectural interest.

J.

JESUITI, CHURCH OF THE. The basest Renaissance ; but worth a visit in order to examine the imitations of curtains in white marble inlaid with green.

It contains a Tintoret, " The Assumption," which I have not examined ; and a Titian, " The Martyrdom of St. Lawrence," originally, it seems to me, of little value, and now, having been restored, of none.

L.

LIBRERIA VECCHIA. A graceful building of the central Renaissance, designed by Sansovino, 1536, and much admired by all architects of the school. It was continued by Scamozzi, down the whole side of St. Mark's Place, adding another story above it, which modern critics blame as destroying the "eurithmia ; " never considering that had the two low stories of the Library been continued along the entire length of the Piazza, they would have looked so low that the entire dignity of the square would have been lost. As it is, the Library is left in its originally good proportions, and the larger mass of the Procuratie Nuove forms a more majestic, though less graceful, side for the great square.

But the real faults of the building are not in its number of stories, but in the design of the parts. It is one of the grossest examples of the base Renaissance habit of turning *keystones* into *brackets*, throwing them out in bold projection (not less than a foot and a half) beyond the mouldings of the arch ; a practice utterly barbarous, inasmuch as it evidently tends to dislocate the entire arch, if any real weight were laid on the extremity of the keystone ; and it is also a very characteristic example of the vulgar and painful mode of filling spandrils by naked figures in alto-relievo, leaning against the arch on each side, and appearing as if they were continually in danger of slipping off. Many of these figures have, however, some merit in themselves ; and the whole building is graceful and effective of its kind. The continuation of the Procuratie Nuove, at the western extremity of St. Mark's

Place (together with various apartments in the great line of the Procuratie Nuove), forms the "Royal Palace," the residence of the Emperor when at Venice. This building is entirely modern, built in 1810, in imitation of the Procuratie Nuove, and on the site of Sansovino's Church of San Geminiano.

In this range of buildings, including the Royal Palace, the Procuratie Nuove, the old Library, and the "Zecca" which is connected with them (the latter being an ugly building of very modern date, not worth notice architecturally), there are many most valuable pictures, among which I would especially direct attention, first to those in the Zecca, namely, a beautiful and strange Madonna, by Benedetto Diana; two noble Bonifazios; and two groups, by Tintoret, of the Provveditori della Zecca, by no means to be missed, whatever may be sacrificed to see them, on account of the quietness and veracity of their unaffected portraiture, and the absolute freedom from all vanity either in the painter or in his subjects.

Next, in the "Antisala" of the old Library, observe the "Sapienza" of Titian, in the centre of the ceiling; a most interesting work in the light brilliancy of its colour, and the resemblance to Paul Veronese. Then, in the great hall of the old Library, examine the two large Tintorets, "St. Mark saving a Saracen from Drowning," and the "Stealing his Body from Constantinople," both rude, but great (note in the latter the dashing of the rain on the pavement, and running of the water about the feet of the figures): then, in the narrow spaces between the windows, there are some magnificent single figures by Tintoret, among the finest things of the kind in Italy, or in Europe. Finally, in the gallery of pictures in the Palazzo Reale, among other good works of various kinds, are two of the most interesting Bonifazios in Venice, the "Children of Israel in their Journeyings," in one of which, if I recollect right, the quails are coming in flights across a sunset sky, forming one of the earliest instances I know of a thoroughly natural and Turneresque effect being felt and rendered by the old masters. The picture struck me chiefly from this circumstance; but, the note-book in which I had described it and its companion having been lost on my way home, I cannot now give a more special account of them, except that they are long, full of crowded figures, and peculiarly light in colour and handling as compared with Bonifazio's work in general.

LIO, CHURCH OF ST. Of no importance, but said to contain a spoiled Titian.

LIO, SALIZZADA DI ST., windows in, II. 253, 257.

LOREDAN, PALAZZO, on the Grand Canal near the Rialto, II. 123, 390. Another palace of this name, on the Campo St. Stefano, is of no importance.

LUCA, CHURCH OF ST. Its campanile is of very interesting and quaint early Gothic, and it is said to contain a Paul Veronese, "St. Luke and the Virgin." In the little Campiello St. Luca, close by, is a very precious Gothic door, rich in brickwork of the thirteenth century; and in the foundations of the houses on the same side of the square, but at the other end of it, are traceable some shafts and arches closely resembling the work of the Cathedral of Murano, and evidently having once belonged to some most interesting building.

M.

MALIPIERO, PALAZZO, on the Campo St. M. Formosa, facing the canal at its extremity. A very beautiful example of the Byzantine Renaissance. Note the management of colour in its inlaid balconies.

MANFRINI, PALAZZO. The architecture is of no interest; and as it is in contemplation to allow the collection of pictures to be sold, I shall take no note of them. But, even if they should remain, there are few of the churches in Venice where the traveller had not better spend his time than in this gallery; as, with the exception of Titian's "Entombment," one or two Giorgiones, and the little John Bellini (St. Jerome), the pictures are all of a kind which may be seen elsewhere.

MANZONI, PALAZZO, on the Grand Canal, near the Church of the Carità. A perfect and very rich example of Byzantine Renaissance; its warm yellow marbles are magnificent.

MARCILIAN, CHURCH OF ST. Said to contain a Titian, "Tobit and the Angel:" otherwise of no importance.

MARIA, CHURCHES OF STA. See FORMOSA, MATER DOMINI, MIRACOLI, ORTO, SALUTE, and ZOBENIGO.

MARCO, SCUOLA DI SAN, III. 16.

MARK, CHURCH OF ST., history of, II. 56; approach to, II. 70; general teaching of, II. 111, 115; measures of façade of, II. 126; balustrades of, II. 244, 247; cornices of, I. 302; horseshoe arches of, II. 250; entrances of, II. 271, III. 223; shafts of, II. 383; base in baptistery of, I. 282; mosaics in atrium of, II. 111; mosaics in cupola of, II. 114, III. 175; lily capitals of, II. 137; Plates illustrative of (Vol. II.), VI., VII., figs. 9, 10, 11, VIII. figs. 8, 9, 12, 13, 15, IX. XI. fig. 1, and Plate III. Vol. III.

their intermediate crosses, all complete, and well worth careful examination.

MICHELE IN ISOLA, CHURCH OF ST.   On the island between Venice and Murano.   The little Cappella Emiliana at the side of it has been much admired, but it would be difficult to find a building more feelingless or ridiculous.   It is more like a German summer-house, or angle turret, than a chapel, and may be briefly described as a bee-hive set on a low hexagonal tower, with dashes of stonework about its windows like the flourishes of an idle penman.

The cloister of this church is pretty; and the attached cemetery is worth entering, for the sake of feeling the strangeness of the quiet sleeping ground in the midst of the sea.

MINELLI, PALAZZO.   In the Corte del Maltese, at St. Paternian.   It has a spiral external staircase, very picturesque, but of the fifteenth century, and without merit.

MIRACOLI, CHURCH OF STA. MARIA DEI.   The most interesting and finished example in Venice of the Byzantine Renaissance, and one of the most important in Italy of the cinque-cento style.   All its sculptures should be examined with great care, as the best possible examples of a bad style.   Observe, for instance, that in spite of the beautiful work on the square pillars which support the gallery at the west end, they have no more architectural effect than two wooden posts.   The same kind of failure in boldness of purpose exists throughout; and the building is, in fact, rather a small museum of unmeaning, though refined sculpture, than a piece of architecture.

Its grotesques are admirable examples of the base Raphaelesque design examined above, III. 135.   Note especially the children's heads tied up by the hair, in the lateral sculptures at the top of the altar steps.   A rude workman, who could hardly have carved the head at all, might have been allowed this or any other mode of expressing discontent with his own doings; but the man who could carve a child's head so perfectly must have been wanting in all human feeling, to cut it off, and tie it by the hair to a vine leaf.   Observe, in the Ducal Palace, though far ruder in skill, the heads always *emerge* from the leaves, they are never *tied* to them.

MISERICORDIA, CHURCH OF.   The church itself is nothing, and contains nothing worth the traveller's time; but the Albergo de' Confratelli della Misericordia at its side is a very interesting and beautiful relic of the Gothic Renaissance.   Lazari says, " del secolo xiv.;" but I believe it to be later.   Its traceries are very curious and rich, and the sculpture of its capitals very fine for the late time. Close to it, on the right-hand side of the canal, which is crossed by the wooden bridge, is one of the richest Gothic doors in Venice, remarkable for the appearance of antiquity in the general design and stiffness of its figures, though it bears its date, 1505. Its extravagant crockets are almost the only features which, but for this written date, would at first have confessed its lateness; but, on examination, the figures will be found as bad and spiritless as they are apparently archaic, and completely exhibiting the Renaissance palsy of imagination.

The general effect is, however, excellent, the whole arrangement having been borrowed from earlier work.

The action of the statue of the Madonna, who extends her robe to shelter a group of diminutive figures, representative of the Society for whose house the sculpture was executed, may be also seen in most of the later Venetian figures of the Virgin which occupy similar situations. The image of Christ is placed in a medallion on her breast, thus fully, though conventionally, expressing the idea of self-support which is so often partially indicated by the great religious painters in their representations of the infant Jesus.

MOISÈ, CHURCH OF ST., III. 124. Notable as one of the basest examples of the basest school of the Renaissance. It contains one important picture, namely, "Christ Washing the Disciples' Feet," by Tintoret; on the left side of the chapel, north of the choir. This picture has been originally dark, is now much faded,—in parts, I believe, altogether destroyed,—and is hung in the worst light of a chapel, where, on a sunny day at noon, one could not easily read without a candle. I cannot, therefore, give much information respecting it; but it is certainly one of the least successful of the painter's works, and both careless and unsatisfactory in its composition as well as its colour. One circumstance is noticeable, as in a considerable degree detracting from the interest of most of Tintoret's representations of our Saviour with His disciples. He never loses sight of the fact that all were poor, and the latter ignorant; and while he never paints a senator or a saint, once thoroughly canonized, except as a gentleman, he is very careful to paint the Apostles, in their living intercourse with the Saviour, in such a manner that the spectator may see in an instant, as the Pharisee did of old, that they were unlearned and ignorant men; and, whenever we find them in a room, it is always such a one as would be inhabited by the lower classes. There seems some violation of this practice in the dais, or flight of steps, at the top of which the Saviour is placed in the present picture; but we are quickly reminded that the guests' chamber or upper room ready prepared was not likely to have been in a palace, by the humble furniture upon the floor, consisting of a tub with a copper saucepan in it, a coffee-pot, and a pair of bellows, curiously associated with a symbolic cup with a wafer, which, however, is in an injured part of the canvas, and may have been added by the priests. I am totally unable to state what the background of the picture is or has been; and the only point farther to be noted about it is the solemnity, which, in spite of the familiar and homely circumstances above noticed, the painter has given to the scene, by placing the Saviour, in the act of washing the feet of Peter, at the top of a circle of steps, on which the other Apostles kneel in adoration and astonishment.

MORO, PALAZZO. See OTHELLO.

MOROSINI, PALAZZO, near the Ponte dell' Ospedaletto, at San Giovanni e Paolo. Outside it is not interesting, though the gateway shows remains of brickwork of the thirteenth century. Its interior court is singularly beautiful; the staircase of early fourteenth century Gothic has originally been superb, and the window in the angle above is the most perfect that I know in Venice of the kind; the lightly sculptured coronet is exquisitely introduced at the top of its spiral shaft.

This palace still belongs to the Morosini family, to whose present representative, the Count Carlo Morosini, the reader is indebted for the note on the character of his ancestors, above, p. 225.

N.

NANI-MOCENIGO, PALAZZO. (Now Hotel Danieli.) A glorious example of the central Gothic, nearly contemporary with the finest parts of the Ducal Palace. Though less impressive in effect than the Casa Foscari or Casa Bernardo, it is of purer architecture than either; and quite unique in the delicacy of the form of the cusps in the central group of windows, which are shaped like broad scimitars, the upper foil of the windows being very small. If the traveller will compare these windows with the neighbouring traceries of the Ducal Palace, he will easily perceive the peculiarity.

O.

ORTO, CHURCH OF STA. MARIA DELL'. An interesting example of

Renaissance Gothic, the traceries of the windows being very rich and quaint.

It contains four most important Tintorets : " The Last Judgment," " The Worship of the Golden Calf," " The Presentation of the Virgin," and " Martyrdom of St. Agnes." The first two are among his largest and mightiest works, but grievously injured by damp and neglect ; and unless the traveller is accustomed to decipher the thoughts in a picture patiently, he need not hope to derive any pleasure from them. But no pictures will better reward a resolute study. The following account of the " Last Judgment," given in the second volume of " Modern Painters," will be useful in enabling the traveller to enter into the meaning of the picture, but its real power is only to be felt by patient examination of it.

" By Tintoret only has this unimaginable event (the Last Judgment) been grappled with in its Verity ; not typically nor symbolically, but as they may see it who shall not sleep, but be changed. Only one traditional circumstance he has received, with Dante and Michael Angelo, the Boat of the Condemned ; but the impetuosity of his mind bursts out even in the adoption of this image ; he has not stopped at the scowling ferryman of the one, nor at the sweeping blow and demon dragging of the other, but, seized Hylas-like by the limbs and tearing up the earth in his agony, the victim is dashed into his destruction ; nor is it the sluggish Lethe, nor the fiery lake, that bears the cursed vessel, but the oceans of the earth and the waters of the firmament gathered into one white, ghastly cataract ; the river of the wrath of God, roaring down into the gulf where the world has melted with its fervent heat, choked with the ruins of nations, and the limbs of its corpses tossed out of its whirling, like water-wheels. Bat-like, out of the holes and caverns and shadows of the earth, the bones gather, and the clay heaps heave, rattling and adhering into half-kneaded anatomies, that crawl, and startle, and struggle up among the putrid weeds, with the clay clinging to their clotted hair, and their heavy eyes sealed by the earth darkness yet, like his of old who went his way unseeing to the Siloam Pool ; shaking off one by one the dreams of the prison-house, hardly hearing the clangour of the trumpets of the armies of God, blinded yet more, as they awake, by the white light of the new Heaven, until the great vortex of the four winds bears up their bodies to the judgment-seat ; the Firmament is all full of them, a very dust of human souls, that drifts, and floats, and falls into the interminable, inevitable light ; the bright clouds are darkened with them as with thick snow, currents of atom life in the arteries of heaven, now soaring up slowly, and higher and higher still, till the eye and the thought can follow no farther, borne up, wingless, by their inward faith and by the angel powers invisible, now hurled in countless drifts of horror before the breath of their condemnation."

Note in the opposite picture the way the clouds are wrapped about the distant Sinai.

The figure of the little Madonna in the " Presentation " should be compared with Titian's in his picture of the same subject in the Academy. I prefer Tintoret's infinitely : and note how much finer is the feeling with which Tintoret has relieved the glory round her head against the pure sky, than that which influenced Titian in encumbering his distance with architecture. [1877. The whole picture has now been daubed over,—chiefly this lovely bit of sky, and is a ghastly ruin and eternal disgrace to modern Venice.]

The " Martyrdom of St. Agnes " *was* a lovely picture. It has been " restored " since I saw it.

OSPEDALETTO, CHURCH OF THE. The most monstrous example of the Grotesque Renaissance which there is in Venice ; the sculptures on its façade representing masses of diseased figures and swollen fruit.

It is almost worth devoting an hour to the successive examination of five buildings, as illustrative of the last degradation of the Renaissance. San Moisè is the most clumsy, Santa Maria Zobenigo the most impious, St. Eustachio the most ridiculous, the Ospedaletto the most monstrous, and the head at Santa Maria Formosa the most foul.

OTHELLO, HOUSE OF, at the CARMINI. The researches of Mr. Brown into the origin of the play of " Othello" have, I think, determined that Shakespeare wrote on definite historical grounds ; and that Othello may be in many points identified with Christopher Moro, the lieutenant of the republic at Cyprus in 1508. See " Ragguagli su Marin Sanuto," i. 226.

His palace was standing till very lately, a Gothic building of the fourteenth century, of which Mr. Brown possesses a drawing. It is now destroyed, and a modern square-windowed house built on its site. A statue, said to be a portrait of Moro, but a most paltry work, is set in a niche in the modern wall.

P.

PANTALEONE, CHURCH OF ST. Said to contain a Paul Veronese ; otherwise of no importance.

PATERNIAN, CHURCH OF ST. Its little leaning tower forms an interesting object, as the traveller sees it from the narrow canal which passes beneath the Porte San Paternian. The two arched lights of the belfry appear of very early workmanship, probably of the beginning of the thirteenth century.

PESARO, PALAZZO, on the Grand Canal. The most powerful and impressive in effect of all the palaces of the Grotesque Renaissance. The heads upon its foundation are very characteristic of the period, but there is more genius in them than usual. Some of the mingled expressions of faces and grinning casques are very clever.

PIAZZETTA, pillars of, see Final Appendix, under head " Capitals." The two magnificent blocks of marble, brought from St. Jean d'Acre, which form one of the principal ornaments of the Piazzetta, are Greek sculpture of the sixth century, and will be described in my folio work.

PIETRO, CHURCH OF ST., at Murano. Its pictures, once valuable, are now hardly worth examination, having been spoiled by neglect.

PIETRO DI CASTELLO, CHURCH OF ST., I. 7, 351. It is said to contain a Paul Veronese, and I suppose the so-called " Chair of St. Peter" must be worth examining.

PISANI, PALAZZO, on the Grand Canal. The latest Venetian Gothic, just passing into Renaissance. The capitals of the first-floor windows are, however, singularly spirited and graceful, very daringly undercut, and worth careful examination. The Paul Veronese, once the glory of this palace, is, I believe, not likely to remain in Venice.* The other picture in the same room, the " Death of Darius," is of no value.

PISANI, PALAZZO, at St. Stefano. Late Renaissance, and of no merit, but grand in its colossal proportions, especially when seen from the narrow canal at its side, which, terminated by the apse of the Church of San Stefano, is one of the most picturesque and impressive little pieces of water scenery in Venice.

POLO, CHURCH OF ST. Of no importance, except as an example of the advantages accruing from restoration. M. Lazari says of it, " Before this church was modernized, its principal chapel was adorned with mosaics, and possessed a pala of silver gilt, of Byzantine workmanship, which is now lost."

POLO, SQUARE OF ST. (Campo San Polo.) A large and important square, rendered interesting chiefly by three palaces on the side of it opposite

* [" The family of Darius at the feet of Alexander after the battle of Issus." It was purchased in 1857 by the English Government, and now hangs in London in the National Gallery.]

the church, of central Gothic (1360), and fine of their time, though small. One of their capitals has been given in Plate II. of this volume, fig. 12. They are remarkable as being decorated with sculptures of the Gothic time, in imitation of the Byzantine ones ; the period being marked by the dog-tooth, and cable being used instead of the dentil round the circles.

PANL, PALAZZO, at San G. Grisostomo (the House of Marco Polo), II. 139. Its interior court is full of interest, showing fragments of the old building in every direction, cornices, windows, and doors, of almost every period, mingled among modern rebuilding and restoration of all degrees of dignity.

POLO, PALAZZO, at San G. Grisostomo (the House of Marco Polo), II. 139. Its interior court is full of interest, showing fragments of the old building in every direction, cornices, windows, and doors, of almost every period, mingled among modern rebuilding and restoration of all degrees of dignity.

PORTA DELLA CARTA, II. 302.

PRIULI, PALAZZO. A most important and beautiful early Gothic palace, at San Severo ; the main entrance is from the Fondamento San Severo, but the principal façade is on the other side, towards the canal. The entrance has been grievously defaced, having had winged lions filling the spandrils of its pointed arch, of which only feeble traces are now left ; the façade has very early fourth-order windows in the lower story, and, above, the beautiful range of fifth-order windows drawn at the bottom of Plate XVIII. Vol. II., where the heads of the fourth-order range are also seen (note their inequality, the larger one at the flank). This palace has two most interesting traceried angle windows also, which, however, I believe are later than those on the façade ; and, finally, a rich and bold interior staircase.

PROCURATIE NUOVE, see " LIBRERIA." VECCHIE : A graceful series of buildings, of late fifteenth century design, forming the northern side of St. Mark's Place, but of no particular interest.

Q.

QUERINI PALAZZO, now the Beccherie, II. 255, III. 244.

R.

RAFFAELLE, CHIESA DELL' ANGELO. Said to contain a Bonifazio : otherwise of no importance.

REDENTORE, CHURCH OF THE, II. 377. It contains three interesting John Bellinis, and also, in the sacristy, a most beautiful Paul Veronese.

REMER, CORTE DEL, house in, II. 251.

REZZONICO, PALAZZO, on the Grand Canal. Of the Grotesque Renaissance time, but less extravagant than usual.

RIALTO, BRIDGE OF THE. The best building raised in the time of the

Grotesque Renaissance; very noble in its simplicity, in its proportions, and in its masonry. Note especially the grand way in which the oblique archstones rest on the butments of the bridge, safe, palpably both to the sense and eye: note also the sculpture of the Annunciation on the southern side of it; how beautifully arranged, so as to give more lightness and grace to the arch—*the dove, flying towards the Madonna, forming the keystone,*—and thus the whole action of the figures being parallel to the curve of the arch, while all the masonry is at right angles to it. Note, finally, one circumstance which gives peculiar firmness to the figure of the angel, and associates itself with the general expression of strength in the whole building; namely, that the sole of the advanced foot is set perfectly level, as if placed on the ground, instead of being thrown back behind like a heron's, as in most modern figures of this kind.

The sculptures themselves are not good; but these pieces of feeling in them are very admirable. The two figures on the other side, St. Mark and St. Theodore, are inferior, though all by the same sculptor, Girolamo Campagna.

The bridge was built by Antonio da Ponte, in 1588. It was anciently of wood, with a drawbridge in the centre, a representation of which may be seen in one of Carpaccio's pictures at the Accademia delle Belle Arti: and the traveller should observe that the interesting effect, both of this and the Bridge of Sighs, depends in great part on their both being *more* than bridges; the one a covered passage, the other a row of shops, sustained on an arch. No such effect can be produced merely by the masonry of the roadway itself.

RIO DEL PALAZZO, II. 283.

ROCCO, CAMPIELLO DI SAN, windows in, II. 258.

ROCCO, CHURCH OF ST. Notable only for the most interesting pictures by Tintoret which it contains, namely:

1. *San Rocco before the Pope.* (On the left of the door as we enter.) A delightful picture in his best manner, but not much laboured; and, like several other pictures in this church, it seems to me to have been executed at some period of the painter's life when he was either in ill-health, or else had got into a mechanical way of painting, from having made too little reference to nature for a long time. There is something stiff and forced in the white draperies on both sides, and a general character about the whole which I can feel better than I can describe; but which, if I had been the painter's physician, would have immediately caused me to order him to shut up

his painting-room, and take a voyage to the Levant and back again. The figure of the Pope is, however, extremely beautiful, and is not unworthy, in its jewelled magnificence, here dark against the sky, of comparison with the figure of the high priest in the " Presentation," in the Scuola di San Rocco.

2. *Annunciation*. (On the other side of door, on entering.) A most disagreeable and dead picture, having all the faults of the age, and none of the merits of the painter. It must be a matter of future investigation to me, what could cause the fall of his mind from a conception so great and so fiery as that of the " Annunciation " in the Scuola di San Rocco, to this miserable reprint of an idea worn out centuries before. One of the most inconceivable things in it, considered as the work of Tintoret, is that where the angel's robe drifts away behind his limb ; one cannot tell by the character of the outline, or by the tones of the colour, whether the cloud comes in before the robe, or whether the robe cuts upon the cloud. The Virgin is uglier than that of the Scuola, and not half so real ; and the draperies are crumpled in the most commonplace and ignoble folds. It is a picture well worth study, as an example of the extent to which the greatest mind may be betrayed by the abuse of its powers, and the neglect of its proper food in the study of nature.

3. *Pool of Bethesda*. (On the right side of the church, in its centre, the lowest of the two pictures which occupy the wall.) A noble work, but eminently disagreeable, as must be all pictures of this subject ; and with the same character in it of undefinable want, which I have noticed in the two preceding works. The main figure in it is the cripple, who has taken up his bed ; but the whole effect of this action is lost by his not turning to Christ, but flinging it on his shoulder like a triumphant porter with a huge load ; and the corrupt Renaissance architecture, among which the figures are crowded, is both ugly in itself, and much too small for them. It is worth noticing, for the benefit of persons who find fault with the perspective of the Pre-Raphaelites, that the perspective of the brackets beneath these pillars is utterly absurd ; and that, in fine, the presence or absence of perspective has nothing to do with the merits of a great picture ; not that the perspective of the Pre-Raphaelites *is* false in any case that I have examined, the objection being just as untenable as it is ridiculous.

4. *San Rocco in the Desert*. (Above the last-named picture.) A single recumbent figure in a not very interesting landscape, deserving less attention than a picture of St. Martin just opposite to it,—a noble

and knightly figure on horseback by Pordenone, to which I cannot pay a greater compliment than by saying that I was a considerable time in doubt whether or not it was another Tintoret.

5. *San Rocco in the Hospital.* (On the right-hand side of the altar.) There are four vast pictures by Tintoret in the dark choir of this church, not only important by their size (each being some twenty-five feet long by ten feet high), but also elaborate compositions; and remarkable, one for its extraordinary landscape, and the other as the most studied picture in which the painter has introduced horses in violent action. In order to show what waste of human mind there is in these dark churches of Venice, it is worth recording that, as I was examining these pictures, there came in a party of eighteen German tourists, not hurried, nor jesting among themselves, as large parties often do, but patiently submitting to their cicerone, and evidently desirous of doing their duty as intelligent travellers. They sat down for a long time on the benches of the nave, looked a little at the " Pool of Bethesda," walked up into the choir, and there heard a lecture of considerable length from their *valet-de-place* upon some subject connected with the altar itself, which, being in German, I did not understand; they then turned and went slowly out of the church, not one of the whole eighteen ever giving a single glance to any of the four Tintorets, and only one of them, as far as I saw, even raising his eyes to the walls on which they hung, and immediately withdrawing them, with a jaded and *nonchalant* expression, easily interpretable into " Nothing but old black pictures." The two Tintorets above noticed, at the end of the church, were passed also without a glance; and this neglect is not because the pictures have nothing in them capable of arresting the popular mind, but simply because they are totally in the dark, or confused among easier and more prominent objects of attention. This picture, which I have called " St. Rocco in the Hospital," shows him, I suppose, in his general ministrations at such places, and is one of the usual representations of disgusting subjects from which neither Orcagna nor Tintoret seems ever to have shrunk. It is a very noble picture, carefully composed and highly wrought; but to me gives no pleasure, first, on account of its subject, secondly, on account of its dull brown tone all over,—it being impossible, or nearly so, in such a scene, and at all events inconsistent with its feeling, to introduce vivid colour of any kind. So it is a brown study of diseased limbs in a close room.

6. *Cattle Piece.* (Above the picture last described.) I can give no

other name to this picture, whose subject I can neither guess nor
discover, the picture being in the dark, and the guide-books leaving
me in the same position.   All I can make out of it is, that there is
a noble landscape, with cattle and figures.   It seems to me the best
landscape of Tintoret's in Venice, except the " Flight into Egypt ; "
and is even still more interesting from its savage character, the principal trees being pines, something like Titian's in his " St. Francis
receiving the Stigmata," and chestnuts on the slopes and in the hollows
of the hills : the animals also seem first-rate.   But it is too high, too
much faded, and too much in the dark to be made out.   It seems never
to have been rich in colour, rather cool and grey, and very full of light.

 7. *Finding of Body of San Rocco.* (On the left-hand side of the
altar.)   An elaborate, but somewhat confused picture, with a flying
angel in a blue drapery ; but it seemed to me altogether uninteresting,
or, perhaps, requiring more study than I was able to give it.

 8. *San Rocco in Campo d' Armata.* So this picture is called by the
sacristan.   I could see no San Rocco in it ; nothing but a wild group of
horses and warriors in the most magnificent confusion of fall and flight
ever painted by man.   They seem all dashed different ways as if by a
whirlwind ; and a whirlwind there must be, or a thunderbolt, behind
them, for a huge tree is torn up and hurled into the air beyond the central figure as if it were a shivered lance.   Two of the horses meet in the
midst, as if in a tournament ; but in madness or fear, not in hostility : on
the horse to the right is a standard-bearer, who stoops as from some foe
behind him, with the lance laid across his saddle-bow, level, and the flag
stretched out behind him as he flies, like the sail of a ship drifting from
its mast ; the central horseman, who meets the shock, of storm, or
enemy, whatever it be, is hurled backwards from his seat, like a stone
from a sling ; and this figure, with the shattered tree trunk behind it,
is the most noble part of the picture.   There is another grand horse
on the right, however, also in full action.   Two gigantic figures on foot,
on the left, meant to be nearer than the others, would, it seems to me,
have injured the picture, had they been clearly visible ; but time has
reduced them to perfect subordination.

Rocco, Scuola di San, bases of, I. 283, 411 ; soffit ornaments of, I.
327.   An interesting building of the early Renaissance (1517), passing
into Roman Renaissance.   The wreaths of leafage about its shafts are
wonderfully delicate and fine, though misplaced.

 As regards the pictures which it contains, it is one of the three most
precious buildings in Italy ; buildings, I mean, consistently decorated

with a series of paintings at the time of their erection, and still exhibit-ing that series in its original order.   I suppose there can be little question but that the three most important edifices of this kind in Italy are the Sistine Chapel, the Campo Santo of Pisa, and the Scuola di San Rocco at Venice : the first painted by Michael Angelo ; the second by Orcagna, Benozzo Gozzoli, Pietro Laurati, and several other men whose works are as rare as they are precious ; and the third by Tintoret.

Whatever the traveller may miss in Venice, he should, therefore, give unembarrassed attention and unbroken time to the Scuola di San Rocco ; and I shall, accordingly, number the pictures, and note in them, one by one, what seemed to me most worthy of observation.

They are sixty-two in all, but eight of these are merely of children or children's heads, and two of unimportant figures.   The number of valuable pictures is fifty-two ; arranged on the walls and ceilings of three rooms, so badly lighted, in consequence of the admirable arrange-ments of the Renaissance architect, that it is only in the early morning that some of the pictures can be seen at all, nor can they ever be seen but imperfectly.   They were all painted, however, for their places in the dark, and, as compared with Tintoret's other works, are therefore, for the most part, nothing more than vast sketches, made to produce, under a certain degree of shadow, the effect of finished pictures.   Their treat-ment is thus to be considered as a kind of scene-painting ; differing from ordinary scene-painting only in this, that the effect aimed at is not *that of a natural scene,* but *of a perfect picture.*   They differ in this respect from all other existing works ; for there is not, as far as I know, any other instance in which a great master has consented to work for a room plunged into almost total obscurity.   It is probable that none but Tintoret would have undertaken the task, and most fortunate that he was forced to it.   For in this magnificent scene-painting we have, of course, more wonderful examples, both of his handling and knowledge of effect, than could ever have been exhibited in finished pictures ; while the necessity of doing much with few strokes keeps his mind so completely on the stretch throughout the work (while yet the velocity of production prevented his being wearied), that no other series of his works exhibits powers so exalted.   On the other hand, owing to the velocity and coarseness of the painting, it is more liable to injury through drought or damp ; and as the walls have been for years con-tinually running down with rain, and what little sun gets into the place contrives to fall all day right on one or other of the pictures, they are nothing but wrecks of what they were ; and the ruins of paintings originally coarse are not likely ever to be attractive to the public mind. Twenty or thirty years ago they were taken down to be re-touched ; but the man to whom the task was committed providentially died, and only one of them was spoiled. I have found traces of his work upon another, but not to an extent very seriously destructive. The rest of the sixty-two, or, at any rate, all that are in the upper room, appear entirely intact.

Although, as compared with his other works, they are all very scenic in execution, there are great differences in their degrees of finish ; and, curiously enough, some on the ceilings and others in the darkest places in the lower room are very nearly finished pictures, while the "Agony in the Garden," which is in one of the best lights in the upper room, appears to have been painted in a couple of hours with a broom for a brush.

For the traveller's greater convenience I shall give a rude plan of the arrangement, and list of the subjects, of each group of pictures before examining them in detail.

First group.   On the walls of the room on the ground floor.

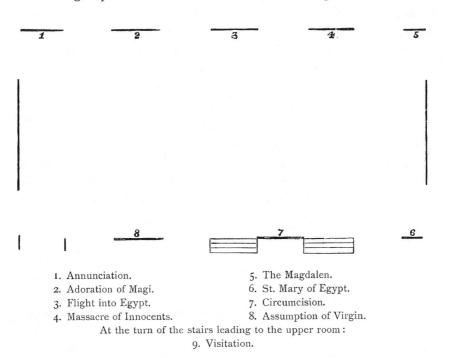

1. Annunciation.
2. Adoration of Magi.
3. Flight into Egypt.
4. Massacre of Innocents.
5. The Magdalen.
6. St. Mary of Egypt.
7. Circumcision.
8. Assumption of Virgin.

At the turn of the stairs leading to the upper room :
9. Visitation.

1. *The Annunciation.* This, which first strikes the eye, is a very just representative of the whole group, the execution being carried to the

utmost limits of boldness consistent with completion. It is a well-known picture, and need not therefore be specially described, but one or two points in it require notice. The face of the Virgin is very disagreeable to the spectator from below, giving the idea of a woman about thirty, who had never been handsome. If the face is untouched, it is the only instance I have ever seen of Tintoret's failing in an intended effect, for, when seen near, the face is comely and youthful, and expresses only surprise, instead of the pain and fear of which it bears the aspect in the distance. I could not get near enough to see whether it had been retouched. It looks like Tintoret's work, though rather hard ; but, as there are unquestionable marks of the re-touching of this picture, it is possible that some slight restoration of lines supposed to be faded, entirely alters the distant expression of the face. One of the evident pieces of repainting is the scarlet of the Madonna's lap, which is heavy and lifeless. A far more injurious one is the strip of sky seen through the doorway by which the angel enters, which has originally been of the deep golden colour of the distance on the left, and which the blundering restorer has daubed over with whitish blue, so that it looks like a bit of the wall ; luckily he has not touched the outlines of the angel's black wings, on which the whole expression of the picture depends. This angel and the group of small cherubs above form a great swinging chain, of which the dove representing the Holy Spirit forms the bend. The angels in their flight seem to be attached to this as the train of fire is to a rocket ; all of them appearing to have swooped down with the swiftness of a falling star.

2. *Adoration of the Magi.* The most finished picture in the Scuola except the " Crucifixion," and perhaps the most delightful of the whole. It unites every source of pleasure that a picture can possess ; the highest elevation of principal subject, mixed with the lowest detail of picturesque incident ; the dignity of the highest ranks of men, opposed to the simplicity of the lowest ; the quietness and serenity of an incident in cottage life, contrasted with the turbulence of troops of horsemen and the spiritual power of angels. The placing of the two doves as principal points of light in the front of the picture, in order to remind the spectator of the poverty of the mother whose child is receiving the offerings and adoration of three monarchs, is one of Tintoret's master touches ; the whole scene, indeed, is conceived in his happiest manner. Nothing can be at once more humble or more dignified than the bearing of the kings : and there is a sweet reality given to the whole incident by the Madonna's stooping forward and lifting her hand in admiration of

the vase of gold which has been set before the Christ, though she does so with such gentleness and quietness that her dignity is not in the least injured by the simplicity of the action. As if to illustrate the means by which the Wise Men were brought from the East, the whole picture is nothing but a large star, of which the Christ is the centre; all the figures, even the timbers of the roof, radiate from the small bright figure on which the countenances of the flying angels are bent, the star itself, gleaming through the timbers above, being quite subordinate. The composition would almost be too artificial were it not broken by the luminous distance, where the troop of horsemen are waiting for the kings. These, with a dog running at full speed, at once interrupt the symmetry of the lines, and form a point of relief from the over-concentration of all the rest of the action.

3. *Flight into Egypt.* One of the principal figures here is the donkey. I have never seen any of the nobler animals—lion, or leopard, or horse, or dragon—made so sublime as this quiet head of the domestic ass, chiefly owing to the grand motion in the nostril and writhing in the ears. The space of the picture is chiefly occupied by lovely landscape, and the Madonna and St. Joseph are pacing their way along a shady path upon the banks of a river at the side of the picture. I had not any conception, until I got near, how much pains had been taken with the Virgin's head; its expression is as sweet and as intense as that of any of Raffaelle's, its reality far greater. The painter seems to have intended that everything should be subordinate to the beauty of this single head; and the work is a wonderful proof of the way in which a vast field of canvas may be made conducive to the interest of a single figure. This is partly accomplished by slightness of painting, so that on close examination, while there is everything to astonish in the masterly handling and purpose, there is not much perfect or very delightful painting; in fact, the two figures are treated like the living figures in a scene at the theatre, and finished to perfection, while the landscape is painted as hastily as the scenes, and with the same kind of opaque size colour. It has, however, suffered as much as any of the series, and it is hardly fair to judge of its tones and colours in its present state.

4. *Massacre of the Innocents.* The following account of this picture, given in "Modern Painters," may be useful to the traveller, and is therefore here repeated. " I have before alluded to the painfulness of Raffaelle's treatment of the Massacre of the Innocents. Fuseli affirms of it, that, ' in dramatic gradation he disclosed all

the mother through every image of pity and of terror.' If this be so, I think the philosophical spirit has prevailed over the imaginative. The imagination never errs ; it sees all that is, and all the relations and bearings of it : but it would not have confused the mortal frenzy of maternal terror with various development of maternal character. Fear, rage, and agony, at their utmost pitch, sweep away all character : humanity itself would be lost in maternity, the woman would become the mere personification of animal fury or fear. For this reason all the ordinary representations of this subject are, I think, false and cold : the artist has not heard the shrieks, nor mingled with the fugitives ; he has sat down in his study to convulse features methodically, and philosophize over insanity. Not so Tintoret. Knowing, or feeling, that the expression of the human face was, in such circumstances, not to be rendered, and that the effort could only end in an ugly falsehood, he denies himself all aid from the features, he feels that if he is to place himself or us in the midst of that maddened multitude, there can be no time allowed for watching expression. Still less does he depend on details of murder or ghastliness of death ; there is no blood, no stabbing or cutting, but there is an awful substitute for these in the chiaroscuro. The scene is the outer vestibule of a palace, the slippery marble floor is fearfully barred across by sanguine shadows, so that our eyes seem to become bloodshot and strained with strange horror and deadly vision ; a lake of life before them, like the burning seen of the doomed Moabite on the water that came by the way of Edom : a huge flight of stairs, without parapet, descends on the left ; down this rush a crowd of women mixed with the murderers ; the child in the arms of one has been seized by the limbs ; *she hurls herself over the edge, and falls head downmost, dragging the child out of the grasp by her weight ;*—she will be dashed dead in a second :—close to us is the great struggle ; a heap of the mothers, entangled in one mortal writhe with each other and the swords ; one of the murderers dashed down and crushed beneath them, the sword of another caught by the blade and dragged at by a woman's naked hand ; the youngest and fairest of the women, her child just torn away from a death grasp, and clasped to her breast with the grip of a steel vice, falls backwards, helplessly over the heap, right on the sword points ; all knit together and hurled down in one hopeless, frenzied, furious abandonment of body and soul in the effort to save. Far back, at the bottom of the stairs, there is something in the shadow like a heap of clothes. It is a woman, sitting quiet,—quite quiet,—still as any stone ; she looks down steadfastly on her dead child, laid along on the floor before her, and her hand is pressed softly upon her brow."*

I have nothing to add to the above description of this picture, except that I believe there may have been some change in the colour of the shadow that crosses the pavement. The chequers of the pavements are, in the light, golden white and pale grey; in the shadow, red and dark grey, the white in the sunshine becoming red in the shadow. I formerly supposed that this was meant to give greater horror to the scene, and it is very like Tintoret if it be so; but there is a strangeness and discordance in it which makes me suspect the colours may have changed.

5. *The Magdalen.* This and the picture opposite to it, "St. Mary of Egypt," have been painted to fill up narrow spaces between the windows which were not large enough to receive compositions, and yet in which single figures would have looked awkwardly thrust into the corner. Tintoret has made these spaces as large as possible by filling them with landscapes, which are rendered interesting by the introduction of single figures of very small size. He has not, however, considered his task, of making a small piece of wainscot look like a large one, worth the stretch of his powers, and has painted these two landscapes just as carelessly and as fast as an upholsterer's journeyman finishing a room at a railroad hotel. The colour is for the most part opaque, and dashed or scrawled on in the manner of a scene-painter; and as during the whole morning the sun shines upon the one picture, and during the afternoon upon the other, hues, which were originally thin and imperfect, are now dried in many places into mere dirt upon the canvas. With all these drawbacks the pictures are of very high interest, for although, as I said, hastily and carelessly, they are not languidly painted; on the contrary, he has been in his hottest and grandest temper; and in this first one (Magdalen) the laurel-tree, with its leaves driven hither and thither among flakes of fiery cloud, has been probably one of the greatest achievements that his hand performed in landscape: its roots are entangled in underwood, of which every leaf seems to be articulated, yet all is as wild as if it had grown there instead of having been painted; there has been a mountain distance, too, and a sky of stormy light, of which I infinitely regret the loss, for though its masses of light are still discernible, its variety of hue is all sunk into a withered brown. There is a curious piece of execution in the striking of the

* ["Modern Painters," vol. ii., p. 174, of the old edition, and pp. 103—5 of vol. ii. of the revised edition in two vols.]

light upon a brook which runs under the roots of the laurel in the foreground : these roots are traced in shadow against the bright surface of the water : another painter would have drawn the light first, and drawn the dark roots over it.   Tintoret has laid in a brown ground which he has left for the roots, and painted the water through their interstices with a few mighty rolls of his brush laden with white.

6. *St. Mary of Egypt*.   This picture differs but little, in the plan, from the one opposite, except that St. Mary has her back towards us, and the Magdalen her face, and that the tree on the other side of the brook is a palm instead of a laurel.   The brook (Jordan ?) is, however, here much more important ; and the water painting is exceedingly fine.   Of all painters that I know, in old times, Tintoret is the fondest of running water ; there was a sort of sympathy between it and his own impetuous spirit.   The rest of the landscape is not of much interest, except so far as it is pleasant to see trunks of trees drawn by single strokes of the brush.

7. *The Circumcision of Christ*.   The custode has some story about this picture having been painted in imitation of Paul Veronese.   I much doubt if Tintoret ever imitated anybody ; but this picture is the expression of his perception of what Veronese delighted in, the nobility that there may be in mere golden tissue and coloured drapery. It is, in fact, a picture of the moral power of gold and colour ; and the chief use of the attendant priest is to support upon his shoulders the crimson robe, with its square tablets of black and gold ; and yet nothing is withdrawn from the interest or dignity of the scene.   Tintoret has taken immense pains with the head of the high priest.   I know not any existing old man's head so exquisitely tender, or so noble in its lines. He receives the infant Christ in his arms kneeling, and looking down upon the child with infinite veneration and love ; and the flashing of golden rays from its head is made the centre of light and all interest. The whole picture is like a golden charger to receive the Child ; the priest's dress is held up behind him, that it may occupy larger space ; the tables and floor are covered with chequer-work ; the shadows of the temple are filled with brazen lamps ; and above all are hung masses of curtains, whose crimson folds are strewn over with golden flakes.   Next to the "Adoration of the Magi" this picture is the most laboriously finished of the Scuola di San Rocco, and it is unquestionably the highest existing type of the Sublimity which may be thrown into the treatment of accessories of dress and decoration.

8. *Assumption of the Virgin*.   On the tablet or panel of stone which

forms the side of the tomb out of which the Madonna rises, is this
inscription, in large letters, REST. ANTONIUS FLORIAN, 1834.
Exactly in proportion to a man's idiocy is always the size of the letters
in which he writes his name on the picture that he spoils.   The old
mosaicists in St. Mark's have not, in a single instance, as far as I
know, signed their names ; but the spectator who wishes to know who
destroyed the effect of the nave, may see his name inscribed twice over,
in letters half a foot high, BARTOLOMEO BOZZA.   I have never seen
Tintoret's name signed, except in the great " Crucifixion ; " but this
Antony Florian, I have no doubt, repainted the whole side of the tomb
that he might put his name on it.   The picture is, of course, ruined
wherever he touched it, that is to say, half over : the circle of cherubs
in the sky is still pure ; and the design of the great painter is palpable
enough yet in the grand flight of the horizontal angel, on whom the
Madonna half leans as she ascends.   It has been a noble picture, and
is a grievous loss ; but, happily, there are so many pure ones, that we
need not spend time in gleaning treasures out of the ruins of this.

   9. *Visitation*.   A small picture, painted in his very best manner ;
exquisite in its simplicity, unrivalled in vigour, well preserved, and,
as a piece of painting, certainly one of the most precious in Venice.
Of course, it does not show any of his high inventive powers : nor can
a picture of four middle-sized figures be made a proper subject of
comparison with large canvases containing forty or fifty ; but it is, for
this very reason, painted with such perfect ease, and yet with no
slackness either of affection or power, that there is no picture that I
covet so much.   It is, besides, altogether free from the Renaissance
taint of dramatic effect. The gestures are as simple and natural as
Giotto's, only expressed by grander lines, such as none but Tintoret
ever reached.   The draperies are dark, relieved against a light sky, the
horizon being excessively low, and the outlines of the drapery so severe
that the intervals between the figures look like ravines between great
rocks, and have all the sublimity of an alpine valley at twilight.
This precious picture is hung about thirty feet above the eye, but
by looking at it in a strong light, it is discoverable that the St.
Elizabeth is dressed in green and crimson, the Virgin in the peculiar
red which all great colourists delight in,—a sort of glowing brick
colour or brownish scarlet, opposed to a rich golden brownish
black ; and both have white kerchiefs, or drapery, thrown over their
shoulders.   Zacharias leans on his staff behind them in a black dress
with white sleeves.   The stroke of brilliant white light, which outlines

the knee of St. Elizabeth, is a curious instance of the habit of the
painter to relieve his dark forms by a sort of halo of more vivid light
which, until lately, one would have been apt to suppose a somewhat
artificial and unjustifiable means of effect. The daguerreotype has
shown—what the naked eye never could—that the instinct of the
great painter was true, and that there is actually such a sudden and
sharp line of light round the edges of dark objects relieved by luminous
space.

Opposite this picture is a most precious Titian, the "Annunciation,"
full of grace and beauty. I think the Madonna one of the sweetest
figures he ever painted. But if the traveller has entered at all into
the spirit of Tintoret, he will immediately feel the comparative feebleness and conventionality of the Titian. Note especially the mean and
petty folds of the angels' drapery, and compare them with the draperies
of the opposite picture. The larger pictures at the sides of the stairs
by Zanchi and Negri are utterly worthless.

Second group.   On the walls of the upper room.

10. Adoration of Shepherds.   17. Resurrection of Lazarus.
11. Baptism.   18. Ascension.
12. Resurrection.   19. Pool of Bethesda.
13. Agony in Garden.   20. Temptation.
14. Last Supper.   21. St. Rocco.
15. Altar Piece : St. Rocco.   22. St. Sebastian.
16. Miracle of Loaves.

10. *The Adoration of the Shepherds.*   This picture commences the
series of the upper room, which, as already noticed, is painted with far

less care than that of the lower. It is one of the painter's inconceivable caprices that the only canvases that are in good light should be covered in this hasty manner, while those in the dungeon below, and on the ceiling above, are all highly laboured. It is, however, just possible that the covering of these walls may have been an after-thought, when he had got tired of his work. They are also, for the most part, illustrative of a principle of which I am more and more convinced every day, that historical and figure pieces ought not to be made vehicles for effects of light. The light which is fit for a historical picture is that tempered semi-sunshine of which, in general, the works of Titian are the best examples, and of which the picture we have just passed, "The Visitation," is a perfect example from the hand of one greater than Titian ; so also the three "Crucifixions," of San Rocco, San Cassano, and St. John and Paul ; the "Adoration of the Magi" here ; and, in general, the finest works of the master ; but Tintoret was not a man to work in any formal or systematic manner ; and, exactly like Turner, we find him recording every effect which Nature herself displays. Still, he seems to regard the pictures which deviate from the great general principle of colourists rather as "tours de force" than as sources of pleasure ; and I do not think there is any instance of his having worked out one of these tricky pictures with thorough affection, except only in the case of the "Marriage of Cana." By tricky pictures, I mean those which display light entering in different directions, and attract the eye to the effects rather than to the figure which displays them. Of this treatment, we have already had a marvellous instance in the candlelight picture of the "Last Supper" in San Giorgio Maggiore. This "Adoration of the Shepherds" has probably been nearly as wonderful when first painted ; the Madonna is seated on a kind of hammock floor, made of rope netting, covered with straw ; it divides the picture into two stories, of which the uppermost contains the Virgin, with two women who are adoring Christ, and shows light entering from above through the loose timbers of the roof of the stable, as well as through the bars of a square window ; the lower division shows this light falling behind the netting upon the stable floor, occupied by a cock and a cow, and against this light are relieved the figures of the shepherds, for the most part in demi-tint, but with flakes of more vigorous sunshine falling here and there upon them from above. The optical illusion has originally been as perfect as in one of Hunt's best interiors : but it is most curious that no part of the work seems to have been taken any pleasure in by the painter ; it is all by his hand, but it looks as if he had been bent only on getting over the ground. It is literally a piece of scene-painting, and is exactly what we might fancy Tintoret to have done, had he been forced to paint scenes at a small theatre at a shilling a day. I cannot think that the whole canvas, though fourteen feet high and ten wide, or thereabouts, could have taken him more than a couple of days to finish : and it is very noticeable that exactly in proportion to the brilliant effects of light is the coarseness of the execution, for the figures of the Madonna, and of the women above, which are not in any strong effect, are painted with some care, while the shepherds and the cow are alike slovenly ; and the latter, which is in full sunshine, is recognizable for a cow more by its size and that of its horns, than by any care given to its form. It is interesting to contrast this slovenly and mean sketch with the ass's head in the "Flight into Egypt," on which the painter exerted his full power ; as an effect of light, however, the work is, of course, most interesting. One point in the treatment is especially noticeable : there is a peacock in the rack beyond the cow ; and, under other circumstances, one cannot doubt that Tintoret would have liked a peacock in full colour, and would have painted it green and blue with great satisfaction. It is sacrificed to the light, however, and is painted in warm grey, with a dim eye or two in the tail : this process is exactly analogous to Turner's taking the colours out of the flags of his ships in the "Gosport." Another striking point is the litter with which the whole picture is filled in order more to confuse the eye : there is straw sticking from the roof, straw all over the hammock floor, and straw struggling hither and thither all over the floor itself ; and, to add to the confusion, the glory round the head of the infant, instead of being united and serene, is broken into little bits, and is like a glory of chopped straw. But the most curious thing, after all, is the want of delight in any of the principal figures, and the comparative meanness and commonplaceness of even the folds of the drapery. It seems as if Tintoret had determined to make the shepherds as uninteresting as possible ; but one does not see why their very clothes should be ill painted, and their disposition unpicturesque. I believe, however, though it never struck me until I had examined this picture, that this is one of the painter's fixed principles : he does not, with German sentimentality, make shepherds and peasants graceful or sublime, but he purposely vulgarizes them, not by making their actions or their faces boorish or disagreeable, but rather by painting them ill, and composing their draperies tamely. As far as I recollect at present, the principle is universal with him ; exactly in proportion to the dignity of character is the beauty of the painting. He will not put out his strength upon any man belonging to the lower classes ; and, in order to know what the painter is, one must see him at work on a king, a senator, or a saint. The curious connexion of this with the aristocratic tendencies of the Venetian nation, when we remember that Tintoret was the greatest man whom that nation produced, may become very interesting, if followed out. I forgot to note that, though the peacock is painted with great regardlessness of colour, there is a feature in it which no common painter would have observed,—the peculiar flatness of the back and undulation of the shoulders : the bird's body is all there, though its feathers are a good deal neglected ; and the same thing is noticeable in a cock who is pecking among the straw near the spectator, though in other respects a shabby cock enough. The fact is, I believe he had made his shepherds so commonplace that he dared not paint his animals well, otherwise one would have looked at nothing in the picture but the peacock, cock, and cow. I cannot tell what the shepherds are offering ; they look like milk-bowls, but they are awkwardly held up, with such twistings of body as would have certainly spilt the milk. A woman in front has a basket of eggs ; but this I imagine to be merely to keep up the rustic character of the scene, and not part of the shepherds' offerings.

11. *Baptism.* There is more of the true picture quality in this work than in the former one, but still very little appearance of enjoyment or care. The colour is for the most part grey and uninteresting, and the figures are thin and meagre in form, and slightly painted ; so much so, that, of the nineteen figures in the distance, about a dozen are hardly worth calling figures, and the rest are so sketched and flourished in that one can hardly tell which is which. There is one point about it very interesting to a landscape painter : the river is seen far into the distance, with a piece of copse bordering it : the sky beyond is dark, but the water nevertheless receives a brilliant reflection from some unseen rent in the clouds, so brilliant, that when I was first at Venice, not being accustomed to Tintoret's slight execution, or to see pictures so much injured, I took this piece of water for a piece of sky. The effect, as Tintoret has arranged it, is indeed somewhat unnatural, but it is valuable as showing his recognition of a principle unknown to half the historical painters of the present day,—that the reflection seen in water is totally different from the object seen above it, and that it is very possible to have a bright light in reflection where there appears nothing

but darkness to be reflected. The clouds in the sky itself are round, heavy, and lightless ; and in a great degree spoil what would otherwise be a fine landscape distance. Behind the rocks on the right a single head is seen, with a collar on the shoulders : it seems to be intended for a portrait of some person connected with the picture.

12. *Resurrection.* Another of the "effect of light" pictures, and not a very striking one, the best part of it being the two distant figures of the Maries seen in the dawn of the morning. The conception of the Resurrection itself is characteristic of the worst points of Tintoret. His impetuosity is here in the wrong place : Christ bursts out of the rock like a thunderbolt, and the angels themselves seem likely to be crushed under the rent stones of the tomb. Had the figure of Christ been sublime, this conception might have been accepted ; but, on the contrary, it is weak, mean, and painful ; and the whole picture is languidly or roughly painted, except only the fig-tree at the top of the rock, which, by a curious caprice, is not only drawn in the painter's best manner, but has golden ribs to all its leaves, making it look like one of the beautiful crossed or chequered patterns, of which he is so fond in his dresses : the leaves themselves being a dark olive brown.

13. *The Agony in the Garden.* I cannot at present understand the order of these subjects ; but they may have been misplaced. This, of all the San Rocco pictures, is the most hastily painted, but it is not, like those we have been passing, *clodly* painted ; it seems to have been executed altogether with a hearth-broom, and in a few hours. It is another of the "effects," and a very curious one ; the angel who bears the cup to Christ is surrounded by a red halo ; yet the light which falls upon the shoulders of the sleeping disciples, and upon the leaves of the olive-trees, is cool and silvery, while the troop coming up to seize Christ are seen by torchlight. Judas, who is the second figure, points to Christ, but turns his head away as he does so, as unable to look at him. That is a noble touch ; the foliage is also exceedingly fine, though what kind of olive-tree bears such leaves I know not, each of them being about the size of a man's hand. If there be any which bear such foliage, their olives must be of the size of cocoa-nuts. This, however, is true only of the underwood, which is, perhaps, not meant for olive. There are some taller trees at the top of the picture, whose leaves are of a more natural size. On closely examining the figures of the troop on the left, I find that the distant ones are concealed, all but the limbs, by a sort of arch of dark colour, which is now so injured, that I cannot tell whether it was foliage or ground : I suppose it to have

been a mass of close foliage, through which the troop is breaking its way; Judas rather showing them the path, than actually pointing to Christ, as it is written, " Judas, who betrayed Him, knew the place." St. Peter, as the most zealous of the three disciples, the only one who was to endeavour to defend his Master, is represented as wakening and turning his head towards the troop, while James and John are buried in profound slumber, laid in magnificent languor among the leaves. The picture is singularly impressive, when seen far enough off, as an image of thick forest gloom amidst the rich and tender foliage of the South : the leaves, however, tossing as in disturbed night air, and the flickering of the torches, and of the branches, contrasted with the steady flame which from the angel's presence is spread over the robes of the disciples. The strangest feature in the whole is that the Christ also is represented as sleeping. The angel seems to appear to Him in a dream.

14. *The Last Supper.* A most unsatisfactory picture; I think about the worst I know of Tintoret's, where there is no appearance of retouching. He always makes the disciples in this scene too vulgar; they are here not only vulgar, but diminutive, and Christ is at the end of the table, the smallest figure of them all. The principal figures are two mendicants sitting on steps in front, a kind of supporters, but I suppose intended to be waiting for the fragments : a dog, in still more earnest expectation, is watching the movements of the disciples, who are talking together, Judas having but just gone out. Christ is represented as giving what one at first supposes is the sop to Judas, but as the disciple who receives it has a glory, and there are only eleven at table, it is evidently the sacramental bread. The room in which they are assembled is a sort of large kitchen, and the host is seen employed at a dresser in the background. This picture has not only been originally poor, but is one of those exposed all day to the sun, and is dried into mere dusty canvas ; where there was once blue, there is now nothing.

15. *St. Rocco in Glory.* One of the worst order of Tintorets, with apparent smoothness and finish, yet languidly painted, as if in illness or fatigue ; very dark and heavy in tone also ; its figures, for the most part, of an awkward middle size, about five feet high, and very uninteresting. St. Rocco ascends to Heaven, looking down upon a crowd of poor and sick persons who are blessing and adoring him. One of these, kneeling at the bottom, is very nearly a repetition, though a careless and indolent one, of that of St. Stephen, in St. Giorgio Maggiore, and of the central figure in the " Paradise " of the Ducal

Palace. It is a kind of lay figure of which he seems to have been fond; its clasped hands are here shockingly painted,—I should think unfinished. It forms the only important light at the bottom, relieved on a dark ground; at the top of the picture, the figure of St. Rocco is seen in shadow against the light of the sky, and all the rest is in confused shadow. The commonplaceness of this composition is curiously connected with the languor of thought and touch throughout the work.

16. *Miracle of the Loaves.* Hardly anything but a fine piece of landscape is here left; it is more exposed to the sun than any other picture in the room, and its draperies having been, in great part, painted in blue, are now mere patches of the colour of starch; the scene is also very imperfectly conceived. The twenty-one figures, including Christ and His disciples, very ill represent a crowd of seven thousand; still less is the marvel of the miracle expressed by the perfect ease and rest of the reclining figures in the foreground, who do not so much as look surprised: considered merely as reclining figures, and as pieces of effect in half light, they have once been fine. The landscape, which represents the slope of a woody hill, has a very grand and far-away look. Behind it is a great space of streaky sky, almost prismatic in colour, rosy and golden clouds covering up its blue, and some fine vigorous trees thrown against it; painted in about ten minutes each, however, by curly touches of the brush, and looking rather more like seaweed than foliage.

17. *Resurrection of Lazarus.* Very strangely, and not impressively, conceived. Christ is half reclining, half sitting, at the bottom of the picture, while Lazarus is disencumbered of his grave-clothes at the top of it; the scene being the side of a rocky hill, and the mouth of the tomb probably once visible in the shadow on the left; but all that is now discernible is a man having his limbs unbound, as if Christ were merely ordering a prisoner to be loosed. There appears neither awe nor agitation, nor even much astonishment, in any of the figures of the group: but the picture is more vigorous than any of the three last mentioned, and the upper part of it is quite worthy of the master, especially its noble fig-tree and laurel, which he has painted, in one of his usual fits of caprice, as carefully as that in the " Resurrection of Christ," opposite. Perhaps he has some meaning in this; he may have been thinking of the verse, " Behold the fig-tree, and all the trees; when they now shoot forth," etc. In the present instance, the leaves are dark only, and have no golden veins. The uppermost figures

also come dark against the sky, and would form a precipitous mass, like a piece of the rock itself, but that they are broken in upon by one of the limbs of Lazarus, bandaged and in full light, which, to my feeling, sadly injures the picture, both as a disagreeable object, and a light in the wrong place. The grass and weeds are, throughout, carefully painted, but the lower figures are of little interest, and the face of the Christ a grievous failure.

18. *The Ascension.* I have always admired this picture, though it is very slight and thin in execution, and cold in colour ; but it is remarkable for its thorough effect of open air, and for the sense of motion and clashing in the wings of the angels which sustain the Christ: they owe this effect a good deal to the manner in which they are set, edge on ; all seem like sword-blades cutting the air. It is the most curious in conception of all the pictures in the Scuola, for it represents, beneath the Ascension, a kind of epitome of what took place before the Ascension. In the distance are two apostles walking, meant, I suppose, for the two going to Emmaus ; nearer are a group round a table, to remind us of Christ appearing to them as they sat at meat : and in the foreground is a single reclining figure of, I suppose, St. Peter, because we are told that " He was seen of Cephas, then of the twelve :" but this interpretation is doubtful ; for why should not the vision by the Lake of Tiberias be expressed also ? And the strange thing of all is the scene, for Christ ascended from the Mount of Olives ; but the disciples are walking, and the table is set, in a little marshy and grassy valley, like some of the bits near Maison Neuve on the Jura, with a brook running through it, so capitally expressed, that I believe it is this which makes me so fond of the picture. The reflections are as scientific in the diminution, in the image, of large masses of bank above, as any of Turner's, and the marshy and reedy ground looks as if one would sink into it ; but what all this has to do with the Ascension I cannot see. The figure of Christ is not undignified, but by no means either interesting or sublime.

19. *Pool of Bethesda.* I have no doubt the principal figures have been repainted ; but as the colours are faded, and the subject disgusting, I have not paid this picture sufficient attention to say how far the injury extends ; nor need any one spend time upon it, unless after having first examined all the other Tintorets in Venice. All the great Italian painters appear insensible to the feeling of disgust at disease ; but this study of the population of an hospital is without any points of contrast, and I wish Tintoret had not condescended to paint it.

This and the six preceding paintings have all been uninteresting,—I believe chiefly owing to the observance in them of Sir Joshua's rule for the heroic, "that drapery is to be mere drapery, and not silk, nor satin, nor brocade." However wise such a rule may be when applied to works of the purest religious art, it is anything but wise as respects works of colour. Tintoret is never quite himself unless he has fur or velvet, or rich stuff of one sort or the other, or jewels, or armour, or something that he can put play of colour into, among his figures, and not dead folds of linsey-wolsey; and I believe that even the best pictures of Raffaelle and Angelico are not a little helped by their hems of robes, jewelled crowns, priests' copes, and so on; and the pictures that have nothing of this kind in them, as for instance the "Transfiguration," are to my mind not a little dull.

20. *Temptation.* This picture singularly illustrates what has just been observed; it owes great part of its effect to the lustre of the jewels in the armlet of the evil angel, and to the beautiful colours of his wings. These are slight accessories apparently, but they enhance the value of all the rest, and they have evidently been enjoyed by the painter. The armlet is seen by reflected light, its stones shining by inward lustre; this occult fire being the only hint given of the real character of the Tempter, who is otherways represented in the form of a beautiful angel, though the face is sensual: we can hardly tell how far it was intended to be therefore expressive of evil; for Tintoret's good angels have not always the purest features; but there is a peculiar subtlety in this telling of the story by so slight a circumstance as the glare of the jewels in the darkness. It is curious to compare this imagination with that of the mosaics in St. Mark's, in which Satan is a black monster, with horns, and head, and tail, complete. The whole of the picture is powerfully and carefully painted, though very broadly; it is a strong effect of light, and therefore, as usual, subdued in colour. The painting of the stones in the foreground I have always thought, and still think, the best piece of rock drawing before Turner, and the most amazing instance of Tintoret's perceptiveness afforded by any of his pictures.

21. *St. Rocco.* Three figures occupy the spandrils of the windows above this and the following picture, painted merely in light and shade, two larger than life, one rather smaller. I believe these to be by Tintoret; but as they are quite in the dark, so that the execution cannot be seen, and very good designs of the kind have been furnished by other masters, I cannot answer for them. The figure of St. Rocco, as well as its companion, St. Sebastian, is

coloured; they occupy the narrow intervals between the windows, and are of course invisible under ordinary circumstances. By a great deal of straining of the eyes, and sheltering them with the hand from the light, some little idea of the design may be obtained. The " St. Rocco" is a fine figure, though rather coarse, but at all events, worth as much light as would enable us to see it.

22. *St. Sebastian.* This, the companion figure, is one of the finest things in the whole room, and assuredly the most majestic St. Sebastian in existence, as far as mere humanity can be majestic, for there is no effort at any expression of angelic or saintly resignation; the effort is simply to realize the fact of the martyrdom, and it seems to me that this is done to an extent not even attempted by any other painter. I never saw a man die a violent death, and therefore cannot say whether this figure be true or not, but it gives the grandest and most intense impression of truth. The figure is dead, and well it may be, for there is one arrow through the forehead and another through the heart; but the eyes are open, though glazed, and the body is rigid in the position in which it last stood, the left arm raised and the left limb advanced, something in the attitude of a soldier sustaining an attack under his shield, while the dead eyes are still turned in the direction from which the arrows came : but the most characteristic feature is the way these arrows are fixed. In the common martyrdoms of St. Sebastian they are stuck into him here and there like pins, as if they had been shot from a great distance and had come faltering down, entering the flesh but a little way, and rather bleeding the saint to death than mortally wounding him ; but Tintoret had no such ideas about archery. He must have seen bows drawn in battle, like that of Jehu when he smote Jehoram between the harness : all the arrows in the saint's body lie straight in the same direction, broad-feathered and strong-shafted, and sent apparently with the force of thunderbolts ; every one of them has gone through him like a lance, two through the limbs, one through the arm, one through the heart, and the last has crashed through the forehead, nailing the head to the tree behind, as if it had been dashed in by a sledge-hammer. The face, in spite of its ghastliness, is beautiful, and has been serene ; and the light which enters first and glistens on the plumes of the arrows, dies softly away upon the curling hair, and mixes with the glory upon the forehead. There is not a more remarkable picture in Venice, and yet I do not suppose that one in a thousand of the travellers who pass through the Scuola so much as perceive there is a picture in the place which it occupies.

Third Group.   On the roof of the upper room.

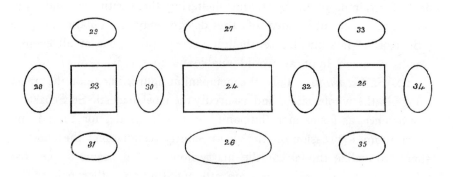

23. Moses Striking the   27. Ezekiel's Vision.   32. Sacrifice of Isaac.
      Rock.   28. Fall of Man.   33. Elijah at the Brook.
24. Plague of Serpents.   29. Elijah.   34. Paschal Feast.
25. Fall of Manna.   30. Jonah.   35. Elisha Feeding the
26. Jacob's Dream.   31. Joshua.   People.

23. *Moses Striking the Rock.* We now come to the series of pictures
upon which the painter concentrated the strength he had reserved
for the upper room ; and in some sort wisely, for, though it is not
pleasant to examine pictures on a ceiling, they are at least distinctly
visible without straining the eyes against the light.   They are carefully conceived, and thoroughly well painted in proportion to their
distance from the eye.   This carefulness of thought is apparent
at a glance: the "Moses Striking the Rock" embraces the whole
of the seventeenth chapter of Exodus, and even something more,
for it is not from that chapter, but from parallel passages that we
gather the facts of the impatience of Moses and the wrath of God
at the waters of Meribah ; both which facts are shown by the
leaping of the stream out of the rock half-a-dozen ways at once,
forming a great arch over the head of Moses, and by the partial veiling of the countenance of the Supreme Being.   This latter is the most
painful part of the whole picture, at least as it is seen from below ;
and I believe that in some repairs of the roof this head must have been
destroyed and repainted.   It is one of Tintoret's usual fine thoughts
that the lower part of the figure is veiled, not merely by clouds, but
in a kind of watery sphere, showing the Deity coming to the Israelites
at that particular moment as the Lord of the Rivers and of the Fountain

of the Waters.   The whole figure, as well as that of Moses, and the greater number of those in the foreground, is at once dark and warm, black and red being the prevailing colours, while the distance is bright gold touched with blue, and seems to open into the picture like a break of blue sky after rain.   How exquisite is this expression, by mere colour, of the main force of the fact represented ! that is to say, joy and re-freshment after sorrow and scorching heat.   But, when we examine of what this distance consists, we shall find still more cause for admiration. The blue in it is not the blue of sky, it is obtained by blue stripes upon white tents glowing in the sunshine ; and in front of these tents is seen that great battle with Amalek of which the account is given in the remainder of the chapter, and for which the Israelites received strength in the streams which ran out of the rock in Horeb. Considered merely as a picture, the opposition of cool light to warm shadow is one of the most remarkable pieces of colour in the Scuola, and the great mass of foliage which waves over the rocks on the left appears to have been elaborated with his highest power and his most sublime invention. But this noble passage is much injured, and now hardly visible.

24. *Plague of Serpents.*   The figures in the distance are remark-ably important in this picture, Moses himself being among them ; in fact, the whole scene is filled chiefly with middle-size figures, in order to increase the impression of space.   It is interesting to observe the difference in the treatment of this subject by the three great painters, Michael Angelo, Rubens, and Tintoret.   The first two, equal to the latter in energy, had less love of liberty : they were fond of binding their compositions into knots, Tintoret of scattering his far and wide ; they all alike preserve the unity of composition, but the unity in the first two is obtained by binding, and that of the last by springing from one source ; and, together with this feeling, comes his love of space, which makes him less regard the rounding and form of objects themselves than their relations of light and shade and distance. Therefore Rubens and Michael Angelo made the fiery serpents huge boa-constrictors and knotted the sufferers together with them.   Tintoret does not like to be so bound ; so he makes the serpents little flying and fluttering monsters, like lampreys with wings ; and the children of Israel, instead of being thrown into convulsed and writhing groups, are scattered, fainting in the fields, far away in the distance.   As usual, Tintoret's conception, while thoroughly characteristic of himself, is also truer to the words of Scripture.   We are told that "the Lord sent fiery serpents among the people, and they *bit* the people ;" we are not

told that they crushed the people to death.   And, while thus the truest,
it is also the most terrific conception.   M. Angelo's would be terrific
if one could believe in it : but our instinct tells us that boa-constrictors
do not come in armies ; and we look upon the picture with as little
emotion as upon the handle of a vase, or any other form worked out of
serpents, where there is no probability of serpents actually occurring.
But there is a probability in Tintoret's conception.   We feel that it is
not impossible that there should come up a swarm of these small winged
reptiles ; and their horror is not diminished by their smallness : not that
they have any of the grotesque terribleness of German invention ; they
might have been made infinitely uglier with small pains, but it is their
veritableness which makes them awful.   They have triangular heads with
sharp beaks or muzzles ; and short, rather thick bodies, with bony
processes down the back like those of sturgeons ; and small wings
spotted with orange and black ; and round glaring eyes, not very large,
but very ghastly, with an intense delight in biting expressed in them.
(It is observable that the Venetian painter has got his main idea of
them from the sea-horses and small reptiles of the Lagoons.)   These
monsters are fluttering and writhing about everywhere, fixing on whatever
they come near with their sharp venomous heads ; and they are coiling
about on the ground, and all the shadows and thickets are full of them,
so that there is no escape anywhere : and, in order to give the idea of
greater extent to the plague, Tintoret has not been content with one
horizon ; I have before mentioned the excessive strangeness of this composition, in having a cavern open in the right of the foreground, through
which is seen another sky and another horizon.   At the top of the picture,
the Divine Being is seen borne by angels, apparently passing over the
congregation in wrath, involved in masses of dark clouds ; while, behind,
an angel of mercy is descending towards Moses, surrounded by a globe
of white light.   This globe is hardly seen from below ; it is not a common
glory, but a transparent sphere, like a bubble, which not only envelopes
the angel, but crosses the figure of Moses, throwing the upper part of
it into a subdued pale colour, as if it were crossed by a sunbeam.
Tintoret is the only painter who plays these tricks with transparent
light, the only man who seems to have perceived the effects of sunbeams,
mists, and clouds in the far-away atmosphere, and to have used what
he saw on towers, clouds, or mountains, to enhance the sublimity of his
figures.   The whole upper part of this picture is magnificent, less with
respect to individual figures, than for the drift of its clouds, and originality and complication of its light and shade ; it is something like

Raffaelle's " Vision of Ezekiel," but far finer.   It is difficult to understand how any painter, who could represent floating clouds so nobly as he has done here, could ever paint the odd, round, pillowy masses, which so often occur in his more carelessly designed sacred subjects.   The lower figures are not so interesting, and the whole is painted with a view to effect from below, and gains little by close examination.

25. *Fall of Manna.*   In none of these three large compositions has the painter made the slightest effort at expression in the human countenance ; everything is done by gesture, and the faces of the people who are drinking from the rock, dying from the serpent-bites, and eating the manna, are all alike as calm as if nothing was happening ; in addition to this, as they are painted for distant effect, the heads are unsatisfactory and coarse when seen near, and perhaps in this last picture the most so, and yet the story is exquisitely told.   We have seen in the Church of San Giorgio Maggiore another example of his treatment of it, where, however, the gathering of manna is a subordinate employment, but here it is principal.   Now, observe, we are told of the manna, that it was found in the morning ; that then there lay round about the camp a small round thing like the hoar-frost, and that " when the sun waxed hot it melted."   Tintoret has endeavoured, therefore, first of all, to give the idea of coolness ; the congregation are reposing in a soft green meadow, surrounded by blue hills, and there are rich trees above them, to the branches of one of which is attached a great grey drapery to catch the manna as it comes down.   In any other picture such a mass of drapery would assuredly have had some vivid colour, but here it is grey ; the fields are cool frosty green, the mountains cold blue, and, to complete the expression and meaning of all this, there is a most important point to be noted in the form of the Deity seen above, through an opening in the clouds.   There are at least ten or twelve other pictures in which the form of the Supreme Being occurs, to be found in the Scuola di San Rocco alone ; and in every one of these instances it is richly coloured, the garments being generally red and blue, but in this picture of the manna the figure is *snow white.* Thus the painter endeavours to show the Deity as the Giver of Bread, just as in the " Striking of the Rock " we saw that he represented Him as the Lord of the Rivers, the Fountains, and the Waters.   There is one other very sweet incident at the bottom of the picture ; four or five sheep, instead of pasturing, turn their heads aside to catch the manna as it comes down, or seem to be licking it off each other's fleeces.   The tree above, to which the drapery is tied, is the most

delicate and delightful piece of leafage in all the Scuola ; it has a large sharp leaf, something like that of a willow, but five times the size.

26. *Jacob's Dream*. A picture which has good effect from below, but gains little when seen near. It is an embarrassing one for any painter, because angels always look awkward going up and down stairs ; one does not see the use of their wings. Tintoret has thrown them into buoyant and various attitudes, but has evidently not treated the subject with delight ; and it is seen to all the more disadvantage because just above the painting of the " Ascension," in which the full fresh power of the painter is developed. One would think this latter picture had been done just after a walk among hills, for it is full of the most delicate effects of transparent cloud, more or less veiling the faces and forms of the angels, and covering with white light the silvery sprays of the palms, while the clouds in the " Jacob's Dream " are the ordinary rotundities of the studio.

27. *Ezekiel's Vision*. I suspect this has been repainted, it is so heavy and dead in colour ; a fault, however, observable in many of the smaller pictures on the ceiling, and perhaps the natural result of the fatigue of such a mind as Tintoret's. A painter who threw such intense energy into some of his works can hardly but have been languid in others in a degree never experienced by the more tranquil minds of less powerful workmen ; and when this languor overtook him whilst he was at work on pictures where a certain space had to be covered by mere force of arm, this heaviness of colour could hardly but have been the consequence : it shows itself chiefly in reds and other hot hues, many of the pictures in the Ducal Palace also displaying it in a painful degree. This " Ezekiel's Vision " is, however, in some measure worthy of the master, in the wild and horrible energy with which the skeletons are leaping up about the prophet ; but it might have been less horrible and more sublime, no attempt being made to represent the space of the Valley of Dry Bones, and the whole canvas being occupied only by eight figures, of which five are half skeletons. It is strange that, in such a subject, the prevailing hues should be red and brown.

28. *Fall of Man*. The two canvases last named are the most considerable in size upon the roof, after the centre pieces. We now come to the smaller subjects which surround the " Striking the Rock ; " of these, this " Fall of Man " is the best, and I should think it very fine anywhere but in the Scuola di San Rocco : there is a grand light on the body of Eve, and the vegetation is remarkably rich, but the faces are coarse, and the composition uninteresting. I could not get near

enough to see what the grey object is upon which Eve appears to be sitting, nor could I see any serpent. It is made prominent in the picture of the Academy of this same subject, so that I suppose it is hidden in the darkness, together with much detail which it would be necessary to discover in order to judge the work justly.

29. *Elijah* (?). A prophet holding down his face, which is covered with his hand. God is talking with him, apparently in rebuke. The clothes on his breast are rent, and the action of the figures might suggest the idea of the scene between the Deity and Elijah at Horeb : but there is no suggestion of the past magnificent scenery,—of the wind, the earthquake, or the fire ; so that the conjecture is good for very little. The painting is of small interest ; the faces are vulgar, and the draperies have too much vapid historical dignity to be delightful.

30. *Jonah.* The whale here occupies fully one half of the canvas ; being correspondent in value with a landscape background. His mouth is as large as a cavern, and yet, unless the mass of red colour in the foreground be a piece of drapery, his tongue is too large for it. He seems to have lifted Jonah out upon it, and not yet drawn it back, so that it forms a kind of crimson cushion for him to kneel upon in his submission to the Deity. The head to which this vast tongue belongs is sketched in somewhat loosely, and there is little remarkable about it except its size, nor much in the figures, though the submissiveness of Jonah is well given. The great thought of Michael Angelo renders one little charitable to any less imaginative treatment of this subject.

31. *Joshua* (?). This is a most interesting picture, and it is a shame that its subject is not made out, for it is not a common one. The figure has a sword in its hand, and looks up to a sky full of fire, out of which the form of the Deity is stooping, represented as white and colourless. On the other side of the picture there is seen among the clouds a pillar apparently falling, and there is a crowd at the feet of the principal figure, carrying spears. Unless this be Joshua at the fall of Jericho, I cannot tell what it means ; it is painted with great vigour, and worthy of a better place.

32. *Sacrifice of Isaac.* In conception, it is one of the least worthy of the master in the whole room, the three figures being thrown into violent attitudes, as inexpressive as they are strained and artificial. It appears to have been vigorously painted, but vulgarly ; that is to say, the light is concentrated upon the white beard and upturned countenance of Abraham, as it would have been in

one of the dramatic effects of the French school, the result being that the head is very bright and very conspicuous, and perhaps, in some of the late operations upon the roof, recently washed and touched. In consequence, every one who comes into the room is first invited to observe the " bella testa di Abramo." The only thing characteristic of Tintoret is the way in which the pieces of ragged wood are tossed hither and thither in the pile upon which Isaac is bound, although this scattering of the wood is inconsistent with the scriptural account of Abraham's deliberate procedure, for we are told of him that " he set the wood in order." But Tintoret had probably not noticed this, and thought the tossing of the timber into the disordered heap more like the act of the father in his agony.

33. *Elijah at the Brook Cherith* (?). I cannot tell if I have rightly interpreted the meaning of this picture, which merely represents a noble figure couched upon the ground, and an angel appearing to him ; but I think that between the dark tree on the left, and the recumbent figure, there is some appearance of a running stream ; at all events, there is of a mountainous and stony place. The longer I study this master, the more I feel the strange likeness between him and Turner, in our never knowing what subject it is that will stir him to exertion. We have lately had him treating Jacob's Dream, Ezekiel's Vision, Abraham's Sacrifice, and Jonah's Prayer (all of them subjects on which the greatest painters have delighted to expend their strength), with coldness, carelessness, and evident absence of delight ; and here, on a sudden, in a subject so indistinct that one cannot be sure of its meaning, and embracing only two figures, a man and an angel, forth he starts in his full strength. I believe he must somewhere or another, the day before, have seen a kingfisher ; for this picture seems entirely painted for the sake of the glorious downy wings of the angel,—white clouded with blue as the bird's head and wings are with green,—the softest and most elaborate in plumage that I have seen in any of his works : but observe also the general sublimity obtained by the mountainous lines of the drapery of the recumbent figure, dependent for its dignity upon these forms alone, as the face is more than half hidden, and what is seen of it expressionless.

34. *The Paschal Feast.* I name this picture by the title given in the guide-books ; it represents merely five persons watching the increase of a small fire lighted on a table or altar in the midst of them. It is only because they have all staves in their hands that one may conjecture this fire to be that kindled to consume the Paschal offer-

ing. The effect is of course a firelight; and, like all mere firelights that I have ever seen, totally devoid of interest.

35. *Elisha Feeding the People.* I again guess at the subject; the picture only represents a figure casting down a number of loaves before a multitude; but, as Elisha has not elsewhere occurred, I suppose that these must be the barley-loaves brought from Baal-shalisha. In conception and manner of painting, this picture and the last, together with the others above mentioned, in comparison with the "Elijah at Cherith," may be generally described as "dregs of Tintoret:" they are tired, dead, dragged out upon the canvas apparently in the heavy-hearted state which a man falls into when he is both jaded with toil and sick of the work he is employed upon. They are not hastily painted; on the contrary, finished with considerably more care than several of the works upon the walls; but those, as, for instance, the "Agony in the Garden," are hurried sketches with the man's whole heart in them, while these pictures are exhausted fulfilments of an appointed task. Whether they were really amongst the last painted, or whether the painter had fallen ill at some intermediate time, I cannot say; but we shall find him again in his utmost strength in the room which we last enter.

36 to 39. *Four Children's Heads,* which it is much to be regretted should be thus lost in filling small vacuities of the ceiling.

40. *St. Rocco in Heaven.* The central picture of the roof, in the inner room. From the well-known anecdote respecting the production of this picture, whether in all its details true or not, we may at least gather that, having been painted in competition with Paul Veronese and other powerful painters of the day, it was probably Tintoret's endeavour to make it as popular and showy as possible. It is quite different from his common works; bright in all its tints and tones; the faces carefully drawn, and of an agreeable type; the outlines firm, and the shadows few; the whole resembling Correggio more than any Venetian painter. It is, however, an example of the danger, even to the greatest artist, of leaving his own style; for it lacks all the great virtues of Tintoret, without obtaining the lusciousness of Correggio. One thing, at all events, is remarkable in it,—that, though painted while the competitors were making their sketches, it shows no sign of haste or inattention.

41 to 44. *Figures of Children,* merely decorative.

45 to 56. *Allegorical Figures on the Roof.* If these were not in the same room with the "Crucifixion," they would attract more public attention than any works in the Scuola, as there are here no

Fourth Group.   Inner room on the upper floor.

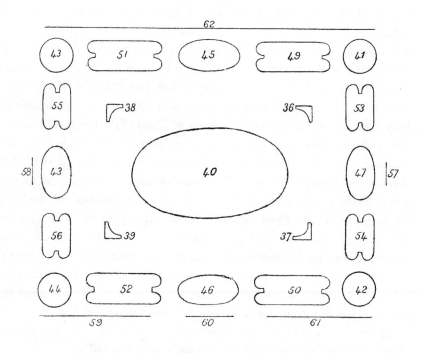

On the Roof.

36 to 39. Children's Heads.   41 to 44. Children.
40. St. Rocco in Heaven.   45 to 56. Allegorical Figures.

On the Walls.

57. Figure in Niche.   60. Ecce Homo.
58. Figure in Niche.   61. Christ Bearing His Cross.
59. Christ before Pilate.   62. CRUCIFIXION.

black shadows, nor extravagances of invention, but very beautiful figures richly and delicately coloured, a good deal resembling some of the best works of Andrea del Sarto. There is nothing in them, however, requiring detailed examination. The two figures between the windows are very slovenly, if they are his at all ; and there are bits of marbling and fruit filling the cornices, which may or may not be his : if they are, they are tired work, and of small importance.

59. *Christ before Pilate.* A most interesting picture, but, which is unusual, best seen on a dark day, when the white figure of Christ alone draws the eye, looking almost like a spirit; the painting of the rest of the picture being both somewhat thin and imperfect. There is a certain meagreness about all the minor figures, less grandeur and

largeness in the limbs and draperies, and less solidity, it seems, even in the colour, although its arrangements are richer than in many of the compositions above described. I hardly know whether it is owing to this thinness of colour, or on purpose, that the horizontal clouds shine through the crimson flag in the distance; though I should think the latter, for the effect is most beautiful. The passionate action of the Scribe in lifting his hand to dip the pen into the ink-horn is, however, affected and over-strained, and the Pilate is very mean; perhaps intentionally, that no reverence might be withdrawn from the person of Christ. In work of the thirteenth and fourteenth centuries, the figures of Pilate and Herod are always intentionally made contemptible.

60. *Ecce Homo.* As usual, Tintoret's own peculiar view of the subject. Christ is laid fainting on the ground, with a soldier standing on one side of him; while Pilate, on the other, withdraws the robe from the scourged and wounded body, and points it out to the Jews. Both this and the picture last mentioned resemble Titian more than Tintoret in the style of their treatment.

61. *Christ Bearing His Cross.* Tintoret is here recognizable again in undiminished strength. He has represented the troops and attendants climbing Calvary by a winding path of which two turns are seen, the figures on the uppermost ledge, and Christ in the centre of them, being relieved against the sky; but instead of the usual simple expedient of the bright horizon to relieve the dark masses, there is here introduced, on the left, the head of a white horse, which blends itself with the sky in one broad mass of light. The power of the picture is chiefly in effect, the figure of Christ being too far off to be very interesting, and only the malefactors being seen on the nearer path; but for this very reason it seems to me more impressive, as if one had been truly present at the scene, though not exactly in the right place for seeing it.

62. *The Crucifixion.* I must leave this picture to work its will on the spectator; for it is beyond all analysis, and above all praise.

S.

SAGREDO, PALAZZO, on the Grand Canal, II. 257. Much defaced, but full of interest. Its sea story is restored: its first floor has a most interesting arcade of the early thirteenth century third-order windows; its upper windows are the finest fourth and fifth orders of early fourteenth century : the group of fourth orders in the centre being brought into some resemblance to the late Gothic traceries by the subsequent introduction of the quatrefoils above them.

SALUTE, CHURCH OF STA. MARIA DELLA, on the Grand Canal, II. 377. One of the earliest buildings of the Grotesque Renaissance, rendered impressive by its position, size, and general proportions. These latter are exceedingly good ; the grace of the whole building being chiefly dependent on the inequality of size in its cupolas, and pretty grouping of the two campaniles behind them. It is to be generally observed that the proportions of buildings have nothing whatever to do with the style or general merits of their architecture. An architect trained in the worst schools, and utterly devoid of all meaning or purpose in his work, may yet have such a natural gift of massing and grouping as will render all his structures effective when seen from a distance : such a gift is very general with the late Italian builders, so that many of the most contemptible edifices in the country have good stage effect so long as we do not approach them. The Church of the Salute is farther assisted by the beautiful flight of steps in front of it down to the canal ; and its façade is rich and beautiful of its kind, and was chosen by Turner for the principal object in his well-known view of the Grand Canal. The principal faults of the building are the meagre windows in the sides of the cupola, and the ridiculous disguise of the buttresses under the form of colossal scrolls ; the buttresses themselves being originally a hypocrisy, for the cupola is stated by Lazari to be of timber, and therefore needs none. The sacristy contains several precious pictures : the three on its roof by Titian, much vaunted, are indeed as feeble as they are monstrous ; but the small Titian, " St. Mark, with Sts. Cosmo and Damian," was, when I first saw it, to my judgment, by far the first work of Titian's in Venice. It has since been restored by the Academy, and it seemed to me entirely destroyed, but I had not time to examine it carefully.

At the end of the larger sacristy is the lunette which once decorated the tomb of the Doge Francesco Dandolo (see above, page 74) ; and, at the side of it, one of the most highly finished Tintorets in Venice, namely :

The Marriage in Cana. An immense picture, some twenty-five feet long by fifteen high, and said by Lazari to be one of the few which Tintoret signed with his name. I am not surprised at his having done so in this case. Evidently the work has been a favourite with him, and he has taken as much pains as it was ever

necessary for his colossal strength to take with anything.   The subject
is not one which admits of much singularity or energy in composition.
It was always a favourite one with Veronese, because it gave dramatic
interest to figures in gay costumes and of cheerful countenances ; but
one is surprised to find Tintoret, whose tone of mind was always grave,
and who did not like to make a picture out of brocades and diadems,throw-
ing his whole strength into the conception of a marriage feast ; but so
it is, and there are assuredly no female heads in any of his pictures in
Venice elaborated so far as those which here form the central light.
Neither is it often that the works of this mighty master conform themselves to any of the rules acted upon by ordinary painters ; but in this
instance the popular laws have been observed, and an Academy student
would be delighted to see with what severity the principal light is
arranged in a central mass, which is divided and made more brilliant by
a vigorous piece of shadow thrust into the midst of it, and which dies
away in lesser fragments and sparkling towards the extremities of the
picture.   This mass of light is as interesting by its composition as by
its intensity.   The cicerone, who escorts the stranger round the sacristy
in the course of five minutes, and allows him some forty seconds for
the contemplation of a picture which the study of six months would not
entirely fathom, directs his attention very carefully to the " bell' effetto
di prospettivo," the whole merit of the picture being, in the eyes of the
intelligent public, that there is a long table in it, one end of which looks
farther off than the other ; but there is more in the " bell' effetto di prospettivo " than the observance of the common laws of optics.   The table
is set in a spacious chamber, of which the windows at the end let in the
light from the horizon, and those in the side wall the intense blue of
an eastern sky.   The spectator looks all along the table, at the farther
end of which are seated Christ and the Madonna, the marriage guests
on each side of it,—on one side men, on the other women ; the men are
set with their backs to the light, which, passing over their heads and
glancing slightly on the tablecloth, falls in full length along the line
of young Venetian women, who thus fill the whole centre of the picture
with one broad sunbeam, made up of fair faces and golden hair.   Close
to the spectator a woman has risen in amazement, and stretches across
the table to show the wine in her cup to those opposite ; her dark red
dress intercepts and enhances the mass of gathered light.   It is rather
curious, considering the subject of the picture, that one cannot distinguish either the bride or the bridegroom ; but the fourth figure from
the Madonna in the line of women, who wears a white head-dress of

lace and rich chains of pearls in her hair, may well be accepted for the former, and I think* that between her and the woman on the Madonna's left hand the unity of the line of women is intercepted by a male figure : be this as it may, this fourth female face is the most beautiful, as far as I recollect, that occurs in the works of the painter, with the exception only of the Madonna in the "Flight into Egypt." It is an ideal which occurs indeed elsewhere in many of his works, a face at once dark and delicate, the Italian cast of feature moulded with the softness and childishness of English beauty some half a century ago ; but I have never seen the ideal so completely worked out by the master. The face may best be described as one of the purest and softest of Stothard's conceptions, executed with all the strength of Tintoret. The other women are all made inferior to this one, but there are beautiful profiles and bendings of breasts and necks along the whole line. The men are all subordinate, though there are interesting portraits among them ; perhaps the only fault of the picture being that the faces are a little too conspicuous, seen like balls of light among the crowd of minor figures which fill the background of the picture. The tone of the whole is sober and majestic in the highest degree ; the dresses are all broad masses of colour, and the only parts of the picture which lay claim to the expression of wealth or splendour are the head-dresses of the women. In this respect the conception of the scene differs widely from that of Veronese, and approaches more nearly to the probable truth. Still the marriage is not an unimportant one ; an immense crowd, filling the background, forming superbly rich mosaic of colour against the distant sky. Taken as a whole, the picture is perhaps the most perfect example which human art has produced of the utmost possible force and sharpness of shadow united with richness of local colour. In all the other works of Tintoret, and much more of other colourists, either the light and shade or the local colour is predominant ; in the one case the picture has a tendency to look as if painted by candlelight, in the other it becomes daringly conventional, and approaches the conditions of glass-painting. This picture unites colour as rich as Titian's with light and shade as forcible as Rembrandt's, and far more decisive.

There are one or two other interesting pictures of the early Venetian schools in this sacristy, and several important tombs in the adjoining cloister ; among which that of Francesco Dandolo, transported

* (A correspondent writes that, with a good glass, a beard is discernible on the face of this figure. Note, 1884.)

here from the Church of the Frari, deserves especial attention. See above, p. 74.

SALVATORE, CHURCH OF ST. Base Renaissance, occupying the place of the ancient church, under the porch of which the Pope Alexander III. is said to have passed the night. M. Lazari states it to have been richly decorated with mosaics ; now, all is gone.

In the interior of the church are some of the best examples of Renaissance sculptural monuments in Venice. (See above, Chap. II., § LXXX.) It is said to possess an important pala of silver, of the thirteenth century, one of the objects in Venice which I much regret having forgotten to examine ; besides two Titians, a Bonifazio, and a John Bellini. The latter ("The Supper at Emmaus") must, I think, have been entirely repainted : it is not only unworthy of the master, but unlike him ; as far, at least, as I could see from below, for it is hung high.

SANUDO, PALAZZO. At the Miracoli. A noble Gothic palace of the fourteenth century, with Byzantine fragments and cornices built into its walls, especially round the interior court, in which the staircase is very noble. Its door, opening on the quay, is the only one in Venice entirely uninjured ; retaining its wooden valve richly sculptured, its wicket for examination of the stranger demanding admittance, and its quaint knocker in the form of a fish.

SCALZI, CHURCH OF THE. It possesses a fine John Bellini, and is renowned through Venice for its precious marbles. I omitted to notice above, in speaking of the buildings of the Grotesque Renaissance, that many of them are remarkable for a kind of dishonesty, even in the use of *true* marbles, resulting not from motives of economy, but from mere love of juggling and falsehood for their own sake. I hardly know which condition of mind is meanest, that which has pride in plaster made to look like marble, or that which takes delight in marble made to look like silk. Several of the later churches in Venice, more especially those of the Jesuiti, of San Clemente, and this of the Scalzi, rest their chief claims to admiration on their having curtains and cushions cut out of rock. The most ridiculous example is in San Clemente, and the most curious and costly are in the Scalzi ; which latter church is a perfect type of the vulgar abuse of marble in every possible way, by men who had no eye for colour, and no understanding of any merit in a work of art but that which arises from costliness of material, and such powers of imitation as are devoted in England to the manufacture of peaches and eggs out of Derbyshire spar.

SEBASTIAN, CHURCH OF ST. The tomb, and of old the monument, of Paul Veronese. It is full of his noblest pictures, or of what once were such; but they seemed to me for the most part destroyed by repainting. I had not time to examine them justly, but I would especially direct the traveller's attention to the small Madonna over the second altar on the right of the nave, still a perfect and priceless treasure.

SERVI, CHURCH OF THE. Only two of its gates and some ruined walls are left, in one of the foulest districts of the city. It was one of the most interesting monuments of the early fourteenth century Gothic; and there is much beauty in the fragments yet remaining. How long they may stand I know not, the whole building having been offered me for sale, ground and all, or stone by stone, as I chose, by its present proprietor, when I was last in Venice. More real good might at present be effected by any wealthy person who would devote his resources to the preservation of such monuments wherever they exist, by freehold purchase of the entire ruin, and afterwards by taking proper charge of it, and forming a garden round it, than by any other mode of protecting or encouraging art. There is no school, no lecturer, like a ruin of the early ages.

SEVERO, FONDAMENTA SAN, palace at, II. 264.

SILVESTRO, CHURCH OF ST. Of no importance in itself, but it contains two very interesting pictures: the first, a " St. Thomas of Canterbury with the Baptist and St. Francis," by Girolamo Santa Croce, a superb example of the Venetian religious school; the second by Tintoret, namely:

The Baptism of Christ. (Over the first altar on the right of the nave.) An upright picture, some ten feet wide by fifteen high; the top of it is arched, representing the Father supported by angels. It requires little knowledge of Tintoret to see that these figures are not by his hand. By returning to the opposite side of the nave, the join in the canvas may be plainly seen, the upper part of the picture having been entirely added on : whether it had this upper part before it was repainted, or whether originally square, cannot now be told, but I believe it had an upper part which has been destroyed. I am not sure if even the dove and the two angels which are at the top of the older part of the picture are quite genuine. The rest of it is magnificent, though both the figures of the Saviour and the Baptist show some concession on the part of the painter to the imperative requirement of his age, that nothing should be done except in an attitude; neither are there any of his usual fantastic imaginations. There is simply the Christ in the water and the St. John on the shore, without attendants, disciples, or witnesses of any kind; but the power of the light and shade, and the splendour of the landscape, which on the whole is well preserved, render it a most interesting example. The Jordan is represented as a mountain brook, receiving a tributary stream in a cascade from the rocks, in which St. John stands : there is a rounded stone in the centre of the current ; and the parting of the water at this, as well as its rippling among the roots of some dark trees on the left, are among the most accurate remembrances of nature to be found in any of the works of the great masters. I hardly know whether most to wonder at the power of the man who thus broke through the neglect of nature which was universal at his time ; or at the evidences, visible throughout the whole of the conception, that he was still content to paint from slight memories of what he had seen in hill countries, instead of following out to its full depth the fountain which he had opened. There is not a stream among the hills of Priuli which in any quarter of a mile of its course would not have suggested to him finer forms of cascade than those which he has idly painted at Venice.

SIMEONE, PROFETA, CHURCH OF ST. Very important, though small, possessing the precious statue of St. Simeon, above noticed, II. 309. The rare early Gothic capitals of the nave are only interesting to the architect; but in the little passage by the side of the church, leading out of the Campo, there is a curious Gothic monument built into the wall, very beautiful in the placing of the angels in the spandrils, and rich in the vine-leaf moulding above.

SIMEONE, PICCOLO, CHURCH OF St. One of the ugliest churches in Venice or elsewhere. Its black dome, like an unusual species of gasometer, is the admiration of modern Italian architects.

SOSPIRI, PONTE DE'. The well-known "Bridge of Sighs," a work of no merit, and of a late period (see Vol. II., p. 304), owing the interest it possesses chiefly to its pretty name, and to the ignorant sentimentalism of Byron.

STEFANO, CHURCH OF ST. An interesting building of central Gothic, the best ecclesiastical example of it in Venice. The west entrance is much later than any of the rest, and is of the richest Renaissance Gothic, a little anterior to the Porta della Carta, and first-rate of its kind. The manner of the introduction of the figure of the angel at the top of the arch is full of beauty. Note the extravagant crockets and cusp finials as signs of decline.

STEFANO, CHURCH OF ST., at Murano (pugnacity of its abbot), II. 33. The church no longer exists.

STROPE, CAMPIELLO DELLA, house in, II. 266.

T.

TANA, windows at the, II. 260.

TOLENTINI, CHURCH OF THE. One of the basest and coldest works of the late Renaissance. It is said to contain two Bonifazios.

TOMA, PONTE SAN. There is an interesting ancient doorway opening on the canal close to this bridge, probably of the twelfth century, and a good early Gothic door, opening upon the bridge itself.

TORCELLO, general aspect of, II. 11; Santa Fosca at, I. 113, II. 13; duomo, II. 14; mosaics of, II. 197; measures of, II. 378; date of, II. 379.

TREVISAN, PALAZZO, I. 358, III. 224.

TROVASO, CHURCH OF ST. Itself of no importance, but containing two pictures by Tintoret, namely:

1. *The Temptation of St. Anthony.* (Altar piece in the chapel on the left of the choir.) A small and very carefully finished picture, but marvellously temperate and quiet in treatment, especially considering the subject, which one would have imagined likely to inspire the painter with one of his most fantastic visions. As if on purpose to disappoint us, both the effect and the conception of the figures are perfectly quiet, and appear the result much more of careful study than of vigorous imagination. The effect is one of plain daylight; there are a few clouds drifting in the distance, but with no wildness in them, nor is there any energy or heat in the flames which mantle about the waist of one of the figures. But for the noble workmanship, we might almost fancy it the production of a modern academy: yet, as we begin to read the picture, the painter's mind becomes felt. St. Anthony is surrounded by four figures, one of which only has the form of a demon, and he is in the background, engaged in no more terrific act of violence towards St. Anthony, than endeavouring to pull off his mantle; he has, however, a scourge over his shoulder, but this is probably intended for St. Anthony's weapon of self-discipline, which the fiend, with a very Protestant turn of mind, is carrying off. A broken staff, with a bell hanging to it, at the saint's feet, also expresses his interrupted devotion. The three other figures beside him are bent on more cunning mischief: the woman on the left is one of Tintoret's best portraits of a young and bright-eyed Venetian beauty. It is curious that he has given so attractive a countenance to a type apparently of the temptation to violate

the vow of poverty, for this woman places one hand in a vase full of coins, and shakes golden chains with the other. On the opposite side of the saint, another woman, admirably painted, but of a far less attractive countenance, is a type of the lusts of the flesh, yet there is nothing gross or immodest in her dress or gesture. She appears to have been baffled, and for the present to have given up addressing the saint : she lays one hand upon her breast, and might be taken for a very respectable person, but that there are flames playing about her loins. A recumbent figure on the ground is of less intelligible character, but may perhaps be meant for Indolence ; at all events, he has torn the saint's book to pieces. I forgot to note, that, under the figure representing Avarice, there is a creature like a pig ; whether actual pig or not is unascertainable, for the church is dark, the little light that comes on the picture falls on it the wrong way, and one-third of the lower part of it is hidden by a white case, containing a modern daub, lately painted by way of an altar-piece ; the meaning, as well as the merit, of the grand old picture being now far beyond the comprehension both of priests and people.

2. *The Last Supper.* (On the left-hand side of the Chapel of the Sacrament.) A picture which has been through the hands of the Academy, and is therefore now hardly worth notice. Its conception seems always to have been vulgar, and far below Tintoret's usual standard. There is singular baseness in the circumstance that one of the near Apostles, while all the others are, as usual, intent upon Christ's words, " One of you shall betray me," is going to help himself to wine out of a bottle which stands behind him. In so doing he stoops towards the table, the flask being on the floor. If intended for the action of Judas at this moment, there is the painter's usual originality in the thought ; but it seems to me rather done to obtain variation of posture, in bringing the red dress into strong contrast with the tablecloth. The colour has once been fine, and there are fragments of good painting still left ; but the light does not permit these to be seen, and there is too much perfect work of the master's in Venice to permit us to spend time on retouched remnants. The picture is only worth mentioning, because it is ignorantly and ridiculously referred to by Kugler as characteristic of Tintoret.

V.

VITALI, CHURCH OF ST. Said to contain a picture by Vittor Carpaccio, over the high altar : otherwise of no importance.

Volto Santo, Church of the. An interesting but desecrated ruin of the fourteenth century ; fine in style. Its roof retains some fresco colouring, but, as far as I recollect, of later date than the architecture.

Z.

Zaccaria, Church of St. Early Renaissance, and fine of its kind; a Gothic chapel attached to it is of great beauty. It contains the best John Bellini in Venice, after that of San G. Grisostomo, " The Virgin, with Four Saints ;" and is said to contain another John Bellini and a Tintoret, neither of which I have seen.

Zobenigo, Church of Santa Maria, III. 124. It contains one valuable Tintoret, namely :

Christ with Sta. Justina and St. Augustin. (Over the third altar on the south side of the nave.) A picture of small size, and upright, about ten feet by eight. Christ appears to be descending out of the clouds between the two saints, who are both kneeling on the sea-shore. It is a Venetian sea, breaking on a flat beach, like the Lido, with a scarlet galley in the middle distance, of which the chief use is to unite the two figures by a point of colour. Both the saints are respectable Venetians of the lower class, in homely dresses and with homely faces. The whole picture is quietly painted, and somewhat slightly ; free from all extravagance, and displaying little power except in the general truth or harmony of colours so easily laid on. It is better preserved than usual, and worth dwelling upon as an instance of the style of the master when *at rest.*

THE END.

GENERAL INDEX.

NOTE.

The References used in this Index are these :—

(*a*) *The figures refer to the volume, chapter, and section* (*not to the page*) ; I. ix. 3
thus standing for Vol. I. chap. ix. § 3.

(*b*) A. *to the appendices ; I. A. i. thus standing for Vol. I. Appendix I.*

V.I. *to the Venetian Index at the end of the third volume.*

C.F. *to the " Castelfranco " chapter added in the Travellers' Edition, and reprinted
as chapter v. in the third volume of the edition of* 1886.

T.E. *n. to the notes added in the Travellers' Edition, especially throughout the
Venetian Index. These notes are reprinted in the edition of* 1886, *partly in
the Venetian Index, and partly in the form of appendices* 26 (*Vol. I.*), |13
(*Vol. II.*), *and* 11 (*Vol. III.*) ; *thus,* I. i. 5. T.E. *n. will be found either on
reference to the reprint of* I. i. 5 *in the Travellers' Edition, or in appendix* 26
to Vol. I. of the 1886 *edition ; and* V.I. T.E. *n. will be found in the Venetian
Index of either the Travellers' or the* 1886 *edition.*

GENERAL INDEX.

Author : books of, quoted or referred to, *continued :*

Bible, the, *continued:*

Ananias' sin, *ib.*, *ib.*, *ib.*
Araunah, threshing floor of, III. iii. 41.
Babel, tower of, II. viii. 46.
David and the shewbread, I. xxi. 31.
Ebal, III. iii. 42.
Elisha (2 Kings iv. 31), "once trusted his staff too far," II. A. 10 *n.*
Evangelists, symbolized by four beasts, III. iii. 63.
Ezekiel, scenery of the Book of, III. iii. 62.
Genesis (and Ghiberti's gates), III. iii. 50.
Gerizim, III. iii. 42.
Gomorrah, fall of, III. iii. 76.
High priest's breastplate, III. i. 47.
Japheth, meaning of name, II. v. 34.
Job, Book of. See s. Job.
S. Paul on inspiration, III. iii. 60 *n.*
Revelations, scenery of the Book of, III. iii. 62.

(*b*) *Passages quoted:*

Gen. i. 30—"Every green herb for meat," II. vi. 71.
  ,, i. 31—"Behold it was very good," II. vi. 40.
  ,, viii. 11—"Lo, in her mouth was an olive leaf," II. vi. 71.
  ,, viii. 20—"Every clean beast and every clean fowl," I. A. 6.
  ,, ix. 27—"God shall enlarge Japheth," II. v. 34.
  ,, xi. i. *seqq.*—"The tower of Babel," II. viii. 46.
  ,, xviii. 19—"To do justice and judgment," II. iv. 71.
  ,, xxviii. 18—"And Jacob took the stone . . . and set it up for a pillar,"
        I. vii. 8.
  ,, xxxvii. 3—"Joseph's 'coat of many colours,'" II. v. 33.
  ,, xli. 57—"All countries came to Joseph to buy corn," III. ii. 27.
2 Sam. xiii. 18—"With such robes were the king's daughters . . . apparelled,"
        II. v. 53.
  ,, xxiv. 18—"The threshing floor of Araunah," III. iii. 41.
1 Kings vi. 7—"Neither the hammer . . . was heard while . . . building,"
        I. v. 5.
  ,, vii. 17—9—"The chapiters of Solomon's temple," I. xxvii. 47.
  ,, vii. 17—9—"   ,,   ,,   ,,   ,,   " II. v. 24.
  ,, xvii. 14—"The barrel of meal . . . cruse of oil fail," III. ii. 27.
2 Kings v. 18—"When I bow myself in the house of Rimmon," II. A. 10.
  ,, viii. 15—"Hazael took a cloth and dipped it . . . and spread it on
        his face," III. i. 5.
Job iii. 17—"There the wicked cease from troubling," etc., II. ii. 9.
  ,, viii. 11—3—"Can the rush grow without mire . . . hypocrite's hope
        perish," I. viii. 25.
  ,, xv. 31—"Let not him that is deceived trust in vanity," II. viii. 92.
  ,, xxxi. 26—8—"The moon walking in brightness . . . should have
        denied the God above, III. ii. 101 *n.*
  ,, xxxviii. 11—"Hitherto shalt thou come . . . and ⎰ III. ii. 103.
        here thy (proud) waves be stayed" ⎱ I. xxi. 17.
  ,, xl. 15—"Behold now behemoth, which I made with thee," III. ii. 31.
Psalm iv. 8—"I will lay me down in peace . . . dwell in safety," III. ii. 46.
  ,, v. 5—"The foolish shall not stand in thy sight," II. viii. 56.
  ,, xiv. 1—"The fool hath said . . . 'There is no God' . . ." II. iii. 40.
  ,, xiv. 1—"   ,,   ,,   ,,   ,,   ,,   " II. viii. 56.
  ,, xiv. 1—"   ,,   ,,   ,,   ,,   ,,   " III. ii. 92.
  ,, xix. 5, 6—"As a bridegroom . . . hid from the heat thereof," III. ii. 9.

Breadth in art, good and bad, III. i. 13.

Brenta, villas on the, I. xxx. 7 ; II. i. 6.

Brentford gas company, *ed.* 1873 *pref.*

Brick, chequering of, I. xxvi. 4.

    ,,   decoration by pointing, I. xxvi. 4.

    ,,   real use of, II. vii. 38.

    ,,   yellow, of Murano Cathedral, II. iii. 19.

Brides of Venice, III. iii. 7 *seqq.*

Bridge, building of a, I. ii. 7.

    ,,   buttresses of a, I. xv. 3.

———— of Sighs. See s. Venice, IV. (3).

Bridging over of spaces, by lintels, arches, gables, II. vi. 87.

British Museum, base of the, I. xxv. 4.

    ,,   ,,   contents of :

          Assyrian bulls at, I. A. 8.

          Elgin marbles, I. xxviii. 5.

          Egyptian sculpture, I. xxi. 7.

          Erectheum architrave, I. xxviii. 5.

          Greek mirror, I. xx. 25.

          Parthenon, capital of, I. xxvii. 7.

          water, ancient representation of, in, I. A. 21.

British Quarterly, review of " Seven Lamps," I. xxi. 31 *n.*

    ,,   ,,   August 1849, quoted, I. xxv. 5 *n ;* I. xxvi. 17 *n.*

Britomart. See s. Spenser.

Brotherhood, a principle of art, as of life, III. i. 26.

Brown, Rawdon, II. viii. 26 *n ;* C.F. 3.

    ,,   ,,   III. V.I., s. Contarini.

    ,,   ,,   quoted anonymously, I. A. 5.

    ,,   ,,   author helped by, I. A. 20.

    ,,   ,,   on Casa Dario and Ca' Trevisan, III. A. 4.

    ,,   ,,   on Othello's House, V.I., s. Othello.

    ,,   ,,   on Venetian archives, III. iii. 10 *n.*

    ,,   ,,   his translations of Sanuto, etc., II. vii. 14 *n.*

    ,,   ,,   ,,   ,,   III. A. 9.

Browne, Sir Thomas, quoted, II. A. 10.

Browning, Eliz. Barrett, I. xvii. 14.

    ,,   ,,   ,,   on Florence, II. vi. 77 *n.*

Brunel, and the Thames Tunnel, I. xi. 1.

Builder, quoted on death of workman, II. iv. 24.

    ,,   (Jan. 1853), on fall of a house, II. vii. 47 *n.*

Builders, ungratefully forgotten, whilst founders are remembered, I. ii. 5.

Buildings : *

---

* For buildings (especially cathedrals and churches) particularly referred to see s. Saints (*h*) and also as follows :—Abbeville, Abbeys, Alhambra, Amiens, Antwerp, Bayeux, Beauvais, Belgium, Bergamo, Bologna, Borgund, Bourges, Chartres, Cologne, Como, Coutances, Crystal Palace, Dijon, Dolo, Durham, Edinburgh, Egypt, Erectheum, Florence,

Giovanni e Paolo, SS., Church of, Venice : tombs in, *continued :*

of Cornaro (Marco), III. ii. 65.
,,   ,, (Pietro), I. xxvii. 28.
,, Dolfino, III. ii. 62 *seqq.*
,, Faliero (worst Renaissance), III. ii. 84.
,, Giustiniani (Marco), I. xxvii. 21.
,, Mocenigo (Giov. and Pietro), III. ii. 78·
,,   ,, (Tomaso), I. i. 9, 40.
,, Morosini (Andrea and Michele), I. xxvii. 28; III. i. 15; III. ii. 65.
,, Steno (Michele), III. ii. 70.
,, Tiepolo (Jacopo and Lorenzo), III. ii. 50 *seqq.*
,, Vendramin (Andrea), I. i. 41 ; III. ii. 77.

————, Grisostomo, in Bragora, e Paolo, etc., Churches of. See s. Venice, IV. (1).
Giudecca, derivation of the word, V.I., s. Giudecca.
Giulio Romano, I. i. 36.
Giustiniani, Doge Marco (1684), his tomb in SS. Giov. e Paolo. See s. Venice, IV. (1) s.v.
Glacier, line of, I. xxvii. 9.
Glass, architectural use of, I. A. 17.
  ,, ductility and transparency of, its main qualities, II. A. 12.
  ,, painted, characteristics of, I. A. 17.
  ,,   ,, development of, II. iv. 45.
  ,,   ,, French 1100—1300, the best possible, II. A. 12.
  ,,   ,, not used by Renaissance builders, II. v. 32.
  ,,   ,, not to be pretty pictures, II. A. 12.
  ,, -work, II. A. 12.
  ,, cut, barbarous, *ib., ib., ib.*
  ,, modern English, II. vi. 20.
  ,, Venetian, II. iii. 5.
Gloucester Cathedral, buttresses of, I. xviii. 16.
    ,,   ,, tracery, I. xvii. 16.
Gluttony, Ducal Palace capital, II. viii. 87.
God " creates without toil," I. A. 17.
  ,, permits His gifts to be wasted, II. v. 36.
  ,, just as well as kind, III. iii. 42.
  ,, laws of, are those of art, I. xxi. 26, 31.
  ,,   ,, expressed by everything beautiful, III. i. 26.
  ,, representation of, effort at, Dolfino's tomb, III. ii. 63.
  ,, works of, the real object of honest delight, I. ii. 14.
  ,,   ,, the subject of noble ornament, I. xx. 3.
Godfrey, of Bouillon, receiving Emirs, III. ii. 42, 44.
    ,,   ,, scorn of flattery, *ib., ib.*, 44.
Gold, use of, in tree painting, III. iv. 25.
Golden fruit, idea of, III. iv. 16.
Goldsmith's work, design in, II. vi. 18.
Gondolas, approach to Venice in, I. xxx. 10
    ,, carriages of Venice, II. iii. 1.

Gondolas, *continued :*
   ,,   management of, II. A. 1.
   ,,   motion of, II. i. 1.
   ,,   steam, C.F. 3.
Gondolier's cry, II. i. 1 and *n. ;* II. A. 1.
Good, delight in, really universal, I. ii. 16.
   ,, evil and, mingled in all things, II. vi. 56.
   ,,   ,, pursuit of, in art, II. vi. 51 *seqq.*
Gorne, the, or battlements of the Ca' d'Oro, II. vii. 14.
Gothic architecture :—
    I. Generally. II. Its Characteristics. III. Its Details.
    I. Generally :
        definition of, II. vi. 81, 82, and (finally) 98.
        divisions of, II. vi. 89, 90.
        ,, critical period of (1350), II. vi. 100.
        ,, early and late meet (1300—1400), II. vi. 100.
        kinds of :
           Flamboyant, I. ix. 30 *seqq.*
           ,, I. xxiv. 6 *seqq.*
           Northern, I. viii. 14.
           Venetian, contest between Byzantine, II. iv. 5.
           ,,   ,,   ,, II. vii. 14, 26.
           ,, early, I. i. 33.
           ,, ,, I. xxiii. 14.
           ,, ,, II. chaps. vi.—viii.
           Veronese and French, II. vi. 103.
        modern architects, their dislike of, I. xv. 12.
        origin of, Corinthian, I. i. 17.
        Renaissance, effects of the, on, I. i. 35.
        ,,   ,,   ,, II. iv. 5.
        ruin of, caused by the Renaissance and luxury, III. i. 4, 18.
        rules for fixing date of, by the doors, III. A. 10.
        ,, judging merits of, II. vi. 107 *seqq.*
        spirit of "Gothicness," II. vi. 2—5.
        systematized schools have no place in, I. xiv. 16 *n.*
        term, history of the, II. vi. 7.
    II. Its characteristics :
        general summary of, II. vi. 1 *seqq.,* 107 *seqq.*
        adaptability of, to the requirements of buildings, II. vi. 38.
        by no means barbarous, III. ii. 3.
        centaurism traceable in, I. xxvii. 24.
        colour, its love of, II. iv. 43.
        its delightfulness, and that of modern English architecture, II. vii. 46.
        domestic, not only ecclesiastical, II. iv. 56.
        ,, author's plea for its domestic use, II. vii. 47.
        expression, its power of, II. vi. 4 *seqq.*
        fact, its love of, II. vi. 64 ; and realization of, *ib.* 65.

---

* Misprinted " Andrea " in this passage.

Salvia leaf, line of its curvature, I. xx. 19 (plate vii.) ; I. xxv. 12 ; II. v. 14.

„ „ as applied to the cornice line, I. xxvii. 3.

„ „ „ to head of a capital, I. xxvii. 42.

Salviati, restoration of S. Mark's, mosaics by, II. iv. 48. T.E. *n.*

Sammichele, builds Casa Grimani, III. ii. 3.

„ power of, absorbed in fortification, III. ii. 91.

Samson, Ducal Palace capital, II. viii. 79.

Sandwich islanders, grotesque art of, III. iii. 70.

Sansovino, as an architect :

Libreria Vecchia, Venice, designed by, V.I. s.v.

Palladio and, head the Renaissance, I. i. 36, 38.

subjects of his ornament, I. xx. 5.

as an historian :

cautious, II. viii. 13.

not explicit, II. viii. 18 *n.*

quoted :

on election of the doge, I. i. 4 and *n.*

„ F. Dandolo, " The Dog," III. ii. 59.

„ M. Cornaro, III. ii. 70.

„ Morosini (Doge), III. ii. 67.

„ the jewel shaft, in S. Giacomo dell' Orio, II. iv. 33 *n.*

„ Venice :

derivation of the word, I. A. 1.

dress of people, II. iii. 39 *n.* ; II. A. 7.

Ducal Palace, II. viii. 1—20 *passim.*

„ „ opposed to rebuilding it (1574), II. viii. 28.

S. Maria Formosa, rebuilding of, III. iii. 5.

Sanuto, " precious diaries " of, II. vii. 14 *n.*

„ saints and kings confused by, *ib., ib., ib.*

„ quoted, on lily falling from Ducal Palace (1511), II. vii. 13, 14 *n.*

„ „ „ rebuilding of Ducal Palace (1419), II. viii. 22.

Saracens, the arch in architecture of, I. ii. 7.

„ lessons to Europe of the, II. v. 34.

Sarcophagus, of Early Gothic and Italian tombs, III. ii. 46 *seqq.*, 49.

„ Renaissance change of form from Gothic, III. ii. 79.

Sardinia, King of, proposes Mont Cenis tunnel (1851), I. xi. 1.

Satire and playfulness, III. iii. 26, 29.

„ vulgar delight in, III. iii. 52.

Savageness of Gothic, II. vi. 7 *seqq.*

Savages, grotesque art of, III. iii. 70.

Saxon, rough building of, III. ii. 41.

Scalelike decoration of roof, I. xxix. 6.

Scaligers', palace, window of 4th order in, II. vii. 34.

tombs :

of Can Grande, Mastino II., and Signorio, decoration of, I. xx. 31.

„ „ „ „ „ described, III. ii. 53—6.

„ „ its brickwork, 1873 *ed. pref.*

„ „ „ summit, II. vi. 86, 87 (fig. 10 *a*).

Venice : character, *continued* :

honesty (placed among the virtues, only at Venice), II. viii. 99.
individual heroism, I. i. 5, 7.
not hypocritical, II. ii. 128.
oriental feeling (love of colour), II. iv. 28, 43.
playful not frivolous, III. iii. 75.
Roman race of, I. i. 6.
serious, III. iii. 75.
strong and refined, II. vii. 46.
temper of early Venice, II. v. 30.
training, I. i. 7.
the true heart of Venice, I. i. 9. T.E. *n.*
unity of families, I. i. 12.

religion :

early Venice and, II. v. 35 ; II. viii. 9 *n.*
individual not public, I. i. 8, 9.
irreligion begins (1400—1500), I. i. 14.
   ,,   its period fixed, III. iii. 17.
   ,,   ,, result, II. vii. 14 *n.*
Jesuits in, I. A. 5.
part of life of Venice, I. i. 10—16.
priests excluded from her councils, I. i. 11.
   ,,   ,,   ,, I. A. 5,
struggle with Church of Rome, *ib., ib., ib.*

Chronological list of events :

Aquileia, the true mother of, II. ii. 3. T.E. *n.*
Cf. Roman race of, I. i. 6.

foundation of, I. A. 1 ; II. i. 6 ; II. A. 4.
809 A.D., Ducal residence fixed at, I. i. 31.
813 ,, capital of the Rialto, II. viii. 9.
1159 ,, Barbarossa and Alexander III., I. i. 9.
1193 ,, conquest of Zara, I. i. 9.
,, ,, under Dandolo, II. vii. 41 *n.*
1250—1400 ,, central epoch and struggle of, I. i. 3, 4.
1297 ,, change of government, II. viii. 12.
1311 ,, Council of Ten created, II. viii. 16.
,, ,, ,, ,, its secrecy, II. viii. 128.
1352 ,, war with Hungary, III. ii. 62.
1355 ,, Marino Faliero's conspiracy, I. i. 5.
1373 ,, war with Austria, III. ii. 69.
1380 ,, Chiozza, her most fatal war, I. i. 5.
,, ,, ,, ,, ,, III. iii. 13.
1406 ,, murder of Carrara, her worst crime, I. i. 5.
1418 ,, Carlo Zeno's death, I. i. 5, 6.
,, ,, fall of Venice. See below, s. Fall.
1454 ,, war with Turkey, I. i. 5.
1497 ,, ,, ,, *ib., ib., ib.* (cf. II. vii. 41).

Venice, *continued :*

windows of early Gothic palaces, II. vii. 35 (plate xvii.).

IV. Buildings, etc., mentioned* (including pictures they contain) :

(1) *churches :*

Alvise, S., V.I. s.v.

Andrea, S., V.I. s.v.

Angeli (Murano), V.I. s.v.

(Antonino, S., V.I. s.v.)

(Apollinare, S., V.I. s.v.)

        ,,   porch of, destroyed, I. xviii. 6.

Apostoli, SS., V.I. s.v.

(Barnaba, S., V.I. s.v.)

Bartolomeo, S., V.I. s.v.

(Basso, S., V.I. s.v.)

(Benedetto, S., V.I. s.v.)

(Canciano, S., V.I. s.v.)

Carita, Church of the, V.I. s.v.

Carmini, finialed porch of, III. i. 14.

Cassano, S., V.I. s.v.

(Cattarina, S., V.I. s.v.)

Clemente, S.

Cristoforo della Pace, S., II. iii. 1.

Donato of Murano, V.I. s.v.

Eufemia, S., V.I. s.v.

Eustachio, S., example of keystone near, II. vii. 31.

        ,,   sculpture of façade, III. iii. 22.

        ,,   ,,   ,,   V.I., s. Ospedaletto.

(Fantino, V.I. s.v.)

(Fava, V.I. s.v.)

(Felice, V.I. s.v.)

Formosa, S. Maria, the first church in Venice to the Virgin, III. iii. 3.

        ,,   ,,   the first church, with no religious decoration, III. iii. 17.

        ,,   ,,   grotesque head on, III. iii. 14, 16, 39.

        ,,   ,,   ,,   V.I., s. Ospedaletto.

Fosca, S. (Torcello). See s. Torcello.

Francesco della Vigna, S., V.I. s.v.

Frari. See above, s. Frari.

Geminiano, S., old church of, II. iv. 3.

(Geremia, S., V.I. s.v.)

        ,,   ,,   barren brickwork of, II. v. 2.

(Gesuati, V.I. s.v.)

Giacomo dell' Orio, S., V.I. s.v.

        ,,   ,,   Arabian character of, I. i. 33.

        ,,   ,,   jewel shaft, II. iv. 33.

        ,,   di Rialto, S., V.I. s.v.

        ,,   ,,   Byzantine character in, I. i. 30.

Giobbe, S., V.I. s.v.

Giorgio dei Greci, S., V.I. s.v.

        ,,   ,, Schiavoni, S., V.I. s.v.

        ,,   in Aiga, V.I. s.v.

        ,,   Maggiore, V.I. s.v.

---

* The bracketed references are to the buildings of little or no importance omitted from the Venetian Index, as revised in the Travellers' and 1886 Edition.

Venice, *continued :*

Scalzi, V.I. s.v.
Sebastian, S., architecture and painting of, III. i. 36. T.E. *n.*
   ,,   ,,   ,,   ,,   V.I. s.v.
Servi, V.I. s.v.
Silvestro, S., V.I. s.v.
Simeone Piccolo, V.I. s.v.
   ,,   Profeta, V.I. s.v
(Spirito Santo, V.I. s.v.)
Stefano (Murano), V.I. s.v.
———— (Venice), V.I. s.v.
   ,,   ,,   base from, I. xxv. 5, 14, 6.
   ,,   ,,   chamfers on windows, I. xxii. 11.
   ,,   ,,   finials of, III. i. 14.
Tolentini, Church of the, V.I. s.v.
(Toma, S., V.I. s.v.)
Torcello. See s. Torcello.
Trovaso, S., V.I. s.v.
Vitali, S., V.I. s.v.
Volto, Santo, V.I. s.v.
Zaccaria, S., V.I. s.v.
(Zitelle, S., V.I. s.v.)   .
Zobenigo, S. Maria, V.I. s.v., and s. Ospedaletto.
   ,,   ,,   its insolent atheism, III. iii. 19.

(2) *palaces :*

Apostoli, palace near, SS., V.I. s.v.
Badoer Participazio, its disc ornament (Plate VIII.), I. xxi. 10 ; V.I. s.v.
Baffo, V.I. s.v.
(Balbi, V.I. s.v.)
Barbarigo, II. vii. 57 (legend on) ; V.I. s.v.
Barbaro, V.I. s.v.
(Battagia, V.I. s.v.)
Bembo (*a*), on Grand Canal, V.I. s.v.
   ,,   (*b*), in Calle Magno, V.I. s.v.
Bernardo { (*a*), on Grand Canal.
{ (*b*), at S. Polo, " the best after the Ducal," V.I. s.v.
Braided House, II. v. 4 *n. ;* 19 (capital) ; II. A. 11.
Businello, II. v. 4 ; II. A. 11.
Camerlenghi, II. i. 1 ; V.I. s.v.
Cappello, V.I. s.v.
Cavalli (*a*), V.I. s.v.
   ,,   (*b*), V.I. s.v.
Cicogna, II. vii. 43 ; traceries of, III. A. 10 (6).
Contarini dai Scrigni, V.I. s.v.
———— della Figure, III. i. 23 ; V.I. s.v.
———— Fasan, II. vii. 18 ; V.I. s.v.
———— Porta di Ferro, V.I. s.v.
———— (of S. Luca, V.I. s.v.)
Corner della Ca' Grande, V.I. s.v.
———— ,, Regina, III. iii. 22, 71.
———— (Mocenigo, V.I. s.v.)
———— Spinelli, V.I. s.v.
———— Raccolta, V.I. s.v.
Dandolo, V.I. s.v.
Dario, III. i. 23, and T.E. *n. ;* I. A. 6 ; III. A. 4 (date).

Wall, *continued :*

,,   base, like life, I. xxv. 1 *seqq.*

,,   body of a, equally thick throughout, I. iv. 4.

,,   ,,   but moderately thick in good architecture, I. iv. 4.

,,   cornice of a, I. vi. 1 *seqq.*

,,   decoration of a London brick wall, I. xxvi. 2.

,,   definition of a, I. iii. 3.

,,   use of, between pillars, I. vii. 7.

,,   shafts and, their due proportion, I. xix. 8.

—— -veil, I. v. 1 *seqq.*

,,   ,,   its decoration by colour and chiselling, I. xxvi. 1, 3.

,,   ,,   ,,   spaces adapted to, I. xxvi. 8.

,,   ,,   meaning of the term, I. iv. 4.

War, the art of, I. A. 14.

,,   number of soldiers in, I. xxi. 35.

Warwick Castle, buttresses of Guy's Tower, I. xv. 4.

Waste of God's gifts, permitted by God, II. v. 36.

Water, ancient representations of, I. xx. 25 ; I. A. 21.

—————— -lily, compared with capitals, II. v. 14.

—————— -spouts in architecture, I. xiv. 3.

Waterloo House, I. xx. 13.

Watts, G. F., painter, III. i. 35, 39 *n.*

Weaving, art of, II. v. 22.

Weight, requirements of support, how met in early and late architecture,
           I. xv. 6.

,,   to be borne by capitals. See s. Capital.

Wellington statue, window under, I. xxi. 34.

Wells, Byzantine, at Venice, II. vii. 59.

Wenlock Abbey, I. vi. 9 ; I. xxiii. 8.

West, Benjamin, II. iv. 58.

Western and Eastern temper compared, II. v. 35.

,,   door of a cathedral, religious idea of, I. xvi. 6.

Westminster, fall of a house in (1853), II. vii. 47 *n.*

,,   Abbey, II. vi. 3.

,,   ,,   piers of, II. A. 9.

,,   ,,   shafts at, I. viii. 22.

,,   ,,   spandrils of, I. xxvi. 10.

,,   ,,   upper windows, II. vi. 109.

,,   Henry VII.'s chapel, turrets of, I. x. 17.

Whitehall, I. v. 7.

,,   I. xix. 10.

,,   windows of, I. xviii. 8.

,,   ,,   I. A. 18.

,,   ,,   III. ii. 3.

Whitewash and restoration, III. i. 32. T.E. *n*

Wilfrid," "Bishop, Eddy's, I. A. 9.

Wilkinson's Egypt, quoted, I. xx. 33 *n.*

THE END.